Re: Mix

University of North Florida

Department of English Writing Program
ENC1101

FOUNTAINHEAD
PRESS

Our green initiatives include:

Electronic Products
We deliver products in non-paper form whenever possible. This includes pdf downloadables, flash drives, & CDs.

Electronic Samples
We use Xample, a new electronic sampling system. Instructor samples are sent via a personalized web page that links to pdf downloads.

FSC Certified Printers
All of our printers are certified by the Forest Service Council which promotes environmentally and socially responsible management of the world's forests. This program allows consumer groups, individual consumers, and businesses to work together hand-in-hand to promote responsible use of the world's forests as a renewable and sustainable resource.

Recycled Paper
Most of our products are printed on a minimum of 30% post-consumer waste recycled paper.

Support of Green Causes
When we do print, we donate a portion of our revenue to green causes. Listed below are a few of the organizations that have received donations from Fountainhead Press. We welcome your feedback and suggestions for contributions, as we are always searching for worthy initiatives.
>   Rainforest 2 Reef
>   Environmental Working Group

Cover Artwork by Misty Fuller
Cover Designer: Lori Bryan
Book Designer: Doris Bruey

Books may be purchased for educational purposes. For information, please call or write:
>   1-800-586-0330
>   Fountainhead Press
>   Southlake, TX 76092
>   Web site: www.fountainheadpress.com
>   E-mail: customerservice@fountainheadpress.com

ISBN: 978-1-68036-431-6
Printed in the United States of America

TABLE OF CONTENTS

INTRODUCTION

TOWARDS CARE, CONSIDERATION, COMPETENCE, & CONFIDENCE: AN INTRODUCTION TO FIRST-YEAR WRITING AT UNF

(2017 update)

WHAT IS GENERAL EDUCATION?

As you begin your university work, you no doubt have many questions about your classes:

- Will they be at all similar to your high school classes?
- Will your professors know you by name?
- Will your professors be tough graders?
- Do you need to buy the textbook?
- When do they bring puppies to campus to play with?

Part of joining a new community is asking questions, just as part of participating in a new community is seeking answers to your questions. Sometimes, though, it's the questions people don't ask that prove more interesting. Students often wonder but are hesitant to ask "Why do I have to take this class?" That question seems like as good a place as any to introduce you to the class—not in answering the question but in asking it and letting you answer the question.

Below is a blank area for you to write out some notes or your thoughts on the questions: **Why** am I in this writing class? **Why** do I have to take this class? **How** does a class like this one fit with my major? **How** do I value this class? **How** do my friends value this class? **How** do my parents value this class?

That's not to say we don't have an answer for you. In fact, we have many answers. In the following pages, we offer some common answers, as well as our own towards the end, but it's up to you to situate your answer among these ideas.

COMPETING IDEAS

You can imagine that you're not the first person to question why you have to take a class. In fact, this question is one that—as it relates to first-year writing and other first-year and sophomore courses—many have discussed. For example, in his 2011 *Psychology Today* article, Dr. Michael W. Austin assigns a high value to general education, explaining, "[i]t is in the interests of students, employers, colleges and universities, and society at large to keep this important element of a college education."[1] To support his point, he lists four ends of general education courses:

1. to help students become better people

2. to produce capable, participating citizens in a democracy

3. to cultivate critical thinking skills that transcend fields

4. to help students be successful across a lifetime.

Some of these goals seem pretty lofty. And when you contrast them with someone who doesn't agree with Dr. Austin, you start to see a conversation unfolding. Let's take Jaime Wandschneider's January 2014 *Iowa State Daily*[2] opinion piece on the topic. Wandschneider, a university senior studying public relations, argues that students "come to college in search of one thing: knowledge in our chosen program of study," but they "are being cheated out of valuable course hours by taking classes that will never be of much use in their future careers." In her next sentence, she clarifies: "These precious hours are wasted on what are known as general education requirements."

Do you imagine that a 15-week writing course is going to help you become a better person, as Dr. Austin explains? **How** do you feel about the

---

1   Austin, Michael W. "The Value of General Education." *Psychology Today Online*, 13 Apr. 2011. Web. 12 May 2016. https://www.psychologytoday.com/blog/ethics-every-one/201104/the-value-general-education.

2   Wandschneider, Jamie. "General education requirements waste students' time." *Iowa State Daily*, 29 Jan. 2014. Web. 12 May 2016. http://www.iowastatedaily.com/opinion/article_0f2b155a-8875-11e3-add2-001a4bcf887a.html

suggestion that your 15-week general education courses connect to your success in life? **Do** you find any common ground with Ms. Wandschneider? On the previous page, where you responded to that question of "Why do I have to take this class?" did any of these two authors' points or some variation of them make it into your notes? Perhaps they complement or overlap some of your ideas.

Use the table below to map out how your thoughts on the questions above fit into this larger conversation about the goals and values of general education courses.

Critic's Ideas	Your Ideas

Before we share our answers, we should point out that this process you've begun—placing your ideas in conversation with existing ideas—is a small example of the scholastic model that you're moving towards by way of your general education courses. No matter your major, you'll be expected to be able to participate in a specific kind of conversation (i.e., a discourse) and create content in that conversation so that you can contribute to your field: whether you're an engineering student, a nursing student, a biology student, or a business student.

You can further this process, too, by talking with your classmates about their responses. As you can imagine, we all come here from various backgrounds and with different expectations. In speaking with your peers, then, you could complete the same chart as above to continue to map out how your ideas relate to others'.

GENERAL EDUCATION WRITING COURSES AT UNF

Casually called English courses, these courses are more accurately composition courses that are often found being taught in English departments. Why split this hair? When you start in one of these classes, you may appreciate knowing that the course is not a literature or reading class. Instead: these are writing courses that place rhetoric at their core. In completing these courses, you'll read a variety of texts, but these courses don't focus on the texts and how well you understand them. Yes, reading and understanding texts *is* an important and significant aspect of the courses, but these courses call on you to read and understand these texts in service to a greater purpose: to use the texts and put them to work for you to synthesize new ideas. New ideas that you'll be asked to share via the written word and, often, other print media.

Course Themes

Each year a new theme is presented in ENC 1101 – Rhetoric & Writing and ENC 1143 – Rhetoric and Narrative. The themes work together and, yet, stand very much apart from each other. In ENC 1101 students will encounter texts that focus on identifying discourses and discourse communities and moving between rhetorical situations. Readings in ENC 1101 are chiefly scholarly texts from peer-reviewed journals and publications. In ENC 1143 students will encounter texts that focus on a narrative-driven theme. Readings for ENC 1143 straddle many disciplines from philosophy to psychology to poetry.

Within both courses, writing instructors have the opportunity to build their courses from the texts in the textbook and other supplementary materials, so it's possible that two sections may call on different sets of texts. Students in all sections will nonetheless practice specific reading and writing techniques, techniques that may at first seem obvious and familiar—and for this reason unnecessary. However, we focus on these techniques to make the later steps of the course and major writing assignments less complicated in process so you can focus your energies on developing and presenting complicated ideas well.

Rhetorical Reading

When we read a text, we read differently by purpose. Consider for a moment how you read a text from a friend versus how you read a letter from an auto manufacturer about a car recall. These two situations couldn't be more different, but if you read the auto manufacturer's recall notice as you read a text, you might miss important information. Often, in such a situation, you're likely to make notes on such a piece of mail: circling a phone number, using the blank space to write a reminder for yourself, etc. In this comparison, you might start to see how active and passive reading are two different methods.

In your first-year writing courses, you'll read many texts that range in topic and difficulty, and to support your reading efforts, we provide you with a worksheet called a rhetorical reading notes worksheet (or RRN). You might think of these documents like a SparkNotes/crib sheet for your reading. The worksheet contains questions to help you focus your reading for certain kinds of information: specifically, rhetorical information. For example

- Who wrote the text?

- For what audience(s) did the author(s) write the text?

- On what occasion was the text written?

- What was going on historically during the composition of the text?

- How has the author(s) broken the text up?

When we read a text, we see this information and we absorb that information, but as gifted as the human mind is in retaining information, we're not perfect sponges. Enter the RRN. This document becomes a place for us to record important information about the text and compels us to interact with the text actively. If only a book could be read and its information put into our minds. Reading and learning don't work that way, so with the RRN, we practice asking questions of the text in order to get more than what's on the surface of the text.

Summary

In the same way that we as readers use the rhetorical reading notes worksheet to record a snapshot of a text, we can in turn create a summary description of the text. Have you ever read a text and then immediately composed a summary of that text? That practice may not be a common one outside the classroom, but it's the second step in the active reading process. In fact, I would bet that if you were asked to summarize a text after reading it, you'd have no problem doing so. But imagine being asked to explain a text a week or two after you've read it—without notes. In this moment, you might start to see the value of the summary.

With the summary step, you effectively create a narrative snapshot of your reading of a text. Imagine now being asked to explain a text a week or two after you've read it *but this time* you have a summary in front of you for notes. How much more confident might you be in the completeness of your summary? In your accuracy?

Analysis & Synthesis

Both of the above steps are prefatory and technical steps. They're both steps you already do—but instead of doing them in your mind *while you read*, you're doing them as part of the reading process and noting your thoughts, insights, and comments. With that information, you're able to refine how you understand a text, focus in on parts you understand well and return to parts you don't, perhaps, understand as well. With that information, you're able to reread a text and find more information that sheds light on your first or earlier readings.

In these first-year courses, then, these two steps are prefatory to your major writing assignments. If you're not able to read, digest, and explain the texts you're reading, imagine how difficult your projects might end up. During the semester, you'll complete three projects specific to your course and theme, and your course readings will be the bedrock on which you build out your ideas and enter a conversation.

Whether you discuss digital literacies in ENC 1101 or your place in the world in ENC 1143, your success in the course depends on your willingness to try out new techniques and to consider how you can improve something you already know how to do. We know that's a difficult step: admitting that you do something well but can improve it, but we're also confident that if you put time into those steps, you'll find that the writing assignments will interest you that much more and that they become less onerous.

OUR PROGRAM PHILOSOPHY

If you flip back to the title page of this chapter, you'll see that we've titled this chapter "Towards Care, Consideration, Competence, & Confidence: An Introduction to First-Year Writing at UNF." The four Cs in our title underpin the principles and philosophy from which each writing course is created. The UNF Writing Program sees general education writing courses as the opportunity for students to learn and practice care and consideration in their work in order to demonstrate competence and build confidence in themselves as writers. If you want to situate our belief between Dr. Austin's and Ms. Wandschneider's beliefs, you can place us closer to Dr. Austin's position. We do believe that general education courses are important, and we go to great efforts to make our general education writing program courses valuable to you.

As you enter this first-year writing course, the question of value may very well be an important one to you. You and the state of Florida are paying a sum of money for a specific outcome, and we want you to see the value that we see in our courses. They will not transform you or make you into a better person or a better writer. But, in engaging the courses, in asking questions, in determining how you can take advantage of the course, you position yourself to determine how you might transform, how you might change as a person, how you might work on your writing.

THE FOUR Cs

The Writing Program at UNF values four core principles called "The Four Cs," which are Care, Consideration, Confidence, and Competence. Everyone in the program—the administrators, the Writing Center staff, the instructors, and the students—are asked to embody these principles. The 4Cs are explained below.

> **Care**: Ideally, you are in college because you care about, or put value in, education. You care about your future and hope that higher education will help you achieve your future goals. Your instructor will look for indications that you care about your studies.

> Your instructor cares about your education and will show that through careful instruction and availability in office hours. Careful instruction is demonstrated when instructors prepare a lesson plan; they consider the learning styles and personalities of the students in a particular course in order to present the material in the best possible way for that set of students. Instructors also demonstrate care through individualized feedback on assignments. Additionally, the instructor will care about you as an individual and will often email you if you miss a course and will work with you on reaching your personal learning goals in the course.

Additionally, you should take care of yourself as a person and work to be healthy and happy as you cannot achieve your educational goals if you, as an individual, have not been cared for.

Consideration: It is important to consider the education we are being given by attending to the course, attending to the readings, and attending to the ideas of our peers and instructor. Attendance means more than simply showing up and reading. Attendance means to be present, to pay attention, and to carefully consider. It is when we consider the ideas/teaching presented in the course that we grow as intellectuals.

Note: to consider other viewpoints does not mean you have to accept them. But you should listen and think about those viewpoints in order to consider your own viewpoints more thoroughly.

Confidence: As we learn new information, we grow as intellectuals, and, hopefully, our confidence in ourselves as learners, thinkers, and future employees/employers grows. Your instructor will work to instill confidence in you as a reader, a writer, a student, and an individual by providing you with the tools you need to succeed, giving you individualized feedback, and meeting with you during office hours. However, not all confidence comes from external (extrinsic) factors such as feedback and grades. Think about what inside of you motivates you (intrinsic factors) and how you can use those factors to help you build your confidence.

Competence: Of course, everyone hopes that you will learn a lot in college and become more competent in a number of skills and knowledge areas. That is no different in the Writing Program. It is hoped that you will become a more competent reader, writer, peer reviewer, and student. Your competence is measured through a number of rubrics.

There are a series of questions across the top of this chart. They are asking you to reflect on the core principle listed down the left-hand side of the chart. Write a few notes in answer to the questions. You may be asked to complete this chart more fully in the first few weeks of the course.

CORE PRINCIPLES	In your own words, define this core principle in the context of academic habits.	In the past, how have you displayed this core principle in your academic life? Did you find these habits to be successful or unsuccessful?	How might you display this core principle in this course? Why might you display this core principle in this course?	How might you develop this core principle further in order to help you in other courses you are currently taking and in future courses?
CARE				
CONSIDERATION				
CONFIDENCE				
COMPETENCE				

YOUR LEARNING PHILOSOPHY

As you've read through this introduction, you've been asked to consider a great deal of information—much of it coming from you. As this chapter concludes, then, and you begin to approach the course with—we hope— some new information, we'd ask you to take a moment to consider: What do you want out of this class? How are you going to accomplish that goal(s)? How do your goals differ from your peers'? How do your goals differ from your family's expectations? What do these goals say about you as a learner?

Using your notes here on the above questions, compose a paragraph that summarizes your learning philosophy. Why are you enrolled at a university? How do you approach your classes? What principles support your decision-making? How does learning matter to you, inside and outside of the classroom? And how does making these principles explicit and clear support your agenda in life?

NEXT STEPS

What follows is an anthology of texts that your faculty have compiled to create the framework of a conversation. During the course of the semester, you'll work inside this framework to encounter how you see yourself in the world. The preceding sections have asked you to consider who you are, where you've been, and what you value. In moving forward into the semester in earnest, you will encounter challenges: some course material may not interest you, other obligations may interrupt your schedule, you may receive writing feedback that doesn't match how you judge your writing. Your response to each, small situation adds up to your experience of the course, and in the end you are responsible for that experience. Shape your experience and make the course useful to you as best you can. Ask questions and mark yourself as someone who cares.

Framing Remix Rhetorically: Toward a Typology of Transformative Work

Dustin W. Edwards

Abstract Since it entered the critical lexicon in composition and rhetoric, remix has become an increasingly popular topic for scholarly work and pedagogical focus. Despite its pervasiveness, remix remains a cumbersome and overwhelming conceptual category. As such, this article has two interconnected purposes: To develop a pliable and useable framework for understanding the rhetorical significance of remix, and to begin to chart some of the major types of remix writers compose today. I open by arguing that the rhetorical concept of imitation (*imitatio*) can serve as a malleable frame both to understand the rhetorical importance of remix and to help map the many ways in which remix writers accomplish their rhetorical goals. After developing this frame, I offer a four-part typology of remix: assemblage, reappropriation, redistribution, and genre play. Finally, I close by providing strategies for teaching and directions for future research.

Keywords: remix; imitation; digital rhetoric; composition pedagogy; invention

1. INTRODUCTION

Allow me to start with four scenarios:

1. A composer compiles a video using several already-existing materials, including images, film footage, sound bytes, music, animations, and so on. The final text, though patched together from many different source texts, is a coherent five-minute argument that claims political change cannot happen by simply voting for a particular candidate.

2. A YouTube user constructs a capitalist critique using an already-made video advertisement. The composer does not shoot any original clips, nor does the composer add an original voiceover. Once complete, the composer does, however, provide a radically different message than the original advertisement by inserting alphabetic writing in strategic moments throughout the video.

3. A presidential nominee makes a comment during a nationally televised debate that sparks a meme-generating frenzy. Within minutes of this occurrence, several texts are made, distributed, redistributed, modified, and re-modified—all relying on variations of the original phrase uttered by the nominee. The widely circulated phrase becomes a famous—if not infamous—catchphrase of the election season.

4. A student designs a standardized test with mock reading passages, questions, and directions that calls into question the current fixation on standardized testing in primary and secondary schools in the United States. By playing with the typified genre conventions of standardized tests, the student asks her readers to interrogate the values and actions of the current testing system and the political contexts in which they emerged.

These scenarios, as our current vocabulary would have them, likely fall under the conceptual umbrella of remix—that is, each explicitly builds upon or repurposes already existing material. Taken together, these scenarios, each real pieces of writing that have impacted real audiences, show the rhetorical potential of *transforming*[1] already-existing materials into new texts for new audiences. My point in sharing these scenarios is not only to emphasize commonality but also to demonstrate difference. Indeed, remix has come to signify a wide range of meaning and practice. Take the above scenarios as cases in point: the first composer assembles an argument by strategically compiling several already existing texts into one coherent narrative; the second radically repurposes a single text to offer critical commentary; writers in the third scenario share, update, and intervene in the

---

1   I use "transformative" for two key reasons: first, to signal that this work has new rhetorical purpose, and second, to argue that this work adheres to fair use guidelines. As Patricia Aufderheide and Peter Jaszi (2012) noted, work that is transformative—that is, work "recontextualied and re-presented for a new purpose, and to a new audience" (p. 81)—is more likely to be deemed fair in U.S. courts.

rhetorical velocity (Ridolfo & DeVoss, 2009; Sheridan, Ridolfo, & Michel, 2012) of an already circulating text; and the fourth composer playfully refashions a common genre for the purposes of critique. In effect, these texts—each a kind of remix—are distinctive in purpose, delivery, design, and style.

Similarly, remix has come to represent an expansive range of meaning in computers and writing scholarship. Recent work has positioned remix—as a concept, as a practice, as a genre, as a method—in wide and varied ways: as a means to enter and participate in political exchanges (e.g., Dietel-McLaughlin, 2009; Dubisar & Palmeri, 2010), as a method of making arguments, solving problems, and effecting social change (e.g., Johnson-Eilola & Selber, 2007; Kuhn, 2012), as a way to participate in communities (Jenkins, 2009; Stedman, 2012), as a research and conceptual method (e.g., Palmeri, 2012; Pough, 2010; Yancey, 2009), and as a theoretical frame to view culture, authorship, and intellectual property (e.g., DeVoss & Porter, 2006; Lessig, 2008; Ridolfo & DeVoss, 2009). In short, remix is a loaded term. It has, nevertheless, emerged as an increasingly significant writing practice in digital culture. Although scholars have importantly noted that remix need not only refer to the digital (e.g, Delagrange, 2009; Hesse, Sommers, & Yancey, 2012; Palmeri, 2012), the relative ease of manipulating material in the ever-expanding digital archives hosted online, coupled with the possibility for mentorship and participation in community networks, has allowed remix to flourish in digitally mediated contexts. From the emergence of online remix communities, such as Vidders.net, TotalRecut.com, and ccMixter.com, to the rise of remix artists of public intellectual renown, such as Jonathan McIntosh and Elisa Kreisinger, it appears remix has secured itself as an enduring and profound practice worthy of continued inquiry. It is perhaps because of its relatively quick ascendance to such heightened popularity in scholarly pursuits and public spheres that remix remains a cumbersome, if not overwhelming, concept.

How might we better harness the pedagogical usefulness of remix in more accessible and illustrative ways? If we are to accept remix as a valid and important composing practice, one that has the potential to teach a wealth of rhetorical knowledge for a digital age, we need to further develop and refine approaches to discuss the many nuances involved in transforming already existing material. A possible way to reconcile the sprawling posture of remix in writing practice is to develop a typology that begins to delineate the rhetorical distinctions among types of remixed compositions. Here, I work toward such a typology by outlining four varieties of remix—assemblage, reappropriation, redistribution, and genre play—in an effort to alleviate confusion about a term encumbered with excessive meaning.

In addition to relieving obfuscation, writing specialists would benefit from developing a remix typology for two other interconnected reasons. First, a remix typology does valuable work in asserting the often-touted epistemological commitments that undergird the fields of rhetoric and composition and computers and writing. These commitments, predicated on values of collaboration (e.g., Lunsford & Ede, 1992), sharing (e.g., DeVoss & Porter, 2006), and problem solving (e.g., Johnson-Eilola & Selber, 2007), suggest that we need to lend serious consideration to the task of teaching what constitutes meaningful and productive authorship in a digital economy of writing. Such a task, as many scholars have argued (e.g., Johnson-Eiloa & Selber, 2007; Howard, 1999; Lunsford, 1999; Robbins, 2003), involves reconceptualizing notions of originality and ownership that have persisted since the Romantic era, and replacing them with, to echo Andrea Lunsford (1999), "a new rhetoric of authorship, one that rejects the naïve construction of author as originary genius or as entrepreneurial corporate entity, without diminishing the importance of agency, and of difference, to the lives of working writers" (p. 534). To delineate a typology of remix embraces these social and ethical commitments, and, in turn, provides a needed foundation for writing in a remix culture.

Second, a remix typology can be used as a powerful pedagogical tool. As Henry Jenkins (2009) asserted, "schools remain hostile to overt signs of repurposed content [. . .] and they often fail to provide the conceptual tools needed to analyze and interpret works produced in this appropriative process" (p. 57). This typology addresses this dismissal. It suggests that remix practices can be used to accomplish many ends (i.e., offer critique, participate in publics, propel arguments to new audiences, and so on) and, as such, that variations of remix engender different rhetorical, composing, and ethical issues. A typology provides teachers and students of writing with a heuristic that serves to guide them through the process of composing transformative work. To this end, it can also emphasize the need to design and compose with an eye toward the potential for future remixability, an increasingly important delivery concern that a series of publications has called "rhetorical velocity" (Ridolfo & DeVoss, 2009; Sheridan, Ridolfo, & Michel, 2012).

purpose

Although this article aims to map the differences among remix practices, the rhetorical variations of any typology would benefit from an overarching frame, one that affirms the rhetorical, social, and ethical benefits of composing transformative work. My argument proceeds from the acknowledgment that the practice of remix—culling, stitching, merging, and redeploying texts from one's culture—is not new. As I will show, rhetoricians have been practicing and theorizing remix, or something akin to it, for thousands of years under the frame of imitation. Thus, by recalling noteworthy practices, metaphors, and theories from rhetorical traditions, I argue that imitation, if reimagined and remediated for composing in digital contexts, can serve as a pliable framework for understanding the rhetorical significance of remix. It likewise can help build a typology of remix. As scholarship has shown (Lanham, 2012; Muckelbauer, 2003; Pigman, 1980; Porter, 2005), variations of imitation—indeed typologies of imitation—have existed throughout history (i.e., compilation, paraphrase, reproduction, inspiration, and so on). The task now is reconfiguring these typologies for a digital age.

audience

We also need to unpack the significance of imitation. In classical rhetoric, imitation (*mimesis/imitatio*) was deeply connected to invention, style, memory, ethics, and being. It is in this sense of imitation that we should position remix within our classrooms today. This frame situates remix practices as inherently rhetorical, suggesting that composers have a myriad of choices, concerns, and constraints to consider before, during, and after they construct their texts and disperse them throughout varied distribution networks. Further, it celebrates a sort of community stockpile from which composers can continuously invent and reinvent. In this way, the move to locate remix practices within the classical Greco-Roman sense of imitation works to displace the headlock of the lone genius creating texts *ex nihilo*. As remix so clearly demonstrates, we do not create texts out of nowhere but we build them through the discovery of other texts (Johnson-Eilola & Selber, 2007). Finally, to position remix within a revived frame of imitation encourages a sense of ethical mindfulness. It positions remix writers as producers, evaluators, and collaborators, and thereby demonstrates that responsible textual production matters, that the materials of remixes have histories, and that remixed texts might themselves be repurposed. In other words, it positions remix as a process whereby rhetors are productively and ethically—not haphazardly—working with other texts, communities, and people.

In this article, I employ two methodological approaches. In the first half, by surveying historiographical work on imitation theory and practice, I seek to recast imitation for a digital age. In so doing, my aim is to forge a relationship between remix and imitation to emphasize how the rhetorical considerations of imitation (i.e., invention, ethics, and collaboration) are integral in expressing and advocating for the usefulness of remix practices today. My methodology for this section is informed by recovery work in writing studies that aims to re-theorize rhetorical concepts for a digital age (e.g., Brooke, 2009; Porter, 2009; Welch, 1999). In the second half of the article, I establish a four-part typology of remix by analyzing what I consider to be particularly illustrative cases that highlight fundamental distinctions among the four types of remix practices. By close reading a representation of each type of remix, I work to provide a set of nuanced terms and concepts to consider when teaching and composing transformative work. Because remix is necessarily entangled in matters of ethics (i.e., negotiating how—and if—to reuse texts), Heidi McKee and James Porter's (2009) rhetorical-casuistic framework also informed my analysis. Although McKee and Porter's framework was intended to aid Internet researchers in contemplating and working through ethically complex cases, I see great value in extending their approach to the classroom. For McKee and Porter, such a framework entailed identifying and testing against "cases about which there is common agreement" (p. 24). As McKee and Porter explained, these agreed upon cases, also known as paradigmatic cases, serve as clear-cut examples against which more difficult cases can be compared. Here is where the work of rhetoric—of comparison, of inquiry, of action—comes into play: "rhetoric is [a useful art for] resolution of conflict, for negotiation of differences, and for analysis of tough cases (McKee & Porter, 2009, p. 12). Taken together, then, rhetoric and casuistry provide a lens through which ethically perplexing examples of remix can be grappled. My hope is that the cases offered here are representative of paradigmatic cases of remix today—that is, the intent is to offer individual cases that serve as exemplars not only for distinguishing remix approaches, but also for considering how to tease out the ethical uptake of others' work.

2. RECOVERING IMITATION: SITUATING REMIX RHETORICALLY

To say imitation has a complex and diverse history would be an under-
statement. Theorists, practitioners, and pedagogues have developed and
deployed imitation in many (sometimes disparate) ways, at times promoting it as a central basis for invention and art, while at other times bemoan-
ing it as a derivative and unsophisticated mechanical approach. As such,
like any recovery work, to adopt imitation in a modern sense is to submit
a *partial* interpretation.[2] Although imitation today is often stripped of its
rhetorical, social, and inventive heritage,[3] scholars have argued that imitation once played a central role in rhetoric education and thought (Clark,
1957; Corbett, 1971; Murphy, 2012; Sullivan, 1989). The significance
of imitation rests on early observations from classical thinkers, including Isocrates, Plato, and Aristotle, each of whom observed that humans
tended to model those they admire (Bender, 1996). Moreover, most con-
tend that imitation was part of a larger *process*—not merely a skill-and-drill
exercise—that prepared students to be ethical and well-informed citizens.
As Dale Sullivan (1989) put it, "imitation was more than a simple-minded
approach to teaching rhetoric: It was an integral part of the classical mindset which held great respect for the accomplishments of the past and saw
in imitation a basis for ontology, art, political action, and ethics" (p. 14).
It is this collaborative approach—more than particular training exercises—
that we should yoke into discussions of digital remix. In particular, I want
to suggest that the process of classical imitation, that is, the connections
to be made among imitation, invention, and community, is valuable when
discussing the significance and importance of remix within our composition classrooms today.

    Although most historiographical accounts of imitation often begin
with Roman rhetoric, likely because rhetoricians such as Cicero, Quintil-

---

2   In this way, I have come to value James Berlin's *Octalog* (1988) statement on historiography: "All histories are partial accounts, are both biased and incomplete. The good histories admit this and then tell their stories. The bad attempt to dominant the past, pretend-
ing at the same time to be mere recorders of the facts" (p. 12).

3   Scholars point to romanticism, scientism, changes in technology, the racial politics of
the 19th century, and, more recently, expressivist and cognitivist composition pedagogies
as factors leading to the fallout of imitative pedagogy and practice (Farmer & Arrington,
1993; Howard, 1999; Wilson, 2003). The romantic formulation of "author as genius" is
perhaps the most pervasive account for imitation's decline (Howard, 1999; Randall,2001;
Sullivan, 1989).

ian, and others further systematized it, imitation has its roots in the Greek *mimesis*. Several scholars (see, for example, Crowley, 1985; Haskins, 2000) have explained that *mimesis*, from its very origin, was a vexed concept, and thus have offered complex historical accounts connected to both rhetorical and poetic traditions, exploring how Isocrates, Plato, and Aristotle treated *mimesis* in their rhetoric and poetic treatises. Largely, most noted that *mimesis* in antiquity dealt with poetic artists imitating nature (Crowley, 1985; Haskins, 2000; Sullivan, 1989). In other words, the project of *mimesis* involved replicating reality by mimicking its features—that is, under poetic mimetic theory, art is always an imitation, one that can never genuinely reproduce reality. Sharon Crowley (1985) and Dale Sullivan (1989) both noted that it was not until later in the classical tradition that imitation became prominently known in its highly rhetorical sense: rhetors studying, memorizing, internalizing, recalling, and recasting models. Scholars typically refered to this process as *imitatio*, not *mimesis*, as it was the Romans who more overtly developed this rhetoric theory. Typically, then, scholarship on *mimesis* often, but not always, related to literary work (i.e., Erich Auerbach's [1953] *Mimesis: The Representation of Reality in Western Literature*), whereas scholarship on *imitatio* often engaged rhetorical practice.[4] Largely, I will refer to the latter.

To begin a historical recovery of *imitatio*, it is important to clarify an unfortunate translation issue—imitation, as it was practiced in the Roman rhetoric tradition, did not always mean reproducing exact replicas of models. In fact, Edward Corbett (1971) noted that "imitate" in our current lexicon is perhaps the wrong verb to account for the process the Romans practiced, and instead suggested the verb "emulate" is perhaps a more useful signifier. As Corbett described it, "imitation asked the student to observe the manner or pattern or form or means used by a model and then attempt to emulate the model" (p. 244). Crucially, imitation, for the Romans, was part of a process that asked rhetors to navigate, decipher, and critically examine a cultural reservoir of knowledge, components of which were to be redeployed to fit the occasion of future speech acts. All parts of this process, not just the final emulation of texts, were important. As James Murphy (2012) put it, imitation was "a carefully plotted sequence

---

4   Though, as John Muckelbauer (2003) asserted, perhaps these disciplinary boundaries have outrun their usefulness. The neat divides between poetic *mimesis* and rhetorical *imitatio* might serve to further split imitation from invention. It remains, nevertheless, a favorable way to taxonomize imitation.

of interpretive and re-creational activities using preexisting texts to teach students how to create their own original texts" (p. 54). Murphy's description was striking, as it resembled rationales many contemporary theorists provide when justifying the practice of remix. The purpose of imitation is not to produce highly derivative or plagiaristic work, but rather to construct new work based on preexisting models. The same has been argued for remix (see especially Johnson-Eilola & Selber, 2007).

To further understand the significance of imitation and to thus draw forward practices useful for today, it is helpful to examine the writing instruction students practiced as part of the Quintilian-influenced Roman education system. James Murphy (2012) found the process of imitation included seven steps: reading aloud, analysis of the text, memorization of models, paraphrase of models, transliteration of models, recitation of paraphrase/transliteration, and correction of paraphrase/transliteration. Donald Leman Clark (1957) limited the process to three central steps: memorizing models, translating from Greek to Latin, and paraphrasing. For the purposes of relating imitation to remix, I want to focus on—and revive—three steps: analysis of the text, memorization, and paraphrase. These three practices, if reimagined for present-day composers, closely resemble the process of inventing, composing, and distributing remixes.

The first component, analysis of the text, asked students to literally dissect given texts: "The immediate intent is to show the student how the author made good or bad choices in wording, in organization, in the use of figures, and the like" (Murphy, 2012, p. 55). This activity, Murphy explained, was not unlike the practice of "close reading" commonly employed in English studies today. As a beginning stage in the process, we see that imitation is not simply the rehashing of authoritative texts; rather, the practice asked students to be critical of the texts they encountered.[5] For the memorization approach, students were taught to memorize great works not to repeat them verbatim but to, as Quintilian (2006) remarked, "set before our eyes the excellences of several, that different qualities from different writers may fix themselves in our minds and that we may adopt, for any subject, the style which is most suitable to it" (10.2.26). This approach can be considered a "storehouse" method—that is, students were asked to retain the works of great authors in order to recall their

---

5   Mary Minock (1995) made a similar argument, suggesting a postmodern imitation pedagogy as a "kind of serious play" that pushes students to locate "authoritative" texts within their unconscious memories (p. 502). The goal, for Minock, was not merely to recall authoritative texts from one's unconscious but to potentially transgress and challenge those authoritative texts.

best words, figures, and phrases, all of which were to be used in future rhetorical situations to fit the particular occasion of a given speech. This storehouse, if externalized, remediated, and reimagined for modern-day composers, is not unlike discussions of building a public domain inspired by an economy of sharing (see DeVoss & Porter, 2006; Lessig, 2001).[6] Finally, with paraphrase, the production aspect of imitation, students were asked to redeploy and restructure models, allowing for a "personal style in narration" (Murphy, 2012, p. 58). All of these steps, as I see them, are essential for composing effective remixes today: first, reading widely and critically, then gathering and collecting materials, and finally, repurposing and redeploying selected materials. It is by no coincidence that many prominent rhetoric theorists have used variations of the metaphor of a bee transforming pollen into honey to conceptualize such a process (Pigman, 1980): just as the bee collects pollen from several flowers to be transformed into honey, the writer assembles materials from several sources to be amalgamated into a single work. The composer as an industrious and transformative bee no doubt serves as a potent metaphor for remix.

Invention

As this process shows, imitation is highly connected to the rhetorical canon of invention. Karen Burke LeFevre (1987) famously defined invention as a social act "best understood as occurring when individuals interact dialectically with socioculture in a distinctive way to generate something" (p. 33). Although LeFevre did not explicitly mention imitation in her argument, her positioning of invention as a social process whereby individuals work dialectically with society and culture, is, as I see it, highly aligned with the classical mindset of imitation. As John Muckelbauer (2003) pointed out, to see imitation as a mode of invention forces us to recalibrate the often-asserted understanding of imitation as the task of a writer mechanically replicating a model. Instead, we should see imitation as inventive action—that is, as paying attention to the "*movement* through which [a] model is encountered" (p. 88, my emphasis). Indeed, if we are to gain anything from recalling classical imitation, we should foremost approach the process of inventing transformative work as a movement through complex ecologies.

---

6   Although I do not have the space here, a much deeper discussion on digital memory would prove useful. For instance, Colin Gifford Brooke's (2009) work on retheorizing memory as persistence might productively complicate my discussion. In his ecological approach, Brooke likened the act of "practicing" memory, what he called persistence, as an act of bricolage—taking bits of information from disparate sources to forward a new rhetorical object. As such, a more developed treatment of memory would efficaciously add to any discussion of remix and imitation.

The undergoing of this movement, moreover, has the potential to inspire ethical effects. Robert Terrill (2011) argued that an imitation pedagogy cultivates what he called a productive "form of duality" that "encourages students to divide their attention between the exemplar and their own rhetorical production" (p. 297). In other words, imitation pedagogy calls on students to set themselves in relation to others as they closely analyze and emulate others' texts. In the process of doing so, Terrill claimed that students learn valuable resources for democratic citizenship. For Terrill, the constant outward thinking required of an imitative pedagogy called on students to be, in Terrill's words, "extraordinarily culturally literate" (p. 308). To put it another way, asking writers to be mindful of the movement of invention—the material, social, temporal, spatial, cultural aspects of textual construction and distribution—calls on them to be in dialogue with, and thus attentive to, the multiple stakeholders and competing interests of a given argument or idea. In terms of remix, evaluating texts—along with the sociocultural contexts from which they arise—and then theorizing about how those ought to be remixed becomes an exercise of ethical mindfulness.

So far I have spent considerable time discussing the significance and process of imitation in classical rhetoric. My aim in doing so is to pull out useful concepts, metaphors, and practices to better situate the purpose and need for teaching the rhetorically complex practice of remix. To position remix within the framework of imitation suggests remix is neither a new nor an unsophisticated composing approach. It implies that the *process* of constructing remixes is just as—or even more—important than the finished "product." In addition, it suggests rhetoric has long held a relationship with what we now call remix, and that past orators and language theorists have spent consider-able time theorizing about how imitation can be leveraged pedagogically and rhetorically. With this framework in mind, my focus turns to the problem with which I began this article: how to begin to chart the various types of remix.

3. MAPPING REMIX PRACTICES: TOWARD A TYPOLOGY OF TRANSFORMATIVE WORK

Drawing upon and aggregating both recent scholarship and prominent remix practices, I present a four-part typology to parse out digital transformative work: assemblage, reappropriation, redistribution, and genre play.

The typology at which I arrive is hardly my own; it borrows from the rich line of scholarship on remix within rhetoric and composition, and pulls from work in critical theory and media studies. Although this typology categorizes many types of remix (see Table 1), it in no way claims to be exhaustive. Moreover, individual texts may cross borders and be categorized in multiple ways—for example, a YouTube video may compile various film clips of a particular television show (assemblage) but repurpose them in a way that offers a nuanced critique of the show's patriarchal themes (reappropriation). In keeping with a rhetorical-caustic approach (McKee & Porter, 2009), this typology seeks to lay out rather clear-cut exemplars of ethically *productive* forms of remix. Another consideration, which is outside the scope of this article, would examine, like much contemporary scholarship does, the transgressive and, in many ways, unproductive form of imitation for a modern economy of writing: plagiarism (for extended discussions, see Eisner & Vicinus, 2008; Howard, 1999; Randall,2001). My hope, however, is that the cases offered here might help teachers and students puzzle through more ethically challenging types of remix.

The proposed typology is intended to be a starting point for talking about the wide-ranging rhetorical effects of remix. That is, exploring this typology within composition classrooms is one possible way to introduce the various rhetorical purposes—both subtle and overt—of remix. After discussing some of the key differences, similarities, and purposes of each type, students can decide what they want their text to accomplish, whom they want their text to reach, and how they want to achieve their rhetorical goals. To explicate a heuristic to teach the major remix types practiced today, the following section discusses how we might pedagogically begin to describe and explain each type. As such, each genus of the typology includes 1) a brief description, 2) a few common rhetorical purposes, and 3) a discussion of pertinent theory and scholarship. To further account for these distinctions, I return to the scenarios I posed at the start of this article to narrate how each type operates at a conceptual and rhetorical level.

Table 1 Typology of transformative work.			
	Description	Common Rhetorical Purposes	Exemplary Case
Assemblage	Building a new text by compiling, aggregating, and juxtaposing a combination of already existing texts	Builds arguments by pulling (often disparate) materials into one coherent narrative or text; Reveals reoccurring or perhaps undetected themes	"You Can't Vote-In Change" political video remix
Reappropriation	Slightly altering an existing text and/or reclaiming or "taking back" already existing texts	Shows power relationships; Inverts/challenges dominant discourse; Offers commentary or critique	"GoForth and Destroy Capitalism" advertisement commentary
Redistribution	Sharing and updating an already circulating text	Reaches new audiences; Expresses opinions and/or mobilizes collective action	"Binders Full of Women" meme
Genre play	Deploying a text that blends, repurposes, or moves in and out of genre expectations	Disrupts how we commonly view the world	Student-designed standardized test

3.1 Assemblage

Assemblage is a method of composing wherein a composer builds a new text by gathering, repurposing, and redeploying a combination of already-existing texts. Remixers using this approach often weave together a coherent narrative or argument that does not necessarily correlate with the ways in which the source texts were originally deployed. To put it another way, assemblage can be likened to the common metaphor used to explain imitation: a bee collecting pollen from multiple flowers to be transformed into honey. Assemblage is perhaps the most widely recognized method of remix; it fits nicely with the "taking old texts to build something new" stock definition provided by many popular sources (i.e., Lessig, 2008; Ferguson, 2010; Gaylor, 2009). In writing studies, Johndan Johnson-Eilolaand Stuart Selber (2007) defined assemblages as texts "built primarily and explicitly from existing texts" (p. 381). Henry Jenkins (2009) helped to narrow this definition by providing a useful description of what I consider assemblages: "[the]creative juxtaposition of materials that otherwise occupy very different cultural niches" (p. 57). Importantly, Jenkins mentioned that materials may be—and are very likely to be—disparate.

For a prime example of assemblage, I examine remix artist Elisa Kreisinger's "You Can't Vote-In Change," a video remix published on YouTube in 2009. In this work, Kreisinger argued that social change must happen by people's movements, reasoning that the ever-present promises made by U.S. politicians are inept methods of enacting social change. To make her argument, Kreisinger used a series of presidential ads and campaign speeches from past U.S. Presidents. The materials she gathered, snippets from the campaign speeches of Dwight D. Eisenhower, John F. Kennedy, Lyndon B. Johnson, Richard Nixon, Jimmy Carter, George H. W. Bush, Bill Clinton, and George W. Bush, were all carefully selected clips that verbalized the "changes" each president claimed to implement upon taking office. After Kreisinger selectively compiled these clips, she mixed in an audio clip from an unidentified political analyst, which stated, "Historically, whenever important issues of peace and justice had to be solved, they were not solved by electing one party or the other. They were solved by people's movements." As these words were vocalized, news footage rolled that showed scenes of social demonstrations and protests. From here, Kreisigner replayed, in an almost robotic tone, the words "you can't vote-in change," stitching the phrase together from various sources. As these words were being repeated, Kreisinger used an image of a burning match and a massive crowd of people running through a street to imply citizens must ignite change on their own terms. In effect, Kreisinger pulled in source material from a wide range of sources—each with its own historical, social, political, and rhetorical connotation—for the purposes of building a coherent and well-supported argument.

3.2. Reappropriation

Reappropriation involves making tactical changes to an existing text (or set of texts) to signal resistance or offer a critique of the original text or the concept for which it stands. That is, reappropriation is often used to

challenge, invert, counter, or draw attention to oppressive discourse.[7] As
such, composers using reappropriation tactics typically play on or with
source materials to expose oppressive, harmful, or problematic ideologies.
To explain how reappropriation works rhetorically, I borrow concepts
from critical and rhetorical theorists, namely Judith Butler's (1997a, 1997b)
concept of resignification and Kenneth Burke's (1954) notion of perspective by incongruity. That is, I see reappropriation happening in two key
ways: first, a "taking back" of an oppressive text or term, and second, a reusing of a text to expose its damaging effects. Butler's work elucidates the
former—how the reclaiming of a potentially oppressive or injurious term
can often work to signal resistance. Working from the Althusserian notion
of interpellation, Butler (1997) argued, "the terms by which we are hailed
are rarely the ones we choose.. but these terms we never really choose
are the occasion for something we might still call agency, the repetition
of an originally subordination for another purpose, one whose future is
partially open" (p. 38). Thus, by embracing a term—accepting it, altering
its meaning, and then redeploying it—a rhetor has the potential to gain
agency to resist oppressive discourse. As an example of the potential of
reappropriation, Butler has turned to the word queer and the movement
to recast the originally oppressive word into one of resistance. In an interview conducted by Gary Olson and Lynn Worsham (2000), for example,
Butler detailed an experience she encountered walking down the streets
of Berkeley wherein a passerby harassingly shouted from a car window,
"Are you a lesbian?" In the interview, Butler explained how she accepted
the term in the affirmative, which shocked and stunted the person whom
asked the question. Of her acceptance of the term, Butler stated, ". .it
was a very powerful thing to do. It wasn't that I authored that term: I
received the term and gave it back; I replayed it, reiterated it" (p. 760). The
power Butler claimed in this moment stemmed from a reappropriating of
a word—and of a lager social, cultural, and historical practice—aimed at
excluding, disenfranchising, and harming the one it interpellates. Hence,
Butler illustrated that purposefully reusing a word (or, I would argue, a
text) can be a powerful means of resistance.

---

7   This rhetorical tactic is hardly new. The 19th century abolitionist Frederick
Douglass is a prime example of a rhetor who used appropriation to challenge oppressive
views of the dominant culture (see for example, Bacon, 1998; Bizzell, 1997; Miller &
Quashie, 1998).

While Butler showed how embracing a term and turning it on its head is a powerful rhetorical act of resistance, Burke's (1954) "perspective by incongruity" explained how re-positioning source texts can serve to *expose* oppressive discourse. For Burke, perspective by incongruity involved breaking "piety"—what Burke described as "the sense of what properly goes with what" (p. 74). In Burkean terms, piety, as Julia Allen and Lester Faigley (1995) explained, does not signal religious connotations; rather, Allen and Faigley described the rhetorical practice as such:

> By juxtaposing incongruous ideas, Burke says, we "shatter pieties." In other words, by juxtaposing one ideological correctness together with another, of a different ideological stripe, the two call each other into question. And it is more likely that the less powerful one will act upon the other in such a way as to reduce its power; the piety will thus be shattered. (p. 162)

In terms of remix, then, a composer might redeploy and slightly modify a text to call attention to the original message's ideological stance.

As a prime example of how a remix composer reappropriates a dominant, primary text, I focus here on a Levi's advertisement distributed on YouTube, and a subsequent remake of the ad. In 2011, Levi's released an advertisement with undertones of activism, protest, and revolution. The original ad, part of Levi's "Go Forth" campaign, featured video clips of young people demonstrating and reacting against tacit oppression, which was especially evident near the end of the ad when a young person raised his arms in apparent protest while solitarily facing a wall of heavily armored figures. Providing a voiceover for the advertisement, Charles Bukowski's poem, "The Laughing Heart," was read in its entirety. The advertisement ended with the Levi's logo. A month after the advertisement was released, YouTube user "go4thREVOLT" published a reappropriated version of the Levi's ad. The video, which used the same voiceover, images, and video, added new alphabetic text to challenge themes presented in the original ad. The text read: "Capitalists have stolen the whole world from us. Poetry and protest, even riots, become advertisements for products. Our bodies, our moments of joy, are flattened into images that impoverish our lives. Now their system is collapsing. Let's tear it down. Go forth and destroy capitalism" [punctuation added]. In Butler's formulation, the remix artist here performed a "taking back" of the phrase "go forth" to resist a text that used a subversive tone to sell a product. In other words, through the act of accepting yet recasting the phrase, the remix artist was able to claim a sense of agency. Further, in Burkean parlance, the juxtaposition of the added words with the original ad called the rhetorical effect of the original text into question. The goal for the reappropriation, in Burke's terms, was to reduce the ad's power, to shatter its piety, by suggesting the images of the advertisement did not match the practices of capitalism.

3.3. Redistribution

Redistribution refers to sharing or adding to an already existing text for the purpose of reaching a new audience, offering an updated message, and/or spreading a text further. The chief appeal of redistribution involves drawing on the rhetorical force of a shared and common text, one that is already in circulation.[8] It may seem odd to include redistribution within a typology of remix, as, especially upon first glance, redistribution does not seem to deal with the laborious act of transforming work (i.e., vigorously repurposing a text from multiple source texts); however, as Abby Dubisar and Jason Palmeri (2010) have suggested, the rhetorical act of making *subtle* changes to widely circulating texts is an increasingly important practice for digital composers today. Moreover, as many scholars have pointed out (Porter, 2009; Ridolfo & DeVoss, 2009; Sheridan, Ridolfo, & Michel, 2012), making distribution and delivery choices is a complex and highly rhetorical endeavor that requires writers and designers to have a certain kind of rhetorical knowledge. As such, I include redistribution, which involves redeploying updated texts in new ways and to potentially new audiences, within this typology.

In recent work, many rhetoric scholars have offered valuable contributions to the relatively nascent theorizing of how texts are circulated in digital publics. For instance, James Porter (2009), working from Douglas Eyman (2007), classified a key aspect of delivery by exploring two interrelated concepts: distribution and circulation. Distinguishing the two, Porter noted, "Distribution refers then to the initial decision about how you package a message in order to send it to its intended audience. Circulation refers to the potential for that message to have a document life of its own

---

8   It resembles what we would today call a meme. As Geoffrey Carter and Sarah Arroyo (2011) have noted, "memes differ from dialogue in that the goal is not to come to consensus or resolve a problem once and for all; rather, the goal is to create more content with which users will connect and invest more time in re-purposing, thus participating in spreading ideas and making them more complex" (p. 296).

and be re-distributed without your direct intervention" (p. 214). Whereas Porter's interest rested in the rhetorical act of the initial rhetor, and the decisions she makes to distribute her message, my focus here is what happens *post*-distribution, when the original message is already in circulation: How will a new rhetor redistribute the text? What will she add to the text? How will she alter its circulatory path?

Although circulation rightly has been positioned as a fleeting, recursive, and affective phenomenon (e.g., Chaput, 2010; Edbauer, 2005; Gries, 2013; Warner, 2005), many scholars have contended that rhetors can develop the needed rhetorical knowledge to prepare for the complexity of texts in motion. An especially useful framework to account for circulation is the notion of rhetorical velocity, what Jim Ridolfo and Dànielle Nicole DeVoss (2009) described as "[a] conscious rhetorical concern for distance, travel, speed, and time.." Although it is often used to discuss how individual rhetors can anticipate how their texts might be appropriated and redistributed, I find rhetorical velocity to be a useful concept for thinking about how rhetors might *intervene* in the circulatory paths of texts already in motion. Such intervention, borrowing from David Sheridan, Jim Ridolfo, and Anthony Michel (2012), necessitates the need for rhetors to be "kairotically inventive" by responding to a given situation in a contextually specific and culturally appropriate manner (p. 11).

As an example of redistribution, I recall a discursive moment that occurred during the second 2012 Presidential debate between Mitt Romney and Barack Obama. During the debate, the Republican nominee Romney used a phrase that within minutes became an Internet sensation, spurring iterations of the expression to be distributed and re-distributed on social media, blogs, news programs, and eventually even as a category on *Jeopardy*. The phrase: "binders full of women." The expression was uttered in response to a question about women and pay equity, wherein Romney recalled the experience of appointing members to the Massachusetts cabinet. Disappointed with the lack of women applicants Romney stated, "we took a concerted effort to go out and find women who had backgrounds that could be qualified to become members of our cabinet. I went to a number of women's groups and said, 'can you help us find folks?' And they brought whole binders full of women" (Romney, 2012). Within minutes, the phrase went viral, jolting writers and designers to irreverently memorialize the event on the social web. More than a memorialization, though, the "Binders Full of Women" memes often included sharp critiques of both Romney's stance on social issues as well as broader social and political issues. In other words, the phrase offered rhetors a common launching point from which they could offer their own opinions on political and social issues. For instance, one comment on the "Binders Full of Women" Facebook page read, "Gov. Romney clearly misspoke. What he meant to say was that his platform wants to bind women to the 19th century" (https://www.facebook.com/romneybindersfullofwomen). Another Facebook group, "Binders Full of Women: And Other Subjects Best Left Unbound," has mobilized to discuss inequity in contemporary politics and culture. The "Binders Full of Women" phrase, in effect, became (and arguably remains) a shared *topos* through which rhetors could both express their beliefs and mobilize collective groups for action. And to do so, rhetors needed to kairotically intervene in the rhetorical velocity of a text that was already in wide circulation.

3.4. Genre play

Genre play can be defined as constructing a text that blends, repurposes, or otherwise moves in and out of genre expectations. Signaled by phrases such as "remixing the book," "remixing the essay," or "remixing traditional scholarship," genre play refers to the ways in which rhetors playfully re-conceptualize reified norms, working both within and against those socially constituted ways of doing and knowing. As Carolyn Miller (1984) famously noted, genres are best understood as forms of social action—meaning that the emphasis for studying genres should be on typified *use* rather than particular forms. Years later, Anis Bawarshi (2000) noted that genres are both functional and epistemological: "they help us function within particular situations at the same time they help us shape the ways we come to know these situations" (p. 340). In other words, genres, for Bawarshi, played a constitutive role in our social activities. As such, playfully altering a genre convention can either call into question how such
a convention became valorized in the first place or invite readers to re-experience what might be conceived as an otherwise banal convention. This rhetorical practice, then, has the potential to interrogate and potentially change the ways in which, to borrow from Bawarshi, we come to know situations.

There are many ways to play with genre conventions. Common ways include using conventions that typically fall outside of the genre (e.g., writing one's own poetry within a scholarly work) and writing content that does not quite match genre expectations (e.g., a professor including intimate details of his or her personal life on a course syllabus). Although parody and irreverence are common ways to play with genres, they are not the only strategies writers use. Gloria Anzaldúa's (1987) *Borderlands/ La Frontera: The New Mestiza* is a classic example of a text that played with genre expectations, at once blending poetry, creative non-fiction, autobiography, spiritual texts, sketches and drawings, and theory. Anzaldúa's text played with many things—design, form, content—to invite readers to experience, if even in a fragmented and partial way, what Anzaldúa called a mestiza consciousness. This was one of the key rhetorical moves of what I am calling genre play: the intentional move to disrupt how we commonly view the world through the conscious and playful act of repurposing the (often mundane) genres we read and view every day.

For an example of genre play, I turn to a text constructed by an eighth-grade student who designed a mock standardized test to critique the rigid, inartistic, ablest, classist, and pressure-inducing qualities of New York's testing system (Strauss, 2013). The student made her argument by using the design and genre conventions of standardized tests, which included directions, reading passages, and multiple-choice questions. The student composed a message, however, that highly transgressed the norms of the test genre, keeping with its typical form but radically changing its typical content. Instead of the "usual" reading passages eighth-grade students might expect, the student wrote a pointed letter of critique against standardized testing. For example, the reading passage of her faux test began as such: "I am not fond of your tests. They do not show you who I am, or who my teachers are" (Strauss, 2013). The passage continued in a similar fashion, providing reasons why the focus on testing invoked anxiety and was biased towards certain learners. Similarly, the student wrote questions that scrutinized the objectives of the test—for example, one question asked, "Which group of individuals struggles with the test the *most?*" With answers that included "teachers," "young people," and "children with special needs," the student succinctly critiqued the testing system by playing within—yet against—the genre expectations of standardized tests. What made this powerful as a rhetorical strategy was that it called into question the social and political contexts from which the test genre emerged (Miller, 1984) and simultaneously asked readers to question how the genre works functionally and epistemologically (Bawarshi, 2000).

4. IMPLICATIONS FOR TEACHING AND RESEARCH

The overarching purposes for this article have been twofold: first, to situate remix rhetorically by drawing on theories and pedagogies of imitation, and second, to isolate and explain common types of remix. These two go hand in hand. In order to explain the central needs and uses for remix, which are both productive (i.e., solving a problem or attempting to effect change) and pedagogical (i.e., learning more about ourselves and others), we need a durable yet malleable theory. And in order to make this theory more usable—that is, more productive and more pedagogical—we need to start to chart the ways in which this theory does work in the world. Hence, a revived theory of imitation serves as a pliable frame from which remix types—assemblage, reappropriation, redistribution, genre play, and still others—can emerge.

4.1. Situating remix rhetorically

How do we begin teaching remix in writing classes? There are, of course, several responses to this question (see, for example, Dietel-McLaughlin, 2009; Dubisar & Palmeri, 2010; Ridolfo & DeVoss, 2009; Ray, 2013; Stedman, 2012). I will sketch another possibility here. First, as Dubisar and Palmeri noted (2010), it is important to remember that students will have varying levels of comfort and knowledge when it comes to analyzing and composing remixes. That is, some students might have experience with both consuming and producing remixes, while others might have little background with remix or think of the concept as belonging solely within the realm of music. As such, I suggest first laying a strong foundation for how—and, more importantly, why—composers use remix methods. As many scholars have noted (Jenkins, 1992, 2009; Kuhn, 2012; Lankshear & Knobel, 2011; Stedman, 2012), the reasons for remixing are varied and situated: from recutting a television series to include oppressed or silenced voices/bodies to repurposing video to participate in political debates about copyright and intellectual property. Discussing some of these reasons would be useful in developing an impetus for remixing—after which, students can begin to think about the reasons they may want to remix, and thus how they might go about inventing, constructing, and distributing their remixes. Here is where the process and theory of imitation and the typology can simultaneously come into play: after sketching some possible needs for and uses of remixing, students can begin to think about the process of making their own remixes. What would constructing a remix entail? What texts will be (re)used? What purpose will their remixes serve? What communities will their remix impact? How will they distribute their remixes? These questions, and still others, can be used to spark discussions and writing activities that address some of the rhetorical concerns of imitation—e.g., deciphering a vast bank of texts, materials, and genres, and attending to the ethical dynamics of repurposing public work.

audiene = students

4.2. Teaching (with) the typology

As students begin to outline and plan their remixes, they will likely need to start conceptualizing what kind of remix they want to make and what kind of work they want it to do. Do they want to build an argument out of a multitude of other texts (assemblage)? Do they want to reuse or "take back" a particular text, image, metaphor, or concept (reappropriation)? Do they want to use an image, phrase, meme, concept, etc. that is already in wide circulation to make their argument (redistribution)? Do they want to play with the conventions of a particular genre to draw attention to something absurd, outlandish, or problematic (genre play)? After teasing out some of the possibilities, students can think through some of the potentials and constraints of the various types of remix presented in the typology. As such, embracing critical pedagogy approaches, I imagine productive classes happening *after* the introduction of this typology. Students can ask: Is anything missing? Should we place more value on some remix approaches over others? How might certain communities value some approaches over others? In answering these questions, and still others, I imagine the initial typology might itself be reassembled—expanded, morphed, hierarchized—to account for the concerns of students and the ever-evolving digital and material spaces they inhabit. From here, as students begin composing their remixes, it may be useful for students to record and track the texts they are considering using in their remixes. Such documentation, much like the dissection of texts Roman rhetoric students used to practice (Murphy, 2012), should offer a detailed analysis of the texts students wish to refashion and a rationale for their redeployment. In this way, students are asked to make strategic and mindful choices about how their remix will impact potential audiences. This document, moreover, shows that effective remixes are not developed by happenstance—rather, they are carefully constructed and are highly attuned to the sociocultural dimensions of the materials they use and the contexts from which they arise.

4.3. Considerations for teaching and research

There are a number of issues to consider when teaching and further developing this typology. I focus on three here: issues with stabilization, potential for unethical use, and issues of intellectual property. It could be argued that trying to pin down remix practices—that is, trying to isolate and explain common rhetorical moves used by remix composers—works to stabilize what is otherwise a fluctuating and evolving practice. I am sensitive to this argument. Our goal should not be to offer some "Master Guidebook" of remix. Such a move would ignore the sociocultural nature of writing. Rather, we should aim to offer writers—some of whom may be unfamiliar or uncomfortable with the concept of remix—an entry point for discussing how to reuse already existing material.

Another issue that deserves merit is the claim that remix cannot—should not—be taught in college classrooms. As literacy scholars Colin Lankshear and Michele Knobel (2011) have noted, learning new literacies (like learning how to remix) often entails a community and identity dimension that cannot be easily recreated in the classroom. To add to this, scholars and critics have noted that remix risks losing its subversive power when it gets institutionalized (Coppa, 2010; Manovich, 2009). These are issues that we cannot take lightly. As many within composition and rhetoric have noted, though, there are ways to bridge both what students do outside of the class and what they do within it (e.g., Anderson, 2008; Stedman, 2012; Yancey, 2004). To this end, by situating remix within a frame of imitation and offering "paradigmatic" cases such as the ones presented here, we are in a much better position to responsibly teach and troubleshoot ethics of use. Still, these positions warrant careful scrutiny in writing classes and further discussion in future research.

Lastly, let me address the elephant in the room: intellectual property. Teaching remix practices, especially if final projects will be delivered in online, public venues like YouTube, automatically implicates students in a legal realm. As such, teaching remix should undoubtedly involve teaching intellectual property, and especially teaching writers how to navigate copyright concerns—both in terms of avoiding copyright infringement and responding to feckless copyright takedowns. Indeed, scholars have increasingly called on writing teachers to be aware of intellectual property issues as they pertain to writing and, particularly, digital writing. These have included, among much other important work, teaching students how to conduct fair use analyses (Rife, 2007), situating writing in terms of the value it adds to communities (DeVoss & Porter, 2006), and using and building local codes of "best practices" (Aufderheide & Jaszi, 2011). These are all important ways to teach students the basics of intellectual property and how to avoid copyright infringement. What I would like to suggest, too, is that by situating remix as a rhetorical concern linked to an ethical and collaborative-minded theory of imitation, teachers already begin to lay a strong foundation for teaching the importance of fair use.

Like all writing, remix practices will continue to evolve over time. The social and material means by which remixes get constructed will be subject to constant change, making remix an unstable practice to chart. This, however, does not make the practices of today any less important. My hope is that this article does not close doors to thinking about remix in exciting and new ways. On the contrary, my hope is that it begins to situate remix in a position of potential endurance, change, and growth.

REFERENCES

Anderson, Daniel. (2008). The low bridge to high benefits: Entry-level multimedia, literacies, and motivation. *Computers and Composition, 25*(1),40–60.

Anzaldúa, Gloria. (1987). *Borderlands/La frontera: The new mestiza.* San Francisco, CA: Aunt Lute.

Allen, Julia M., & Faigley, Lester. (1995). Discursive strategies for social change: An alternative rhetoric of argument. *Rhetoric Review, 14*(1),142–172.

Auerbach, Erich. (1953). *Mimesis: The representation of reality in Western literature Princeton.* NJ: Princeton University Press.

Aufderheide, Patricia, & Jaszi, Peter. (2011). *Reclaiming fair use: How to put balance back in copyright.* Chicago, IL: University of Chicago Press.

Bacon, Jacqueline. (1998). Do you understand your own language? Revolutionary topoi in the rhetoric of African-American abolitionists. *Rhetoric Society Quarterly, 28*(2), 55–75.

Bawarshi, Anis. (2000). The genre function. *College English, 62*(3), 335–360.

Bender, Daniel. (1996). *Imitation. In Theresa Enos ed, Encyclopedia of rhetoric and composition: Communication from ancient times to the information age.* pp. 343–346. New York NY: Garland.

Bizzell, Patricia. (1997). The 4th of July and the 22nd of December: The function of cultural archives in persuasion, as shown by Frederick Douglass and William Apess. *College Composition and Communication*, *21*(4), 44–60.

Butler, Judith. (1997a). *Excitable speech: A politics of the performative*. New York, NY: Routledge.

Butler, Judith. (1997b). *The psychic life of power: Theories in subjection*. Stanford, CA: Stanford University Press.

Brooke, Collin Gifford. (2009). *Lingua fracta: Toward a rhetoric of new media*. New York, NY: Hampton.

Burke, Kenneth. (1954). *Permanence and change*. Berkeley, CA: University of California Press.

Carter, Geoffrey V., & Arroyo, Sarah J. (2011). Tubing the future: Participatory pedagogy and YouTube U in 2020. *Computers and Composition*, *28*(4), 292–302.

Chaput, Catherine. (2010). Rhetorical circulation in late capitalism: Neoliberalism and the over determination of affective energy. *Philosophy and Rhetoric*, *43*(1), 1–25.

Clark, Donald Leman. (1957). *Rhetoric in Greco-Roman education*. New York, NY: Columbia University Press.

Coppa, Francesca. (2010). Interview with Elisa Kreisinger. Transformative Works and Cultures 5. Retrieved February 1, 2014, fromhttp://journal. transformativeworks.org/index.php/twc/article/view/234/170.

Corbett, Edward. (1971). The theory and practice of imitation in classical rhetoric. *College Composition and Communication*, *22*(3),243–250.

Crowley, Sharon. (1985). Rhetoric, literature, and the dissociation of invention. *Journal of Advanced Composition*, *6*, 17–32.

Delagrange, Susan. (2009). Wunderkammer, Cornell, and the visual canon of arrangement Kairos, 13(2). Retrieved January 27, 2014, fromhttp://kairos.technorhetoric.net/13.2/topoi/delagrange/index.html.

DeVoss, Dànielle Nicole, & Porter, James E. (2006). Why Naptster matters to writing: Filesharing as a new ethic of digital delivery. *Computers and Composition*, *23*(2), 178–210.

Dietel-McLaughlin, Erin. (2009). Remediating democracy: Irreverent composition and the vernacular rhetorics of Web 2.0. Computers and Com-position Online. Retrieved January 28, 2014, from http://www2.bgsu.edu/departments/english/cconline/Dietel/irreverent.htm.

Dubisar, Abby, & Palmeri, Jason. (2010). Palin/pathos/Peter Griffin: Political remix and composition pedagogy. *Computers and Composition, 27*(2),77-93.

Edbauer, Jenny. (2005). Unframing models of public distribution: From rhetorical situation to rhetorical ecologies. *Rhetoric Society Quarterly, 35*(4), 5-24.

Eisner, Caroline, & Vicinus, Martha. (2008). *Originality, imitation, and plagiarism: Teaching writing in the digital age.* Ann Arbor, MI: University of Michigan Press.

Eyman, Douglas. (2007). Digital rhetoric: Ecologies and economies of digital circulation (Doctoral dissertation). *Available from ProQuest and Theses database.* (UMI No 3282094)

Farmer, Frank, & Arrington, Phillip. (1993). Apologies and accommodations: Imitation and the writing process. *Rhetoric Society Quarterly, 23*(1),12-34.

Ferguson, Kirby. (2010, October 27). Everything is a remix part 1 [Video File]. Retrieved February 3, 2014, from http://www.youtube.com/watch?v=NmwwjikTHxw.

Gaylor, Brett. (2009). *RiP: A remix manifesto* [Documentary]. New York, NY: Disinformation Company.

Go4thREVOLT. (2011, August 17). Go forth and revolt [Video File]. Retrieved February 2, 2014, from http://www.youtube.com/watch?v=UVc8auO1vuA.

Gries, Laurie E. (2013). Iconographic tracking: A digital research method for visual rhetoric and circulation studies. *Computers and Composition, 30*(4), 332-348.

Haskins, Ekaterina V. (2000). Mimesis between poetics and rhetoric: Performance culture and civic education in Plato. *Isocrates, and Aristotle. Rhetoric Society Quarterly, 30*(3), 7-33.

Hesse, Doug, Sommers, Nancy, & Yancey, Kathleen Blake. (2012). Evocative objects: Reflections on teaching, learning, and living in between. *College English*, 74(4), 325–350.

Howard, Rebecca Moore. (1999). *Standing in the shadow of giants: Plagiarists, authors, collaborators*. Stanford, CT: Albex.

Jenkins, Henry. (2009). *Confronting the challenges of participatory culture: Media education for the 21st century*. Cambridge, MA: The MIT Press.

Jenkins, Henry. (1992). *Textual poachers: Television fans and participatory culture*. New York, NY: Routledge.

Johnson-Eilola, Johndan, & Selber, Stuart. (2007). Plagiarism, originality, assemblage. *Computers and Composition*, 24(4), 375–403.

Kreisinger, Elisa. (2009, February 2). You can't vote in change [Video file]. Retrieved January 27, 2014 from http://www.youtube.com/watch?v=3PhhCGIFS1E.

Kuhn, Virginia. (2012). The rhetoric of remix. *Transformative Works and Cultures*, 9, 279. Retrieved January 27, 2014, fromhttp://journal.transformativeworks.org/index.php/twc/article/view/358/279

Lanham, Carol Dana. (2012). Writing instruction from late antiquity to the twelfth century. In James Murphy (Ed.), *A short history of writing instruction: From ancient Greece to contemporary America* (3rd Ed., pp. 36–76). New York, NY: Routledge.

Lankshear, Colin, & Knobel, Michele. (2011). *New literacies: Everyday practices and social learning*. New York, NY: McGraw-Hill.

LeFevre, Karen Burke. (1987). *Invention as a social act*. Carbondale, IL: Southern Illinois University Press.

Lessig, Lawrence. (2001). *The future of ideas: The fate of the commons in a connected world*. New York. NY: Random House.

Lessig, Lawrence. (2008). *Remix: Making art and commerce thrive in the hybrid economy*. New York, NY: Penguin Press.

Levi's [Advertisement]. (2011, July 20). Levi's Go Forth 2011 [Video File]. Retrieved January 27, 2014, from http://www.youtube.com/watch?v=KT16DcHcjRA.

Lunsford, Andrea A. (1999). Rhetoric, feminism, and the politics of textual ownership. *College English*, 61, 529–544.

Lunsford, Andrea, & Ede, Lisa. (1992). *Singular texts/plural authors: Perspectives on collaborative writing.* Carbondale, IL: Southern Illinois University Press.

Manovich, Lev. (2009). The practice of everyday (media) life: From mass consumption to mass cultural production? *Critical Inquiry, 35*(2), 319–331.

McKee, Heidi A., & Porter, James E. (2009). *The ethics of Internet research: A rhetorical, case-based process.* New York: Peter Lang.

Minock, Mary. (1995). Toward a postmodern pedagogy of imitation. *JAC, 15*(3), 489–509.

Miller, Carolyn R. (1984). Genre as social action. *Quarterly Journal of Speech, 70*(2), 151–167.

Miller, Keith D., & Quashie, Kevin. (1998). Slave mutiny as argument, argument as fiction, fiction as America: The case of Frederick Douglass's the heroic slave. *Southern Journal of Communication, 63*(3), 199–207.

Muckelbauer, John. (2003). Imitation and invention in antiquity: An historical-theoretical revision. *Rhetorica, 21*(2), 61–88.

Murphy, James J. (2012). Roman writing instruction as described by Quintilian. In James Murphy (Ed.), *A short history of writing instruction: From ancient Greece to contemporary America* (3rd ed., pp. 36–76). New York, NY: Routledge.

Octalog. (1988). The politics of historiography. *Rhetoric Review, 7*(1), 5–49.

Olson, Gary A., & Worsham Lynn. (2000). Changing the subject: Judith Butler's politics of radical resignification. *JAC, 20*(4), 727–765.

Palmeri, Jason. (2012). *Remixing composition: A history of multimodal writing pedagogy.* Carbondale, IL: Southern Illinois University Press.

Pigman, George W. (1980). Versions of imitation in the Renaissance. *Renaissance Quarterly, 33*(1), 1–32.

Porter, James E. (2005). New (and old) modes of production and learning in the post-Napster era: Writing as memory, imitation, compilation (unpublished conference presentation) *Conference on Originality, Imitation, and Plagiarism.* Ann Arbor, MI.

Porter, James E. (2009). Recovering delivery for digital rhetoric. *Computers and Composition, 25*(4), 207–224.

Pough, Gwendolyn. (2010). The remix: Revisit, rethink, revise, renew, CFP for Conference on College Composition and Communication. Louisville, KY,

Quintilian. (2006). Institutes of oratory. Lee Honeycutt, Ed., (John Shelby Watson, Trans.) Retrieved February 4, 2014, fromhttp://rhetoric. eserver.org/quintilian/.

Randall, Marilyn. (2001). *Pragmatic plagiarism: Authorship, profit, and power.* Toronto, ON: University of Toronto Press.

Robbins, Sarah. (2003). Distributed authorship: A feminist case-study framework for studying intellectual property. *College English, 66*(2), 155–171.

Romney, Mitt. (2012, October 16). The second presidential debate 2012. Hempstead, New York Retrieved February 4, 2014, fromhttp://www. youtube.com/watch?v=QEpCrcMF5Ps.

Ray, Brian. (2013). More than just remixing: Uptake and new media composition. *Computers and Composition, 30*(3), 183–195.

Ridolfo, Jim, & DeVoss, Dànielle Nicole. (2009). Composing for recomposition: Rhetorical velocity and delivery. *Kairos 13*(2). Retrieved January27, 2014 from http://www.technorhetoric.net/13.2/topoi/ridolfo devoss/intro.html.

Rife, Martine Courant. (2007). The fair use doctrine: History, application, and implications for (new media) writing teachers. *Computers and Composition, 24*(2), 154–178.

Sullivan, Dale. (1989). Attitudes toward imitation: Classical culture and the modern temper. *Rhetoric Review, 8,* 5–21.

Sheridan, David M., Ridolfo, Jim, & Michel, Anthony J. (2012). *The available means of persuasion: Mapping a theory and pedagogy of multimodal public rhetoric.* Anderson, SC: Parlor Press.

Stedman, Kyle. (2012). Remix literacy and fan compositions. *Computers and Composition, 29*(2), 107–123.

Strauss, Valerie. (2013, April 17). Eighth-grader designs standardized test that slams standardized tests. *The Washington Post*. Retrieved February 3, 2014, from http://www.washingtonpost.com/blogs/answer-sheet/wp/2013/04/17/eighth-grader-designs-standardized-test-that-slams-standardized-tests/.

Terrill, Robert. (2011). Mimesis, duality, and rhetorical education. *Rhetoric Society Quarterly, 41*(4), 295–315.

Warner, Michael. (2005). *Publics and counterpublics.* New York, NY: Zone Books.

Welch, Kathleen E. (1999). *Electric rhetoric: Classical rhetoric, oralism, and a new literacy.* Cambridge, MA: MIT Press.

Wilson, Kirt H. (2003). The racial politics of imitation in the nineteenth century. *Quarterly Journal of Speech, 89*(2), 89–108.

Yancey, Kathleen Blake. (2004). Made not only in words: Composition in a new key. *College Composition and Communication, 56*(2), 297–328.

Yancey, Kathleen Blake. (2009). Re-designing graduate education in composition and rhetoric: The use of remix as concept, material, and method. *Computers and Composition, 26*(1), 4–12.

MODULE ONE

Remixing the Text

Introduction: What is Plagiarism?

Marilyn Randall

THE PROBLEM

There is a wealth of received wisdom about plagiarism, transmitted most effectively through countless aphorisms coined primarily by authors, that is, virtual plagiarists, in their own defence. The 'history' of plagiarism can be divided roughly into discourses of apology and of condemnation: the first generally argues that all literature, or art—in fact, all of human activity—is essentially repetitive, and that 'plagiarism,' therefore, is inevitable. The second, ascribing an ethical content to aesthetic activity, defends notions of intellectual property, originality, and individual authenticity, which are seen to be transgressed by certain types of appropriation of intellectual products. These opposing positions meet, however, in their judgment of 'great authors': copying that achieves a superior level of aesthetic approval may escape the negative implications inherent in the accusation of plagiarism. Discursive repetition may be seen either as ubiquitous and essentially benign, producing in some instances great art for which the qualifier 'plagiaristic' becomes inappropriate; or else as exceptional and fundamentally malignant, a transgression of whatever ethical, aesthetic, or legal conventions or laws are available to provide sanctions for it. In fact, the overwhelming consensus about literary plagiarism is that it is bad only when it is not good, and the canonical examples of good plagiarists far outweigh those of the bad variety.

The considerable efforts engaged in by authors to justify 'plagiarism'—or, rather, to recast it in another light—are a significant indication that 'plagiarism' has always marked a definite frontier between the acceptable and the odious, between good writing and bad, between legitimate and illegitimate aesthetic practices. Both the word and the practice have a long and, if not venerable, at least important history, stretching back to antiquity in Western culture and spanning the centuries with a consistency perhaps unknown in any other literary category. Plagiaristic texts ('real' ones), however, are rarely studied, or only inadvertently, precisely because their qualification as plagiaristic automatically excludes them from the domain of appropriate objects of literary attention. Admittedly, a pure and bona fide case of plagiarism, such as Borges imagines in 'Pierre Menard, Author of *Don Quixote*,' would be of little textual significance, and would have mainly artefactual, legal, or biographical interest—in fact, in the real world, plagiarism committed on such a scale would constitute a case of piracy, which is largely outside my domain. In Borges's fictional example, the literary critic's preference for Menard's 'version' of *Don Quixote* over Cervantes's opens up a whole range of fascinating questions to the sociologist or historian of literature. As in so many of Borges's fictions, the hypothetical example is not so far from reality, if one considers the judgment rendered by the Académie française about Corneille's *Le Cid* compared with its Spanish 'original,' or the fortunes of Shakespeare's plays compared with that of their sources. The Borgesian fiction sets the stage for the premise that 'plagiarism' is not, in fact, primarily a textual category, but a *pragmatic* one, principally determined by a wide variety of extratextual criteria that constitute the aesthetic, institutional, and cultural contexts of production and reception of the work. In other words, 'plagiarism' (especially literary plagiarism) does not in fact 'exist' in any positive or objective sense, accompanied by textual criteria that would allow us to recognize it in the same way that we can a lyric poem, a sonnet, or even, however tenuously, a novel.

Far from being controversial, this premise is actually rather self-evident, since disputes about plagiarism and court battles determining breach of copyright depend directly on the undecidable status of explicit repetitions or apparent copies. The question to be answered in such debates is not whether repetition has occurred, but whether, in fact, the repetition that can be seen to have occurred qualifies as one of the sanctionable, unethical, or even illegal forms that we have come to call plagiarism or breach of copyright. The consequence of this evidence is that 'plagiarism' (I use the term, for the time being, in its general sense, to include copyright infractions) is not an immanent feature of texts, but rather the result of judgments involving, first of all, the presence of some kind of textual repetition, but also, and perhaps more important, a conjunction of social, political, aesthetic, and cultural norms and presuppositions that motivate accusations or disculpations, elevating some potential plagiarisms to the level of great works of art, while censuring others and condemning the perpetrators to ignominy. Particular controversies provide clear evidence of the non-textual criteria mobilized in decisions about plagiarism: the status and perceived genius of the author, both plagiarizing and plagiarized; the statues achieved by the plagiaristic text before the discovery of the 'plagiarism'; the national and patriotic interests of accuser and accused; and, of course, the aesthetic and legal norms dominating at the various moments of production, reception, and judgment of the text.

Although the distinction between 'literature' and other forms of discourse is increasingly meaningless as one moves back in history, I have chosen to concentrate mainly on what we now call 'literature' for several reasons, not the least of which is as a means of limiting the field somewhat. The first reason for focusing (primarily) on literary plagiarism arises from my interest in studying the construction of literature *qua* literature, which is what I take to be the fundamental aim of institutional analysis. In this sense, literary plagiarism demonstrates, as do literature and other forms of aesthetic production, certain pragmatic specificities that are not generalizable across the spectrum of discursive or cultural fields, and these specificities arise primarily from institutional differences that are pertinent to the construction of literary plagiarism.

First, non-literary plagiarism—scientific, journalistic, academic, for example—present particular problems and solutions that can sometimes seem more straightforward than in literary plagiarism, since the institutions in which they occur often have more stringent, or at least explicit, internal standards of behaviour for their members, standards that allow them to judge 'plagiarism' not only as a punctual infraction involving theft of intellectual property, but as an ethical breach of norms or laws that constitute the institution. Student plagiarism, to take one example, is explicitly sanctionable within the terms of the contract of the academy, where it is usually defined and proscribed in student handbooks that lay out the proper use of citations, quotation marks, and other techniques of attribution. The contractual agreement into which students enter is clear, if not always to them, at least to the institution, and when infractions can be identified they are always sanctionable. Academia allows for mitigating circumstances that may attenuate the seriousness of the individual offence, but has no official provision for considering some forms of student copying to be brilliant or inspired, or for considering some student plagiarisms to be indicative of genius, regardless of the fact that some student 'geniuses' may, in fact plagiarize—the academic plagiarisms of Martin Luther King, Jr., which I examine in Part Three, are a case in point.

The literary institution has a much more difficult time, first, identifying plagiarism, and, second, condemning it. Literary plagiarism is, in fact, not always bad: the brilliant plagiarism and plagiarist-as-genius are much more common in the literary domain than in any other. While the semantic force of the term usually entails negative connotations, 'plagiarism' has often been used to describe the imitative practices of great writers: 'literary plagiarism' is a kind of pleasing oxymoron expressing the transformative power of aesthetic genius and distinguishing between inspired and servile imitation. In postmodernism, 'plagiarism' (firmly framed by quotation marks) has become both a practice and a critical category for which are claimed aesthetic intentions and effects. This blurring of the use of the term 'plagiarism' to describe explicit and intentionally aesthetic forms of repetition is one of the features of contemporary production that I explore.

A second aspect of the institutional specificity of 'literature' is that today, and since what Bourdieu would call its 'autonomization' during the nineteenth century, it is considered to exist quite independently of any extra-aesthetic function to which it may be put, and which many other kinds of writing—academic, journalistic, political, and so on—entail by definition. Modern authorship exists within a market or institutional structure and may serve multiple purposes where the fact of authorship may be the only one in a complex of functions defining the writer's role. Professional authors may be engaged by contract or in order to fulfill a specific end; their texts may produce both symbolic and material advantages, the two not necessarily coinciding. Texts produced in a professional academic setting, for example, may have an exceedingly strong symbolic value, and a rather indirect market value, only cumulatively leading to tenure and promotion, and occasionally to financial rewards. Both types of value lead, however, to the fulfilment of a contract that exceeds the condition of authorship. The theft of such professional discourse often not only entails the theft of an individual's intellectual property, but may involve either the legal property or the symbolic values of the institution; such theft is quite often considered a transgression of the explicit institutional norms governing the behaviour of the members.

A third aspect of the specificity of the literary institution is the nebulous nature of its existence. It has no membership lists, no official code of ethics regulating the behaviour of its members, no criteria for legitimacy other than 'authorship' itself; it is a fuzzy and tautological structure whose conditions for inclusion are unregulated and indeterminate. There is no external or institutional necessity requiring literary writers to write literature; the activity and its product are, on the one hand, self-imposed by the author and, on the other, somehow superfluous, or at least autotelic. While literary authors may indeed write under contract, this contract is erected on the expectation of authorship alone, and not on other functions (such as teaching or research) from which it derives or for which it is supposed to account. There are no rules defining the criteria for success or failure to which putative literary authors can adhere. And, as Bourdieu points out, the market and the symbolic value of literary works may be so far detached as to be antonymous. The literary institution lacks, as well, official bodies invested with a legislative role for providing sanctions for internal transgressions, whereas other arenas of professional authorship may have their own internal courts of justice, such as one witnesses within the academic field. The plagiarized literary author seeking justice must ultimately turn to civil law, or else rely on the literary press and other informal means of sanction. In this sense, the discourse surrounding literary plagiarism is itself often the only court wherein the greatest number of putative cases are tried.

While the literary institution is clearly a highly regulated field subject to economic forces and depending for its existence on strongly rule-governed organisms such as the publishing industry and the academic institution, the actual content of the literary, as with any aesthetic domain, is largely constructed from within: the various 'rules' and conventions to which literature has to conform in order to become 'literary' in various historico-cultural situations are normally derived from the constitutive elements of the field itself, which reshapes its contours in a continuing contest for legitimacy that Bourdieu has described: 'There is no other criterion of membership of a field than the objective fact of producing effects within it. One of the difficulties of the orthodox defence against heretical transformation of the field by a redefinition of the tacit or explicit terms of entry is the fact that polemics imply a form of recognition; adversaries whom one would prefer to destroy by ignoring them cannot be combated without consecrating them' ('The Field of Cultural Production' 42).

Once values such as 'originality' and 'authenticity' have been established as constitutive of the nature of an institution like the university, they can be raised to the level of explicit rules that exist not only in the minds of individuals, but in regulative documents that prescribe the behaviour and norms of the members of the institution. These rules exist independently of the actual behaviour of the institutional agents, and their codification lends them relative stability and autonomy. The aesthetic field, on the other hand, despite various degrees of regulation, is much less subject to reification by codification. It has been well demonstrated by theorists, from the early Russian formalists to Bourdieu, that the contours of the literary are continually being reshaped from the inside, most often by forces of contestation and revolution that intend to transgress and overturn precisely those conventions that are perceived to be the most highly codified. In this way, while a concept of 'plagiarism' has always been situated solidly beyond the acceptable limits of the literary, the tolerance for actual literary practices is constantly being reformed by the force of those practices themselves. When techniques of aesthetic 'appropriation,' for example, become so widespread as to be largely conventionalized rather than contestatory, they redefine the limits of the acceptable within the norms of the institution without substantially modifying the proscription against 'plagiarism.' In the aesthetic field, it is the relative weakness of its regulative rules, versus the strong force of its constitutive rules, which results in the fact that the concept of plagiarism, a kind of relative rule, is fairly stable, while its constitutive features are in constant flux.

If the construction of literature is a function of institutional, that is, extratextual, constraints and criteria, and their intersection—happily or not—with discursive forms, a most compelling reason for focusing on literary plagiarism is its functioning as a barometer of shifting literary norms and aesthetic conventions, and of the power struggles to institute authority that attend the construction of the literary field. What is at one time called 'plagiarism' constitutes, at others, the exact definition of 'good literature,' and an examination and comparison of some of the more radical moments in this history will reveal not only what is 'plagiarism' for a specific historico-cultural period but, perhaps more importantly, what is 'literature' for that same period. In taking debates about plagiarism to be symptomatic of the power struggles inherent in cultural formations, I am in agreement with Foucault, who states:

Rather than analyzing power from the point of view of its internal rationality, it [a new economy of power relations] consists of analyzing power relations through the antagonism of strategies.

For example, to find out what our society means by sanity, perhaps we should investigate what is happening in the field of insanity.

And what we mean by legality in the field of illegality. ('The Subject and Power' 419)

And, I would add, what we mean by 'literature' through an investigation of 'non-literature': disputes about plagiarism can be seen as instances of power struggles within the literary or, more broadly speaking, cultural field; they can be used to trace its contours, its values, and its institutional formation. Within the literary field, 'plagiarism' constitutes this same otherness that elicits what Foucault describes as an 'antagonism of strategies.'

THE PRAGMATICS

The claim that plagiarism is a pragmatic rather than a textual phenomenon is the corollary of the idea that 'literature' itself exists only as an aesthetic judgment imposed on texts—or authors—and subsequently is taken to be an immanent quality of the work. In this, I adhere to Pierre Bourdieu's sociology of the production of the category of aesthetic objects, when he claims that 'the work of art is an object which exists as such only by virtue of the (collective) belief which knows and acknowledges it as a work of art' ('The Field of Cultural Production' 35). If this claim is valid, as I take it to be, then it is also true of the category of non-literature, of which plagiaristic texts form a particular subset. As the products of judgments rendered about texts that subsequently become exemplary instances of positively or negatively valued cultural objects, literature and non-literature both participate in and arise from complex systems of features. Value—or, in the case of plagiarism, 'non-value'—is, as Barbara Herrnstein Smith says, the result of 'the features of literary and aesthetic judgments in relation to the multiple social, political, circumstantial and other constraints and conditions to which they are responsive' (28). In their analyses of taste and value, both Bourdieu and Smith are concerned with showing the *contingency* of value judgments despite evidence indicating the overwhelming consensus about cultural objects among groups over time.

As Smith explains, and as Bourdieu demonstrates in *Distinction* (1979), 'a coincidence of contingencies among individual subjects who interact as members of some community will operate for them as noncontingency and be interpreted by them accordingly' (Smith, 40). In other words, aesthetic 'value' is specific to communities who share presuppositions about what constitutes the appropriate features of the artistic or literary. I will pursue, with examples, this line of argumentation throughout the course of this study.

In Bourdieu's language, the investigation being undertaken here intends to explore the historical shift that has occurred over centuries in the strategies of legitimate symbolic and material appropriation of cultural capital within the specific field of literary production (with occasional exemplary forays into other domains). In the most general terms, this shift will be seen to follow the historical development of literary production from conventions of legitimization by *identification* with authoritative cultural norms, towards an aesthetic of *dissociation* from previous cultural production and an increased emphasis on the value of individuality, as the literary field gains autonomy throughout the eighteenth and nineteenth centuries. And as Bourdieu points out, the twentieth century has witnessed an increasing return to an aesthetics of recycling of past production, but he warns:

> In fact, these returns are always *apparent*, since they are separated from what they repeat by the negative reference (when it is not by a parodic intention) to something that was itself the negation (of the negation of the negation, etc.) of what they repeat. In the literary or artistic field at the present moment of its history, all acts, all gestures, all manifestations are, as one painter has well said 'kinds of "*clins d'oeil*" towards the inside of the milieu': these *clins d'oeil*, silent and hidden references to other artists, present or past, affirm, in and by games of distinction, a complicity which excludes the uninitiated, always condemned to miss the essential, that is precisely the interrelations and the interactions of which the work is nothing but the silent trace. Never has the structure of the field itself been as present in each act of production.

While Bourdieu provides us with a structure for understanding the macro-developments of institutional formation, it is the principles of discourse analysis arising from the field of literary pragmatics that allow us to examine the presuppositions embedded in discourses situated in terms of their historical, cultural, and aesthetic determinants. These discourses reveal the contextual conditions at the foundation of perceptions of plagiarism for various historical periods. My method attempts to be transhistorical while avoiding ahistoricity: in crossing vast stretches of time, I endeavor to uncover, despite the historical specificity governing differences in judgments about plagiarism, the transhistorical constants that inform them. This move is motivated only in part by the practical difficulty of performing, for each period of literary history, the kind of specific investigations offered by White, Welslau, and Rosenthal (all centered, significantly, on the Renaissance). While these studies provide essential insights about the about the social and aesthetic specificity of plagiarism in a particular historical context, I am here less interested in the cultural *differences* and aesthetic preferences that various periods manifest in relation to plagiarism than in the rather more surprising *similarities* among opinions and the stability of criteria for determining plagiarism, despite the variations in cultural presuppositions and the practices that express and produce them. While my fundamental premises are in agreement with the principles of *contingency* in judgments of value (Bourdieu *Distinction: A Social Critique of the Judgment of Taste*; Smith *Contingencies of Value: Alternative Perspectives for Critical Theory*), I assume this position as self-evident, and explore, rather than cultural difference, the transmission of cultural presuppositions that culminate in a certain stability of features characterizing plagiarism, and subsequently literature, for the Western tradition. The exemplarity and excessiveness of plagiarism make it particularly pertinent as an index of these features.

By considering discourse to be of the order of a 'linguistic act,' pragmatics postulates a communicative situation that, while not necessarily intersubjective (as in the case of literary discourse), is perceived by the receiver as an attempt on the part of the producer of the discourse to 'cause the "receiver" to think or do something' (Levinson 16). In other words, it is an act that generates another. It is essential to point out, for the case of written discourse, especially literary discourse, the irreducibly unidirectional nature both of this 'communication' and of the attribution of intentionality to the producer. If, in fact, literary discourse can at all be said to be a kind of communication, it is so only to the extent that the receiver attributes communicative intentionality to the absent subject of discourse. The pragmatic model that I am adopting understands the intentions of

the producer to be largely subsumed by the presuppositions of the receiver
about those intentions, based on the expectation of discursive conventions
similar to those posited by Grice's Conversational Maxims. The pragmatic assumption that felicitous communication requires a minimal level
of mutual knowledge is replaced by the notion of *relevance* (Sperber and
Wilson, *Relevance*), in which it is necessary for the reader only to *presuppose* the existence or possibility of communal knowledge. Sperber and
Wilson provide the example of a question to which the answer is literally
or semantically non-sequential. The receiver, presupposing, first, that the
interlocutor has understood the question, and then, that he or she understands and shares the convention of *relevance*, will attempt to repair the
apparent deviation by appealing to contextual factors such as encyclopedic
knowledge, or discursive conventions such as irony or sarcasm.

In literary discourse, the role of the receiver in constructing meaning and intentionality is crucial, since the intentions of the producer are
normally not available for verification (or may be considered irrelevant).
The act of reception is, however, inevitably accompanied by a postulate
concerning the production of discourse, specifically that at its origin is
an author-subject motivated by communicative intentions for which the
discourse is the evidence. The construction of meaning on the part of the
reader is also often accompanied by a presupposition that the meaning
discovered or received was in fact intended by the producer; the receiver
might also attribute to the author intentions of an aesthetic or ideological
nature, presuppositions derived either from prior knowledge or from textual evidence. While modern literary theory has identified and denounced
this communicative illusion under which readers labour by isolating, for
example, the 'intentional fallacy' (Wimsatt 3–18) and by turning away
from authorially based forms of interpretation, more subtle effects of reading as a communicative simulacrum are still very much with us. The very
presupposition of the existence of something like 'literary communication'
is a testimony to the continuing power of the notion that literary discourse
is a form of intersubjective communication, necessarily entailing the presence of two subjects of intentionality.

Literary discourse is a *linguistic act* in the sense that it entails presuppositions on the part of readers about the communicative intentions of
the producer of discourse. These intentions can be minimal ('the author
intended to write a novel') or fairly powerful ('the author intended to use
a story of a man and a whale as an allegory for the human condition'). In

the case of plagiarism, the consequences are evident: first, the perceived presence of plagiarism will be interpreted as an authorial intention to plagiarize; second, the intention to plagiarize will subsequently be seen as an intention that the plagiarism produce specific effects, normally of an illegitimate kind.

A fundamental postulate of the pragmatic approach is that conventions (discursive, literary, social, etc.) are normally invisible precisely because of their conventionality: it is usually only in the event that conventional expectations are flouted that, first, the convention becomes identified, and second, the discursive act requires the status of a transgression. The adherence to conventionalized forms of behaviour results from the internalization of expectations that are not easily recognized as such: most particularly in their transgression do they become visible as 'rules' that have been broken. Rarely in the case of literary acts are transgressions of convention liable to be raised to a level involving civil, or even criminal, law: plagiarism is, in this sense, interesting because it is one of the few areas in which aesthetic activity can fall into criminality.

The defining element of pragmatic linguistics is the importance accorded to contextual features in the creation of meaning. The function of *context* is intimately related to the notion of mutual knowledge to which I have alluded: it is presumed that a minimal degree of shared knowledge or presupposition is fundamental to all communication, the most elementary condition being the existence of a code common to producer and receiver. And to the extent that a shared language entails a certain mutual knowledge about the world of reference, about discursive conventions, and about the social behaviour underlying them, the notion of discourse immediately entails contextual features that extend the boundaries of language beyond itself. But if the role of context is considered crucial to pragmatic analysis, it is also sufficiently vague and complex to be fraught with the menace of insignificance.

A brief summary of the varieties of context that are supposed to contribute to the construction of meaning includes both linguistic and non-linguistic elements. In the first category, which remains relatively manageable for the purposes of discourse analysis, are micro-textual structures such as discursive coherence, narrative schemas, and thematic developments. Notions of connotation and discursive convention are also constitutive of this category. But context most problematically entails non-discursive elements as well, such as the enunciative situation (which, for written communication, normally implies a more or less radical separation between producer and receiver); the context of reference; the personal (autobiographical) situation of the producer and receiver; as well as the social, cultural, and economic conditions of both. Clearly, the non-linguistic context of the construction of meaning is not only potentially unlimited and aleatory, but, to a large extent, inaccessible and, many would argue, irrelevant. Nonetheless, the pertinence of a contextual pragmatics for literary analysis has long been recognized, and is implicit in the developments of literary theories that exploit, each in its own manner, various non-linguistic elements that are seen to contribute to the construction of meaning in the text. Whether it be autobiographical criticism, theories of reception, historical criticism, or various forms of sociological and institutionally based criticism, diverse kinds of 'contexts' are clearly felt to be essential to the understanding of literary discourse. These are the conditions that push pragmatics into the realm of institutional analysis or, perhaps, allow the former to recuperate the latter.

Literary pragmatics has been defined as an 'attitude' rather than as a unified and specific set of methodological procedures, and it is this *pragmatic attitude* towards the phenomenon of literary plagiarism that motivates the present study. The defining features of this attitude are that literary discourse is a linguistic act in which the reader is the most important agent, and in which contextual components are essential elements of the reader's construction of literary signification or, more precisely in the present context, of 'literariness.' Specifically, I postulate that the identification of discursive repetition as 'plagiarism' is an act of reception that, first, imputes a particular form of intentionality to the producer and, second, is itself inscribed in a complex of readerly intentions that may or may not be conscious. *Context* is a determining factor in constructing this web of intentions: among the various contextual features that contribute to the reception of discursive repetition as plagiarism are notably, but not exclusively, the literary conventions and horizon of aesthetic expectations of the historical period in question; the personal, aesthetic, and institutional motivations of producer and receiver; and the position of both within the aesthetic, political, academic (etc.) institutions to which the literary is related, or subject. Repetition becomes plagiarism when it is seen to transgress a set of conventional expectations governing discursive behaviour; the identification of such a transgression is simultaneously an unveiling of these conventions. While, at first glance, the principal convention required to generate accusations of plagiarism might seem to be 'thou shalt not copy,' other expectations, as we shall see, are just as important, or according to the dominant aesthetic conventions of a given period, perhaps even more so.

THE DEFINITION

Of course, plagiarism has never been the only criterion used to discriminate between good and bad literary art. Its value lies, however, in its exemplarity or excessiveness. In the contemporary period—except for contexts in which hate literature, pornography, and sedition constitute discursive crimes—literary theft remains one of the worst possible crimes in a domain that, largely restricted to the symbolic, has a tenuous relationship to the 'real' world in which crimes are normally committed and punished. It will be necessary to divide the field of plagiarism into two distinct realms: the first depends on the symbolic or aesthetic value of a discourse, and the second is governed by its market value, today circumscribed by law. The development of copyright legislation and the commercialization of intellectual property over the course of the eighteenth and nineteenth centuries elicit an apparently easy historical division between pre- and post-copyright notions of plagiarism, the first period corresponding to the symbolic, and the second to the commercial realm governed by legislation. However, the historical divide introduced by the development of modern copyright does not entirely capture the coexistence throughout the nineteenth and twentieth centuries of both plagiarism and breach of copyright as two distinct concepts: as David Saunders points out, 'the legal and aesthetic personalities stand in no general relation one to the other' (15). Heuristically, however, and for purposes of economy, our examination of twentieth-century debates about plagiarism will be preceded by an overview of pre-copyright discussions of plagiarism, where the questions posed are primarily ethical and aesthetic. These discussions will be subsequently useful as a means of establishing the continuity in notions about plagiarism across the historical divide provided by the establishment of modern copyright over the course of the eighteenth century.

As plagiarism is judged by its effects (Schneider 102), the wide variety of consequences it can entail points to the fact that instances of plagiarism, either across history or in any given context, are not always considered to be examples of the same phenomenon. The gravity of the plagiarism problem depends on the structure of the ethical, aesthetic, institutional, legal, or economic contexts in which the alleged act has occurred, as well as on the status of the suspected perpetrator and victim. Its consequences are similarly various. Within the academic institution, for example, plagiarism in a doctoral thesis may be more heavily sanctioned than in a first-year essay; the discovery of journalistic plagiarism may be followed by a reprimand, by firing, or, as in at least one Canadian case, by a suicide. Literary imitators may be praised for the alleged brilliance of their 'borrowings,' or may be stripped of their claims to the glory of authorship and expelled from legitimate membership in the literary institution. While plagiarism may be seen to be always a 'problem,' dealt with in different ways by different institutions and individuals, its widely various consequences should be a sufficient indication that the real problem with plagiarism is, in fact, deciding what kind of problem it is.

If plagiarism is necessarily deemed to be an infraction, the realm in which it is historically most consistently located is that of the ethical, rather than the legal or aesthetic. While the terms according to which plagiarism is seen to be an infraction of ethical codes are themselves various, two fundamental features can be distilled from definitions and discussions of plagiarism throughout history. Primarily, plagiarism is unethical because it contravenes the fundamental right to the exclusive enjoyment of and control over one's property, either real or symbolic— that is, it is a form of *theft*—and, second, it is a misrepresentation of one's self in situations where the justified expectations of others entail honesty and authenticity; in other words, it is a form of *fraud*. This definition of plagiarism is immediately problematic in that it presupposes the existence of the two values it appears to contravene: theft entails a notion of *intellectual property*; fraud, a notion of *authenticity* (sometimes confusingly called 'originality'), which is based on the assumption of a necessary and unique causal relation between an author and a work. An obvious difficulty with this definition is that notions of intellectual property and of the originality entailed by authorship are often seen to be modern, that is, eighteenth-century attributes, leading to the common belief that 'plagiarism' did not exist in pre-copyright eras such as Antiquity and the Renaissance. However, concepts of *ownership* and of *authenticity* clearly pre-date the copyright legislation that sets out to regulate them, and they form the basis for the continuing existence of plagiarism since the beginning of recorded history in the West. One of the effects of the history of plagiarism is to modify our understanding of this development, and to show that, far from being a modern invention, the proprietary relationship between authors and the fruits of their labour and/or genius—namely, glory, immortality, fame—is an ancient one, and it is to this relationship that accusations and complaints of plagiarism throughout history point.

The fundamental pragmatic problem involved in questions of plagiarism is not definition, but recognition. Historical descriptions and definitions generally present a rather small and surprisingly stable range of elements to be considered when faced with the possibility that plagiarism has taken place: the issues involved are almost always practical rather than theoretical. While it is relatively simple to agree on the intensional definition of plagiarism, its extensional definition—the actual texts that fit the descriptions proposed—is the problem that all definitions, including legal ones, fail to solve. Plagiarism clearly refers to different practices over time, and sometimes to different practices at the same time; but it is most problematic in the way that it polarizes contemporaneous opinions about a single text. In examining some of these opinions, I do not attempt to distill from them a definitive description of literary plagiarism. My aim in reading the discourse surrounding plagiarism is to consider it symptomatic of cultural norms for literariness and its opposite, as the institution of literature successfully constructs itself by processes of inclusion and exclusion.

We have said that the 'What is plagiarism?' question, in so far as it usually elicits either a text- or an author-based response, is not our object. However, descriptions and definitions, proceeding as they inevitably do from readers, constitute the corpus of our study. In order to clear the path for what follows, and to provide a point of departure, we will pursue the 'definition' of plagiarism as it has been provided at two very different points in history. While metaphoric and euphemistic treatments of literary theft characterize the pre-copyright period, more formal definitions of plagiarism arise during the eighteenth century and continue into the present. Not all definitions of plagiarism are equally interesting, nor equally helpful in determining its precise theoretical contours. Contemporary legal definitions are the least interesting for the purposes of identifying plagiarism, since they are restricted to the terms of breach of copyright, which is a small and historically limited subset of the possible types of plagiarism. The French, English, and German eighteenth and nineteenth centuries demonstrated a most fervent interest in the matter, producing some of the most complete and interesting definitions of literary plagiarism; some of these definitions provide the basis for the ensuing discussion, which is particularly intended to underscore the stability of descriptions of plagiarism over time.

The ubiquitous nature of plagiarism, and its occasional ability to produce great literature, often lead to an irreducible ambiguity in the expression of what is, and what is not, properly called plagiarism. Charles Nodier's definition demonstrates such a confusion: 'Let us define plagiarism, strictly speaking, as the action of taking from an author (particularly a modern and national author, which makes the crime more serious) the content of a work of invention, the development of a new idea or one yet little known, the expression of one of several ideas; for there are ideas which can gain from a new expression; established notions which a more felicitous development can clarify; certain works whose content can be improved through the form; and it would be unjust to qualify as plagiarism that which is really only an extension or a useful amendment.' It will be noted that half of the definition is devoted to enumerating what is not plagiarism—namely, imitation by improvement, extension, amendment, what modern definitions call 'significant enhancement.' At the same time, the paragraph presents a convoluted argument, the 'for' in the middle operating a reversal where the list of plagiarisms, 'properly speaking,' is followed by a list of exceptions that coincide closely with the first.

Two exemplary definitions will serve to identify the finer points of taking for one's own the discursive property of another. The first is a product of the encyclopedic endeavors of the eighteenth century, carried on in the wake of the literary debates between the ancients and the moderns, during the transition between classicism and the beginnings of Romanticism, and which took up the definition of plagiarism as a contribution to the literary theories of imitation and originality in the context of the growing importance of the latter. The most complete of these definitions can be found in Diderot's *Encyclopédie*, in Jaucourt's article 'Plagiarism,' which, for various reasons, serves as my point of departure. First, it has the merit of being compatible with more contemporary definitions while at the same time rendering explicit some elements that later definitions repress, but that still inhabit conceptions of plagiarism. It also dispenses with the metaphorical language so common in descriptions of literary theft and is free, as well, of the polemical quality by which many descriptions of plagiarism reveal themselves as apologies for plagiarism or for certain copiers who are not 'really' plagiarists. Here, then, is the definition in the *Encyclopédie*: 'What then is a *plagiarist*, strictly speaking? He is a man who, wanting at all costs to become an author, and having neither the genius nor the talent necessary, copies not only sentences, but even pages and entire passages of other authors, and has the bad faith not to quote them; or who, by means of a few minor changes in expression or a few additions, presents the productions of others as something that he himself imagined or invented; or who claims for himself the honour of a discovery made by another.'

This is as succinct and complete a definition as is available until the twentieth century, and is more complete than most of these. In particular, it mentions all of the necessary components of 'real' contemporary plagiarism, that is, unacknowledged copying or imitation that is liable to result in moral or legal sanctions against the perpetrator. The essential conditions outlined are: lack of talent; theft of another's property; bad faith and covertness; unearned advantage. Other aspects of this definition will also serve as an inspiration for my analyses: not insignificantly, a plagiarist is a 'man,' but not an author, for he lacks the talent to become one. He copies without giving credit, but the extent of this copying can vary from sentences to whole passages: plagiarism does not seem to be a matter of degree. He usurps property defined according to paternity, therefore accruing to himself the honour due to another. Jaucourt's definition is largely started in ethical terms: the cause of the theft is lack of 'genius,' its criminal element is 'bad faith,' and its advantage is 'honour.'

Translated into more contemporary and juridical language, the same elements appear in the following contemporary proposal for a definition of plagiarism, *The Melancholy Anatomy of Plagiarism*. The differences between the two are also significant: 'Plagiarism is an *intentional* verbal *fraud* committed by the *psychologically competent* that consists of *copying significant and substantial uncredited* written materials for *unearned advantages* with no *significant enhancement* of the materials copied' (St Onge 101; emphasis added).

The elements retained are 'bad faith' ('intentional ... fraud') and 'copying,' here, as in law, qualified as 'significant and substantial.' 'Unearned advantages' echoes the appropriation of honour due to another, and 'no significant enhancement' returns to the notion of the inadequacy of 'a few minor changes in expression.' So far, the two definitions, taking into account the shift from ethical to legalistic language, are substantially similar. The fundamental and radical difference between them is the suppression in the modern definition of any reference to authorial agency. The author-as-creator or plagiarist has virtually disappeared, and, along with him, the quality of talent and the notion of production resulting in a natural right of paternity. In the eighteenth-century definition, plagiarism has its source in a (non)-author to whom is attributed actions and intentions. In the second, rather than being an infringement of personal rights perpetuated by individuals upon others, plagiarism is seen as a disembodied act perpetuated upon written materials. The human element subsists only implicitly, and is attributed to the plagiarist, a 'psychologically competent fraud.'

There is a significant absence of reference in both definitions to the plagiarizing text itself. What is being judged is not an inanimate object, the text, but rather the agent of a criminal or immoral act. The text is important simply as evidence of the act: as plagiarists are rarely 'caught in the act,' and corroborating evidence in the form of witnesses or other external evidence is rare, the text-as-evidence of plagiarism is substituted for the act itself. In definitions of plagiarism, the focus on acts and agents rather than on the plagiaristic 'text' again indicates that plagiarism is not primarily a textual category, but rather a pragmatic one, involving questions of action, intentions, and consequences, rather than the existence of specific types of discursive objects. The traditional absence of any definition of the 'plagiaristic text,' independently of definitions of the act and the intentions of the agent, is also a feature of contemporary definitions of breach of copyright where the question to be decided is rarely whether or not similarity exists since the evidence of similarity is a requisite for the suspicion of plagiarism in the first place. Rather, it is a question of determining whether the intentions and the act that resulted in the similarity constitute infringement of copyright; whether the similarity in question is evidence of a breach of copyright or of a non-sanctionable form of repetition.

The repressed element in both definitions is the pragmatic component of Reader—critic, accuser, or judge—whose authority invests him with the capacity for *recognition* of the repetition, for *naming* it, thereby constructing it as fraudulent or otherwise, and for *judging* the repetition and the perpetrator as being condemnable, excusable, or in some instances praise-worthy. Even in exploring the Author, my true object is, in fact, the Reader, the source of the judgments that form the corpus of the evidence for and against plagiarism.

Several explanations are called for. First, I do not try to distill any
kind of positive—either specific or universal—definition of the 'plagiaristic'
author or act. These categories are entirely discursive ones relying for their
evidence on texts produced about these categories and, as such, they are
all, as well, pragmatic categories that have as the Reader the implicit point
of origin. Second, in order to avoid the dangers of anachronism, I attempt
to avoid referring to plagiarists as 'subjects' of their discourse, since the
term has connotations inappropriate to premodern periods. It is in the
third part of my exploration, dealing with contemporary uses and accusations of plagiarism, that the notion of the writing or reading 'subject'
becomes pertinent for the examination of certain instances of 'plagiarism.'
The psychological motivations of individual plagiarists do not concern
me directly for various reasons, the most theoretically pertinent one being
that such an approach must necessarily consider 'plagiarism' from the
point of view of production, thus construing it as a positive phenomenon
introduced by the author into the text, and waiting to be discovered by the
right reader—or, more accurately, the wrong one. Considering plagiarism
as a category of reception entails seeing psychological or other production-
oriented explanations of plagiarism as being themselves effects of the
judgment of readers, and when we speak of 'motivations' for plagiarism it
is always from the perspective of the reader's perception or presumptions
of these motives. Contemporary contributions from psychoanalysis and
philosophy of language to the understanding of the crucial role played by
language in the construction of subjectivity—and consequently of the uses
of plagiarism in this complex—are relevant in the third part of this essay.
My principal aim throughout is, rather, to unpack some of the cultural
presuppositions governing the possibility of literary accusations of plagiarism. As psychological explanations are themselves culturally determined,
they emerge most significantly in the later part of the twentieth century, in
concert with the rise of psychologically based literary theories. Psychological explanations of plagiarism belong to a historically delimited discourse
of reception that chooses to situate plagiarism in the realm of an authorial
act for which motives or causes can be assumed and, perhaps, found.

What is, however, always necessary for plagiarism to be perceived is a
notion of authorship entailing concepts of propriety, if not property, over
discursive or intellectual products. The author as agent is a social, economic, and cultural construct rather than a psychological one and, as Foucault has taught us, the author's attributes are those of a discursive func-

tion, rather than of an individual subject. Plagiarists, as we shall see, are essentially failed or false authors—those who are seen to have transgressed or left unfulfilled the cultural function authorship defines for them. Thus, according to the aesthetic and critical assumptions adopted, the plagiarist may be judged either a thief or a kleptomaniac; an imperialist or a victim of imperialism; a cultural industrialist or revolutionary; the plagiarist is variously seen as a 'subject' striving towards the creation of an 'authentic,' unified identity, or one radically decentered and divided against itself.

This is not to say that all, or even any, 'plagiarists' are innocent victims of cultural prejudices or literary correctness. The intention to commit literary fraud exists, as does the intention to produce legitimate works of literary art. But the fate of both intentions rests solely in the hands of readers. In this sense, 'plagiarism' is the result of culturally determined presuppositions governing the role and the attributions of authorship. It is the role of plagiarist as cultural function, rather than as a psychological subject, that I explore now.

From *Mark Twain's Letters*

Mark Twain

Riverdale-on-the-Hudson
St. Patrick's Day, '03

Dear Helen,—

I *must* steal half a moment from my work to say how glad I am to have your book, and how highly I value it, both for its own sake and as a remembrance of an affectionate friendship which has subsisted between us for nine years without a break, and without a single act of violence that I can call to mind. I suppose there is nothing like it in heaven; and not likely to be, until we get there and show off. I often think of it with longing, and how they'll say, "There they come—sit down in front!" I am practicing with a tin halo. You do the same. I was at Henry Roger's last night, and of course we talked of you. He is not at all well;—you will not like to hear that; but like you and me, he is just as lovely as ever.

I am charmed with your book—enchanted. You are a wonderful creature, the most wonderful in the world—you and your other half together—Miss Sullivan, I mean, for it took the pair of you to make a complete and perfect whole. How she stands out in her letters! her brilliancy, penetration, originality, wisdom, character, and the fine literary competencies of her pen—they are all there.

Oh, dear me, how unspeakably funny and owlishly idiotic and grotesque was that "plagiarism" farce! As if there was much of anything in any human utterance, oral or written, *except* plagiarism! The kernel, the soul—let us go further and say the substance, the bulk, the actual and valuable

material of *all* human utterances—is plagiarism. For substantially all ideas
are second-hand, consciously and unconsciously drawn from a million
outside sources, and daily use by the garnerer with a pride and satisfaction
born of the superstition that he originated them; whereas there is not a
rag of originality about them anywhere except the little discoloration they
get from his mental and moral calibre and his temperament, and which is
revealed in characteristics of phrasing. When a great orator makes a great
speech you are listening to ten centuries and ten thousand men—but we
call it *his* speech, and really some exceedingly small portion of it *is* his. But
not enough to signify. It is merely a Waterloo. It is Wellington's battle,
in some degree, and we call it his; but there are others that contributed.
It takes a thousand men to invent a telegraph, or a steam engine, or a
phonograph, or a telephone or any other important thing—and the last
man gets the credit and we forget the others. He added his little *mite*—that
is all he did. These object lessons should teach us that ninety-nine parts of
all things that proceed from the intellect are plagiarisms, pure and simple;
and the lesson ought to make us modest. But nothing can do that.

Then why don't we unwittingly reproduce the *phrasing* of a story, as well
as the story itself? It can hardly happen—to the extent of fifty words except
in the case of a child; its memory-tablet is not lumbered with impressions,
and the actual language can have graving-room there, and preserve the
language a year or two, but a grown person's memory-tablet is a palimpsest,
with hardly a bare space upon which to engrave a phrase. It must be a very
rare thing that a whole page gets so sharply printed on a man's mind, by a
single reading, that it will stay long enough to turn up some time or other
to be mistaken by him for his own. No doubt we are constantly littering
our literature with *disconnected* sentences borrowed from books at some
unremembered time and now imagined to be our own, but that is about
the most we can do. In 1866 I read Dr. Holmes's poems, in the Sandwich
Islands. A year and a half later I stole his dedication, without knowing it,
and used it to dedicate my "Innocents Abroad" with. Then years afterward I was talking with Dr. Holmes about it. He was not an ignorant
ass—no, not he; he was not a collection of decayed human turnips, like
your "Plagiarism Court;" and so when I said, "I know now where I stole it,
but whom did you steal it from," he said, "I don't remember; I only know
I stole it from somebody, because I have never originated anything alto-
gether myself, nor met anyone who had."

To think of those solemn donkeys breaking a little child's heart with their ignorant rubbish about plagiarism! I couldn't sleep for blaspheming about it last night. Why, their whole lives, their whole histories, all their learning, all their thoughts, all their opinions were one solid rock of plagiarism, and they didn't know it and never suspected it. A gang of dull and hoary pirates piously setting themselves the task of disciplining and purifying a kitten that they think they've caught filching a chop! Oh, dam—

But you finish it, dear, I am running short of vocabulary today.

Every lovingly your friend
Mark

Executive Summary

Institute of Medicine

Public opinion on the medical value of marijuana has been sharply divided. Some dismiss medical marijuana as a hoax that exploits our natural compassion for the sick; others claim it is a uniquely soothing medicine that has been withheld from patients through regulations based on false claims. Proponents of both views cite "scientific evidence" to support their views and have expressed those views at the ballot box in recent state elections. In January 1997, the White House Office of National Drug Control Policy (ONDCP) asked the Institute of Medicine (IOM) to conduct a review of the scientific evidence to assess the potential health benefits and risks of marijuana and its constituent cannabinoids (see the Statement of Task on page 9). That review began in August 1997 and culminates with this report.

The ONDCP request came in the wake of state "medical marijuana" initiatives. In November 1996, voters in California and Arizona passed referenda designed to permit the use of marijuana as medicine. Although Arizona's referendum was invalidated five months later, the referenda galvanized a national response. In November 1998, voters in six states (Alaska, Arizona, Colorado, Nevada, Oregon, and Washington) passed ballot initiatives in support of medical marijuana. (The Colorado vote will not count, however, because after the vote was taken a court ruling determined there had not been enough valid signatures to place the initiative on the ballot.)

Can marijuana relieve health problems? Is it safe for medical use? Those straightforward questions are embedded in a web of social concerns, most of which lie outside the scope of this report. Controversies concerning the nonmedical use of marijuana spill over into the medical marijuana debate and obscure the real state of scientific knowledge. In contrast with the many disagreements bearing on social issues, the study team found substantial consensus among experts in the relevant disciplines on the scientific evidence about potential medical uses of marijuana.

This report summarizes and analyzes what is known about the medical use of marijuana; it emphasizes evidence-based medicine (derived from knowledge and experience informed by rigorous scientific analysis), as opposed to belief-based medicine (derived from judgment, intuition, and beliefs untested by rigorous science).

Throughout this report, *marijuana* refers to unpurified plant substances, including leaves or flower tops whether consumed by ingestion or smoking. References to the "effects of marijuana" should be understood to include the composite effects of its various components; that is, the effects of tetrahydrocannabinol (THC), which is the primary psychoactive ingredient in marijuana, are included among its effects, but not all the effects of marijuana are necessarily due to THC. *Cannabinoids* are the group of compounds related to THC, whether found in the marijuana plant, in animals, or synthesized in chemistry laboratories.

Three focal concerns in evaluating the medical use of marijuana are:

1. Evaluation of the effects of isolated cannabinoids;

2. Evaluation of the risks associated with the medical use of marijuana; and

3. Evaluation of the use of smoked marijuana.

EFFECTS OF ISOLATED CANNABINOIDS

Cannabinoid Biology

Much has been learned since the 1982 IOM report *Marijuana and Health*. Although it was clear then that most of the effects of marijuana were due to its actions on the brain, there was little information about how THC acted on brain cells (neurons), which cells were affected by THC, or even what general areas of the brain were most affected by THC. In addition, too little was known about cannabinoid physiology to offer any scientific insights into the harmful or therapeutic effects of marijuana. That all changed with the identification and characterization of cannabinoid receptors in the 1980s and 1990s. During the past 16 years, science has

advanced greatly and can tell us much more about the potential medical
benefits of cannabinoids.

CONCLUSION: At this point, our knowledge about the biology of
marijuana and cannabinoids allows us to make some general conclusions:

- Cannabinoids likely have a natural role in pain modulation,
  control of movement, and memory.

- The natural role of cannabinoids in immune systems is likely multifaceted and remains unclear.

- The brain develops tolerance to cannabinoids.

- Animal research demonstrates the potential for dependence, but
  this potential is observed under a narrower range of conditions
  than with benzodiazepines, opiates, cocaine, or nicotine.

- Withdrawal symptoms can be observed in animals but appear to be
  mild compared to opiates or benzodiazepines, such as
  diazepam (Valium).

CONCLUSION: The different cannabinoid receptor types found in
the body appear to play different roles in normal human physiology. In
addition, some effects of cannabinoids appear to be independent of those
receptors. The variety of mechanisms through which cannabinoids can
influence human physiology underlies the variety of potential therapeutic
uses for drugs that might act selectively on different cannabinoid systems.

RECOMMENDATION 1: Research should continue into the
physiological effects of synthetic and plant-derived cannabinoids and
the natural function of cannabinoids found in the body. Because
different cannabinoids appear to have different effects, cannabinoid
research should include, but not be restricted to, effects attributable
to THC alone.

Efficacy of Cannabinoid Drugs

The accumulated data indicate a potential therapeutic value for cannabinoid drugs, particularly for symptoms such as pain relief, control of nausea
and vomiting, and appetite stimulation. The therapeutic effects of cannabinoids are best established for THC, which is generally one of the two most
abundant of the cannabinoids in marijuana. (Cannabidiol is generally the
other most abundant cannabinoid.)

[handwritten: relies Nausea, vomiting]

The effects of cannabinoids on the symptoms studied are generally modest, and in most cases there are more effective medications. However, people vary in their responses to medications, and there will likely always be a subpopulation of patients who do not respond well to other medications. The combination of cannabinoid drug effects (anxiety reduction, appetite stimulation, nausea reduction, and pain relief) suggests that cannabinoids would be moderately well suited for particular conditions, such as chemotherapy-induced nausea and vomiting and AIDS wasting.

Defined substances, such as purified cannabinoid compounds, are preferable to plant products, which are of variable and uncertain composition. Use of defined cannabinoids permits a more precise evaluation of their effects, whether in combination or alone. Medications that can maximize the desired effects of cannabinoids and minimize the undesired effects can very likely be identified.

Although most scientists who study cannabinoids agree that the pathways to cannabinoid drug development are clearly marked, there is no guarantee that the fruits of scientific research will be made available to the public for medical use. Cannabinoid-based drugs will only become available if public investment in cannabinoid drug research is sustained and if there is enough incentive for private enterprise to develop and market such drugs.

CONCLUSION: Scientific data indicate the potential therapeutic value of cannabinoid drugs, primarily THC, for pain relief, control of nausea and vomiting, and appetite stimulation; smoked marijuana, however, is a crude THC delivery system that also delivers harmful substances. *[handwritten: both opinis, smoked=bad]*

RECOMMENDATION 2: Clinical trials of cannabinoid drugs for symptom management should be conducted with the goal of developing rapid-onset, reliable, and safe delivery systems.

Influence of Psychological Effects on Therapeutic Effects

The psychological effects of THC and similar cannabinoids pose three issues for the therapeutic use of cannabinoid drugs. First, for some patients—particularly older patients with no previous marijuana experience—the psychological effects are disturbing. Those patients report experiencing unpleasant feelings and disorientation after being treated with THC, generally more severe for oral THC than for smoked marijuana. Second, for conditions such as movement disorders or nausea, in which anxiety exacerbates the symptoms, the antianxiety effects of can-

other ∙ are ∙ bad (handwritten)

good (handwritten, left margin)

nabinoid drugs can influence symptoms indirectly. This can be beneficial or can create false impressions of the drug effect. Third, for cases in which symptoms are multifaceted, the combination of THC effects might provide a form of adjunctive therapy; for example, AIDS wasting patients would likely benefit from a medication that simultaneously reduces anxiety, pain, and nausea while stimulating appetite.

X opinion of drug (handwritten, left margin)

CONCLUSION: The psychological effects of cannabinoids, such as anxiety reduction, sedation, and euphoria can influence their potential therapeutic value. Those effects are potentially undesirable for certain patients and situations and beneficial for others. In addition, psychological effects can complicate the interpretation of other aspects of the drug's effect.

RECOMMENDATION 3: **Psychological effects of cannabinoids such as anxiety reduction and sedation, which can influence medical benefits, should be evaluated in clinical trials.**

RISKS ASSOCIATED WITH MEDICAL USE OF MARIJUANA

Physiological Risks

Marijuana = bad (handwritten, left margin)

Marijuana is not a completely benign substance. It is a powerful drug with a variety of effects. However, except for the harms associated with smoking, the adverse effects of marijuana use are within the range of effects tolerated for other medications. The harmful effects to individuals from the perspective of possible medical use of marijuana are not necessarily the same as the harmful physical effects of drug abuse. When interpreting studies purporting to show the harmful effects of marijuana, it is important to keep in mind that the majority of those studies are based on *smoked* marijuana, and cannabinoid effects cannot be separated from the effects of inhaling smoke from burning plant material and contaminants.

For most people the primary adverse effect of *acute* marijuana use is diminished psychomotor performance. It is, therefore, inadvisable to operate any vehicle or potentially dangerous equipment while under the influence of marijuana, THC, or any cannabinoid drug with comparable effects. In addition, a minority of marijuana users experience dysphoria, or unpleasant feelings. Finally, the short-term immunosuppressive effects are not well established but, if they exist, are not likely great enough to preclude a legitimate medical use.

The *chronic* effects of marijuana are of greater concern for medical use and fall into two categories: the effects of chronic smoking and the effects of THC. Marijuana smoking is associated with abnormalities of cells lining the human respiratory tract. Marijuana smoke, like tobacco smoke, is associated with increased risk of cancer, lung damage, and poor pregnancy outcomes. Although cellular, genetic, and human studies all suggest that marijuana smoke is an important risk factor for the development of respiratory cancer, proof that habitual marijuana smoking does or does not cause cancer awaits the results of well-designed studies.

CONCLUSION: Numerous studies suggest that marijuana smoke is an important risk factor in the development of respiratory disease.

RECOMMENDATION 4: Studies to define the individual health risks of smoking marijuana should be conducted, particularly among populations in which marijuana use is prevalent.

how should be tested

Marijuana Dependence and Withdrawal

A second concern associated with chronic marijuana use is dependence on the psychoactive effects of THC. Although few marijuana users develop dependence, some do. Risk factors for marijuana dependence are similar to those for other forms of substance abuse. In particular, antisocial personality and conduct disorders are closely associated with substance abuse.

illicit - always)

CONCLUSION: A distinctive marijuana withdrawal syndrome has been identified, but it is mild and short lived. The syndrome includes restlessness, irritability, mild agitation, insomnia, sleep disturbance, nausea, and cramping.

Marijuana as a "Gateway" Drug

Patterns in progression of drug use from adolescence to adulthood are strikingly regular. Because it is the most widely used illicit drug, marijuana is predictably the first illicit drug most people encounter. Not surprisingly, most users of other illicit drugs have used marijuana first. In fact, most drug users begin with alcohol and nicotine before marijuana—usually before they are of legal age.

In the sense that marijuana use typically precedes rather than follows initiation of other illicit drug use, it is indeed a "gateway" drug. But because underage smoking and alcohol use typically precede marijuana use, marijuana is not the most common, and is rarely the first, "gateway" to illicit drug use. There is no conclusive evidence that the drug effects of marijuana are causally linked to the subsequent abuse of other illicit drugs. An important caution is that data on drug use progression cannot be assumed to apply to the use of drugs for medical purposes. It does not follow from those data that if marijuana were available by prescription for medical use, the pattern of drug use would remain the same as seen in illicit use.

Finally, there is a broad social concern that sanctioning the medical use of marijuana might increase its use among the general population. At this point there are no convincing data to support this concern. The existing data are consistent with the idea that this would not be a problem if the medical use of marijuana were as closely regulated as other medications with abuse potential.

CONCLUSION: Present data on drug use progression neither support nor refute the suggestion that medical availability would increase drug abuse. However, this question is beyond the issues normally considered for medical uses of drugs and should not be a factor in evaluating the thera-peutic potential of marijuana or cannabinoids.

Use of Smoked Marijuana

Because of the health risks associated with smoking, smoked marijuana should generally not be recommended for long-term medical use. Nonethe-less, for certain patients, such as the terminally ill or those with debili-tating symptoms, the long-term risks are not of great concern. Further, despite the legal, social, and health problems associated with smoking marijuana, it is widely used by certain patient groups.

RECOMMENDATION 5: Clinical trials of marijuana use for medi-cal purposes should be conducted under the following limited circum-stances: trials should involve only short-term marijuana use (less than six months), should be conducted in patients with conditions for which there is reasonable expectation of efficacy, should be approved by insti-tutional review boards, and should collect data about efficacy.

The goal of clinical trials of smoked marijuana would not be to develop marijuana as a licensed drug but rather to serve as a first step toward the possible development of nonsmoked rapid-onset cannabinoid delivery systems. However, it will likely be many years before a safe and effective cannabinoid delivery system, such as an inhaler, is available for patients. In the meantime there are patients with debilitating symptoms for whom smoked marijuana might provide relief. The use of smoked marijuana for those patients should weigh both the expected efficacy of marijuana and ethical issues in patient care, including providing information about the known and suspected risks of smoked marijuana use.

RECOMMENDATION 6: Short-term use of smoked marijuana (less than six months) for patients with debilitating symptoms (such as intractable pain or vomiting) must meet the following conditions:

[handwritten: all other medications don't work]

- failure of all approved medications to provide relief has been documented,

- the symptoms can reasonably be expected to be relieved by rapid-onset cannabinoid drugs,

- such treatment is administered under medical supervision in a manner that allows for assessment of treatment effectiveness, and

- involves an oversight strategy comparable to an institutional review board process that could provide guidance within 24 hours of a submission by a physician to provide marijuana to a patient for a specified use.

Until a nonsmoked rapid-onset cannabinoid drug delivery system becomes available, we acknowledge that there is no clear alternative for people suffering from *chronic* conditions that might be relieved by smoking marijuana, such as pain or AIDS wasting. One possible approach is to treat patients as n-of-1 clinical trials (single-patient trials), in which patients are fully informed of their status as experimental subjects using a harmful drug delivery system and in which their condition is closely monitored and documented under medical supervision, thereby increasing the knowledge base of the risks and benefits of marijuana use under such conditions.

Statement of Task

The study will assess what is currently known and not known about the medical use of marijuana. It will include a review of the science base regarding the mechanism of action of marijuana, an examination of the peer-reviewed scientific literature on the efficacy of therapeutic uses of marijuana, and the costs of using various forms of marijuana versus approved drugs for specific medical conditions (e.g., glaucoma, multiple sclerosis, wasting diseases, nausea, and pain).

The study will also include an evaluation of the acute and chronic effects of marijuana on health and behavior; a consideration of the adverse effects of marijuana use compared with approved drugs; an evaluation of the efficacy of different delivery systems for marijuana (e.g., inhalation vs. oral); an analysis of the data concerning marijuana as a gateway drug; and an examination of the possible differences in the effects of marijuana due to age and type of medical condition.

Specific Issues

Specific issues to be addressed fall under three broad categories: science base, therapeutic use, and economics.

Science Base

- Review of the neuroscience related to marijuana, particularly the relevance of new studies on addiction and craving
- Review of the behavioral and social science base of marijuana use, particularly an assessment of the relative risk of progression to other drugs following marijuana use
- Review of the literature determining which chemical components of crude marijuana are responsible for possible therapeutic effects and for side effects

Therapeutic Use

- Evaluation of any conclusions on the medical use of marijuana drawn by other groups
- Efficacy and side effects of various delivery systems for marijuana compared to existing medications for glaucoma, wasting syndrome, pain, nausea, or other symptoms
- Differential effects of various forms of marijuana that relate to age or type of disease

Economics

- Costs of various forms of marijuana compared with costs of existing medications for glaucoma, wasting syndrome, pain, nausea, or other symptoms
- Assessment of differences between marijuana and existing medications in terms of access and availability

Recommendations

RECOMMENDATION 1: Research should continue into the physiological effects of synthetic and plant-derived cannabinoids and the natural function of cannabinoids found in the body. Because different cannabinoids appear to have different effects, cannabinoid research should include, but not be restricted to, effects attributable to THC alone.

Scientific data indicate the potential therapeutic value of cannabinoid drugs for pain relief, control of nausea and vomiting, and appetite stimulation. This value would be enhanced by a rapid onset of drug effect.

RECOMMENDATION 2: Clinical trials of cannabinoid drugs for symptom management should be conducted with the goal of developing rapid-onset, reliable, and safe delivery systems.

The psychological effects of cannabinoids are probably important determinants of their potential therapeutic value. They can influence symptoms indirectly which could create false impressions of the drug effect or be beneficial as a form of adjunctive therapy.

RECOMMENDATION 3: *Psychological* effects of cannabinoids such as anxiety reduction and sedation, which can influence medical benefits, should be evaluated in clinical trials.

Numerous studies suggest that marijuana smoke is an important risk factor in the development of respiratory diseases, but the data that could conclusively establish or refute this suspected link have not been collected.

RECOMMENDATION 4: Studies to define the individual health risks of smoking marijuana should be conducted, particularly among populations in which marijuana use is prevalent

Because marijuana is a crude THC delivery system that also delivers harmful substances, smoke marijuana should generally not be recommended for medical use. Nonetheless, marijuana is widely used by certain patient groups, which raises both safety and efficacy issues.

RECOMMENDATION 5: Clinical trials of marijuana use for medical purposes should be conducted under the following limited circumstances: trials should involve only short-term marijuana use (less than six months), should be conducted in patients with conditions for which there is reasonable expectation of efficacy, should be approved by institutional review boards, and should collect data about efficacy.

If there is any future for marijuana as a medicine, it lies in its isolated components, the cannabinoids and their synthetic derivatives. Isolated cannabinoids will provide more reliable effects than crude plant mixtures. Therefore, the purpose of clinical trials of smoked marijuana would not be to develop marijuana as a licensed drug but rather to serve as a first step toward the development of nonsmoked rapid-onset cannabinoid delivery systems.

RECOMMENDATION 6: Short-term use of smoked marijuana (less than six months) for patients with debilitating symptoms (such as intractable pain or vomiting) must meet the following conditions:

- **failure of all approved medications to provide relief has been documented,**

- **the symptoms can reasonably be expected to be relieved by rapid-onset cannabinoid drugs,**

- **such treatment is administered under medical supervision in a manner that allows for assessment of treatment effectiveness, and**

- **involves an oversight strategy comparable to an institutional review board process that could provide guidance within 24 hours of a submission by a physician to provide marijuana to a patient for a specified use.**

Government Study of Marijuana Sees Medical Benefits

March 18, 1999, *The New York Times*

Sheryl Gay Stolberg

The active ingredients in marijuana appear to be useful for treating pain, nausea and the severe weight loss associated with AIDS, according to a new study commissioned by the Government that is inflaming the contentious debate over whether doctors should be permitted to prescribe the drug.

The report, the most comprehensive analysis to date of the medical literature about marijuana, said there was no evidence that giving the drug to sick people would increase illicit use in the general population. Nor is marijuana a "gateway drug" that prompts patients to use harder drugs like cocaine and heroin, the study said.

The authors of the study, a panel of 11 independent experts at the Institute of Medicine, a branch of the National Academy of Sciences, cautioned that the benefits of smoking marijuana were limited because the smoke itself was so toxic. Yet at the same time, they recommended that the drug be given, on a short-term basis under close supervision, to patients who did not respond to other therapies.

The release of the delicately worded report, at a morning news conference here, prompted a flurry of political maneuvering. Proponents of state initiatives to legalize marijuana for medical purposes seized upon the findings as long-awaited evidence that it had therapeutic value. They called on the Clinton Administration, and in particular Gen. Barry R. McCaffrey, director of the Office of National Drug Control Policy, which requested the study, to ease its steadfast opposition to the initiatives.

(wana)

"This report has proved McCaffrey wrong," said Chuck Thomas, a spokesman for the Marijuana Policy Project, a nonprofit organization in Washington that lobbies for the legalization of medical marijuana. "We never said marijuana was a panacea and a be-all or end-all. What we have said is there are some patients who don't respond to existing medications, and this report confirms that."

But the study is unlikely to change the Administration's position. The Department of Health and Human Services, which is already financing some research involving medical marijuana, issued a written statement noting simply that it would continue to finance the work. And General McCaffrey, speaking in a telephone interview from Los Angeles, said, "This study seems to suggest that there is little future in smoked marijuana."

General McCaffrey politely praised the analysis as a "superb piece of work" and said he would take the recommendations under advisement. But he said there was "enormous confusion in law enforcement" about how to handle the issue, and added, "We've got people with mischievous agendas at work."

While the study's authors said they had been surprised to discover "an explosion of new scientific knowledge about how the active components of marijuana affect the body," they added pointedly that the future of marijuana as a medicine did not lie in smoking it. Marijuana smoke, they said, is even more toxic than tobacco smoke, and can cause cancer, lung damage and complications during pregnancy.

The true benefits of marijuana, the experts said, would only be realized when alternative methods, like capsules, patches and bronchial inhalers, were developed to deliver its active components, called cannabinoids, to the body without the harmful effects of smoke.

So far there is only one cannabinoid-based drug on the market, Marinol, manufactured by Unimed of Somerville, N.J. It comes in pill form and was approved in May 1985 by the Food and Drug Administration for nausea and vomiting associated with chemotherapy, as well as for anorexia and weight loss associated with AIDS. Some patients have complained that Marinol is more expensive than marijuana and that they do not feel its effects as quickly.

The researchers recommended that the Government pay for research that would speed the development of more cannabinoid drugs, and were particularly keen on the promise of inhalers. But, recognizing that such methods might take years to perfect, they also recommended that people who did not respond to other therapy be permitted to smoke marijuana in the interim.

"Marijuana should only be smoked in circumstances where the long-term risks are not of great concern, such as for terminally ill patients or those with debilitating symptoms that do not respond to approved medications," said Dr. John A. Benson Jr., former dean of the Oregon Health Sciences University School of Medicine and one of the study's two lead authors. "Even in these cases, smoking should be limited to carefully controlled situations."

Dr. Benson and his co-author, Dr. Stanley J. Watson Jr. of the Mental Health Research Institute of the University of Michigan, announced their findings in a wood-paneled lecture hall at the Institute of Medicine here. As the two scientists spoke, a handful of people sat quietly in the audience, wearing fire-engine red T-shirts with white block lettering that blared: "Medical Marijuana Patient."

Among them was Jim Hardin, a 48-year-old Virginia man who testified before the panel and whose story was among several personal anecdotes included in the report. Mr. Hardin suffers from Hepatitis C, a disease that is destroying his liver, and uses a wheelchair. He said smoking marijuana helped him cope with the intense nausea and rapid weight loss the disease has caused.

"I lost 95 pounds," Mr. Hardin said. "I tried everything: 35 different pills. Finally, doctors told me to go to Europe and try marijuana." He did just that, in November 1997, visiting the Netherlands, where a doctor prescribed one to two grams of marijuana per day. Here in the United States, Mr. Hardin said, he obtains the drug "from a network of care providers that are willing to grow a safe and clean cannabis."

Also in the audience was Joyce Nalepka of America Cares, a parents' anti-drug group based in Maryland that has been critical of efforts to legalize marijuana for medical use.

"I'm concerned about the message we are sending," Ms. Nalepka said. "Kids interpret things differently than adults. What they're going to hear is, 'Marijuana is good for something.'"

The report contained some surprising findings. It concluded that, despite popular belief, marijuana was not useful in treating glaucoma. While the drug can reduce some of the eye pressure associated with glaucoma, the effects were short-lived, the report found, and did not outweigh the long-term hazards of using the drug.

In addition, the study found that there was little evidence for marijuana's potential in treating movement disorders like Parkinson's disease or Huntington's disease, but that it was effective in combating the muscle spasms associated with multiple sclerosis.

So far, voters in seven states—California, Alaska, Arizona, Colorado, Nevada, Oregon and Washington—have approved initiatives intended to make marijuana legal for medical purposes. But doctors are often afraid to write prescriptions because the Federal Government has threatened to prosecute them, and patients often have difficulty obtaining the drug, in part because the Government has moved to shut the marijuana buyers' clubs that had been distributing it. In the District of Columbia, meanwhile, the November ballot contained a proposal to legalize medical marijuana, but Congress intervened and prevented the vote from being counted.

Correction: *March 25, 1999, Thursday An article last Thursday about a Government report that outlined risks and benefits of the medical use of marijuana misstated the location of the office of Unimed Pharmaceuticals Inc., the manufacturer of the drug Marinol, which delivers the active components of marijuana. The company is in Buffalo Grove, Ill., not Somerville, N.J.*

Medical Messages in the Media – Barriers and Solutions to Improving Medical Journalism

Anna Larsson, Andrew D. Oxman MD, Cheryl Carling,
and Jeph Herrin PhD

ABSTRACT

Context Medical issues are widely reported in the mass media. These reports influence the general public, policy makers and health-care professionals. This information should be valid, but is often criticized for being speculative, inaccurate and misleading. An understanding of the obstacles medical reporters meet in their work can guide strategies for improving the informative value of medical journalism.

the extent to which healthcare reports provide valid and useful info — explain

Objective To investigate constraints on improving the informative value of medical reports in the mass media and elucidate possible strategies for addressing these.

Design We reviewed the literature and organized focus groups, a survey of medical journalists in 37 countries, and semi-structured telephone interviews. .

Results We identified nine barriers to improving the informative value of medical journalism; lack of time, space and knowledge; competition for space and audience; difficulties with terminology;

problems finding and using sources; problems with editors and
commercialism. Lack of time, space and knowledge were the most
common obstacles. The importance of different obstacles varied
with the type of media and experience. Many health reporters feel
that it is difficult to find independent experts willing to assist journalists, and also think that editors need more education in critical
appraisal of medical news. Almost all of the respondents agreed
that the informative value of their reporting is important. Nearly
everyone wanted access to short, reliable and up-to-date background
information on various topics available on the Internet. A majority
(79%) was interested in participating in a trial to evaluate strategies
to overcome identified constraints.

Conclusion Medical journalists agree that the validity of medical
reporting in the mass media is important. A majority acknowledge many constraints. Mutual efforts of health-care professionals
and journalists employing a variety of strategies will be needed to
address these constraints.

BACKGROUND

Extensive interest in reports on health and medicine in the mass media
and wide coverage raises concerns for many health professionals as well
as medical reporters.[1] Journalists working in the medical field are often
accused of being sensational, speculative or of paying too much attention
to anecdotal findings.[2-4] Reporters, on the other hand, find scientists
unable to describe their research in understandable terms, or interested in
using mass media to promote their own interests. Contact between journalists and physicians is often a meeting between two cultures with rather
little in common and with many possibilities for misunderstanding.[5,6]
Despite this, very little attention has been paid to the working processes
of journalists covering medicine (used broadly here and in the rest of this
paper to include coverage of health and health-care) and how these processes affect what is reported.

The mass media are an important source of medical information.
Medical reports can increase or diminish the willingness of individuals
to seek medical care (or participate in clinical trials), may raise expecta-

tions (sometimes falsely), may dash hopes, or may provoke alarm (sometimes unnecessarily). Press coverage of dramatic medical stories, such as organ transplants, often raise unrealistic expectations and may promote new technologies that have not been adequately evaluated. Although the impact of health-care reporting is difficult to measure[7,8] the mass media can influence individual health behaviour, health-care utilization, health-care practices, health policy and the stock market.[8-13] In many countries new legislation on patient's rights includes the right to make informed decisions about one's own health-care. The ability to exercise this right effectively depends on exposure to good information. Policy makers and physicians also get medical information from the mass media and this can affect their work both directly and indirectly.[8, 14, 15] This information should be valid.

Journalists struggle to provide accurate and relevant information about health and medicine, but there are many obstacles between a research report and a short, easy-to-understand and entertaining article.[7] The aim of this study was to identify and elucidate obstacles that hinder journalists from improving the informative value[16] (Box 1) of their work and possible strategies for overcoming these obstacles.

We found few articles and very few empirical studies on barriers to improving the quality of medical reporting or interventions to improve the informative value of medical reporting. Several authors have discussed problems with the dissemination of health information to the general public through the mass media and recommend better education for journalists.[1, 2] Lack of training in critical appraisal and translation of scientific jargon have been reported as factors that limit the scientific quality of medical reporting. Demands from editors for sensational stories have also been identified as a problem in the literature.[17] Other constraints that have been identified in the literature include: lack of time and space, competition among journalists and problems finding reliable information.[18] The structure of news stories, the need for something newsworthy, and problems negotiating with editors and headline writers have also been identified as barriers.[7]

> **Box 1 Definition of 'informative value'**
>
> The following definition was used in this study, in both the telephone interviews and the survey:
>
> By 'informative value' we mean the extent to which health-care reports provide valid and useful information. 'Informative value' also signifies that the basis or evidence for what is reported is apparent. A report with high 'informative value' allows the audience to draw conclusions about:
>
> - the applicability of the information to personal or policy decisions
>
> - the strength of the evidence upon which the report is based (or the degree of uncertainty)
>
> - the size of the effects, risks, associations, or costs that are reported

METHODS

Focus groups

In June 1999 we organized two focus groups with a total of 20 participants in two different countries. In Sweden journalists were identified by personal contacts and senior British Medical Journal (BMJ) staff assembled a group in the UK. Journalists in both groups were chosen to represent different media and different levels of education and experience. Inclusion criteria were that participants were full-time health or medical reporters, either employed or freelancers, who had been working with health issues for at least 3 years. The focus groups were open forums with possibilities for free exchange of views on working situations. We had previously constructed lists of possible barriers and strategies for addressing them, based on our review of the literature and personal experience. Each possible barrier was presented orally and thoroughly discussed, with possible solutions for different types of media. These lists were expanded and modified based on the focus group discussions. These group discussions were tape recorded, transcribed and reviewed by two of us (AL and CC).

Survey

The data produced by the focus groups and background literature search were used to design a survey instrument (available from the authors) comprising 28 closed questions, including some four-point Likkert scales with a possibility for writing in comments for all questions. The survey was put up on a website. Journalists with an e-mail address as shown on the membership lists of associations for science and medical journalists (687 people in 37 countries) were invited to respond to the survey or to contact us if they preferred receiving a paper copy of the survey. The target group for this study was professional journalists specializing in health and science reporting. To be included in the study a journalist had to produce at least 10 stories on health or medicine per year. A hard copy of the survey was mailed to a sample of the first 100 people on the lists without e-mail addresses.

For each respondent, we assigned a 'dominant media', according to the media for which that respondent claimed to use the highest percentage of her time. Respondents with no dominant media (i.e. with a tie between two or more different types of media) were assigned dominant media 'None'. Responses on the four-point Likkert scales to statements about each barrier were categorized as 'Yes' if the respondent either agreed or strongly agreed that the barrier existed. All survey responses were summarized, with frequencies tabulated for dichotomous responses and means, standard deviations, and ranges for continuous responses.

Telephone interviews

To elucidate or explain responses in the survey, we then conducted semi-structured, in-depth interviews by telephone with 10 health reporters from Europe, Canada and Australia. The subjects were chosen through our network of contacts, with the aim to reach people from different countries and with different levels of education and experience. The goal of the telephone interviews was to elicit a broad and in-depth picture of the interviewees' working situation in their own words by probing deeply into their experiences. The interviewers followed an interview guide including questions to elicit background information, experienced constraints and strategies that might overcome them, factors that they found enabling, and their definition of scientific quality in health reporting. A preliminary review conducted when 10 interviews had been completed suggested that data saturation was reached. The interviews were recorded on mini-disc and transcripts were reviewed by two of us (AL and CC).

RESULTS

Focus groups

The participants in the focus groups were invited to speak freely of their experiences and to exchange views on problems in daily work. The British group pointed out competition and commercialism as major obstacles: 'Someone said that a journalist's job is to explain the world. That's the kind way of putting it. The unkind way is to say that a journalist's job is to sell newspapers. This is a commercial business, you know. If we don't sell newspapers we are out of our job.' Public relation agents and lobby groups that want to promote certain ideas, studies or a special issue were also seen as obstacles.

Possibly due to their being highly experienced, most of the reporters in the UK group did not identify lack of time or knowledge as major concerns. 'A professional reporter learns to work very fast.'

Journalists writing for magazines claimed that there were problems with editors and the structure of the media. 'Editors are not interested in what is accurate and what isn't accurate. As long as it doesn't kill anybody, they're not bothered if it's not actually spot on.'

The Swedish group indicated greater concern about the lack of time and problems finding reliable sources. 'It can be that something arrives on my desk in the morning and I need to have a story ready in the afternoon and in addition I will be interrupted by all sorts of other things.'

Some of the Swedish people were concerned about how to choose the right subject in the enormous flow of information from different sources. The selection process was thought to be difficult, given the demand for something newsworthy, not too complicated and relevant to a big audience. 'People don't read newspapers sitting in armchairs in front of a fire. They read them on station platforms, crowded subways, stuck on the street, etcetera. So the stories have got to grab them by the throat.'

Survey

The 148 journalists that answered the survey were quite experienced (Table 1). Most of them worked in magazines or newspapers and the average journalist had been working almost 10 years with health matters. Twenty-one reporters had worked for more than 20 years with health stories.

Table 1 Characteristics of survey respondents				
	Number	Stories/year*	Proportion on health (%)*	Years*
Magazine	39	30	80	9
Newspaper	37	60	90	7
Television	17	40	70	7
Internet	12	50	100	9
Radio	11	50	40	6
Books	4	12	90	16
Other	16	18	90	6
None (tied) †	12	40	55	12
Total	148	35	80	8

* Median number of stories prepared per year; proportion of those stories thate were on medicine, health or health-care; and number of years workng as a medical journalist.
† Journalists who worked on equal proportion of time in two or more media.

We identified nine barriers to improving the informative value of medical reporting (Fig. 1). The predominant ones were lack of time, space and knowledge. Some reporters felt that competition for space and audience were important obstacles, while others had difficulties with terminology, editors and problems finding and using sources. Commercialism was also perceived to be an obstacle.

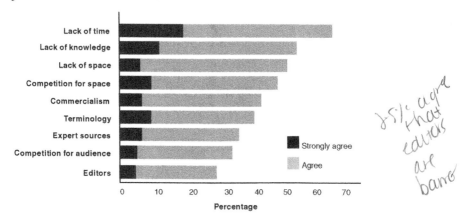

Figure 1 Barriers to improved medical reporting. Percentage of respondents who indicated strong agreement or agreement that the indicated constraint was a barrier to their improving the informative value of their work.

Barriers varied relative to the media in which the reporters worked (Table 2). Almost half (47.4%) of the journalists working at magazines felt that editors were an obstacle to preparing high qualitative reports. Lack of time to prepare a report was an obstacle most often to radio reporters (91.0%), while expert sources (70.6%), terminology (76.5%) and competition for audiences (58.8%) were noted as barriers most often by TV-reporters.

Table 2 Relationship between specific barriers and the dominant media in which journalists worked	
Barrier	**Dominant media with highest score (% agree)***
Lack of time	Radio (91)
Lack of knowledge	Internet (75)
Lack of space	Radio (82)
Competition for space	Radio/TV (64)
Commercialism	Internet (64)
Terminology	TV/books (75)
Expert sources	TV (67)
Competition for audience	TV/books (75)
Editors	Magazine (47)

*The percentage of respondents who reported worked predominantly in each of the specified media who either agreed or strongly agreed that this was a barrier for them.

The respondents were asked about several suggested strategies for improving the informative value of their work (Fig. 2). Almost everyone wanted access to reliable, up-to-date background information on various topics available on the Internet and 90% were interested in access to experts in diverse areas of health and roughly the same proportion were interested in learning strategies to prepare more informative reports that are still entertaining and 'saleable'. A high proportion (over 80%) were interested in strategies for presenting research results simply, in access to help translating scientific and medical terminology, and access to methodological experts. Most (> 70%) were also interested in other possible aids to improving the informative value of stories about health and 79% were interested in participating in a trial to evaluate strategies to overcome the identified barriers.

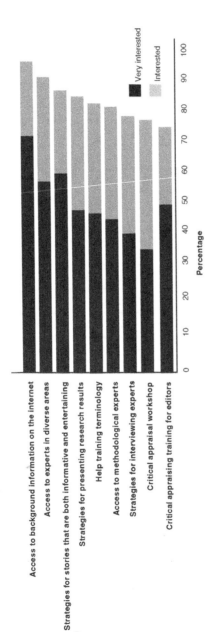

Figure 2 Interest in possible strategies to improve the informative value of medical reporting. Percentage of respondents who indicated they would be very interested or somewhat interested in the indicated strategies to help improve the informative value of their work.

Telephone interviews

Ten in-depth interviews were conducted to include journalists from other countries and media and to broaden our understanding of journalists' working situations. The respondents lived in Europe (Finland, Denmark, Germany, Bulgaria), Australia and Canada. The interviews showed that working conditions varied a lot among the reporters, primarily due to type of media, but also in relation to cultural and political circumstances. The health-care situation in a given country also appeared as an important factor that impacts on the daily work of reporters.

The attitudes of experts who were contacted by journalists were a source of concern for reporters: 'Half of them are really helpful and others are really afraid of bad press. One example was a dentist who said he only wanted to communicate via fax with me. Things like this are really not helpful.' Others thought that the scientific jargon could be difficult: 'Even though I have grown a bit used to it, sometimes the vocabulary is pretty obscure and you don't know what they are talking about.'

Lack of independent researchers was reported as an obstacle by several reporters: 'Well, I am not sure if there are any left. Some few elderly professors in the universities, but they are getting rare. Even university research is getting more and more subsidized and when people know something that might be detrimental for the ones who subsidize them they will not talk. Or they will talk off the record, which is not very useful. That is a sad thing, not having any sources left.' Another reporter claimed: 'an expert that can give you the whole picture with risks, costs and benefits of a treatment for example, is a rare species of whom you should take good care if you find one.'

There was a consensus that the shortage of independent researchers and experts is a serious threat to reliable medical journalism, meaning that most reporters find it difficult to reveal someone's hidden interests and therefore could be tricked into writing a story with a less critical view.

DISCUSSION

The results of this study represent the perceptions of experienced medical journalists. Although the response rate to our survey was low (22%, with no difference in response rate for those receiving email invitation or paper copy in mail), this needs to be viewed in light of the fact that the majority of people who were invited to respond were not eligible. The membership of the organizations that we contacted includes science writers who do not specialize in health, editors, and others who do not write a minimum of 10 articles about health per year. The breadth of the included sample and the consistency of the findings from the various methods that were used strengthen our confidence in the results.

The journalists included in this study were clearly defined as medical reporters and most of them were quite experienced. The results may not apply to less experienced reporters who do not specialize in medical reporting. Nonetheless, the participants were very heterogeneous. They represent a wide range of media, experience and level of education. They worked in countries with different cultural, economic, political and health-care situations.

Despite the fact that the respondents' backgrounds differed, there was a consensus on the three most prominent constraints: a majority agreed that lack of time, space and knowledge were major obstacles in their work. This is not surprising given that journalists must work quickly and be brief. Perhaps more unexpected is the self-reported lack of knowledge, as the sample of reporters had been working for many years and had long experience with medical reporting. The steadily increasing flow of information in the medical field, the breadth of material that journalists must cover, and difficulties finding reliable sources could explain this.

Problems with sources were expressed as being of considerable importance. Many journalists reported difficulties finding experts willing to assist the media and to explain scientific jargon. Another problem is that experts often have conflicts of interest and these frequently are not revealed.[19] Interactions between journalists and experts has been described as a meeting between two professional cultures, with very little knowledge about the participants' different roles and with great tension as a result.[6, 20] In general, experts see their appearance in the media as an opportunity to educate and give advice to the public and therefore have a more paternalistic view than the journalist who emphasizes the holistic picture of a problem, take a patient's perspective and apply a critical view. This is well-reflected in our study, both in comments from the survey and in the in-depth interviews.

This problem could be dealt with using different strategies. One would be to try to reduce the cultural differences between the groups, which

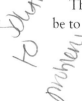

likely would be rejected by both journalists and experts, and would be difficult, at best, given differences in time scales, languages, audiences and motivations between journalists and experts. Another way of dealing with the problem would be to improve the communicating skills of the counterparts. The differences would still be there, but greater competency in dealing with them might improve journalistic processes and outcomes. There is a great need for a deeper understanding of each other's roles in the interview situation. The journalists in our survey did not, however, have any expectations of this happening. They rather emphasized the importance of their own improved education and interviewing skills, and had less interest in the situation of the interviewee. There is clearly a need for interventions that are targeted at both groups—experts and journalists.[21] The different solutions were discussed both in the focus groups and in the telephone interviews.

Another important obstacle to improving the informative value of medical reporting is the attitudes of editors. These people seldom have any higher education in medicine or health matters, nor have they understanding of the scientific process as a whole. Many respondents in our study would welcome training for editors in critical appraisal. Meanwhile, they indicated that editors would be unlikely to prioritize such training for themselves. How to reach editors is a considerable challenge, but potentially an important one to address.[15, 22]

The finding that there is great interest among journalists to improve the quality of their work by, for example, participating in a trial to evaluate strategies to overcome the identified barriers should be welcomed by the medical profession. However, to be effective interventions should be tailored to address identified barriers and the effectiveness of such interventions should be properly evaluated before being widely implemented. Simply offering advice and courses to journalists is unlikely to suffice.

Although this study did not set out to compare these groups, we nevertheless noted striking similarities in the barriers that medical journalists confront in trying to improve the informative value of their work and those that health professionals face in trying to ensure that the care they provide is based on current best evidence (Table 3).[23]

Table 3 Similarities between constraints on journalists and physicians		
Journalists	**Physicians**[23]	**Explanations**
Lack of time	Time constraints	Journalists have little time to prepare stories. Physicians have little time to read.
Lack of space		Journalists have little space in which to report complex information. Physicians have little time in which to explain complex information to patients.
Lack of knowledge	Information overload	Journalists have difficulties mastering the breadth of topics they must cover. Physicians have difficulties coping with the flood of biomedical literature.
Competition for space	Standard of practice	Journalists are compelled to compete with colleagues for space for their stories. Physicians are compelled to adhere with local standards of practice (right or wrong).
Commercialism	Financial disincentives	The need for journalists to sell stories can conflict with providing balanced information. Financial incentives for physicians can conflict with providing good care.
Expert sources	Advocacy	Journalists are bombarded by sources with conflicts of interest. Physicians are bombarded by sources with conflicts of interest.
Terminology	Patient expectations	Journalists have difficulties making jargon understandable. Physicians have difficulties communicating with patients.
Competition for audience		Journalists may compete for their audiences' attention. Physicians may compete for patients.
Editors	Organizational constraints	Journalists are confronted with a number of organizational constraints, including editors, which can restrict their ability to improve the informative value of their work. Physicians are confronted with a number of organizational constraints that can restrict their ability to provide evidence-based care for their patients.

CONCLUSIONS

Health-care professionals and researchers aim to improve the quality of health-care. Ensuring that information about health-care is valid is essential to this aim. Journalists have other priorities. Their aim is not to promote science or effective and efficient health-care. Overcoming the constraints that journalists face will require efforts from both journalists and health-care professionals, as well as an understanding of fundamental differences between the two cultures. A variety of strategies will likely be needed to address these constraints.

ACKNOWLEDGEMENTS

We would like to thank the BMJ staff for their assistance with convening the focus group of British journalists and all of the journalists who contributed to this study. The Norwegian Research Council funded this research.

REFERENCES

1 Johnson T. Shattuck lecture - medicine and the media. *New England Journal of Medicine*, 1998; 339: 87-92.

2 Schuchman M. Wilkes MS. Medical scientists and health news reporting: a case of miscommunication. *Annals of Internal Medicine*, 1997; 126: 976-982.

3 Wilkes MS, Kravitz RL. Medical researchers and the media. Altitudes toward public dissemination of research. *Journal of the American Medical Association*, 1992; 268: 999-1003.

4 Koshland DE Jr. Credibility in science and the press. *Science*, 1991; 254: 629.

5 Peters HP. The interaction of journalists and scientific experts: co-operation and conflict between two professional cultures. *Media, Culture and Society*, 1995; 17: 31-48.

6 Nelkin D. An uneasy relationship: the tension between medicine and the media. *Lancet*, 1996; 347: 1600-1603.

7 Winsten JA. Science and the media: the boundaries of truth. *Health Affairs*, 1985; Spring: 5-23.

8 Grilli R, Freemantle N, Minozzi S, Domenighetti G, Finer D. Mass media interventions: effects on health services utilisation (Cochrane Review). In: *The Cochrane Library*, 2003, Issue 2. Oxford: Update Software.

9 Kristiansen CM, Harding CM. Mobilization of health behavior by the press in Britain. *Journalism Quarterly*, 1984; 61: 364-370, 398.

10 Nelkin D. Selling Science. *How the Press Covers Science and Technology.* Revised edition. New York: WH Freeman and Co, 1995.

11 Gorman C. The hope & the hype. *Time*, 1998; 151: 40-46.

12 Gawande A. Mouse Hunt. Forget cancer. Is there a cure for hype? *The New Yorker*, 1998; (May 18) 5-6.

13 Kolata G. A cautious awe greets drugs that eradicate tumors in mice. *The New York Times*, 1998; (May 3) A1.

14 Shaw DL, Van Nevel JP. The informative value of medical science news. *Journalism Quarterly*, 1967; 44: 548.

15 O'keefe MT. The mass media as sources of medical information for doctors. *Journalism Quarterly*, 1970; 47: 95-100.

16 Oxman AD, Guyatt GH, Cook DJ, Jaeschke R, Heddle N, Keller J. An index of scientific quality for health reports in the lay press. *Journal of Clinical Epidemiology*, 1993; 46: 987-1001.

17 Levi R. Bættre medicinjournalistik kræver bættre kællor. *Vetenskap and praxis*, 1998; 3-4: 8.

18 Matz R. Health news reporting. *Annals of Internal Medicine*, 1997; 11: 948.

19 Moynihan R, Bero L, Ross-Degnan D *et al.* Coverage by the news media of the benefits and risks of medications. *New England Journal of Medicine*, 2000; 342: 1645-1650.

20 de Semir V. Medicine and the media: What is newsworthy? *Lancet*, 1996; 347: 1063-1066.

21 Entwistle V, Watt IS. Judging journalism: how should the quality of news reporting about clinical interventions be assessed and improved? *Quality in Health Care*, 1999; 8: 172-176.

22 Michel K, Frey C, Wyss K, Valach L. An exercise in improving suicide reporting in print media. *Crisis*, 2000; 21: 71-79.

23 Oxman AD, Flottorp S. An overview of strategies to promote implementation of evidence based health care. In: Silagy C, Haines A (eds) *Evidence Based Practice*. 2nd Edition. London: BMJ Publishers, 2001: 101-119.

The Ecstasy of Influence

Jonathan Lethem

All mankind is of one author, and is one volume; when one man dies, one chapter is not torn out of the book, but translated into a better language; and every chapter must be so translated. . . .

—John Donne

LOVE AND THEFT

Consider this tale: a cultivated man of middle age looks back on the story of an *amour fou*, one beginning when, traveling abroad, he takes a room as a lodger. The moment he sees the daughter of the house, he is lost. She is a preteen, whose charms instantly enslave him. Heedless of her age, he becomes intimate with her. In the end she dies, and the narrator — marked by her forever — remains alone. The name of the girl supplies the title of the story: *Lolita*.

The author of the story I've described, Heinz von Lichberg, published his tale of Lolita in 1916, forty years before Vladimir Nabokov's novel. Lichberg later became a prominent journalist in the Nazi era, and his youthful works faded from view. Did Nabokov, who remained in Berlin until 1937, adopt Lichberg's tale consciously? Or did the earlier tale exist for Nabokov as a hidden, unacknowledged memory? The history of literature is not without examples of this phenomenon, called cryptomnesia. Another hypothesis is that Nabokov, knowing Lichberg's tale perfectly well, had set himself to that art of quotation that Thomas Mann, himself a master of it, called "higher cribbing." Literature has always been a crucible in which familiar themes are continually recast. Little of what we admire in Nabokov's *Lolita* is to be found in its predecessor; the former is in no way deducible from the latter. Still: did Nabokov consciously borrow and quote?

"When you live outside the law, you have to eliminate dishonesty." The line comes from Don Siegel's 1958 film noir, *The Lineup*, written by Stirling Silliphant. The film still haunts revival houses, likely thanks to Eli Wallach's blazing portrayal of a sociopathic hit man and to Siegel's long, sturdy auteurist career. Yet what were those words worth — to Siegel, or Silliphant, or their audience — in 1958? And again: what was the line worth when Bob Dylan heard it (presumably in some Greenwich Village repertory cinema), cleaned it up a little, and inserted it into "Absolutely Sweet Marie"? What are they worth now, to the culture at large?

Appropriation has always played a key role in Dylan's music. The songwriter has grabbed not only from a panoply of vintage Hollywood films but from Shakespeare and F. Scott Fitzgerald and Junichi Saga's *Confessions of a Yakuza*. He also nabbed the title of Eric Lott's study of minstrelsy for his 2001 album *Love and Theft*. One imagines Dylan liked the general resonance of the title, in which emotional misdemeanors stalk the sweetness of love, as they do so often in Dylan's songs. Lott's title is, of course, itself a riff on Leslie Fiedler's *Love and Death in the American Novel*, which famously identifies the literary motif of the interdependence of a white man and a dark man, like Huck and Jim or Ishmael and Queequeg — a series of nested references to Dylan's own appropriating, minstrel-boy self. Dylan's art offers a paradox: while it famously urges us not to look back, it also encodes a knowledge of past sources that might otherwise have little home in contemporary culture, like the Civil War poetry of the Confederate bard Henry Timrod, resuscitated in lyrics on Dylan's newest record, *Modern Times*. Dylan's originality and his appropriations are as one.

The same might be said of *all* art. I realized this forcefully when one day I went looking for the John Donne passage quoted above. I know the lines, I confess, not from a college course but from the movie version of 84, *Charing Cross Road* with Anthony Hopkins and Anne Bancroft. I checked out 84, *Charing Cross Road* from the library in the hope of finding the Donne passage, but it wasn't in the book. It's alluded to in the play that was adapted from the book, but it isn't reprinted. So I rented the movie again, and there was the passage, read in voice-over by Anthony

Hopkins but without attribution. Unfortunately, the line was also abridged so that, when I finally turned to the Web, I found myself searching for the line "all mankind is of one volume" instead of "all mankind is of one author, and is one volume."

My Internet search was initially no more successful than my library search. I had thought that summoning books from the vasty deep was a matter of a few keystrokes, but when I visited the website of the Yale library, I found that most of its books don't yet exist as computer text. As a last-ditch effort I searched the seemingly more obscure phrase "every chapter must be so translated." The passage I wanted finally came to me, as it turns out, not as part of a scholarly library collection but simply because someone who loves Donne had posted it on his homepage. The lines I sought were from Meditation 17 in *Devotions upon Emergent Occasions*, which happens to be the most famous thing Donne ever wrote, containing as it does the line "never send to know for whom the bell tolls; it tolls for thee." My search had led me from a movie to a book to a play to a website and back to a book. Then again, those words may be as famous as they are only because Hemingway lifted them for his book title.

Literature has been in a plundered, fragmentary state for a long time. When I was thirteen I purchased an anthology of Beat writing. Immediately, and to my very great excitement, I discovered one William S. Burroughs, author of something called *Naked Lunch*, excerpted there in all its coruscating brilliance. Burroughs was then as radical a literary man as the world had to offer. Nothing, in all my experience of literature since, has ever had as strong an effect on my sense of the sheer possibilities of writing. Later, attempting to understand this impact, I discovered that Burroughs had incorporated snippets of other writers' texts into his work, an action I knew my teachers would have called plagiarism. Some of these borrowings had been lifted from American science fiction of the Forties and Fifties, adding a secondary shock of recognition for me. By then I knew that this "cut-up method," as Burroughs called it, was central to whatever he thought he was doing, and that he quite literally believed it to be akin to magic. When he wrote about his process, the hairs on my neck stood up, so palpable was the excitement. Burroughs was interrogating the universe with scissors and a paste pot, and the least imitative of authors was no plagiarist at all.

CONTAMINATION ANXIETY

In 1941, on his front porch, Muddy Waters recorded a song for the folklorist Alan Lomax. After singing the song, which he told Lomax was entitled "Country Blues," Waters described how he came to write it. "I made it on about the eighth of October '38," Waters said. "I was fixin' a puncture on a car. I had been mistreated by a girl. I just felt blue, and the song fell into my mind and it come to me just like that and I started singing." Then Lomax, who knew of the Robert Johnson recording called "Walkin' Blues," asked Waters if there were any other songs that used the same tune. "There's been some blues played like that," Waters replied. "This song comes from the cotton field and a boy once put a record out — Robert Johnson. He put it out as named 'Walkin' Blues.' I heard the tune before I heard it on the record. I learned it from Son House." In nearly one breath, Waters offers five accounts: his own active authorship: he "made it" on a specific date. Then the "passive" explanation: "it come to me just like that." After Lomax raises the question of influence, Waters, without shame, misgivings, or trepidation, says that he heard a version by Johnson, but that his mentor, Son House, taught it to him. In the middle of that complex genealogy, Waters declares that "this song comes from the cotton field."

Blues and jazz musicians have long been enabled by a kind of "open source" culture, in which pre-existing melodic fragments and larger musical frameworks are freely reworked. Technology has only multiplied the possibilities; musicians have gained the power to *duplicate* sounds literally rather than simply approximate them through allusion. In Seventies Jamaica, King Tubby and Lee "Scratch" Perry deconstructed recorded music, using astonishingly primitive pre-digital hardware, creating what they called "versions." The recombinant nature of their means of production quickly spread to DJs in New York and London. Today an endless, gloriously impure, and fundamentally social process generates countless hours of music.

Visual, sound, and text collage — which for many centuries were relatively fugitive traditions (a cento here, a folk pastiche there) — became explosively central to a series of movements in the twentieth century: futurism, cubism, Dada, musique concrète, situationism, pop art, and appropriationism. In fact, collage, the common denominator in that list, might be called *the* art form of the twentieth century, never mind the twenty-first. But forget, for the moment, chronologies, schools, or even

centuries. As examples accumulate — Igor Stravinsky's music and Daniel
Johnston's, Francis Bacon's paintings and Henry Darger's, the novels of
the Oulipo group and of Hannah Crafts (the author who pillaged Dickens's *Bleak House* to write *The Bondwoman's Narrative*), as well as cherished
texts that become troubling to their admirers after the discovery of their
"plagiarized" elements, like Richard Condon's novels or Martin Luther
King Jr.'s sermons — it becomes apparent that appropriation, mimicry, quotation, allusion, and sublimated collaboration consist of a kind of sine qua
non of the creative act, cutting across all forms and genres in the realm of
cultural production.

In a courtroom scene from *The Simpsons* that has since entered into
the television canon, an argument over the ownership of the animated
characters Itchy and Scratchy rapidly escalates into an existential debate on
the very nature of cartoons. "Animation is built on plagiarism!" declares
the show's hot-tempered cartoon-producer-within-a-cartoon, Roger Mey-
ers Jr. "You take away our right to steal ideas, where are they going to
come from?" If nostalgic cartoonists had never borrowed from *Fritz the
Cat*, there would be no *Ren & Stimpy Show*; without the Rankin/Bass
and Charlie Brown Christmas specials, there would be no *South Park*;
and without *The Flintstones* — more or less *The Honeymooners* in cartoon
loincloths — The Simpsons would cease to exist. If those don't strike you
as essential losses, then consider the remarkable series of "plagiarisms"
that links Ovid's "Pyramus and Thisbe" with Shakespeare's *Romeo and
Juliet* and Leonard Bernstein's *West Side Story*, or Shakespeare's description
of Cleopatra, copied nearly verbatim from Plutarch's life of Mark Antony
and also later nicked by T. S. Eliot for *The Waste Land*. If these are examples of plagiarism, then we want more plagiarism.

Most artists are brought to their vocation when their own nascent
gifts are awakened by the work of a master. That is to say, most artists are
converted to art by art itself. Finding one's voice isn't just an emptying and
purifying oneself of the words of others but an adopting and embracing
of filiations, communities, and discourses. Inspiration could be called
inhaling the memory of an act never experienced. Invention, it must be
humbly admitted, does not consist in creating out of void but out of chaos.
Any artist knows these truths, no matter how deeply he or she submerges
that knowing.

What happens when an allusion goes unrecognized? A closer look
at *The Waste Land* may help make this point. The body of Eliot's poem

is a vertiginous mélange of quotation, allusion, and "original" writing. When Eliot alludes to Edmund Spenser's "Prothalamion" with the line "Sweet Thames, run softly, till I end my song," what of readers to whom the poem, never one of Spenser's most popular, is unfamiliar? (Indeed, the Spenser is now known largely because of Eliot's use of it.) Two responses are possible: grant the line to Eliot, or later discover the source and understand the line as plagiarism. Eliot evidenced no small anxiety about these matters; the notes he so carefully added to *The Waste Land* can be read as a symptom of modernism's contamination anxiety. Taken from this angle, what exactly is postmodernism, except modernism without the anxiety?

SURROUNDED BY SIGNS

The surrealists believed that objects in the world possess a certain but unspecifiable intensity that had been dulled by everyday use and utility. They meant to reanimate this dormant intensity, to bring their minds once again into close contact with the matter that made up their world. André Breton's maxim "Beautiful as the chance encounter of a sewing machine and an umbrella on an operating table" is an expression of the belief that simply placing objects in an unexpected context reinvigorates their mysterious qualities.

This "crisis" the surrealists identified was being simultaneously diagnosed by others. Martin Heidegger held that the essence of modernity was found in a certain technological orientation he called "enframing." This tendency encourages us to see the objects in our world only in terms of how they can serve us or be used by us. The task he identified was to find ways to resituate ourselves vis-à-vis these "objects," so that we may see them as "things" pulled into relief against the ground of their functionality. Heidegger believed that art had the great potential to reveal the "thingness" of objects.

The surrealists understood that photography and cinema could carry out this reanimating process automatically; the process of framing objects in a lens was often enough to create the charge they sought. Describing the effect, Walter Benjamin drew a comparison between the photographic apparatus and Freud's psychoanalytic methods. Just as Freud's theories "isolated and made analyzable things which had heretofore floated along unnoticed in the broad stream of perception," the photographic apparatus focuses on "hidden details of familiar objects," revealing "entirely new structural formations of the subject."

It's worth noting, then, that early in the history of photography a series of judicial decisions could well have changed the course of that art: courts were asked whether the photographer, amateur or professional, required permission before he could capture and print an image. Was the photographer *stealing* from the person or building whose photograph he shot, pirating something of private and certifiable value? Those early decisions went in favor of the pirates. Just as Walt Disney could take inspiration from Buster Keaton's *Steamboat Bill, Jr.*, the Brothers Grimm, or the existence of real mice, the photographer should be free to capture an image without compensating the source. The world that meets our eye through the lens of a camera was judged to be, with minor exceptions, a sort of public commons, where a cat may look at a king.

Novelists may glance at the stuff of the world too, but we sometimes get called to task for it. For those whose ganglia were formed pre-TV, the mimetic deployment of pop-culture icons seems at best an annoying tic and at worst a dangerous vapidity that compromises fiction's seriousness by dating it out of the Platonic Always, where it ought to reside. In a graduate workshop I briefly passed through, a certain gray eminence tried to convince us that a literary story should always eschew "any feature which serves to date it" because "serious fiction must be Timeless." When we protested that, in his own well-known work, characters moved about electrically lit rooms, drove cars, and spoke not Anglo-Saxon but postwar English — and further, that fiction he'd himself ratified as great, such as Dickens, was liberally strewn with innately topical, commercial, and timebound references — he impatiently amended his proscription to those explicit references that would date a story in the "frivolous Now." When pressed, he said of course he meant the "trendy mass-popular-media" reference. Here, transgenerational discourse broke down.

I was born in 1964; I grew up watching Captain Kangaroo, moon landings, zillions of TV ads, the Banana Splits, M*A*S*H, and *The Mary Tyler Moore Show.* I was born with words in my mouth — "Band-Aid," "Q-tip," "Xerox" — object-names as fixed and eternal in my logosphere as "taxicab" and "toothbrush." The world is a home littered with pop-culture products and their emblems. I also came of age swamped by parodies that stood for originals yet mysterious to me — I knew Monkees before Beatles, Belmondo before Bogart, and "remember" the movie *Summer of '42* from a *Mad* magazine satire, though I've still never seen the film itself. I'm not alone in having been born backward into an incoherent realm of texts, products, and images, the commercial and cultural environment with which we've both supplemented and blotted out our natural world. I can no more claim it as "mine" than the sidewalks and forests of the world, yet I do dwell in it, and for me to stand a chance as either artist or citizen, I'd probably better be permitted to name it.

Consider Walker Percy's *The Moviegoer*:

> Other people, so I have read, treasure memorable moments in their lives: the time one climbed the Parthenon at sunrise, the summer night one met a lonely girl in Central Park and achieved with her a sweet and natural relationship, as they say in books. I too once met a girl in Central Park, but it is not much to remember. What I remember is the time John Wayne killed three men with a carbine as he was falling to the dusty street in *Stagecoach*, and the time the kitten found Orson Welles in the doorway in *The Third Man*.

Today, when we can eat Tex-Mex with chopsticks while listening to reggae and watching a YouTube rebroadcast of the Berlin Wall's fall — i.e., when damn near *everything* presents itself as familiar — it's not a surprise that some of today's most ambitious art is going about trying to *make the familiar strange*. In so doing, in reimagining what human life might truly be like over there across the chasms of illusion, mediation, demographics, marketing, imago, and appearance, artists are paradoxically trying to restore what's taken for "real" to three whole dimensions, to reconstruct a univocally round world out of disparate streams of flat sights.

Whatever charge of tastelessness or trademark violation may be attached to the artistic appropriation of the media environment in which we swim, the alternative — to flinch, or tiptoe away into some ivory tower of irrelevance — is far worse. We're surrounded by signs; our imperative is to ignore none of them.

USE MONOPOLY

The idea that culture can be property — *intellectual* property — is used to justify everything from attempts to force the Girl Scouts to pay royalties for singing songs around campfires to the infringement suit brought by the estate of Margaret Mitchell against the publishers of Alice Randall's *The Wind Done Gone*. Corporations like Celera Genomics have filed for patents for human genes, while the Recording Industry Association of America has sued music downloaders for copyright infringement, reaching out-of-court settlements for thousands of dollars with defendants as young as twelve. ASCAP bleeds fees from shop owners who play background music in their stores; students and scholars are shamed from placing texts face-down on photocopy machines. At the same time, copyright is revered by most established writers and artists as a birthright and bulwark, the source of nurture for their infinitely fragile practices in a rapacious world. Plagiarism and piracy, after all, are the monsters we working artists are taught to dread, as they roam the woods surrounding our tiny preserves of regard and remuneration.

A time is marked not so much by ideas that are argued about as by ideas that are taken for granted. The character of an era hangs upon what needs no defense. In this regard, few of us question the contemporary construction of copyright. It is taken as a law, both in the sense of a universally recognizable moral absolute, like the law against murder, and as naturally inherent in our world, like the law of gravity. In fact, it is neither. Rather, copyright is an ongoing social negotiation, tenuously forged, endlessly revised, and imperfect in its every incarnation.

Thomas Jefferson, for one, considered copyright a necessary evil: he favored providing just enough incentive to create, nothing more, and thereafter allowing ideas to flow freely, as nature intended. His conception of copyright was enshrined in the Constitution, which gives Congress the authority to "promote the Progress of Science and useful Arts, by securing for limited Times to Authors and Inventors the exclusive Right to their respective Writings and Discoveries." This was a balancing act between creators and society as a whole; second comers might do a much better job than the originator with the original idea.

But Jefferson's vision has not fared well, has in fact been steadily eroded by those who view the culture as a market in which everything of value should be owned by someone or other. The distinctive feature of modern American copyright law is its almost limitless bloating — its expansion in both scope and duration. With no registration requirement, every creative act in a tangible medium is now subject to copyright protection: your email to your child or your child's finger painting, both are automatically protected. The first Congress to grant copyright gave authors an initial term of fourteen years, which could be renewed for another fourteen if the author still lived. The current term is the life of the author plus seventy years. It's only a slight exaggeration to say that each time Mickey

Mouse is about to fall into the public domain, the mouse's copyright term is extended.

Even as the law becomes more restrictive, technology is exposing those restrictions as bizarre and arbitrary. When old laws fixed on reproduction as the compensable (or actionable) unit, it wasn't because there was anything fundamentally invasive of an author's rights in the making of a copy. Rather it was because copies were once easy to find and count, so they made a useful benchmark for deciding when an owner's rights had been invaded. In the contemporary world, though, the act of "copying" is in no meaningful sense equivalent to an infringement — we make a copy every time we accept an emailed text, or send or forward one — and is impossible anymore to regulate or even describe.

At the movies, my entertainment is sometimes lately preceded by a dire trailer, produced by the lobbying group called the Motion Picture Association of America, in which the purchasing of a bootleg copy of a Hollywood film is compared to the theft of a car or a handbag — and, as the bullying supertitles remind us, "You wouldn't steal a handbag!" This conflation forms an incitement to quit thinking. If I were to tell you that pirating DVDs or downloading music is in no way different from loaning a friend a book, my own arguments would be as ethically bankrupt as the MPAA's. The truth lies somewhere in the vast gray area between these two overstated positions. For a car or a handbag, once stolen, no longer is available to its owner, while the appropriation of an article of "intellectual property" leaves the original untouched. As Jefferson wrote, "He who receives an idea from me, receives instruction himself without lessening mine; as he who lights his taper at mine, receives light without darkening me."

Yet industries of cultural capital, who profit not from creating but from distributing, see the sale of culture as a zero-sum game. The piano-roll publishers fear the record companies, who fear the cassette-tape manufacturers, who fear the online vendors, who fear whoever else is next in line to profit most quickly from the intangible and infinitely reproducible fruits of an artist's labor. It has been the same in every industry and with every technological innovation. Jack Valenti, speaking for the MPAA: "I say to you that the VCR is to the American film producer and the American public as the Boston Strangler is to the woman home alone."

Thinking clearly sometimes requires unbraiding our language. The word "copyright" may eventually seem as dubious in its embedded purposes as "family values," "globalization," and, sure, "intellectual property."

Copyright is a "right" in no absolute sense; it is a government-granted monopoly on the use of creative results. So let's try calling it that — not a right but a *monopoly on use*, a "usemonopoly" — and then consider how the rapacious expansion of monopoly rights has always been counter to the public interest, no matter if it is Andrew Carnegie controlling the price of steel or Walt Disney managing the fate of his mouse. Whether the monopolizing beneficiary is a living artist or some artist's heirs or some corporation's shareholders, the loser is the community, including living artists who might make splendid use of a healthy public domain.

THE BEAUTY OF SECOND USE

A few years ago someone brought me a strange gift, purchased at MoMA's downtown design store: a copy of my own first novel, *Gun, With Occasional Music*, expertly cut into the contours of a pistol. The object was the work of Robert The, an artist whose specialty is the reincarnation of everyday materials. I regard my first book as an old friend, one who never fails to remind me of the spirit with which I entered into this game of art and commerce — that to be allowed to insert the materials of my imagination onto the shelves of bookstores and into the minds of readers (if only a handful) was a wild privilege. I was paid $6,000 for three years of writing, but at the time I'd have happily published the results for nothing. Now my old friend had come home in a new form, one I was unlikely to have imagined for it myself. The gun-book wasn't readable, exactly, but I couldn't take offense at that. The fertile spirit of stray connection this appropriated object conveyed back to me — the strange beauty of its second use — was a reward for being a published writer I could never have fathomed in advance. And the world makes room for both my novel and Robert The's gun-book. There's no need to choose between the two.

In the first life of creative property, if the creator is lucky, the content is sold. After the commercial life has ended, our tradition supports a second life as well. A newspaper is delivered to a doorstep, and the next day wraps fish or builds an archive. Most books fall out of print after one year, yet even within that period they can be sold in used bookstores and stored in libraries, quoted in reviews, parodied in magazines, described in conversations, and plundered for costumes for kids to wear on Halloween. The demarcation between various possible uses is beautifully graded and

hard to define, the more so as artifacts distill into and repercuss through
the realm of culture into which they've been entered, the more so as they
engage the receptive minds for whom they were presumably intended.

Active reading is an impertinent raid on the literary preserve. Readers
are like nomads, poaching their way across fields they do not own — artists
are no more able to control the imaginations of their audiences than the
culture industry is able to control second uses of its artifacts. In the children's classic *The Velveteen Rabbit*, the old Skin Horse offers the Rabbit a
lecture on the practice of textual poaching. The value of a new toy lies not
it its material qualities (not "having things that buzz inside you and a stick-
out handle"), the Skin Horse explains, but rather in how the toy is used.
"Real isn't how you are made. . . . It's a thing that happens to you. When
a child loves you for a long, long time, not just to play with, but REALLY
loves you, then you become Real." The Rabbit is fearful, recognizing that
consumer goods don't become "real" without being actively reworked:
"Does it hurt?" Reassuring him, the Skin Horse says: "It doesn't happen all
at once. . . . You become. It takes a long time. . . . Generally, by the time
you are Real, most of your hair has been loved off, and your eyes drop out
and you get loose in the joints and very shabby." Seen from the perspective
of the toymaker, the Velveteen Rabbit's loose joints and missing eyes represent vandalism, signs of misuse and rough treatment; for others, these are
marks of its loving use.

Artists and their surrogates who fall into the trap of seeking recom-
pense for every possible second use end up attacking their own best
audience members for the crime of exalting and enshrining their work.
The Recording Industry Association of America prosecuting their own
record-buying public makes as little sense as the novelists who bristle at
autographing used copies of their books for collectors. And artists, or their
heirs, who fall into the trap of attacking the collagists and satirists and
digital samplers of their work are attacking the next generation of creators
for the crime of being influenced, for the crime of responding with the
same mixture of intoxication, resentment, lust, and glee that characterizes
all artistic successors. By doing so they make the world smaller, betraying
what seems to me the primary motivation for participating in the world of
culture in the first place: to make the world larger.

SOURCE HYPOCRISY, OR, DISNIAL

The Walt Disney Company has drawn an astonishing catalogue from
the work of others: *Snow White and the Seven Dwarfs, Fantasia, Pinocchio,
Dumbo, Bambi, Song of the South, Cinderella, Alice in Wonderland, Robin Hood,
Peter Pan, Lady and the Tramp, Mulan, Sleeping Beauty, The Sword in the Stone,
The Jungle Book,* and, alas, *Treasure Planet,* a legacy of cultural sampling that
Shakespeare, or De La Soul, could get behind. Yet Disney's protectorate of
lobbyists has policed the resulting cache of cultural materials as vigilantly
as if it were Fort Knox — threatening legal action, for instance, against the
artist Dennis Oppenheim for the use of Disney characters in a sculpture,
and prohibiting the scholar Holly Crawford from using any Disney-related
images — including artwork by Lichtenstein, Warhol, Oldenburg, and others — in her monograph *Attached to the Mouse: Disney and Contemporary Art.*

This peculiar and specific act — the enclosure of commonwealth culture
for the benefit of a sole or corporate owner — is close kin to what could
be called *imperial plagiarism,* the free use of Third World or "primitive"
artworks and styles by more privileged (and better-paid) artists. Think of
Picasso's Les Demoiselles d'Avignon, or some of the albums of Paul Simon
or David Byrne: even without violating copyright, those creators have
sometimes come in for a certain skepticism when the extent of their out-
sourcing became evident. And, as when Led Zeppelin found themselves
sued for back royalties by the bluesman Willie Dixon, the act can occasionally be an expensive one. *To live outside the law, you must be honest:* perhaps
it was this, in part, that spurred David Byrne and Brian Eno to recently
launch a "remix" website, where anyone can download easily disassembled
versions of two songs from *My Life in the Bush of Ghosts,* an album reliant on vernacular speech sampled from a host of sources. Perhaps it also
explains why Bob Dylan has never refused a request for a sample.

Kenneth Koch once said, "I'm a writer who likes to be influenced." It
was a charming confession, and a rare one. For so many artists, the act of
creativity is intended as a Napoleonic imposition of one's uniqueness
upon the universe — *après moi le déluge* of copycats! And for every James
Joyce or Woody Guthrie or Martin Luther King Jr., or Walt Disney, who
gathered a constellation of voices in his work, there may seem to be some
corporation or literary estate eager to stopper the bottle: cultural debts
flow in, but they don't flow out. We might call this tendency "source
hypocrisy." Or we could name it after the most pernicious source hypo-
crites of all time: Disnial.

YOU CAN'T STEAL A GIFT

My reader may, understandably, be on the verge of crying, "Communist!"
A large, diverse society cannot survive without property; a large, diverse,
and modern society cannot flourish without some form of intellectual
property. But it takes little reflection to grasp that there is ample value
that the term "property" doesn't capture. And works of art exist simultaneously in two economies, a market economy and a *gift economy*.

The cardinal difference between gift and commodity exchange is that
a gift establishes a feeling-bond between two people, whereas the sale of
a commodity leaves no necessary connection. I go into a hardware store,
pay the man for a hacksaw blade, and walk out. I may never see him again.
The disconnectedness is, in fact, a virtue of the commodity mode. We
don't want to be bothered, and if the clerk always wants to chat about the
family, I'll shop elsewhere. I just want a hacksaw blade. But a gift makes a
connection. There are many examples, the candy or cigarette offered to a
stranger who shares a seat on the plane, the few words that indicate good-
will between passengers on the late-night bus. These tokens establish the
simplest bonds of social life, but the model they offer may be extended to
the most complicated of unions — marriage, parenthood, mentorship. If a
value is placed on these (often essentially unequal) exchanges, they degen-
erate into something else.

Yet one of the more difficult things to comprehend is that the gift economies — like those that sustain open-source software — coexist so naturally
with the market. It is precisely this doubleness in art practices that we
must identify, ratify, and enshrine in our lives as participants in culture,
either as "producers" or "consumers." Art that matters to us — which
moves the heart, or revives the soul, or delights the senses, or offers cour-
age for living, however we choose to describe the experience — is received
as a gift is received. Even if we've paid a fee at the door of the museum or
concert hall, when we are touched by a work of art something comes to
us that has nothing to do with the price. The daily commerce of our lives
proceeds at its own constant level, but a gift conveys an uncommodifiable
surplus of inspiration.

The way we treat a thing can change its nature, though. Religions often
prohibit the sale of sacred objects, the implication being that their sanc-
tity is lost if they are bought and sold. We consider it unacceptable to sell
sex, babies, body organs, legal rights, and votes. The idea that something
should never be commodified is generally known as *inalienability* or *unalien-*

ability — a concept most famously expressed by Thomas Jefferson in the phrase "endowed by their Creator with certain unalienable Rights . . ." A work of art seems to be a hardier breed; it can be sold in the market and still emerge a work of art. But if it is true that in the essential commerce of art a gift is carried by the work from the artist to his audience, if I am right to say that where there is no gift there is no art, then it may be possible to destroy a work of art by converting it into a pure commodity. I don't maintain that art can't be bought and sold, but that the gift portion of the work places a constraint upon our merchandising. This is the reason why even a really beautiful, ingenious, powerful ad (of which there are a lot) can never be any kind of real art: an ad has no status as gift; i.e., it's never really *for* the person it's directed at.

The power of a gift economy remains difficult for the empiricists of our market culture to understand. In our times, the rhetoric of the market presumes that everything should be and can be appropriately bought, sold, and owned — a tide of alienation lapping daily at the dwindling redoubt of the unalienable. In free-market theory, an intervention to halt propertization is considered "paternalistic," because it inhibits the free action of the citizen, now reposited as a "potential entrepreneur." Of course, in the real world, we know that child-rearing, family life, education, socialization, sexuality, political life, and many other basic human activities require insulation from market forces. In fact, paying for many of these things can ruin them. We may be willing to peek at *Who Wants to Marry a Multimillionaire* or an eBay auction of the ova of fashion models, but only to reassure ourselves that some things are still beneath our standards of dignity.

What's remarkable about gift economies is that they can flourish in the most unlikely places — in run-down neighborhoods, on the Internet, in scientific communities, and among members of Alcoholics Anonymous. A classic example is commercial blood systems, which generally produce blood supplies of lower safety, purity, and potency than volunteer systems. A gift economy may be superior when it comes to maintaining a group's commitment to certain extra-market values.

THE COMMONS

Another way of understanding the presence of gift economies — which dwell like ghosts in the commercial machine — is in the sense of a *public commons*. A commons, of course, is anything like the streets over which we drive, the skies through which we pilot airplanes, or the public parks or beaches on which we dally. A commons belongs to everyone and no one, and its use is controlled only by common consent. A commons describes resources like the body of ancient music drawn on by composers and folk musicians alike, rather than the commodities, like "Happy Birthday to You," for which ASCAP, 114 years after it was written, continues to collect a fee. Einstein's theory of relativity is a commons. Writings in the public domain are a commons. Gossip about celebrities is a commons. The silence in a movie theater is a transitory commons, impossibly fragile, treasured by those who crave it, and constructed as a mutual gift by those who compose it.

The world of art and culture is a vast commons, one that is salted through with zones of utter commerce yet remains gloriously immune to any overall commodification. The closest resemblance is to the commons of a *language*: altered by every contributor, expanded by even the most passive user. That a language is a commons doesn't mean that the community owns it; rather it belongs between people, possessed by no one, not even by society as a whole.

Nearly any commons, though, can be encroached upon, partitioned, enclosed. The American commons include tangible assets such as public forests and minerals, intangible wealth such as copyrights and patents, critical infrastructures such as the Internet and government research, and cultural resources such as the broadcast airwaves and public spaces. They include resources we've paid for as taxpayers and inherited from previous generations. They're not just an inventory of marketable assets; they're social institutions and cultural traditions that define us as Americans and enliven us as human beings. Some invasions of the commons are sanctioned because we can no longer muster a spirited commitment to the public sector. The abuse goes unnoticed because the theft of the commons is seen in glimpses, not in panorama. We may occasionally see a former wetland paved; we may hear about the breakthrough cancer drug that tax dollars helped develop, the rights to which pharmaceutical companies acquired for a song. The larger movement goes too much unremarked. The notion of a *commons of cultural materials* goes more or less unnamed.

Honoring the commons is not a matter of moral exhortation. It is a practical necessity. We in Western society are going through a period of intensifying belief in private ownership, to the detriment of the public good. We have to remain constantly vigilant to prevent raids by those who would selfishly exploit our common heritage for their private gain.

Such raids on our natural resources are not examples of enterprise and initiative. They are attempts to take from all the people just for the benefit of a few.

UNDISCOVERED PUBLIC KNOWLEDGE

Artists and intellectuals despondent over the prospects for originality can take heart from a phenomenon identified about twenty years ago by Don Swanson, a library scientist at the University of Chicago. He called it "undiscovered public knowledge." Swanson showed that standing problems in medical research may be significantly addressed, perhaps even solved, simply by systematically surveying the scientific literature. Left to its own devices, research tends to become more specialized and abstracted from the real-world problems that motivated it and to which it remains relevant. This suggests that such a problem may be tackled effectively not by commissioning more research but by assuming that most or all of the solution can already be found in various scientific journals, waiting to be assembled by someone willing to read across specialties. Swanson himself did this in the case of Raynaud's syndrome, a disease that causes the fingers of young women to become numb. His finding is especially striking — perhaps even scandalous — because it happened in the ever-expanding biomedical sciences.

Undiscovered public knowledge emboldens us to question the extreme claims to originality made in press releases and publishers' notices: Is an intellectual or creative offering truly novel, or have we just forgotten a worthy precursor? Does solving certain scientific problems really require massive additional funding, or could a computerized search engine, creatively deployed, do the same job more quickly and cheaply? Lastly, does our appetite for creative vitality require the violence and exasperation of another avant-garde, with its wearisome killing-the-father imperatives, or might we be better off ratifying the *ecstasy of influence* — and deepening our willingness to understand the commonality and timelessness of the methods and motifs available to artists?

GIVE ALL

A few years ago, the Film Society of Lincoln Center announced a retrospective of the works of Dariush Mehrjui, then a fresh enthusiasm of mine. Mehrjui is one of Iran's finest filmmakers, and the only one whose subject was personal relationships among the upper-middle-class intelligentsia. Needless to say, opportunities to view his films were — and remain — rare indeed. I headed uptown for one, an adaptation of J. D. Salinger's *Franny and Zooey*, titled *Pari*, only to discover at the door of the Walter Reade Theater that the screening had been canceled: its announcement had brought threat of a lawsuit down on the Film Society. True, these were Salinger's rights under the law. Yet why would he care that some obscure Iranian filmmaker had paid him homage with a meditation on his heroine? Would it have damaged his book or robbed him of some crucial remuneration had the screening been permitted? The fertile spirit of stray connection — one stretching across what is presently seen as the direst of international breaches — had in this case been snuffed out. The cold, undead hand of one of my childhood literary heroes had reached out from its New Hampshire redoubt to arrest my present-day curiosity.

A few assertions, then:

Any text that has infiltrated the common mind to the extent of *Gone With the Wind* or *Lolita* or *Ulysses* inexorably joins the language of culture. A map-turned-to-landscape, it has moved to a place beyond enclosure or control. The authors and their heirs should consider the subsequent parodies, refractions, quotations, and revisions an honor, or at least the price of a rare success.

A corporation that has imposed an inescapable notion — Mickey Mouse, Band-Aid — on the cultural language should pay a similar price.

The primary objective of copyright is not to reward the labor of authors but "to promote the Progress of Science and useful Arts." To this end, copyright assures authors the right to their original expression, but encourages others to build freely upon the ideas and information conveyed by a work. This result is neither unfair nor unfortunate.

Contemporary copyright, trademark, and patent law is presently corrupted. The case for perpetual copyright is a denial of the essential gift-aspect of the creative act. Arguments in its favor are as un-American as those for the repeal of the estate tax.

Art is sourced. Apprentices graze in the field of culture.

Digital sampling is an art method like any other, neutral in itself.

Despite hand-wringing at each technological turn — radio, the Internet — the future will be much like the past. Artists will sell some things but also give some things away. Change may be troubling for those who crave less ambiguity, but the life of an artist has never been filled with certainty.

The dream of a perfect systematic remuneration is nonsense. I pay rent with the price my words bring when published in glossy magazines and at the same moment offer them for almost nothing to impoverished literary quarterlies, or speak them for free into the air in a radio interview. So what are they worth? What would they be worth if some future Dylan worked them into a song? Should I care to make such a thing impossible?

Any text is woven entirely with citations, references, echoes, cultural languages, which cut across it through and through in a vast stereophony. The citations that go to make up a text are anonymous, untraceable, and yet *already read*; they are quotations without inverted commas. The kernel, the soul — let us go further and say the substance, the bulk, the actual and valuable material of all human utterances — is plagiarism. For substantially all ideas are secondhand, consciously and unconsciously drawn from a million outside sources, and daily used by the garnerer with a pride and satisfaction born of the superstition that he originated them; whereas there is not a rag of originality about them anywhere except the little discoloration they get from his mental and moral caliber and his temperament, and which is revealed in characteristics of phrasing. Old and new make the warp and woof of every moment. There is no thread that is not a twist of these two strands. By necessity, by proclivity, and by delight, we all quote. Neurological study has lately shown that memory, imagination, and consciousness itself is stitched, quilted, pastiched. If we cut-and-paste our selves, might we not forgive it of our artworks?

Artists and writers — and our advocates, our guilds and agents — too often subscribe to implicit claims of originality that do injury to these truths. And we too often, as hucksters and bean counters in the tiny enterprises of our selves, act to spite the gift portion of our privileged roles. People live differently who treat a portion of their wealth as a gift. If we devalue and obscure the gift-economy function of our art practices, we turn our works into nothing more than advertisements for themselves. We may console ourselves that our lust for subsidiary rights in virtual perpetuity is some heroic counter to rapacious corporate interests. But the truth is that with artists pulling on one side and corporations pulling on the other, the loser is the collective public imagination from which we were nourished in the first place, and whose existence as the ultimate repository of our offerings makes the work worth doing in the first place.

As a novelist, I'm a cork on the ocean of story, a leaf on a windy day. Pretty soon I'll be blown away. For the moment I'm grateful to be making a living, and so must ask that for a limited time (in the Thomas Jefferson

sense) you please respect my small, treasured usemonopolies. Don't pirate
my editions; do plunder my visions. The name of the game is Give All.
You, reader, are welcome to my stories. They were never mine in the first
place, but I gave them to you. If you have the inclination to pick them up,
take them with my blessing.

KEY: I IS ANOTHER

This key to the preceding essay names the source of every line I stole,
warped, and cobbled together as I "wrote" (except, alas, those sources I for-
got along the way). First uses of a given author or speaker are highlighted
in red. Nearly every sentence I culled I also revised, at least slightly — for
necessities of space, in order to produce a more consistent tone, or simply
because I felt like it.

TITLE

The phrase "the ecstasy of influence," which embeds a rebuking play on
Harold Bloom's "anxiety of influence," is lifted from spoken remarks by
Professor Richard Dienst of Rutgers.

LOVE AND THEFT

". . . a cultivated man of middle age . . ." to ". . . hidden, unacknowledged memory?" These lines, with some adjustments for tone, belong to
the anonymous editor or assistant who wrote the dust-flap copy of Michael
Maar's *The Two Lolitas*. Of course, in my own experience, dust-flap copy
is often a collaboration between author and editor. Perhaps this was also
true for Maar.

"The history of literature . . ." to

". . . borrow and quote?" comes from Maar's book itself.

"Appropriation has always . . ." to ". . . Ishmael and Queequeg . . ." This
paragraph makes a hash of remarks from an interview with Eric Lott conducted by David McNair and Jayson Whitehead, and incorporates both
interviewers' and interviewee's observations. (The text-interview form
can be seen as a commonly accepted form of multivocal writing. Most
interviewers prime their subjects with remarks of their own — leading the
witness, so to speak — and gently refine their subjects' statements in the
final printed transcript.)

"I realized this . . ." to ". . . for a long time." The anecdote is cribbed, with an elision to avoid appropriating a dead grandmother, from Jonathan Rosen's *The Talmud and the Internet*. I've never seen 84, *Charing Cross Road*, nor searched the Web for a Donne quote. For me it was through Rosen to Donne, Hemingway, website, et al.

"When I was thirteen . . ." to ". . . no plagiarist at all." This is from William Gibson's "God's Little Toys," in *Wired* magazine. My own first encounter with William Burroughs, also at age thirteen, was less epiphanic. Having grown up with a painter father who, during family visits to galleries or museums, approvingly noted collage and appropriation techniques in the visual arts (Picasso, Claes Oldenburg, Stuart Davis), I was gratified, but not surprised, to learn that literature could encompass the same methods.

CONTAMINATION ANXIETY

"In 1941, on his front porch . . ." to ". . . 'this song comes from the cotton field.'" Siva Vaidhyanathan, *Copyrights and Copywrongs*.

". . . enabled by a kind . . . freely reworked." Kembrew McLeod, *Freedom of Expression*. In *Owning Culture*, McLeod notes that, as he was writing, he

> happened to be listening to a lot of old country music, and in my casual listening I noticed that **six** country songs shared *exactly* the same vocal melody, including Hank Thompson's "Wild Side of Life," the Carter Family's "I'm Thinking Tonight of My Blue Eyes," Roy Acuff's "Great Speckled Bird," Kitty Wells's "It Wasn't God Who Made Honky Tonk Angels," Reno & Smiley's "I'm Using My Bible for a Roadmap," and Townes Van Zandt's "Heavenly Houseboat Blues." . . . In his extensively researched book, Country: *The Twisted Roots of Rock 'n' Roll*, Nick Tosches documents that the melody these songs share is both "ancient and British." There were no recorded lawsuits stemming from these appropriations. . . .

". . . musicians have gained . . . through allusion." Joanna Demers, *Steal This Music*.

"In Seventies Jamaica . . ." to ". . . hours of music." Gibson.

"Visual, sound, and text collage . . ." to ". . . realm of cultural production." This plunders, rewrites, and amplifies paragraphs from McLeod's

Owning Culture, except for the line about collage being the art form of the twentieth and twenty-first centuries, which I heard filmmaker Craig Baldwin say, in defense of sampling, in the trailer for a forthcoming documentary, *Copyright Criminals*.

"In a courtroom scene . . ." to ". . . would cease to exist." Dave Itzkoff, *New York Times*.

". . . the remarkable series of 'plagiarisms' . . ." to ". . . we want more plagiarism." Richard Posner, combined from The Becker-Posner Blog and *The Atlantic Monthly*.

"Most artists are brought . . ." to ". . . by art itself." These words, and many more to follow, come from Lewis Hyde's *The Gift*. Above any other book I've here plagiarized, I commend *The Gift* to your attention.

"Finding one's voice . . . filiations, communities, and discourses." Semanticist George L. Dillon, quoted in Rebecca Moore Howard's "The New Abolitionism Comes to Plagiarism."

"Inspiration could be . . . act never experienced." Ned Rorem, found on several "great quotations" sites on the Internet.

"Invention, it must be humbly admitted . . . out of chaos." Mary Shelley, from her introduction to *Frankenstein*.

"What happens . . ." to ". . . contamination anxiety." Kevin J.H. Dettmar, from "The Illusion of Modernist Allusion and the Politics of Postmodern Plagiarism."

SURROUNDED BY SIGNS

"The surrealists believed . . ." to the Walter Benjamin quote. Christian Keathley's *Cinephilia and History, or the Wind in the Trees*, a book that treats fannish fetishism as the secret at the heart of film scholarship. Keathley notes, for instance, Joseph Cornell's surrealist-influenced 1936 film *Rose Hobart*, which simply records "the way in which Cornell himself watched the 1931 Hollywood potboiler *East of Borneo*, fascinated and distracted as he was by its B-grade star" — the star, of course, being Rose Hobart herself. This, I suppose, makes Cornell a sort of father to computer-enabled fan-creator reworkings of Hollywood product, like the version of George Lucas's *The Phantom Menace* from which the noxious Jar Jar Binks character was purged; both incorporate a viewer's subjective preferences into a revision of a filmmaker's work.

". . . early in the history of photography" to ". . . without compensating the source." From *Free Culture*, by Lawrence Lessig, the greatest of public advocates for copyright reform, and the best source if you want to get radicalized in a hurry.

"For those whose ganglia . . ." to ". . . discourse broke down." From David Foster Wallace's essay "E Unibus Pluram," reprinted in *A Supposedly Fun Thing I'll Never Do Again*. I have no idea who Wallace's "gray eminence" is or was. I inserted the example of Dickens into the paragraph; he strikes me as overlooked in the lineage of authors of "brand-name" fiction.

"I was born . . . *Mary Tyler Moore Show*." These are the reminiscences of Mark Hosler from Negativland, a collaging musical collective that was sued by U2's record label for their appropriation of "I Still Haven't Found What I'm Looking For." Although I had to adjust the birth date, Hosler's cultural menu fits me like a glove.

"The world is a home . . . pop-culture products . . ." McLeod.

"Today, when we can eat . . ." to ". . . flat sights." Wallace.

"We're surrounded by signs, ignore none of them." This phrase, which I unfortunately rendered somewhat leaden with the word "imperative," comes from Steve Erickson's novel *Our Ecstatic Days*.

USEMONOPOLY

". . . everything from attempts . . ." to "defendants as young as twelve." Robert Boynton, *The New York Times Magazine*, "The Tyranny of Copyright?"

"A time is marked . . ." to ". . . what needs no defense." Lessig, this time from *The Future of Ideas*.

"Thomas Jefferson, for one . . ." to "'. . . respective Writings and Discoveries.'" Boynton.

". . . second comers might do a much better job than the originator . . ." I found this phrase in Lessig, who is quoting Vaidhyanathan, who himself is characterizing a judgment written by Learned Hand.

"But Jefferson's vision . . . owned by someone or other." Boynton.

"The distinctive feature . . ." to ". . . term is extended." Lessig, again from *The Future of Ideas*.

"When old laws . . ." to ". . . had been invaded." Jessica Litman, *Digital Copyright*.

"'I say to you . . . woman home alone.'" I found the Valenti quote in McLeod. Now fill in the blank: Jack Valenti is to the public domain as _____ is to _____.

THE BEAUTY OF SECOND USE

"In the first . . ." to ". . . builds an archive." Lessig.

"Most books . . . one year . . ." Lessig.

"Active reading is . . ." to ". . . do not own . . ." This is a mashup of Henry Jenkins, from his *Textual Poachers: Television Fans and Participatory Culture*, and Michel de Certeau, whom Jenkins quotes.

"In the children's classic . . ." to

". . . its loving use." Jenkins. (Incidentally, have the holders of the copyright to *The Velveteen Rabbit* had a close look at *Toy Story*? There could be a lawsuit there.)

SOURCE HYPOCRISY, OR, DISNIAL

"The Walt Disney Company . . . alas, *Treasure Planet* . . ." Lessig.

"Imperial Plagiarism" is the title of an essay by Marilyn Randall.

". . . spurred David Byrne . . . *My Life in the Bush of Ghosts* . . ." Chris Dahlen, *Pitchfork* — though in truth by the time I'd finished, his words were so utterly dissolved within my own that had I been an ordinary cutting-and-pasting journalist it never would have occurred to me to give Dahlen a citation. The effort of preserving another's distinctive phrases as I worked on this essay was sometimes beyond my capacities; this form of plagiarism was oddly hard work.

"Kenneth Koch . . ." to ". . . *déluge* of copycats!" Emily Nussbaum, *The New York Times Book Review*.

YOU CAN'T STEAL A GIFT

"You can't steal a gift." Dizzy Gillespie, defending another player who'd been accused of poaching Charlie Parker's style: "You can't steal a gift. Bird gave the world his music, and if you can hear it you can have it."

"A large, diverse society . . . intellectual property." Lessig.

"And works of art . . . " to ". . . marriage, parenthood, mentorship." Hyde.

"Yet one . . . so naturally with the market." David Bollier, *Silent Theft*.

"Art that matters . . ." to ". . . bought and sold." Hyde.

"We consider it unacceptable . . ." to "'. . . certain unalienable Rights . . .'" Bollier, paraphrasing Margaret Jane Radin's *Contested Commodities*.

"A work of art . . ." to ". . . constraint upon our merchandising." Hyde.

"This is the reason . . . person it's directed at." Wallace.

"The power of a gift . . ." to ". . . certain extra-market values." Bollier, and also the sociologist Warren O. Hagstrom, whom Bollier is paraphrasing.

THE COMMONS

"Einstein's theory . . ." to ". . . public domain are a commons." Lessig.

"That a language is a commons . . . society as a whole." Michael Newton, in the *London Review of Books*, reviewing a book called *Echolalias: On the Forgetting of Language* by Daniel Heller-Roazen. The paraphrases of book reviewers are another covert form of collaborative culture; as an avid reader of reviews, I know much about books I've never read. To quote Yann Martel on how he came to be accused of imperial plagiarism in his Booker-winning novel *Life of Pi*,

> Ten or so years ago, I read a review by John Updike in the *New York Times Review of Books* [sic]. It was of a novel by a Brazilian writer, Moacyr Scliar. I forget the title, and John Updike did worse: he clearly thought the book as a whole was forgettable. His review — one of those that makes you suspicious by being mostly descriptive . . . oozed indifference. But one thing about it struck me: the premise. . . . Oh, the wondrous things I could do with this premise.

Unfortunately, no one was ever able to locate the Updike review in question.

"The American commons . . ." to

". . . for a song." Bollier.

"Honoring the commons . . ." to

". . . practical necessity." Bollier.

"We in Western . . . public good." John Sulston, Nobel Prize–winner and co-mapper of the human genome.

"We have to remain . . ." to ". . . benefit of a few." Harry S Truman, at the opening of the Everglades National Park. Although it may seem the height of presumption to rip off a president — I found claiming Truman's stolid advocacy as my own embarrassing in the extreme — I didn't rewrite him at all. As the poet Marianne Moore said, "If a thing had been said in the **best** way, how can you say it better?" Moore confessed her penchant for incorporating lines from others' work, explaining, "I have not yet been able to outgrow this hybrid method of composition."

UNDISCOVERED PUBLIC KNOWLEDGE

". . . intellectuals despondent . . ." to ". . . quickly and cheaply?" Steve Fuller, *The Intellectual*. There's something of Borges in Fuller's insight here; the notion of a storehouse of knowledge waiting passively to be assembled by future users is suggestive of both "The Library of Babel" and "Kafka and his Precursors."

GIVE ALL

". . . one of Iran's finest . . ." to ". . . meditation on his heroine?" Amy Taubin, *Village Voice*, although it was me who was disappointed at the door of the Walter Reade Theater.

"The primary objective . . ." to ". . . unfair nor unfortunate." Sandra Day O'Connor, 1991.

". . . the future will be much like the past" to ". . . give some things away." Open-source film archivist Rick Prelinger, quoted in McLeod.

"Change may be troubling . . . with certainty." McLeod.

". . . woven entirely . . ." to ". . . without inverted commas." Roland Barthes.

"The kernel, the soul . . ." to ". . . characteristics of phrasing." Mark Twain, from a consoling letter to Helen Keller, who had suffered distressing accusations of plagiarism (!). In fact, her work included unconsciously memorized phrases; under Keller's particular circumstances, her writing could be understood as a kind of allegory of the "constructed" nature of artistic perception. I found the Twain quote in the aforementioned *Copyrights and Copywrongs*, by Siva Vaidhyanathan.

"Old and new . . ." to ". . . we all quote." Ralph Waldo Emerson. These guys all sound alike!

"People live differently . . . wealth as a gift." Hyde.

". . . I'm a cork . . ." to ". . . blown away." This is adapted from The Beach Boys song "'Til I Die," written by Brian Wilson. My own first adventure with song-lyric permissions came when I tried to have a character in my second novel quote the lyrics "There's a world where I can go and/Tell my secrets to/In my room/In my room." After learning the likely expense, at my editor's suggestion I replaced those with "You take the high road/I'll take the low road/I'll be in Scotland before you," a lyric in the public domain. This capitulation always bugged me, and in the subsequent British publication of the same book I restored the Brian Wilson lyric, without permission. *Ocean of Story* is the title of a collection of Christina Stead's short fiction.

Saul Bellow, writing to a friend who'd taken offense at Bellow's fictional use of certain personal facts, said: "The name of the game is Give All. You are welcome to all my facts. You know them, I give them to you. If you have the strength to pick them up, take them with my blessing." I couldn't bring myself to retain Bellow's "strength," which seemed presumptuous in my new context, though it is surely the more elegant phrase. On the other hand, I was pleased to invite the suggestion that the gifts in question may actually be light and easily lifted.

KEY TO THE KEY

The notion of a collage text is, of course, not original to me. Walter Benjamin's incomplete Arcades Project seemingly would have featured extensive interlaced quotations. Other precedents include Graham Rawle's novel *Diary of an Amateur Photographer*, its text harvested from photography magazines, and Eduardo Paolozzi's collage-novel *Kex*, cobbled from crime novels and newspaper clippings. Closer to home, my efforts owe a great deal to the recent essays of David Shields, in which diverse quotes are made to closely intertwine and reverberate, and to conversations with editor Sean Howe and archivist Pamela Jackson. Last year David Edelstein, in *New York* magazine, satirized the Kaavya Viswanathan plagiarism case by creating an almost completely plagiarized column denouncing her actions. Edelstein intended to demonstrate, through ironic example, how bricolage such as his own was ipso facto facile and unworthy. Although Viswanathan's version of "creative copying" was a pitiable one, I differ with Edelstein's conclusions.

The phrase *Je est un autre*, with its deliberately awkward syntax, belongs to Arthur Rimbaud. It has been translated both as "I is another" and "I is someone else," as in this excerpt from Rimbaud's letters:

For I is someone else. If brass wakes up a trumpet, it is not its fault. To me this is obvious: I witness the unfolding of my own thought: I watch it, I listen to it: I make a stroke of the bow: the symphony begins to stir in the depths, or springs on to the stage.

If the old fools had not discovered only the *false* significance of the Ego, we should not now be having to sweep away those millions of skeletons which, since time immemorial, have been piling up the fruits of their one-eyed intellects, and claiming to be, themselves, the authors!

From *The Grasmere Journals*

April 1802

Dorothy Wordsworth

Monday 12th. Had the mantua-maker the ground covered with snow. Walked to T Wilkinson's & sent for letters. The Woman brought me one from Wm & Mary. It was a sharp windy night. Thomas Wilkinson came with me to Barton, & questioned me like a catechizer all the way, every question was like the snapping of a little thread about my heart I was so full of thoughts of my half-read letter & other things. I was glad when he left me. Then I had time to look at the moon while I was thinking over my own thoughts—the moon travelled through the clouds tinging them yellow as she passed along, with two stars near her, one larger than the other. These stars grew or diminished as they passed from or went into the clouds. At this time William as I found the next day was riding by himself between Middleham & Barnard Castle having parted from Mary. I read over my letter when I got to the house. Mr & Mrs C were playing at Cards.

Tuesday 13th April. I had slept ill & was not well & obliged to go to bed in the afternoon—Mrs C waked me from sleep with a letter from Coleridge. After tea I went down to see the Bank & walked along the Lake side to the field where Mr Smith thought of building his house. The air was become still the lake was of a bright slate colour, the hills darkening. The Bays shot into the low fading shores. Sheep resting all things quiet. When I returned Jane met me—William was come. The surprize shot through me. He looked well but he was tired & went soon to bed after a dish of Tea.

Wednesday 14th. William did not rise till dinner time. I walked with Mrs C. I was ill out of spirits—disheartened. Wm & I took a long walk in the Rain.

Thursday 15th. It was a threatening misty morning—but mild. We set off after dinner from Eusemere—Mrs Clarkson went a short way with us but turned back. The wind was furious & we thought we must have returned. We first rested in the large Boat-house, then under a furze Bush opposite Mr Clarksons, saw the plough going in the field. The wind seized our breath the Lake was rough. There was a Boat by itself floating in the middle of the Bay below Water Millock—We rested again in the Water Millock lane. The hawthorns are black & green, the birches here & there greenish but there is yet more of purple to be seen on the Twigs. We got over into a field to avoid some cows—people working, a few primroses by the roadside, woodsorrel flowers, the anemone, scentless violets, strawberries, & that starry yellow flower which Mrs C calls pile wort. When we were in the woods beyond Gowbarrow park we saw a few daffodils close to the water side, we fancied that the lake had floated the seeds ashore & that the little colony had so sprung up—But as we went along there were more & yet more & at last under the boughs of the trees, we saw that there was a long belt of them along the shore, about the breadth of a country turnpike road. I never saw daffodils so beautiful they grew among the mossy stones about & about them, some rested their heads upon these stones as on a pillow for weariness & the rest tossed & reeled & danced & seemed as if they verily laughed with the wind that blew upon them over the Lake, they looked so gay ever glancing ever changing. This wind blew directly over the Lake to them. There was here & there a little knot & a few stragglers a few yards higher up but they were so few as not to disturb the simplicity & unity & life of that one busy highway—We rested again & again. The Bays were stormy & we heard the waves at different distances & in the middle of the water like the Sea—Rain came on, we were wet when we reached Luffs but we called in. Luckily all was chearless & gloomy so we faced the storm—we *must* have been wet if we had waited— put on dry clothes at Dobson's. I was very kindly treated by a young woman, the Landlady looked sour but it is her way. She gave us a goodish supper, excellent ham & potatoes. We paid 7/ when we came away. William was sitting by a bright fire when I came downstairs he soon made his way to the Library piled up in a corner of the window. He brought out a volume of Enfield's Speaker, another miscellany, & an odd volume of Congreve's plays. We had a glass of warm rum & water—we enjoyed ourselves & wished for Mary. It rained & blew when we went to bed. NB deer in Gowbarrow park like to skeletons.

Friday 16th April (Good Friday). When I undrew my curtains in the morning, I was much affected by the beauty of the prospect & the change. The sun shone, the wind had passed away, the hills looked chearful. The river was very bright as it flowed into the lake. The Church rises up behind a little knot of Rocks, the steeple not so high as an ordinary 3 story house. Bees, in a row in the garden under the wall. After Wm had shaved we set forward. The valley is at first broken by little rocky woody knolls that make retiring places, fairy valleys in the vale, the river winds along under these hills travelling not in a bustle but not slowly to the lake. We saw a fisherman in the flat meadow on the other side of the water he came towards us & threw his line over the two arched Bridge. It is a Bridge of a heavy construction, almost bending inwards in the middle, but it is grey & there is a look of ancientry in the architecture of it that pleased me. As we go on the vale opens out more into one vale with somewhat of a cradle Bed. Cottages with groups of trees on the side of the hills we passed a pair of twin Children 2 years old—& sate on the next bridge which we crossed a single arch, we rested again upon the Turf & looked at the same Bridge— we observed arches in the water occasioned by the large stones sending it down in two streams—a Sheep came plunging through the river, stumbled up the Bank & passed close to us, it had been frightened by an insignifi- cant little Dog on the other side, its fleece dropped a glittering shower under its belly—primroses by the roadside, pile wort that shone like stars of gold in the Sun, violets, strawberries, retired & half buried among the grass. When we came to the foot of Brothers water I left William sitting on the Bridge & went along the path on the right side of the Lake through the wood—I was delighted with what I saw—the water under the boughs of the bare old trees, the simplicity of the mountains & the exquisite beauty of the path. There was one grey cottage. I repeated the Glowworm as I walked along—I hung over the gate, & thought I could have stayed for ever. When I returned I found William writing a poem descriptive of the sights & sounds we saw and heard. There was the gentle flowing of the stream, the glittering lively lake, green fields without a living creature to be seen on them, behind us, a flat pasture with 42 cattle feeding, to our left the road leading to the hamlet, no smoke there, the sun shone on the bare roofs. The people were at work ploughing, harrowing & sowing—Lasses spreading dung, a dogs barking now & then, cocks crowing, birds twitter- ing, the snow in patches at the top of the highest hills, yellow palms, pur- ple & green twigs on the Birches, ashes with their glittering spikes quite bare. The hawthorn a bright green with black stems under, the oak & the moss of the oak glossy. We then went on, passed two sisters at work, *they first passed us*, one with two pitch forks in her hand. The other had a spade. We had some talk with them. They laughed aloud after we were gone perhaps half in wantonness, half boldness. William finished his poem before we got to the foot of Kirkstone. There were hundreds of cattle in the vale. There we ate our dinner. The walk up Kirkstone was very interesting. The Becks among the Rocks were all alive—Wm showed me the little mossy streamlet which he had before loved when he saw its bright green track in the snow. The view above Ambleside, very beautiful. There we sate & looked down on the green vale. We watched the Crows at a little distance from us become white as silver as they flew in the sunshine, & when they went still further they looked like shapes of water passing over the green fields. The whitening of Ambleside Church is a great deduction from the beauty of it seen from this point. We called at the Luffs, the Boddingtons there did not go in & went round by the fields. I pulled of my stockings intending to wade the Beck but I was obliged to put them on & we climbed over the wall at the Bridge. The post passed us. No letters! Rydale Lake was in its own evening brightness, the Islands & points distinct. Jane Ashburner came up to us when we were sitting upon the wall—we rode in her cart to Tom Dawsons—all well. The garden looked pretty in the half moonlight half daylight. As we went up the vale of Brothers Water more & more cattle feeding 100 of them.

Saturday 17th. A mild warm rain. We sate in the garden all the morning. William dug a little. I transplanted a honey suckle. The lake was still the sheep on the island reflected in the water, like the grey deer we saw in Gowbarrow park. We walked after tea by moonlight. I had been in bed in the afternoon & William had slept in his chair. We walked towards Rydale first then backwards & forwards below Mr Olliffs. The village was beautiful in the moonlight—helm crag we observed very distinct. The dead hedge round Benson's field bound together at the top by an interlacing of ash sticks which made a chain of silver when we faced the moon—a letter from C, & also from S.H. I saw a Robin chacing a scarlet Butterfly this morning.

Sunday 18th. I lay in bed late. Again a mild grey morning with rising vapours we sate in the orchard—William wrote the poem on the Robin & the Butterfly. I went to drink tea at Luffs but as we did not dine till 6 o clock it was late. It was mist & small rain all the way but very pleasant.

William met me at Rydale—Aggy accompanied me thither. We sate up late. He met me with the conclusion of the poem of the Robin. I read it to him in Bed. We left out some lines.

Monday 19th. A mild rain very warm Wm worked in the garden, I made pies & bread. After dinner the mist cleared away & sun shone. William walked to Luff's I was not very well & went to bed. Wm came home pale & tired. I could not rest when I got to bed.

Tuesday 20th. A beautiful morning the sun shone—William wrote a conclusion to the poem of the Butterfly, 'I've watch'd you now a full half-hour'. I was quite out of spirits & went into the orchard—When I came in he had finished the poem. We sate in the orchard after dinner, it was a beautiful afternoon. The sun shone upon the Level fields & they grew greener beneath the eye—houses village all chearful, people at work. We sate in the Orchard & repeated the Glowworm & other poems. Just when William came to a Well or a Trough which there is in Lord Darlington's Park he began to write that poem of the Glow-worm not being able to ride upon the long Trot—interrupted in going through the Town of Staindrop. Finished it about 2 miles & a half beyond Staindrop—he did not feel the jogging of the horse while he was writing but when he had done he felt the effect of it & his fingers were cold with his gloves. His horse fell with him on the other side of St Helen's, Auckland.—So much for the Glowworm: It was written coming from Middleham on Monday April 12th 1802. On Tuesday 20th when we were sitting after Tea Coleridge came to the door. I startled Wm with my voice—C came up palish but I afterwards found he looked well. William was not well & I was in low spirits.

Wednesday 21st. William & I sauntered a little in the garden. Coleridge came to us & repeated the verses he wrote to Sara—I was affected with them & was on the whole, not being well, in miserable spirits. The sunshine—the green fields & the fair sky made me sadder; even the little happy sporting lambs seemed but sorrowful to me. The pile wort spread out on the grass a thousand shining stars, the primroses were there & the remains of a few Daffodils. The well which we cleaned out last night is still but a little muddy pond, though full of water. I went to bed after dinner, could not sleep, went to bed again. Read Ferguson's life & a poem or two—fell asleep for 5 minutes & awoke better. We got tea. Sate comfortably in the Evening I went to bed early.

I Wondered Lonely as a Cloud

William Wordsworth

I wandered lonely as a Cloud
That floats on high o'er vales and Hills,
When all at once I saw a crowd,
A host, of golden Daffodils;
Beside the Lake, beneath the trees,
Fluttering and dancing in the breeze.

Continuous as the stars that shine
And twinkle on the milky way,
They stretched in never-ending line
Along the margin of a bay:
Ten thousand saw I at a glance,
Tossing their heads in sprightly dance.

The waves beside them danced; but they
Out-did the sparkling waves in glee:-
A Poet could not but be gay
In such a jocund company:
I gazed—and gazed—but little thought
What wealth the show to me had brought:

For oft when on my couch I lie
In vacant or in pensive mood,
They flash upon that inward eye
Which is the bliss of solitude,
And then my heart with pleasure fills,
And dances with the Daffodils.

MODULE TWO

Remixing the Self

Voice in Academic Writing:
The Rhetorical Construction of Author
Identity in Blind Manuscript Review

Paul Kei Matsuda[1] and Christine M. Tardy

ABSTRACT

Some researchers have argued that voice is irrelevant to academic writing and that the importance of voice has been overstated in the professional literature [Helms-Park, R., & Stapleton, P. (2003); Stapleton, P. (2002). To investigate whether and how a socially oriented notion of *voice*—defined as "the amalgamative effect of the use of discursive and non-discursive features that language users choose, deliberately or otherwise, from socially available yet ever-changing repertoires" [Matsuda, P.K. (2001)—plays a role in academic writing, this study examined the construction of an author's discursive identity by peer reviewers in a simulated blind manuscript review process for an academic journal in the field of rhetoric and composition. The analysis of the written reviews as well as interviews with the two reviewers and the manuscript author indicated that the reviewers' constructions of the author's voice are related to their stance toward the author. The findings suggest that voice does play a role in academic writing and that there is a need for further research into the issue of identity construction from the perspectives of both writers and readers.

---

1   Tel.: +1 603 862 0292/868 8010.

1. INTRODUCTION

In recent years, the notion of identity has come to attract significant attention from applied linguistics researchers. One of the terms that has been used to capture the sense of identity in written discourse is *voice*—a term that has been defined in a wide variety of ways (see Elbow, 1994). In 2001, Belcher and Hirvela (2001) edited a special issue of the *Journal of Second Language Writing* focused on the issue of voice in second language writing. Shortly after voice became a topic of discussion, however, Stapleton (2002) expressed skepticism over the importance of voice in academic writing and sought to demonstrate its irrelevance to academic writing in a study examining the relationship between voice-related textual features and the quality of undergraduate argumentative writing (Helms-Park & Stapleton, 2003).

Is voice, as Stapleton and Helms-Park maintain, irrelevant to academic writing? The answer, of course, depends on how voice is defined and how its relevance is measured and interpreted. In this study, we sought to examine whether and how voice plays a role in academic writing. For this purpose, we studied the construction of voice in blind peer review of a journal article manuscript—a high-stakes academic writing situation. Specifically, we examined whether blind peer reviewers of a journal manuscript perceived the voice of the author and what clued them into the identity of the author.

2. VOICE AND ACADEMIC WRITING

Because the notion has been variously defined, any discussion of voice has to be based on a careful and consistent definition of voice. One of the strongest and most-frequently-cited proponents of the notion, Elbow (1994, p. xx) has identified, in addition to the literal or physical voice, five meanings of voice that are relevant to writing:

1.   audible voice or intonation (the sounds in a text);

2.   dramatic voice (the character or implied author in a text);

3.   recognizable or distinctive voice;

4.   voice with authority;

5.   resonant voice or presence.

Despite the diverse meanings of voice, each of which holds implications for various types of writing, the notion has often been associated almost exclusively with individual or personal quality in writing. Caught in the dichotomy between personal writing and academic writing, the notion of voice has often been relegated to the realm of personal and individual, whereas academic writing has been characterized as relatively impersonal—if not objective or neutral—and therefore voiceless.

As a result of its strong ties to the ideology of Western individualism, voice has come under severe scrutiny in the last decade. Ramanathan and Atkinson (1999), for example, have linked the notion of voice to what they called "the ideology of individualism" (p. 46), pointing out that "the core notion underlying this social practice seems to be that, as individuals, we all have essentially private and isolated inner selves, which we give outward expression to through the use of a metaphorical 'voice'" (p. 47). Bowden (1999) has also argued that "Voice, evolving as it has from its 1970s affiliations with powerful writing, carries with it connotations of an authentic and unitary self" (p. 109). In the special voice issue of the *Journal of Second Language Writing*, Hirvela and Belcher (2001), recognizing the plurality of voice, shift their attention from helping L2 writers develop an L2 voice to recognizing the L1 voice students already possess.

In the same special issue, other contributors sought to move away from the traditional view of voice that is tied exclusively to the individual. Ivanič and Camps (2001), for example, argued for "a way of thinking about 'voice' that does not treat it as an optional extra"; instead, they defined voice as "self-representation" that is inevitable not only in writing but also in "all human activity" (p. 4). Similarly, Prior (2001), taking a sociohistoric perspective influenced by Russian sociocultural theories (Bakhtin, 1986; Volshinov, 1973; Wertsch, 1990), pointed out that "romantic notion of voice as the expression of an autonomous individual are not the only notions of voice available to us" (p. 62). Instead, he argued, "notions of collective or social voices also exist" (p. 62). Matsuda (2001), pointing out that "voice is not necessarily tied to the ideology of individualism" (p. 36), also stressed the inevitability of voice as a result of intentional or unintentional uses of "socially available yet ever-changing repertoires" (p. 40). These views all reflect a growing awareness of the inevitability of identity in discourse as an expression not only of the individual but also the surrounding social relations (Bakhtin, 1981; Fairclough, 1992; Ivanič, 1998).

Prior to the appearance of the special voice issue, the notion of voice had received relatively little attention in second language writing research, except as a target of criticism (Ramanathan & Atkinson, 1999; Ramanathan & Kaplan, 1996). This is partly because of its association with so-called expressivism, a brand of L1 composition pedagogy that has come to be severely stigmatized both in composition studies and applied linguistics (see Matsuda, 2003). Yet, as soon as the exploration of the notion of voice began, some researchers expressed skepticism toward the importance of voice in academic writing (Helms-Park & Stapleton, 2003; Stapleton, 2002). Stapleton (2002), for example, argued that the importance of voice has been "overstated" (p. 177):

> the problem with extended discussions in academic journals and monographs in the L2 writing community that highlight voice is that they lend power to the notion of voice that is far greater than it deserves. It sends the message to teachers that voice is critically important, and this message, if passed down to students, may result in learners who are more concerned with identity than ideas. (Stapleton, 2002, p. 187)

Stapleton's premise that there has been an extended discussion of voice is rather perplexing, given the relative dearth of discussion on this topic in the L2 writing literature. His argument that the prominence of voice in the research literature would lead to teachers and students being concerned with voice at the expense of ideas may also strike some readers as a *non-sequitur* argument. Yet, Stapleton does raise an important question for further exploration: whether and how voice plays a role in academic writing.

In a follow-up study of argumentative writing by undergraduate students, Helms-Park and Stapleton (2003) found no correlation between the presence of what they considered to be voice-related textual features and the overall quality of argumentative writing. Yet, their study does not seem to address the research question they set out to answer: "*Are components of voice, as identified in the L2 writing literature, correlates of high-quality L2 writing?*" (p. 247; italics in the original). First, their definition of voice does not seem to account for the social perspective on voice presented by a number of L2 writing researchers (Ivanič & Camps, 2001; Matsuda, 2001; Prior, 2001). Instead, the study investigated "individualized voice" (p. 247) as defined by a rather narrow set of discursive features: assertiveness, self-identification, reiteration of the central point, authorial presence and autonomy of thought" (pp. 259–260). In other words, the construct being examined in the study does not accurately represent how voice has been "*identified in the L2 writing literature*" (p. 247; italics in the original).

Second, the use of the ESL Composition Profile (Jacobs, Zinkgraf, Wormuth, Hartfiel, & Hughey, 1981) as a measure of overall writing quality in relation to voice-related features is questionable. While it has been heralded as "one of the best known and widely used analytic scales in ESL" (Weigle, 2002, p. 115; cited in Helms-Park & Stapleton, 2003, p. 248), the scale is designed to measure writing quality in terms of five categories: content, organization, vocabulary, language use, and mechanics; in other words, it is not designed to measure writing quality relevant to voice-related features, the effects of which Helms-Park and Stapleton (2003) sought to examine. As Haswell (2005) points out, the choice of which criteria to include in an assessment scale is not "trivial or irrelevant" because "the criteria not chosen shape the outcomes as much as those that are chosen" (p. 110). It may be argued that voice does not play a role in academic writing situations where rubrics similar to the ESL Composition Profile are being used. Yet, that does not mean voice does not affect the quality of writing in those contexts; it may simply mean that the quality of writing is not defined or measured in ways that account for the impact of voice.

Third, and most important, Helms-Park and Stapleton (2003) chose, perhaps inadvertently, a writing situation in which individual voice is not likely to play a major role. They asked students to write in response to "a provocatively worded passage arguing that Canada should abandon its system of allowing refugees and family-class immigrants (e.g., retired parents) into the country since such new arrivals were a drain on the economy" (p. 250). Although this task does resemble some testing situations and some classroom writing situations, especially at the undergraduate level, it is hardly representative of academic writing as a whole. In addition, they assumed in choosing this task that the topic would be " 'real' to new arrivals in Canada" (p. 251). Yet, their participants—"48 Chinese-speaking undergraduate students"—were academically successful students and had only spent an average of "3.5 years in Canada or an English-speaking country" (p. 250). They did not necessarily come to Canada to live there permanently. Even if they had, with their educational achievements, they would be strong contributors to the economy rather than "a drain" (p.

250). Thus, they may not have been in the position to use their personal experience to argue for or against the position. Furthermore, the evanescent nature of the task may have precluded the writers from exerting greater or lesser authority based on their sustained engagement with the topic or with the amount of information they have.

The study by Helms-Park and Stapleton (2003) is, then, far from conclusive. Further research is needed in order to determine whether and how voice plays a role in academic writing. What happens when the presence and implications of voice are examined in a high-stakes academic writing situation where voice, if it can be identified, would matter? The goal of this study is to examine whether voice plays a role in the blind peer review process for an academic journal—a kind of academic writing situation. We chose to examine blind peer review because it is a high-stakes academic writing activity, the outcome of which can make or break a research publication. The manuscript review is also a relatively "occluded genre" (Swales, 1996), and the description of the activities surrounding the genre can contribute to the professional development of novice researchers.

3. METHOD

Research questions for this study were

1. Do readers construct the author's voice when reading an academic text?

2. If so, what are some of the discursive and non-discursive features that readers draw upon when constructing this voice?

In this study, we use a definition of voice that accounts for a broader range of factors that contribute to the construction of voice in written discourse: "Voice is the amalgamative effect of the use of discursive and non-discursive features that language users choose, deliberately or otherwise, from socially available yet ever-changing repertoires"; it is the overall impression associated with particular features that make "impersonation or 'mimicking' possible" (Matsuda, 2001, p. 40). Although Helms-Park and Stapleton (2003) quoted this definition in their study, they did not fully integrate it into the design of the study, which examined a limited set of predetermined discursive features. It is important to note that, in Matsuda's (2001) definition, voice is not a set of certain discursive features; rather, voice is the reader's impression derived from the particular combination of the ways in which both discursive and non-discursive features are used.

Discursive features may include both form (e.g., sentence structures, organization, the use of transition devices, word choice) as well as content (e.g., the choice of topic and specific examples, argumentative strategies). Non-discursive features may include, for example, the use of margins, the choice of font face and size, the use of blank space between words and punctuation marks as well as the use of extra line-breaks between paragraphs and block quotes.[2] Because the effect on the audience is the key in this definition of voice, it would not be appropriate to determine a set of discursive and non-discursive features *a priori*. Instead, we sought to identify the overall impression of the manuscript first and then to identify discursive and non-discursive features that contributed to that impression.

3.1. Simulated blind peer review

In our attempt to examine voice as a social construct resulting from reader-writer interactions, our study focuses on how readers construct an author's voice. To investigate this phenomenon, we set up a simulated blind peer review task, in which we provided an anonymous manuscript to two "reviewers". The reviewers were given the manuscript and asked to read and evaluate it as they would in a typical peer review situation. They were told that the purpose of the study was to understand the blind peer review process, but they were not aware of our specific interest in voice at the beginning of the study. We asked these readers to review the manuscript for a specific well-known journal in rhetoric and composition (the journal to which the manuscript was in fact submitted), thereby providing them with a known audience with which each was familiar. We did not provide guidelines regarding the length, style, or audience (e.g., editor or author) of the written review; we asked only that they compose a typical review and that they include in it a recommendation regarding publication. The reviewers were told that their review would be shared with the manuscript's author, as in an authentic peer review.

Each reviewer was given the manuscript and asked to review it in the time and place of their choosing, in order to simulate a real review task to the extent possible. Our only stipulation was that we needed to conduct an oral interview with the reviewer within the same day that the review had

---

2 Although journals and publishers usually set their own guidelines for the formatting of manuscripts, authors do not always follow those guidelines. Authors from outside North America often do not have a choice but to use A4 size rather than the letter size paper specified by North American publishers. See Canagarajah (1996) for a detailed discussion of how non-discursive features can influence the academic publication process.

been completed. We conducted a second confirmatory interview at a later time to share our analyses with the reviewers.

3.2. Participants

The study involved three participants, including a manuscript author and two anonymous reviewers (Reviewer #1, #2). The author was a male graduate student in rhetoric and composition at a research university in the United States. He provided a manuscript that had been submitted and accepted for publication for a major journal in his field. All three participants were native English speakers.

The two reviewers were both professors of rhetoric and composition at US universities, and they represented varying degrees of experience with peer review. Reviewer #1 was a senior-level professor with extensive experience reviewing manuscripts for a range of rhetoric and composition journals. Furthermore, he was quite interested in the process of blind peer review from a scholarly perspective. Reviewer #2 was newer to the field and was a more inexperienced reviewer. He had received numerous peer reviews of his own work and had been asked to serve on the review board of the journal used in our simulation; however, he had had no first-hand experience as a peer reviewer at the time of our study.

3.3. Data collection and analysis

The data for this study included the author's manuscript, reviews of the manuscript written by the two reviewers (Reviews #R1, #R2), post-task interviews with each of the two reviewers (Interviews #1-R1, #1-R2), subsequent confirmatory interviews with the reviewers (Interviews #2-R1, #2-R2), and an interview with the manuscript author (Interview #A1).

We conducted an oral interview with each reviewer immediately following the completion of the review task (Interview #1; see Appendix A). These post-task interviews were designed to identify the reviewers' reading processes, influences on the reviewers' evaluations of the manuscript, the reviewers' images of the author and the author's credibility, and any information that the reviewers used to construct the author's identity. The interview with Reviewer #1 lasted nearly 1 hour, and the interview with Reviewer #2 lasted approximately 30 minutes.

Each interview was taped and later transcribed. The transcripts and written reviews were coded separately by each of the two researchers according to salient features related to our research questions. Common themes were identified and then shared with each reviewer in a separate confirmatory interview (Interview #2; see Appendix B). In each case, the reviewer agreed with our analysis; Reviewer #1 shed some additional light on his comments in this second interview. These interviews ranged in length from 15 minutes (Reviewer #2) to 45 minutes (Reviewer #1).[3]

In addition, we conducted a follow-up interview with the manuscript's author (Interview #A1; Appendix C). In this interview, the researcher provided the author with the written reviews of his work, shared a summary of each reviewer's construction of the author's identity, and elicited any reactions from the author. This interview lasted approximately 45 minutes.

4. FINDINGS

4.1. Reviewers' construction of the author's voice

The first question we hoped to explore in this study was whether readers do create an image of the author—that is, voice—when reading an academic text, often thought to be less "personal" or "individual" than other discourse registers. It became clear quite early in our interviews with each reviewer that these particular readers had constructed for themselves an image of the author. Reviewer #1 referred to the author with the third person masculine pronoun almost immediately—an assumption he later questioned but then believed did reflect his impression of the author's identity. Reviewer #2 also described aspects of the author's identity before being asked explicitly about any assumptions he may have had. Specifically, he described trying to "figure out what this person's 'bibliographic networks' look like . . . what types of people are they reading, what types of conversations are they attuned to, you know, and as a consequence, what kinds of conversations are they unaware of . . ." (Interview #1-R2).

The reviewers' constructions of the author's identity shared many similarities. Both reviewers believed the author to be male, and both felt that the author was likely a graduate student or at least a relative newcomer to the field. Reviewer #1 believed it was likely that the manuscript had originally been written for a graduate seminar. The reviewers' positioning of the author as a relative novice in comparison with themselves was not only

---

3   Although the interviews were conducted by the same researcher using the same set of questions, the lengths of the actual interviews were different perhaps because Reviewer #1, with more extensive editorial experience and a personal interest in the topic of blind peer review, had much more to say.

found in their oral comments but is also reflected in their written reviews
of the manuscript in various ways. Review #R1, for example, was highly
interpersonal with frequent use of the pronouns *I* and *you*. In addition,
this review contains a high incidence of praise, and criticisms are heavily
hedged throughout, as in the following examples:

> *I wonder if it might not be* a particularly Western (North American?)
> potential to be able to reflect (at leisure?) on [the topic of
> the manuscript].[4]

> *A more effective rhetorical move might be* to reorganize this first section
> to acknowledge initially (rather than on page 5) the extraordinarily
> powerful sway that the ideology of individualism has on the domi-
> nant set of relations that bind up the US university at large. (Review
> #R1, emphases added)

In the first interview, Reviewer #1 acknowledged that in writing any
peer review he tries to avoid harsh criticism. In this particular review
task, however, he admitted that he "could have been more, I don't know,
demeaning or something in suggesting that [a particular section of the
manuscript] could have been handled with greater nuance" (Interview
#1-R1). When asked why he decided not to be more critical, Reviewer #1
responded, "Because I felt pretty certain that this is a young, inexperienced author."

In addition to adopting these rhetorical strategies, Review #R1 includes
several statements which seem to position the author as less of an expert
than the reviewer. It must be acknowledged that the review genre itself
reflects and enacts such positioning, but we identified several statements
that we felt were unlikely to appear in a review of a manuscript that was
believed to be written by an expert in the field. For example:

> You're doing important work here.

> I strongly encourage you. . . not to abandon this work, but to keep
> reading and reworking this piece . . .

> Your earnestness inhabits my reading of your piece. (Review #R1)

---

4   In order to protect anonymity of the author, we have deleted references to specific
content of the manuscript.

These statements, in our view, reflected the reviewer's belief that the writer was a relative novice rather than an experienced authority. Reviewer #1 also acknowledged that he would be less likely to write these statements if he believed the author to be more experienced.

The second review, written by Reviewer #2, similarly positions the writer as someone with less experience and a more limited knowledge base than the reviewer. Statements like the following draw explicit attention to the author's perceived lack of knowledge or experience:

> On the whole, I found the author's points to be a tad bit theoretically naïve.

> Contrary to what the author claims, [the topic of the manuscript] has been thoroughly problematized within certain quarters of Rhetoric and Composition, as well as by critical theorists such as . . .

> Author has too monolithic a conception of the field of Rhetoric and Composition, the audience to which this piece is apparently directed. (Review #R2)

In addition to positioning the author as a relative novice, both reviewers described the author's intentions in similar ways, using adjectives like "earnest" (Review #R1) and "conscientious" (Review #R2). During the interview, Reviewer #2 further described the author as "ambitious", "politically 'progressive'" and "White" (Interview #1-R2). Some of these characterizations were based largely on the content of the manuscript as well as the overall impression reviewers formed in the reading process, while others were tied to specific features of the manuscript. Let us now examine how the reviewers arrived at a particular conception of the author's voice.

4.2. Discursive and non-discursive features and voice construction

After determining that these reviewers did construct a voice for the anonymous manuscript writer, we hoped to identify some of the discursive and non-discursive features that the readers drew upon when constructing this image. To identify these features, we examined the reviewers' statements regarding their evaluation of the manuscript and the author's credibility, and we asked the reviewers explicitly to consider which features of the manuscript may have led them to build their impressions of the author.

Table 1 presents the various features that each reviewer described as influencing his impression in some way. These reviewers focused primarily on influential discursive features, though Reviewer #1 described non-discursive features of document formatting as something that do influence his initial impression, particularly if they do not conform to the expected standard. When these features do conform, as was the case in this manuscript, they seemed to be largely "unmarked" for the reviewer—that is, they did not stand out in the reviewer's mind—confirming an impression of the author as a credible writer in the field. We expand on this issue of markedness later in this paper.

Table 1 Features used by reviewers in constructing author voice	
Reviewer #1	Reviewer #2
• Scope of the manuscript	• Demonstrated knowledge of topic and conversation
• Choice of journal	• Theoretical lens
• (Mis)use of terms	• Personal growth/revelation
• Rhetorical moves	• Gender/race lens
• Representation/positioning of other scholars in the field	• Rhetoric moves/representation of the field
• Breadth of knowledge	• Citations
• Gaps in sustained style	• (Un)awareness of full implications of argument
• Syntax	• Syntax
• Careful editing	• Concision
• Formatting	• Mechanics

As we have mentioned, the two characteristics of the author's identity constructed by both reviewers were that the author was male and relatively new to the field. We were therefore interested in understanding more about what led to these impressions.

Neither reviewer seemed entirely comfortable making the conjecture that the author was male, though both felt fairly certain that this was the case. Reviewer #1 referred to the author using the pronoun *he* from the very start of the post-task interview. He later questioned his assumption, but then explained that he saw the writing as characteristic of "masculine" discourse, both in its positioning of other scholars and in some of its stylistic features:

> . . . there's a kind of an aggressive . . . positioning . . . I think of that as kind of analogous to kind of holding somebody down, you know . . . that kind of what this positioning does is it freezes somebody in a particular kind of way so that you can do what you want with them . . .you see what I mean by masculine, in that it like literally holds on to this person in a particular kind of way until the author does what he or she wants to do with them and let's go, right? And it seems like a masculine kind of move to me, right? . . .And then the way I'm not sure that this translates to the gender of the author is that this move is so embedded in the discourse that I think that it's possible, I suppose, for everybody to pick that up, even if they would ordinarily shy away from that kind of bold, kind of conflict-laden move . . .And then, I'm less committed to this, maybe I'm just thinking about it now, but phrases like . . . "this begs a larger question", "in this regard", "herein lies the disconnect". These phrases just read to me like something that—and maybe that's just my own experience working with students, the way my male master's students are more likely to approximate published scholarship than the women students, I think. I don't know, that's just the way it looks to me. (Interview #1-R1)

The reviewer's response to this particular aspect of the manuscript also piqued the interest of the manuscript author after reading Review #R1. The author explained that the "agonistic positioning" referred to in the review "was one of the things I was working most hard to avoid" (Interview #A1), suggesting a disconnect between the voice he wished to express and that which the reviewer had constructed.

Reviewer #2 did not make any explicit assumptions about the author's sex until the very end of the post-task interview, when he was asked for any final thoughts. At this point, the Reviewer #2 noted, "I guess I'd like to know if it was a he or a she . . . I think it was a man. . . Just a guess" (Interview #1-R2). The reviewer had difficulty pinpointing any feature of the manuscript that led to this "guess", but explained in the second interview that his impression was related to the manuscript's content and issues that had been excluded from the discussion:

I just don't think you can talk about the concept of [topic] and not appreciate how that has different registers along the lines of gender and race. And this person doesn't problematize it along those axes at all. (Interview #2-R2)

While both reviewers seemed somewhat hesitant to make claims about the author's sex, they were more confident in their impressions of the author as a relative novice or newcomer to the field. Reviewer #1 described the author as "fresh" and the paper as something that might be submitted in a doctoral seminar. Reviewer #2 similarly described feeling as though the writer "was a graduate student, but it could easily be an assistant professor". When pressed to explain why he had formed this impression, Reviewer #2 focused on the theoretical framing of the paper and the writer's knowledge of prior disciplinary conversations:

Just the theoretical lens being limited . . . [*describes focus of manuscript*], so I mean that's a conversation you're sort of introduced to in graduate school. And then the fact that this person is now coming to problematize it, and grappling with the implications, especially with the stuff on [topic X], suggests to me that—I mean, the paper demonstrates personal revelation, personal growth, personal inventory of—so, we've had these conversations, I understand these theories, but then what? (Interview #1-R2)

One way in which readers assess an author's rhetorical framing or his or her disciplinary knowledge base is through the use of citations. In our simulated peer review, both reviewers used the manuscript's references to other work as a means of evaluating the text and also constructing the author's voice as a relative newcomer. Reviewer #1, who felt that the paper might have originally been written for a seminar, noted that the references would be impressive for a graduate course paper but were weak in the context of a disciplinary conversation within a major journal:

[I think of the author as] maybe less fluent with the kinds of expectations for a manuscript than you'd hope, I guess. I mean, somebody who's not, who hasn't—who has read a good deal and probably—I mean, if I got this . . . as a seminar paper or something, it would look really good to me. . . But the dearth of references to [topic X] within rhetoric and composition makes me think it's somebody who's fairly fresh to the field. (Interview #1-R1)

Reviewer #2 had also formed the impression of a writer who was somewhat new to a rather long and intertextually complex conversation:

> I think the author is trying to break into a disciplinary conversation and just doesn't quite have enough of a bibliographic base to necessarily know how vast the literature is on the topic they're exploring. (Interview #1-R2)

Both reviewers described the manuscript as generally clear and well written, though the writing style did influence some of Reviewer #1's impressions of the author. Specifically, this reviewer noted some slight inconsistencies in the style, such as repetitive or awkward phrasing, that he felt were less likely to be characteristic of an experienced writer:

> . . . what I mean by "young writers" are people who would not recognize the syntactic problem there when they go back through the text. Or, you know, not recognize the importance of attending to it perhaps . . . So I bet this person sweated over the sentence-level stuff to some degree. At least that's the way it reads to me, because some of it works really well. But then there are these places where it doesn't sound so good, and yet that problem isn't throughout, right? So it makes me think that, you know, that it's a strong representation of revising and editing on this person's part, but it's not the . . . it's not the revising and editing that we'd see from an established scholar who's sending a piece in to a top-tier journal. (Interview #1-R1)

We should note that while Reviewer #1 felt fairly confident of the voice he had constructed, he was less confident in describing the features that had led him to these impressions. He noted that much of his picture of the writer as a novice was a general sense rather than being based on a specific feature or set of features found in the manuscript.

5. DISCUSSION

The reviewers in our study each recommended that the author "revise and resubmit" this manuscript. In their interviews and their written reviews, the primary reasons given for this recommendation centered around the author's rhetorical frames and perceived disciplinary knowledge. Reviewer #1 was most concerned about the ways in which the author had positioned other work in the field, and he also felt that more reading within the field would strengthen the piece. Reviewer #2 felt the manuscript reiterated an argument that had already occurred in the field and overlooked relevant work for building a novel contribution to the discussion. Both critiques mirror the reviewers' construction of the author as a disciplinary newcomer.

We cannot know if the critiques were influenced by the reviewers' sense that the author was a relative novice, if the critiques led the reviewers to see the author as a novice, or even if these two assessments were dialogically constructed. Nevertheless, the reviewers' impressions of the work seem to be congruent with their impressions of the author, suggesting that these two reading processes are not unrelated. Furthermore, both reviewers described actively constructing an identity of the author in the blind review process, making guesses as to the author's status in the field, sex, and, in one case, race. Our discussion with other experienced reviewers suggest, at least anecdotally, that this rhetorical process of identity construction is not unique to these two reviewers, although further research is needed to explore how pervasive this phenomenon is and how it may vary in different disciplinary contexts.

In identifying discursive and non-discursive features that led the reviewers to construct the author's voice in particular ways, the notion of "markedness" is a useful one. As the reviewers evaluated the manuscript and described the author to us, they paid little attention to those textual features which were "unmarked" and therefore conformed to discursive and generic expectations. In this study, for example, the manuscript's formatting, internal consistency, and general topic fit with the readers' expectations for a manuscript submission to this journal; these features, therefore, did not attract the readers' attention in significant ways. Instead, the reviewers attended to "marked" features of the text—that is, those features which departed from the discursive or generic expectations in some way. In this case, marked features included inconsistent style, lack of concision, the framing and representation of related work, and content that was included/excluded (e.g., the *lack* of discussion on race or gender led Reviewer #2 to guess that the author was a white male). Features that depart from the norm could also be perceived positively, of course; manuscripts evaluated very highly may be exceptional in their theoretical lens, their stylistic features, or their research design, to name just a few examples.

Importantly, both the process of evaluating academic writing and constructing voice are likely to draw upon discursive and non-discursive features that are marked *in the readers' eyes*. Therefore, while we might expect an audience of disciplinary peers to share some expectations for a text, we would expect individual readers to construct voice of a single author in divergent ways as well. In our study, for example, Reviewer #1 described viewing the writer as male primarily because of the ways in which he positioned and framed other works within the manuscript; Reviewer #2, on the other hand, guessed that the writer was male because the paper ignored the issue of gender in theorizing this particular topic, which is closely related to the issues of gender and race. Various discursive and non-discursive features, and by extension, voice, are therefore read in both shared and unique ways by readers who are members of a discipline (or multiple disciplines) and also individuals with distinct personal histories and social relations.

It may be useful to consider the development of voice as one strand of the complicated process of discourse acquisition. As writers are socialized into disciplinary ways of doing, they develop a sense of the expectations that readers bring to a text (McNabb, 2001). With this increased knowledge, writers are better able to make purposeful choices in the extent to which they conform or deviate from standards and how they choose to do so. Over time, writers learn to enact and exploit disciplinary genres for multiple agendas, and, importantly, learn how their textual choices may be received and perceived by others.

6. CONCLUSIONS

The study described here was small in scale, examining the ways in which two readers constructed the author's voice through the process of blind peer review. Although we cannot claim that all blind manuscript reviewers would follow the processes and patterns illustrated here, this study shows how voice plays a role in the blind review process for at least some readers. We can make no claims regarding the relationship between the reviewers' constructions of the author's voice and their respective evaluations of the manuscript, though this issue is worthy of future research. We further acknowledge that this study is limited in generic and disciplinary scope, as we have focused on the reading of a theoretical essay within the field of rhetoric and composition. It is certainly possible—and, indeed, likely—

that readers of other genres and/or in other fields may attend to different textual features and construct the author's voice in different ways, if at all. Other important factors for further investigation include the sex/gender and native language background of the authors and reviewers. In addition, the review process in this study was a simulated one, and further research is needed to explore these issues *in situ*. Nevertheless, within the simulated context of this study, we found the issue of voice to pervade the process of blind peer review. The existence of an academic writing context in which voice plays an important role suggests that, contrary to the view held by some researchers (Helms-Park & Stapleton, 2003; Stapleton, 2002), voice can be an element of academic writing—both from the writer's and readers' perspectives—that warrants further research and discussion.

In this study, we have applied a broad definition of "voice", considering not just a set of discursive markers but the more general amalgamation of both discursive and non discursive features. We have examined how readers construct voice within a particular context of social interaction, bringing their own assumptions, beliefs, values, and expectations to bear on the writer's text. Shifting the discussion of voice from the sole province of the writer to the jointly constructed reader-writer interaction can provide rich insight into the readers' role in the process of constructing voice. Furthermore, broadening the scope of voice to an overall impression of the author can bring us closer to the rhetorical processes that readers enact when reading and evaluating academic texts.

APPENDIX A. INTERVIEW GUIDE FOR INTERVIEW #1: POST-TASK INTERVIEWS WITH MANUSCRIPT REVIEWERS

(conducted immediately or shortly after the blind peer review has been completed)

1. In general, what do you think about the manuscript?

2. What was your reading process like?

3. What was the order of reading?

4. What kind of information were you looking for in evaluating the manuscript?

5. What was it like to write this review?

6. What part of this review did you find particularly easy or difficult to write?

7. Who was the audience for your review?

8. What image do you have of the author of the paper you reviewed?

9. What do you think about the writing ability of the author?

10. How credible do you think the author is?

11. What gave you those ideas about the writer's credibility?

12. Did you look for this information? If so, where did you look to find it?

13. Would you say the process of reviewing this manuscript was fairly typical of the usual reviews you do for journals in the field? Explain.

APPENDIX B. INTERVIEW GUIDE FOR INTERVIEW #2: CONFIRMATORY INTERVIEWS WITH MANUSCRIPT REVIEWERS

(conducted within one week of Interview #1)

1. The primary purpose of this interview is to share our interpretations of your review and your comments in Interview #1. Our main interpretations include . . . (explain)

2. Do any of these interpretations seem different from your own? If so, please explain.

3. Is there anything you would like to add at this point?

4. At this point of the study, we would also like to share more specific information with you about our research focus. Our primary aim in the study is to understand how readers construct the author's voice when reading an anonymous manuscript, as is done in the process of blind review. We are interested in identifying what elements of the text led you to construct the author as you did. Knowing this about our research, is there anything more you'd like to share that may give us more insight into this process?

APPENDIX C. INTERVIEW GUIDE FOR INTERVIEW #A1: CONFIRMATORY INTERVIEW WITH MANUSCRIPT AUTHOR

1. When you wrote the manuscript, did you ever consciously consider what type of authorial voice or identity you wanted to project? If so, please explain.

2. (Share the written review from the Faculty Participant.) What is your reaction to the reviews?

3. Based on this review, how do you think the reviewers "read" your voice or identity in this paper? Why do you think this?

4. When we spoke to the reviewers about the reviews that they wrote, they have descriptions of who they imagined you to be, the author of the manuscript. And here are some of the descriptions: One of them said he wasn't sure completely, but he thought it was a male and relatively inexperienced. Graduate student. And, perhaps wrote this as a seminar paper. And the [other] reviewers said this person is a white person, not a person of color. And also an inexperienced graduate student. And perhaps introduced to [scholar X] in a graduate seminar. Do you have any reactions to this? Why do you think the reviewer constructed you in this way?

5. Do you have any other comments that you think will be useful for our study, regarding voice in your own academic writing?

REFERENCES

Bakhtin, M. (1981). Discourse in the novel. In M. Holquist (Ed.), *The dialogic imagination: Four essays.* Austin: University of Texas Press (C. Emerson, & M. Holquist, Trans.; pp. 259–422).

Bakhtin, M. (1986). *Speech genres and other late essays* (V. W. McGee, Trans.). Austin: University of Texas Press.

Belcher, D., & Hirvela, A. (Eds.). (2001). Voice in L2 writing. *Journal of Second Language Writing, 10*(1/2) (Special issue).

Bowden, D. (1999). *The mythology of voice.* Portsmouth, NH: Boynton/Cook.

Canagarajah, A. S. (1996). Nondiscursive requirements in academic publishing, material resources of periphery scholars, and the politics of knowledge production. *Written Communication, 13,* 435–472.

Elbow, P. (1994). Introduction. In P. Elbow (Ed.), *Landmark essays on voice and writing* (pp. xi–xvii). Davis, CA: Hermagoras Press.

Fairclough, N. (1992). *Discourse and social change.* Cambridge: Polity Press.

Haswell, R. (2005). Researching teacher evaluation of second language writing via prototype theory. In P. K. Matsuda & T. Silva (Eds.), *Second language writing research: Perspectives on the process of knowledge construction* (pp. 105–120). Mahwah, NJ: Lawrence Erlbaum Associates.

Helms-Park, R., & Stapleton, P. (2003). Questioning the importance of individualized voice in undergraduate L2 argumentative writing: an empirical study with pedagogical implications. *Journal of Second Language Writing, 12*(3), 245–265.

Hirvela, A., & Belcher, D. (2001). Coming back to voice: the multiple voices and identities of mature multilingual writers. *Journal of Second Language Writing, 10*(1-2), 83–106.

Ivanič, R. (1998). *Writing and identity: the discoursal construction of identity in academic writing.* Amsterdam: John Benjamins.

Ivanič, R., & Camps, D. (2001). I am how I sound: voice as self-representation in L2 writing. *Journal of Second Language Writing, 10*(1-2), 3–33.

Jacobs, H., Zinkgraf, S., Wormuth, D., Hartfiel, V., & Hughey, J. (1981). *Testing ESL composition: a practical approach.* Rowley, MA: Newbury House.

Matsuda, P. K. (2001). Voice in Japanese written discourse: implications for second language writing. *Journal of Second Language Writing, 10*(1-2), 35–53.

Matsuda, P. K. (2003). Process and post-process: a discursive history. *Journal of Second Language Writing, 12*(1), 65–83.

McNabb, R. (2001). Making the gesture: graduate student submissions and the expectations of journal referees. *Composition Studies, 29,* 9–26.

Prior, P. (2001). Voices in text, mind, and society: sociohistoric accounts of discourse acquisition and use. *Journal of Second Language Writing, 10*(1-2), 55–81.

Ramanathan, V., & Atkinson, D. (1999). Individualism, academic writing, and ESL writers. *Journal of Second Language Writing, 8*(1), 45–75.

Ramanathan, V., & Kaplan, R. B. (1996). Audience and voice in current L1 composition texts: some implications for ESL student writers. *Journal of Second Language Writing, 5*(1), 21-34.

Stapleton, P. (2002). Critiquing voice as a viable pedagogical tool in L2 writing: returning the spotlight to ideas. *Journal of Second Language Writing, 11*(3), 177-190.

Swales, J. M. (1996). Occluded genres in the academy: the case of the submission letter. In E. Ventola & A. Mauranen (Eds.), *Academic writing Intercultural and textual issues* (pp. 45-58). Amsterdam: John Benjamins.

Volshinov, V. N. (1973). *Marxism and the philosophy of language.* Cambridge: Harvard University Press (L. Matejka, & I. R. Titunik, Trans.).

Weigle, S. C. (2002). *Assessing writing.* Cambridge, UK: Cambridge University Press.

Wertsch, J. V. (1990). The voice of rationality in a sociocultural approach to mind. In L. Moll (Ed.), *Vygotsky and education* (pp. 111-126). Cambridge, UK: Cambridge University Press.

A Response to Matsuda and Tardy's "Voice in Academic Writing: The Rhetorical Construction of Author Identity in Blind Manuscript Review"

Paul Stapleton and Rena Helms-Park[1]

ABSTRACT

In a recent article in ESP, Matsuda and Tardy (2007) investigate the role of voice in academic writing via a simulated blind manuscript review process. Based on their findings, they claim that voice does play a role in such writing, and call for further research into the issue of the reader's construction of authorial identity. Matsuda and Tardy's study appears to have been triggered in part by articles we wrote several years ago (Helms-Park & Stapleton, 2003; Stapleton, 2002) in which we discussed the extent to which voice should be considered as a pedagogical tool in L2 undergraduate writing. In this rejoinder, we call into question Matsuda and Tardy's characterization of our earlier work and also comment on their research methodology while further focusing on the qualities of voice which continue resonating with writing researchers.

In a recent article published in *English for Specific Purposes*, Paul Matsuda and Christine Tardy revisit the issue of authorial voice (Matsuda & Tardy, 2007), arguing in favor of its importance in academic writing. Their study

---

1   Tel.: +1 416 287 7142 (Office); fax: +1 416 287 7116

appears to have been triggered, at least in part, by two papers we wrote some years ago in which we contended that, in some pedagogical contexts, the issue of voice might be ignored in favor of more fundamental problems that new writers grapple with (Helms-Park & Stapleton, 2003; Stapleton, 2002). To support their opposition, Matsuda and Tardy describe a study that they conducted in which two readers reviewed a simulated manuscript written for publication by a native-speaker graduate student. The reviewers' critiques were then analyzed for evidence that purportedly demonstrated that they had constructed a voice (or identity) associated with the manuscript's author. Based on the findings of this research, Matsuda and Tardy suggest that voice does indeed play a role in academic writing and that further research into authorial identity construction is needed. In this rejoinder to Matsuda and Tardy's article, we would like to clarify some of the points made in our 2003 paper as well as raise a few questions about some of the intractable problems of research on L2 voice, as illustrated by Matsuda and Tardy's study.

At the outset, Matsuda and Tardy pose what we consider a straw man argument, which ostensibly represents our papers: "Is voice, as Stapleton and Helms-Park maintain, irrelevant to academic writing?" This is somewhat perplexing since nowhere in either of our papers do we state that voice (however defined) is irrelevant to all or most academic writing. The quotations below capture some of our original sentiments:

> Voice, in my opinion, is an important part of writing and communicating, and aspects of it are essential at the higher levels of academic writing where authors are aiming to publish. However, the great emphasis that it has been accorded, as assumed by the number of published works in the L2 writing field, appears to be disproportionate in relation to other aspects of writing, particularly the content contained within, and therefore unwarranted. (Stapleton, 2002)

> . . .what the results of this study suggest is that *at least within the context of novice L2 writing*, an undue amount of attention may have been accorded to voice and its linguistic manifestations [emphasis ours]. (Helms-Park & Stapleton, 2003)

We believe that the title of our 2003 article made it clear that it was the role of "individualized voice" in the argumentative writing of L2 undergraduates that we had chosen to investigate (and not "voice in academic writing," as Matsuda and Tardy would have the reader believe). Our study included various caveats regarding the shifting definitions of the abstraction called "voice" and our route was one that is customary in empirical testing in science: Does x (here "individualized voice"), defined in such-and-such manner, correlate with attribute y (here writing "quality"), measured by such-and-such instrument (here an established L2 writing scale)? Furthermore, if x is the sum of sub-components a, b, c, and d (i.e., the four criteria in our rating scale for individualized voice), do any of the subcomponents correlate with y?

Our main finding was that certain pre-selected linguistic and rhetorical elements associated with voice in the L1 and L2 literature (e.g., the use of the first person or of reinforcing deontic modals to make self-generated assertions rather than passive-type constructions, often combined with mitigating phrases) had little bearing on the strength or weakness of L2 students' argumentative writing in a first-year introductory writing course. We suggested that certain native-speaker features of voice could nonetheless be felicitously adopted by L2 writers at higher levels of writing. It seems obvious, however, that most of the L2 writers in our 2003 study were not in the same league as Matsuda and Tardy's participant, who happened to be not only a native speaker of English but also a graduate student whose article had already been accepted by a refereed journal; this is an issue that Matsuda and Tardy do not address.

More difficult to follow, however, is Matsuda and Tardy's logic when, after making a point of defining voice rather differently from the way we did, they proceed to not only validate their hypothesis (which is clearly their prerogative), but to reject our old one – this in spite of the fact that, as they themselves note, their definition of voice (as identity) is essentially different from our criteria-based one. To this end, they devise a study which sets out to discern whether reviewers of academic papers construct the author's voice when reading a text and if so, what discursive and non-discursive features they rely upon to accomplish this. The study includes three participants: a graduate student who wrote the manuscript to be assessed, and two reviewers who were asked to assess the student's paper as if for publication.

Matsuda and Tardy are certainly within their right to express their quarrel with the definition of voice in Helms-Park and Stapleton (2003): We agree that the term is indeed slippery, and debates about its meaning are inevitable. Elbow's identification of voice as a quality that "captures the sound of the individual on the page" (1981, p. 287) continues to be persuasive. However, Elbow (1981) also makes clear that "the sound, rhythm [and] energy" (p. 299) of the writer's voice cannot be pointed to on the page. Given such a definition, this construct of voice cannot be tested empirically any more than can, say, the "certain *je ne sais quoi*" that gives rise to personal charisma, or the exact nature of the brush strokes that separate Andrea de Sarto from Michaelangelo.

Matsuda's (2001) definition of voice in componential terms provides the beginnings of an empirically testable concept of voice: "Voice is the amalgamative effect of the use of discursive and non-discursive features that language users choose, deliberately or otherwise, from socially available yet ever-changing repertoires" (2001, p. 40). However, equating voice with a construct such as identity and then, *a posteriori* and without clearly delineated guidelines, assembling empirical evidence to support the reader's reconstruction of identity can lead to a methodological quagmire. One potential pitfall of the simulated nature of a study such as Matsuda and Tardy's, for instance, lies in the lack of an instrument for regulating data selection and coding, compounded by the cognitive biases that arise when participants are explicitly allocated their roles. In other words, the usual "observer's paradox" is further exaggerated in a study where the two reviewers are aware that their own critiques would be scrutinized. For example, Matsuda and Tardy interpret Reviewer 1's use of the first person singular in his review as an attempt to be more "interpersonal" with the paper's author, whom he assumes to be a novice. However, a distinct possibility is that Reviewer 1 could well have been using the first person in anticipation of his review being analyzed by those who had constructed the simulation (i.e., researchers whom he knew personally).

Yet another troubling aspect of studies without clearly defined parameters for coding textual features correlated with an abstract writing quality is exemplified by the post-review interviewing of the reviewers. One of the questions was: "What image do you have of the author of the paper you reviewed?" (p. 13). It is entirely possible that the reviewers had given little thought to such a question before it was asked. However, upon being questioned in a formalized interview setting, interviewees can begin to feel compelled to justify their earlier responses through various post hoc rationalizations. One example of how the interview questions could well have triggered previously unconceptualized responses concerns the gender of the student author, a point to which considerable discussion is devoted in Matsuda and Tardy's paper. We learn that while neither reviewer was comfortable identifying the student author as a male, they both reached that conclusion nonetheless. Reviewer 1 guessed that the author was a male because of the paper's "aggressive positioning" and various agonistic rhetorical moves. Matsuda and Tardy include an extended quote from Reviewer 1 in which he is clearly struggling to come up with evidence to support his belief that the author is a male:

> . . .you see what I mean by masculine in that it like literally holds on to this person in a particular kind of way until the author does what he or she wants to do with them and let's go, right? And it seems like a masculine kind of move, right? And then the way I'm not sure that this translates to the gender of the author. . . (p. 9)

Beyond the uncertainty expressed here, what is striking is that the reviewer himself uses the terms "he or she" here, perhaps revealing considerable indecision (or discomfort) about his own thought processes. Curiously, Matsuda and Tardy do not problematize the whole notion of Reviewer 1's gender stereotyping, that is, the implied notion that it is men alone who write combatively. Somewhat surprising, too, is that Matsuda and Tardy chose to include such a wavering quotation in support of their argument. If such replies are among the best samples taken from the interview responses, one is forced to wonder about the general quality of the data.

We agree with Matsuda and Tardy about the importance of voice in academic writing. Arguments that are not only compelling but also resonate with "the sound of the individual on the page" (Elbow, 1981, p. 287) have a clear advantage over dry, lifeless prose. Clearly, the sustained interest in voice in L1 and L2 academic writing, as reflected by Matsuda and Tardy's study, suggests that there is a belief in this ineffable quality that distinguishes good writing from mediocre, uninspiring prose. In that sense, we stand on the same page as Matsuda and Tardy. What we disagree on is how one can empirically test the value of a quality that eludes definition and the degree to which "voice pedagogy" plays an active role in the (L2) writing curriculum. As for the latter, we maintain that the large numbers of new L2 writers who are grappling with the fundamentals of syntax, lexis, and textual organization need not be further burdened by (prescriptive) notions of voice.

In fact, in the conclusion of their paper, Matsuda and Tardy also seem to indicate indirectly that studies such as theirs do not yield any identifiable implications for writing pedagogy. "We can make no claims regarding the relationship between the reviewers' constructions of the author's voice and their respective evaluations of the manuscript" (p. 13). This being the case, the ultimate goal of their research on reconstructing the author's identity is not clear. Our study (2003) was largely motivated by the plight of EAP instructors with writing students from various disciplines that strongly prescribe the use or avoidance of rhetorical and linguistic structures such as first person, active or passive voice, or reinforcing or mitigating modals. If Matsuda and Tardy's article was meant to serve an academic purpose other than making a connection between authors' voices and their communicative effectiveness or informing pedagogy (and particularly L2 pedagogy) in some fashion, Matsuda and Tardy might have chosen a better candidate than our 2003 article as the counterargument to their argument.

We should add that there is hardly a piece of writing that does not evoke some image of its author even if this image is fuzzy or counterfactual. Surely, it is not this literal-minded image of the author's identity, encompassing such features as "male" or "graduate student" or "non-professorial," that amount to the abstract quality of "voice" that Matsuda and Tardy claim is important in academic writing. Furthermore, even if this were to be the case, surely these are not the ingredients of voice that one is supposed to take into consideration when rating the quality of L2 undergraduate students' writing. Indeed, there are aspects of the writer's identity that fair-minded raters are supposed to *suppress* when grading a paper (e.g., whether the student writer is masculine or feminine, Asian or European, and so on).

Matsuda and Tardy themselves make a sound observation about the variation of voice with genre and discipline at the end of their paper:

> "We acknowledge that this study is limited in generic and disciplinary scope, as we have focused on the reading of a theoretical essay within the field of rhetoric and composition. It is certainly possible — and, indeed, likely — that readers of other genres and/or in other fields may attend to different textual features and construct the author's voice in different ways, if at all" (p. 13).

Does this mean then that voice is literally "identity" in some genres and fields and not in others? Or does it mean that the identity in question is variously defined? The relative fruitlessness of personifying or concretizing the abstraction called "voice" as the author's identity in a literal-minded way is especially well exemplified by writing within the scientific tradition. This tradition communicates via a "language of proof recognized, used, and understood across national and cultural boundaries" (Landes, 1998, p. 205).[2] The language is not meant to be nice or engaging. In essence, whether an attempt to advance knowledge within a given field holds up to scrutiny over time rests solely upon the persuasiveness of the supporting arguments and the evidence within. While it is certainly true that authors sometimes do engage their readers via non-adversarial, gentler approaches, in the academy, the success of any claim finally rests upon the power of the supporting evidence. Famed scientist Wilson (1998) contends, for example, that "[there is no] better way to strengthen organized knowledge than continually to defend it from hostile forces" (p. 44).

Finally, consider the following key sentence from James Watson and Francis Crick's famous letter to Nature in 1953 detailing the double helix nature of DNA. "We wish to suggest a structure for the salt of deoxyribose nucleic acid (DNA). This structure has novel features which are of considerable biological interest" (p. 964). Clearly what is remarkable is the epoch-making significance of the discovery suggested in this statement. What is unremarkable here is the discursive feature chosen by the authors. Although this sentence was written in a natural sciences journal generations ago, the authors decided to use the first person plural to address their audience. They could have easily begun their sentence, "It is suggested that there is a structure. . ." and this may have slightly altered the nuance to take a bit of focus off of the authors themselves. Or perhaps the use of "we" might have made the authors seem more "interpersonal" in their approach. There might even have been a few structures here and there in this historic publication that could have been associated with a "feminine" style of writing. Perhaps the reviewers of the article reconstructed the authors' identities and conjured up well-defined images of them – or perhaps not. Would anyone have cared, however, in light of what was being stated in the article? We doubt it.

---

2   Needless to say, this does not mean that all scientific genres are the same or that they remain unchanged over time (cf. Atkinson, 1999).

REFERENCES

Atkinson, D. (1999). *Scientific discourse in sociohistorical context: The Philosophical transactions of the Royal Society of London*. Mahwah, NJ: Lawrence Erlbaum Associates, 1675-1975.

Elbow, P. (1981). *Writing with power*. New York: Oxford University Press.

Helms-Park, R., & Stapleton, P. (2003). Questioning the importance of individualized voice in undergraduate L2 argumentative writing: An empirical study with pedagogical implications. *Journal of Second Language Writing, 12*, 245-265.

Landes, D. S. (1998). *The wealth and poverty of nations*. New York: Norton.

Matsuda, P. K. (2001). Voice in Japanese written discourse: Implications for second language writing. *Journal of Second Language Writing, 10*, 35-53.

Matsuda, P. K., & Tardy, C. (2007). Voice in academic writing: The rhetorical construction of author identity in blind manuscript review. *English for Specific Purposes, 12*, 235-249.

Stapleton, P. (2002). Critiquing voice as a viable pedagogical tool in L2 writing: Returning the spotlight to ideas. *Journal of Second Language Writing, 11*, 177-190.

Watson, J. D., & Crick, F. H. C. (1953). Genetical implications of the structure of deoxyribonucleic acid. *Nature, 171*(May), 964-967.

Wilson, E. O. (1998). *Consilience*. New York: Alfred A. Knopf.

Continuing the Conversation on Voice in Academic Writing

Paul Kei Matsuda and Christine M. Tardy

We are grateful to Professors Stapleton and Helms-Park for taking the time to respond to our recent article, "Voice in academic writing: The rhetorical construction of author identity in blind manuscript review" (Matsuda & Tardy, 2007), thus opening up the space for further discussion of voice in written discourse. We would like to take this opportunity to clarify what seem to us to be some of the misunderstandings about our study, particularly those related to our definition of voice—a definition which differs from that used by Stapleton and Helms-Park.

In their response, Stapleton and Helms-Park situate our study as a "counterargument" to their research and believe that we conducted our study to "support [our] opposition". They write:

> It seems obvious . . . that most of the L2 writers in our 2003 study were not in the same league as Matsuda and Tardy's participants. . .; this is an issue that Matsuda and Tardy do not address.

> . . . after making a point of defining voice rather differently from the way we did, they proceed not only to validate their hypothesis (which is clearly their prerogative), but to reject our old one—this in spite of the fact that, as they themselves note, their definition of voice (as identity) is essentially different from our criteria-based one.

We did not address these issues because our study was not a direct response to Helms-Park and Stapleton (2003). While it was in part stimulated by two of the most recent and most vocal attempts to critique the notion of voice (Helms-Park & Stapleton, 2003; Stapleton, 2002), it was not designed to provide any counter evidence. Rather, the main goal of our article was to move beyond the narrow conception of voice as closely, if not essentially, tied to the ideology of individualism. Indeed, we thought of their work not so much as a "straw man" but as a jumping-off point for a more useful exploration of socially-oriented conceptions of voice in written discourse that, in the long run, may have important implications for writing theory and pedagogy. As Stapleton and Helms-Park state in their response, our definition of voice is essentially different from theirs; it therefore becomes quite problematic to draw direct comparisons between our research and theirs.

In the first part of our article, we sought to establish the context for our study by problematizing the tendency to conflate the notion of voice with individual voice—a conflation that seems to permeate Stapleton and Helms-Park's articles on this topic as well as their response to our article. We took issue with Stapleton' (2002) objection to the consideration of voice as an important issue in the field of L2 writing. As we mentioned in our article, we were particularly perplexed by what seemed to be his contention that voice had been discussed extensively, lending "power to the notion of voice that is far greater than it deserves" (Stapleton, 2002, p. 187). As researchers and teachers, we were troubled by the implication that some research topics should be discouraged because teachers might think they are important.

We then considered a recent attempt by Helms-Park and Stapleton (2003) to examine the relationship between voice and writing quality. Contrary to what Stapleton and Helms-Park suggest in their response, our rejection of their hypothesis was not based on the findings of our study. Instead, we focused on theoretical and methodological issues. We fully understood that they took the "route . . . that is customary in empirical testing in science":

> Does x (here 'individualized voice'), defined in such-and-such manner, correlate with attribute y (here, writing 'quality'), measured by such-and-such instrument (here and established L2 writing scale)? Furthermore, if x is the sum of sub-components a, b, c, and d (i.e., the four criteria in our rating scale for individualized voice), do any of the subcomponents correlate with y?

This methodological approach was not a problem in itself. Our concerns, as we explained in our article, were the skewed representation of the *"components of voice as identified in the L2 writing literature"* (Helms-Park & Stapleton, 2003 , p. 247; italics in the original), the discrepancy between what is being measured (the effects of voice-related features) and the choice of instrument (i.e., ESL Composition Profile) that systematically steers readers away from voice-related quality, and the choice of a data elicitation method that did not seem appropriate for studying the effect of voice. Furthermore, when there is no statistically significant correlation, we would expect to see some discussion of alternative hypotheses that may account for the lack of relationship, including possible flaws in the research design; we did not find a sufficient discussion of alternative explanations in Helms-Park and Stapleton (2003) and, therefore, pointed to some possible alternatives in our literature review. In short, we did not feel it was necessary to carry out a study as counter evidence because of the weaknesses that already existed in these two studies.

These shortcomings notwithstanding, however, it seems shortsighted of Helms-Park and Stapleton to use their findings to argue that "in introductory L2 writing courses voice should be treated as a relatively minor concern" (Helms-Park & Stapleton, 2003, p. 256). Again, our definition of voice as socially constructed, by both writers and readers, leads us to the rather different conclusion that voice is not a trivial element of writing. If beginning L2 writers do not use voice features in ways that contribute to the overall effectiveness, would it not be possible to argue that those students might need to learn whether, when, and how to use voice-related features to make their writing more effective? Furthermore, if voice does not make a difference for novice writers but may play an important role for advanced writers, as Stapleton and Helms-Park appear to agree, it seems reasonable to consider the acquisition of voice as an aspect of writing proficiency, possibly related to specialized genre knowledge, that can benefit from instruction as students develop their writing expertise.

Stapleton and Helms-Park's response to our article also highlights another major contradiction in their theoretical framework. Citing Elbow (1981), they claim that "the construct of voice cannot be tested empirically"—the point they also make in their 2003 article. Paradoxically, they went on to use an *a priori* set of discursive features as the component of voice for their analysis. Furthermore, Helms-Park and Stapleton (2003) quoted Matsuda's (2001) definition of voice as a justification for this move, which suggests that they did not fully understand the theoretical framework they were drawing on. The point of Matsuda's definition was to expand the notion of voice to include not only the writers and their uses of discursive features but also the "amalgamative effect"—i.e., the readers' rhetorical construction of voice mediated by discursive and non-discursive features.

A misunderstanding of Matsuda's theoretical framework also becomes apparent when Stapleton and Helms-Park accuse us, in their response, of ". . . equating voice with a construct such as identity and then, *a posteriori* and without clearly delineating guidelines, assembling empirical evidence to support the reader's reconstruction of identity". First, Matsuda (2001) makes clear that "Voice is . . . distinguished from identity, although it is a significant component of identity" (p. 41). In Matsuda and Tardy (2007), we also conceptualized voice as "one of the terms that has been used to capture the sense of identity in written discourse" (p. 236), focusing on the author's identity as constructed rhetorically by the reader. Second, our study was decidedly exploratory in nature, seeking to identify whether blind manuscript reviewers rhetorically construct the author's voice and, if so, what discursive and non-discursive features they might draw on in the process. In other words, our study was what Sasaki (2005) has called a "hypothesis-generating exploratory study" designed to move toward valid criteria for further studies of voice in blind manuscript review rather than a "hypothesis-testing confirmatory study" (p. 79).

We are also troubled by Stapleton and Helms-Park's criticism of our study as "lack[ing] . . . an instrument for regulating data selection and coding". To the contrary, our exploration was carefully guided by our interpretation of Matsuda's (2001) definition of voice:

Discursive features may include both form (e.g., sentence structures, organization, the use of transition devices, word choice) as well as content (e.g., the choice of topic and specific examples, argumentative strategies). Non-discursive features may include, for example, the use of margins, the choice of font face and size, the use of blank space between words and punctuation marks as well as the use of extra line-breaks between paragraphs and block quotes. Because the effect on the audience is the key in this definition of voice, it would not be appropriate to determine a set of discursive and nondiscursive features *a priori*. Instead, we sought to identify the overall impression of the manuscript first and then to identify discursive and non-discursive features that contributed to that impression. (Matsuda & Tardy, 2007, p. 239)

Stapleton and Helms-Park also suggest that "the usual 'observer's paradox' is further exaggerated in a study where the two reviewers are aware that their own critiques would be scrutinized". We must point out that, in designing our study, we were fully aware of this potential pitfall, and carefully planned the data collection procedure to avoid this bias. As we explained in our article, the two reviewers "were told that the purpose of the study was to understand the blind peer review process, but they were not aware of our specific interest in voice at the beginning of the study" (Matsuda & Tardy, 2007, p. 239). We did not disclose our particular interest in voice until the second interview, and the first seven questions of the first interview with the reviewers were specifically designed to avoid hinting at the focus of our study. We also indicated in our article that the reviewers volunteered the information about their rhetorical construction of the author's voice before we had the chance to elicit them:

Reviewer #1 referred to the author with the third person masculine pronoun almost immediately—an assumption he later questioned but then believed did reflect his impression of the author's identity. Reviewer #2 also described aspects of the author's identity before being asked explicitly about any assumptions he may have had. (Matsuda & Tardy, 2007, p. 241)

Reviewer #1 also mentioned that "I sort of imagine this person as a young person" in response to the first question about the general impression of the manuscript, and he began referring to the author as a "guy" and "he" before the second question was introduced. Reviewer #2's comments about the author's bibliographic network was in response to the fourth question: "What kind of information were you looking for in evaluating the manuscript?" (Matsuda & Tardy, 2007, p. 247).

Even if the reviewers had become aware of our interest in voice earlier on, the fact that they did not hesitate to discuss their rhetorical construction of the author throughout the interviews seems to suggest that this was not an issue. If, as Stapleton and Helms-Park suggest, these reviewers had believed that having an image of the authors was a problem, they would probably have hesitated to discuss their assumptions. They did not.

The hesitation about the gender of the author in Reviewer #1's transcript was about the nature of the assumption but not about having that assumption. In other words, Reviewer #1 was being self-reflexive about his own gender biases.

Stapleton and Helms-Park also challenge us for not problematizing "the whole notion of Reviewer 1's gender stereotyping, that is, the implied notion that it is men alone who write combatively". We did not critique reviewers' perceptions because our goal was to identify their perceptions and not to criticize their world view—it was a qualitative study designed to understand rather than to evaluate. We were interested in the reviewers' perceptions of gender as well as their ambivalence. What Stapleton and Helms-Park characterize as the "wavering quotation", we feel, makes our understanding of the reader's rhetorical construction of author identity richer and more nuanced rather than simplistic and sweeping. Readers' ambivalence in their construction of writers' voice is something to emphasize, we believe, not something to overlook.

Stapleton and Helms-Park also seem to assume that one goal of our study was to establish a relationship between the presence of voice and the quality of writing. At this point, we are not making that claim, nor was our study designed to investigate such a relationship. In fact, we explicitly stated that "We can make no claims regarding the relationship between the reviewer's constructions of the author's voice and their respective evaluations of the manuscript, though this issue is worthy of further research" (Matsuda & Tardy, 2007, p. 247). Yet, it would be premature to conclude that voice (à la Matsuda, 2001) has no effect on writing assessment. Rubin and William-James (1997), for example, have shown that the perceived nationality—not the actual nationality of the writers—affect the rating of student writing. While the idea of blind peer review is in part driven by the premise that "fair-minded raters are supposed to *suppress*" their assumptions about the image of the author in evaluating manuscripts, our study shows that at least two reviewers did not do so. Now that we have identified some of the possible factors that contribute to the reader's rhetorical construction of author's voice, we are currently conducting a follow-up survey study to determine whether or not this phenomenon is idiosyncratic to these two reviewers.

Stapleton and Helms-Park conclude their response by arguing how a few changes in discursive features would not have made a difference in the effectiveness of Watson and Crick (1953) letter to *Nature*. Their choice of example is rather ironic because this letter is one of the scientific documents that has been discussed extensively for the impact of the authors' rhetorical choices on their success as scientists (Blakeslee, 1997; Fahnestock, 1986; Gross, 1990; Halloran, 1984; Moore, 1994, 2000; Paul, Charney, & Kendall, 2001; Swales, 2004).

In closing, we would like to make a plea for open-mindedness in research. To argue that a certain topic is overrepresented in the field because it may not apply to a limited population of students seems to impose an unreasonable constraint on the scope of the field, which deals with a wide range of issues related to second language writing at various levels of instruction in various contexts. It would be more productive if researchers focused their efforts on studying what *is* relevant to their own contexts, and building theories useful to those contexts, rather than discouraging others from exploring issues that seem relevant and useful for their own purposes.

REFERENCES

Blakeslee, A. M. (1997). Activity, context, interaction, and authority: Learning to write scientific papers in situ. *Journal of Business and Technical Communication, 11,* 125–169.

Elbow, P. (1981). *Writing with power.* New York: Oxford University Press.

Fahnestock, J. (1986). Accommodating science: The rhetorical life of scientific facts. *Written Communication, 3,* 275–296.

Gross, A. (1990). *The rhetoric of science.* Cambridge, MA: Harvard University Press.

Halloran, S. M. (1984). The birth of molecular biology: An essay in the rhetorical criticism of scientific discourse. *Rhetoric Review, 3,* 70–83.

Helms-Park, R., & Stapleton, P. (2003). Questioning the importance of individualized voice in undergraduate L2 argumentative writing: An empirical study with pedagogical implications. *Journal of Second Language Writing, 12*(3), 245–265.

Matsuda, P. K. (2001). Voice in Japanese written discourse: Implications for second language writing. *Journal of Second Language Writing, 10*(1-2), 35–53.

Matsuda, P. K., & Tardy, C. M. (2007). Voice in academic writing: The rhetorical construction of author identity in blind manuscript review. *English for Specific Purposes, 26,* 235–249.

Moore, R. (1994). Using the literature to teach students about science: Writing, rhetoric, and the structure of DNA. *Journal of College Science Teaching* (November), 114–121.

Moore, R. (2000). Writing about biology: How rhetorical choices can influence the impact of a scientific paper. *Bioscience, 26*(1), 23–25.

Paul, D., Charney, D., & Kendall, A. (2001). Moving beyond the moment: Reception studies in the rhetoric of science. *Journal of Technical and Business Communication, 15,* 372–399.

Rubin, D. L., & William-James, M. (1997). The impact of writer nationality on mainstream teachers' judgments of composition quality. *Journal of Second Language Writing, 6*(2), 139–153.

Sasaki, M. (2005). Hypothesis generation and hypothesis testing: Two complementary studies of EFL writing processes. In P. K. Matsuda & T. Silva (Eds.), *Second language writing research: Perspectives on the process of knowledge construction* (pp. 79–92). Mahwah, NJ: Lawrence Erlbaum.

Stapleton, P. (2002). Critiquing voice as a viable pedagogical tool in L2 writing: Returning the spotlight to ideas. *Journal of Second Language Writing, 11*(3), 177–190.

Swales, J. M. (2004). *Research genres: Exploration and applications.* Cambridge, UK: Cambridge University Press.

Watson, J. D., & Crick, F. H. C. (1953). Molecular structure of nucleic acids: A structure for deoxyribose nucleic acid. *Nature, 171,* 737–738.

Inventing the University[1]

David Bartholomae

Education may well be, as of right, the instrument whereby every indi-
vidual, in a society like our own, can gain access to any kind of discourse.
But we well know that in its distribution, in what it permits and in what
it prevents, it follows the well-trodden battle-lines of social conflict. Every
educational system is a political means of maintaining or of modifying
the appropriation of discourse, with the knowledge and the powers it
carries with it.

Foucault, *"The Discourse on Language"* (227)

Every time a student sits down to write for us, he has to invent the university for the occasion—invent the university, that is, or a branch of it,
like History or Anthropology or Economics or English. He has to learn
to speak our language, to speak as we do, to try on the peculiar ways of
knowing, selecting, evaluating, reporting, concluding, and arguing that
define the discourse of our community. Or perhaps I should say the various discourses of our community, since it is in the nature of a liberal arts
education that a student, after the first year or two, must learn to try on
a variety of voices and interpretive schemes—to write, for example, as a
literary critic one day and an experimental psychologist the next, to work
within fields where the rules governing the presentation of examples or
the development of an argument are both distinct and, even to a professional, mysterious.

The students have to appropriate (or be appropriated by) a specialized
discourse, and they have to do this as though they were easily and comfort-

Pecularity

Writing important

ably one with their audience, as though they were members of the academy, or historians or anthropologists or economists; they have to invent
the university by assembling and mimicking its language, finding some
compromise between idiosyncracy, a personal history, and the requirements of convention, the history of a discipline. They must learn to speak
our language. Or they must dare to speak it, or to carry off the bluff, since
speaking and writing will most certainly be required long before the skill
is "learned." And this, understandably, causes problems.

Let me look quickly at an example. Here is an essay written by a college
freshman, a basic writer:

> In the past time I thought that an incident was creative was when
> I had to make a clay model of the earth, but not of the classical or
> your everyday model of the earth which consists of the two cores,
> the mantle and the crust. I thought of these things in a dimension
> of which it would be unique, but easy to comprehend. Of course,
> your materials to work with were basic and limited at the same time,
> but thought help to put this limit into a right attitude or frame of
> mind to work with the clay.

> In the beginning of the clay model, I had to research and learn the
> different dimensions of the earth (in magnitude, quantity, state of
> matter, etc.) After this, I learned how to put this into the clay and
> come up with something different than any other person in my class
> at the time. In my opinion, color coordination and shape was the
> key to my creativity of the clay model of the earth.

> Creativity is the venture of the mind at work with the mechan-
> ics relay to the limbs from the cranium, which stores and triggers
> this action. It can be a burst of energy released at a precise time a
> thought is being transmitted. This can cause a frenzy of the human
> body, but it depends of the characteristics of the individual and how
> they can relay the message clearly enough through mechanics of the
> body to us as an observer. Then we must determine if it is creative
> or a learned process varied by the individuals thought process.
> Creativity is indeed a tool which has to exist, or our world will not
> succeed into the future and progress like it should.

I am continually impressed by the patience and good will of our students. This student was writing a placement essay during freshman orientation. (The problem set to him was, "Describe a time when you did something you felt to be creative. Then, on the basis of the incident you have described, go on to draw some general conclusions about 'creativity'.") He knew that university faculty would be reading and evaluating his essay, and so he wrote for them.

In some ways it is a remarkable performance. He is trying on the discourse even though he doesn't have the knowledge that makes the discourse more than a routine, a set of conventional rituals and gestures. And he does this, I think, even though he *knows* he doesn't have the knowledge that makes the discourse more than a routine. He defines himself as a researcher, working systematically, and not as a kid in a high school class: "I thought of these things in a dimension of ..."; "had to research and learn the different dimensions of the earth (in magnitude, quantity, state of matter, etc.)." He moves quickly into a specialized language (his approximation of our jargon) and draws both a general, textbook-like conclusion ("Creativity is the venture of the mind at work ... ") and a resounding peroration ("Creativity is indeed a tool which has to exist, or our world will not succeed into the future and progress like it should.") The writer has even, with that "indeed" and with the qualifications and the parenthetical expressions of the opening paragraphs, picked up the rhythm of our prose. And through it all he speaks with an impressive air of authority.

There is an elaborate but, I will argue, a necessary and enabling fiction at work here as the student dramatizes his experience in a "setting"—the setting required by the discourse—where he can speak to us as a companion, a fellow researcher. As I read the essay, there is only one moment when the fiction is broken, when we are addressed differently. The student says, "Of course, your materials to work with were basic and limited at the same time, but thought help to put this limit into a right attitude or frame of mind to work with the clay." At this point, I think, we become students and he the teacher, giving us a lesson (as in, "You take your pencil in your right hand and put your paper in front of you."). This is, however, one of the most characteristic slips of basic writers. It is very hard for them to take on the role—the voice, the person—of an authority whose authority is rooted in scholarship, analysis, or research. They slip, then, into the more immediately available and realizable voice of authority, the voice of a teacher giving a lesson or the voice of a parent lecturing at the dinner table. They offer advice or homilies rather than "academic" conclusions. There is a similar break in the final paragraph, where the conclusion that pushes for a definition ("Creativity is the venture of the mind at work with the mechanics relay to the limbs from the cranium ... ") is replaced by a conclusion which speaks in the voice of an Elder ("Creativity is indeed a tool which has to exist, or our world will not succeed into the future and progress like it should.").

It is not uncommon, then, to find such breaks in the concluding sections of essays written by basic writers. Here is the concluding section of an essay written by a student about his work as a mechanic. He had been asked to generalize about "work" after reviewing an on-the-job experience or incident that "stuck in his mind" as somehow significant.

> How could two repairmen miss a leak? Lack of pride? No incentive? Lazy? I don't know.

At this point the writer is in a perfect position to speculate, to move from the problem to an analysis of the problem. Here is how the paragraph continues however (and notice the change in pronoun reference):

> From this point on, I take *my* time, do it right, and don't let customers get under your skin. If they have a complaint, tell them to call your boss and he'll be more than glad to handle it. Most important, worry about yourself, and keep a clear eye on everyone, for there's always someone trying to take advantage of you, anytime and anyplace.

We get neither a technical discussion nor an "academic" discussion but a Lesson on Life.[2] This is the language he uses to address the general question, "How could two repairmen miss a leak?" The other brand of conclusion, the more academic one, would have required him to speak of his experience in our terms; it would, that is, have required a special vocabulary, a special system of presentation, and an interpretive scheme (or a set of commonplaces) he could use to identify and talk about the mystery of human error. The writer certainly had access to the range of acceptable commonplaces for such an explanation: "lack of pride," "no incentive," "lazy." Each would dictate its own set of phrases, examples, and conclusions, and we, his teachers, would know how to write out each argument, just as we would know how to write out more specialized arguments of our own. A "commonplace," then, is a culturally or institutionally authorized concept or statement that carries with it its own necessary elaboration. We all use commonplaces to orient ourselves in the world; they provide a point of reference and a set of "prearticulated" explanations that are readily available to organize and interpret experience. The phrase "lack of pride" carries with it its own account for the repairman's error just as, at another point in time, a reference to "original sin" would provide an explanation, or just as, in a certain university classroom, a reference to "alienation" would enable a writer to continue and complete the discussion. While there is a way in which these terms are interchangeable, they are not all permissible. A student in a composition class would most likely be turned away from a discussion of original sin. Commonplaces are the "controlling ideas" of our composition textbooks, textbooks that not only insist upon a set form for expository writing but a set view of public life.[3]

When the student above says, "I don't know," he is not saying, then, that he has nothing to say. He is saying that he is not in a position to carry on this discussion. And so we are addressed as apprentices rather than as teachers or scholars. To speak to us as a person of status or privilege, the writer can either speak to us in our terms—in the privileged language of university discourse—or, in default (or in defiance), he can speak to us as though we were children, offering us the wisdom of experience.

I think it is possible to say that the language of the "Clay Model" paper has come *through* the writer and not from the writer. The writer has located himself (he has located the self that is represented by the *I* on the page) in a context that is, finally, beyond him, not his own and not available to his immediate procedures for inventing and arranging text. I would not, that is, call this essay an example of "writer-based" prose. I would not say that it is egocentric or that it represents the "interior monologue of a writer thinking and talking to himself" (Flower 63). It is, rather, the record of a writer who has lost himself in the discourse of his readers. There is a context beyond the reader that is not the world but a way of talking about the world, a way of talking that determines the use of examples, the possible conclusions, the acceptable commonplaces, and the key words of an essay on the construction of a clay model of the earth. This writer has entered the discourse without successfully approximating it.

Linda Flower has argued that the difficulty inexperienced writers have with writing can be understood as a difficulty in negotiating the transition between writer-based and reader-based prose. Expert writers, in other words, can better imagine how a reader will respond to a text and can transform or restructure what they have to say around a goal shared with a reader. Teaching students to revise for readers, then, will better prepare them to write initially with a reader in mind. The success of this pedagogy depends upon the degree to which a writer can imagine and conform to a reader's goals. The difficulty of this act of imagination, and the burden of such conformity, are so much at the heart of the problem that a teacher must pause and take stock before offering revision as a solution. Students like the student who wrote the "Clay Model" paper are not so much trapped in a private language as they are shut out from one of the privileged languages of public life, a language they are aware of but cannot control.

Our students, I've said, have to appropriate (or be appropriated by) a specialized discourse, and they have to do this as though they were easily or comfortably one with their audience. If you look at the situation this way, suddenly the problem of audience awareness becomes enormously complicated. One of the common assumptions of both composition research and composition teaching is that at some "stage" in the process of composing an essay a writer's ideas or his motives must be tailored to the needs and expectations of his audience. A writer has to "build bridges" between his point of view and his readers. He has to anticipate and acknowledge his readers' assumptions and biases. He must begin with "common points of departure" before introducing new or controversial arguments. There is a version of the pastoral at work here. It is assumed that a person of low status (like a shepherd) can speak to a person of power (like a courtier), but only (at least so far as the language is concerned) if he is not a shepherd at all, but actually a member of the court out in the fields in disguise.

Writers who can successfully manipulate an audience (or, to use a less pointed language, writers who can accommodate their motives to their readers' expectations) are writers who can both imagine and write from a position of privilege. They must, that is, see themselves within a privileged discourse, one that already includes and excludes groups of readers. They must be either equal to or more powerful than those they would address. The writing, then, must somehow transform the political and social relationships between basic writing students and their teachers.

If my students are going to write for me by knowing who I am—and if this means more than knowing my prejudices, psyching me out—it means knowing what I know; it means having the knowledge of a professor of English. They have, then, to know what I know and how I know what I know (the interpretive schemes that define the way I would work out the problems I set for them); they have to learn to write what I would write, or to offer up some approximation of that discourse. The problem of audience awareness, then, is a problem of power and finesse. It cannot be addressed, as it is in most classroom exercises, by giving students privilege and denying the situation of the classroom, by having students write to an outsider, someone excluded from their privileged circle: "Write about 'To His Coy Mistress,' not for your teacher, but for the students in your class"; "Describe Pittsburgh to someone who has never been there"; "Explain to a high school senior how best to prepare for college"; "Describe baseball to a Martian."

Exercises such as these allow students to imagine the needs and goals of a reader and they bring those needs and goals forward as a dominant constraint in the construction of an essay. And they argue, implicitly, what is generally true about writing—that it is an act of aggression disguised as an act of charity. What they fail to address is the central problem of academic writing, where students must assume the right of speaking to someone who knows Pittsburgh or "To His Coy Mistress" better than they do, a reader for whom the general commonplaces and the readily available utterances about a subject are inadequate. It should be clear that when I say that I know Pittsburgh better than my basic writing students I am talking about a way of knowing that is also a way of writing. There may be much that they know that I don't know, but in the setting of the university classroom I have a way of talking about the town that is "better" (and for arbitrary reasons) than theirs.

I think that all writers, in order to write, must imagine for themselves the privilege of being "insiders"—that is, of being both inside an established and powerful discourse, and of being granted a special right to speak. And I think that right to speak is seldom conferred upon us—upon any of us, teachers or students—by virtue of the fact that we have invented or discovered an original idea. Leading students to believe that they are responsible for something new or original, unless they understand what those words mean with regard to writing, is a dangerous and counterproductive practice. We do have the right to expect students to be active and engaged, but that is more a matter of being continually and stylistically working against the inevitable presence of conventional language; it is not a matter of inventing a language that is new.

When students are writing for a teacher, writing becomes more problematic than it is for the students who are describing baseball to a Martian. The students, in effect, have to assume privilege without having any. And since students assume privilege by locating themselves within the discourse of a particular community—within a set of specifically acceptable gestures and commonplaces—learning, at least as it is defined in the liberal arts curriculum, becomes more a matter of imitation or parody than a matter of invention and discovery.

What our beginning students need to learn is to extend themselves into the commonplaces, set phrases, rituals, gestures, habits of mind, tricks of persuasion, obligatory conclusions, and necessary connections that determine the "what might be said" and constitute knowledge within the various branches of our academic community. The course of instruction that would make this possible would be based on a sequence of illustrated assignments and would allow for successive approximations of academic or "disciplinary" discourse. Students will not take on our peculiar ways of reading, writing, speaking, and thinking all at once. Nor will the command of a subject like sociology, at least as that command is represented by the successful completion of a multiple choice exam, enable students to write sociology. Our colleges and universities, by and large, have failed to involve basic writing students in scholarly projects, projects that would allow them to act as though they were colleagues in an academic enterprise. Much of the written work students do is test-taking, report or summary, work that places them outside the working discourse of the academic community, where they are expected to admire and report on what we do, rather than inside that discourse, where they can do its work and participate in a common enterprise.[4] This is a failure of teachers and curriculum designers who, even if they speak of writing as a mode of learning, all too often represent writing as a "tool" to be used by an (hopefully) educated mind.

Pat Bizzell is one of the most important scholars writing now on basic writers and on the special requirements of academic discourse.[5] In a recent essay, "Cognition, Convention and Certainty: What We Need to Know About Writing," she argues that the problems of basic writers might be

better understood in terms of their unfamiliarly with the academic
discourse community, combined, perhaps, with such limited
experience outside their native discourse communities that they are
unaware that there is such a thing as a discourse community with
conventions to be mastered. What is underdeveloped is their knowledge both of the ways experience is constituted and interpreted in
the academic discourse community and of the fact that all discourse
communities constitute and interpret experience. (230)

One response to the problems of basic writers, then, would be to
determine just what the community's conventions are, so that those conventions can be written out, "demystified," and taught in our classrooms.
Teachers, as a result, could be more precise and helpful when they ask students to "think," "argue," "describe," or "define." Another response would
be to examine the essays written by basic writers—their approximations of
academic discourse—to determine more clearly where the problems lie. If
we look at their writing, and if we look at it in the context of other student
writing, we can better see the points of discord when students try to write
their way into the university.

The purpose of the remainder of this paper will be to examine some of
the most striking and characteristic problems as they are presented in the
expository essays of basic writers. I will be concerned, then, with university
discourse in its most generalized form—that is, as represented by introductory courses—and not with the special conventions required by advanced
work in the various disciplines. And I will be concerned with the difficult,
and often violent, accommodations that occur when students locate themselves in a discourse that is not "naturally" or immediately theirs.

I have reviewed 500 essays written in response to the "creativity"
question used during one of our placement exams. (The essay cited at the
opening of this paper was one of that group.) Some of the essays were written by basic writers (or, more properly, those essays led readers to identify
the writers as "basic writers"); some were written by students who "passed"
(who were granted immediate access to the community of writers at the
university). As I read these essays, I was looking to determine the stylistic
resources that enabled writers to locate themselves within an "academic"
discourse. My bias as a reader should be clear by now. I was not looking
to see how the writer might represent the skills demanded by a neutral
language (a language whose key features were paragraphs, topic sentences,

transitions, and the like-features of a clear and orderly mind). I was looking to see what happened when a writer entered into a language to locate
himself (a textual self) and his subject, and I was looking to see how, once
entered, that language made or unmade a writer.

Here is one essay. Its writer was classified as a basic writer. Since the
essay is relatively free of sentence level errors, that decision must have been
rooted in some perceived failure of the discourse itself.

I am very interested in music, and I try to be creative in my interpretation of music. While in high school, I was a member of a jazz
ensemble. The members of the ensemble were given chances to
improvise and be creative in various songs. I feel that this was a
great experience for me, as well as the other members. I was proud
to know that I could use my imagination and feelings to create
music other than what was written.

Creativity to me, means being free to express yourself in a way that
is unique to you, not having to conform to certain rules and guidelines. Music is only one of the many areas in which people are given
opportunities to show their creativity. Sculpting, carving, building,
art, and acting are just a few more areas where people can show
their creativity.

Through my music I conveyed feelings and thoughts which were
important to me. Music was my means of showing creativity.
In whatever form creativity takes, whether it be music, art, or science, it is an important aspect of our lives because it enables us to
be individuals.

Notice, in this essay, the key gesture, one that appears in all but a few
of the essays I read. The student defines as his own that which is a commonplace. "Creativity, to me, means being free to express yourself in a way
that is unique to you, not having to conform to certain rules and guidelines." This act of appropriation constitutes his authority; it constitutes his
authority as a writer and not just as a musician (that is, as someone with
a story to tell). There were many essays in the set that told only a story,
where the writer's established presence was as a musician or a skier or
someone who painted designs on a van, but not as a person removed from
that experience interpreting it, treating it as a metaphor for something

else (creativity). Unless those stories were long, detailed, and very well told (unless the writer was doing more than saying, "I am a skier or a musician or a van-painter"), those writers were all given low ratings.

Notice also that the writer of the jazz paper locates himself and his experience in relation to the commonplace (creativity is unique expression; it is not having to conform to rules or guidelines) regardless of whether it is true or not. Anyone who improvises "knows" that improvisation follows rules and guidelines. It is the power of the commonplace (its truth as a recognizable and, the writer believes, as a final statement) that justifies the example and completes the essay. The example, in other words, has value because it stands within the field of the commonplace. It is not the occasion for what one might call an "objective" analysis or a "close" reading. It could also be said that the essay stops with the articulation of the commonplace. The following sections speak only to the power of that statement. The reference to "sculpting, carving, building, art, and acting" attest to the universality of the commonplace (and it attests to the writer's nervousness with the status he has appropriated for himself—he is saying, "Now, I'm not the only one here who's done something unique."). The commonplace stands by itself. For this writer, it does not need to be elaborated. By virtue of having written it, he has completed the essay and established the contract by which we may be spoken to as equals: "In whatever form creativity takes, whether it be music, art, or science, it is an important aspect of *our* lives because it enables *us* to be individuals." (For me to break that contract, to argue that *my* life is not represented in that essay, is one way for me to begin as a teacher with that student in that essay.)

I said that the writer of the jazz paper offered up a commonplace regardless of whether it was "true" or not, and this, I said, was an example of the power of a commonplace to determine the meaning of an example. A commonplace determines a system of interpretation that can be used to "place" an example within a standard system of belief. You can see a similar process at work in this essay.

During the football season, the team was supposed to wear the same type of cleats and the same type socks, I figured that I would change this a little by wearing my white shoes instead of black and to cover up the team socks with a pair of my own white ones. I thought that this looked better than what we were wearing, and I told a few of the other people on the team to change too. They agreed that it did

*appropriation: taking something [for]
one'like w/out ouner's permu(in)*

look better and they changed there combination to go along with
mine. After the game people came up to us and said that it looked
very good the way we wore our socks, and they wanted to know why
we changed from the rest of the team.

Commasplice

I feel that creativity comes from when a person lets his imagination come up with ideas and he is not afraid to express them. Once
you create something to do it will be original and unique because
it came about from your own imagination and if any one else tries
to copy it, it won't be the same because you thought of it first from
your own ideas.

This is not an elegant paper, but it seems seamless, tidy. If the paper
on the clay model of the earth showed an ill-fit between the writer and his
project, here the discourse seems natural, smooth. You could reproduce
this paper and hand it out to a class, and it would take a lot of prompting
before the students sensed something fishy and one of the more aggressive
ones might say, "Sure he came up with the idea of wearing white shoes and
white socks. Him and Billy White-shoes Johnson. Come on. He copied the
very thing he said was his own idea, 'original and unique'."

Do NOT use 'I' in rhetoric

The "I" of this text, the "I" who "figured," "thought," and "felt" is
located in a conventional rhetoric of the self that turns imagination into
origination (I made it), that argues an ethic of production (I made it and it
is mine), and that argues a tight scheme of intention (I made it because I
decided to make it). The rhetoric seems invisible because it is so common.
This "I" (the maker) is also located in a version of history that dominates
classroom accounts of history. It is an example of the "Great Man" theory,
where history is rolling along—the English novel is dominated by a central,
intrusive narrative presence; America is in the throes of a great depression;
during football season the team was supposed to wear the same kind of
cleats and socks—until a figure appears, one who can shape history—Henry
James, FDR, the writer of the football paper—and everything is changed.
In the argument of the football paper, "I figured," "I thought," "I told,"
"They agreed," and, as a consequence, "I feel that creativity *comes from
when* a person lets his imagination come up with ideas and he is not afraid
to express them." The story of appropriation becomes a narrative of cour-
age and conquest. The writer was able to write that story when he was able
to imagine himself in that discourse. Getting him out of it will be difficult
matter indeed.

unter imaging himkeP in ducurse

There are ways, I think, that a writer can shape history in the very act of writing it. Some students are able to enter into a discourse, but, by stylistic maneuvers, to take possession of it at the same time. They don't originate a discourse, but they locate themselves within it aggressively, self-consciously.

Here is one particularly successful essay. Notice the specialized vocabulary, but also the way in which the text continually refers to its own language and to the language of others.

Throughout my life, I have been interested and intrigued by music. My mother has often told me of the times, before I went to school, when I would "conduct" the orchestra on her records. I continued to listen to music and eventually started to play the guitar and the clarinet. Finally, at about the age of twelve, I started to sit down and to try to write songs. Even though my instrumental skills were far from my own high standards, I would spend much of my spare time during the day with a guitar around my neck, trying to produce a piece of music.

Each of these sessions, as I remember them, had a rather set format. I would sit in my bedroom, strumming different combinations of the five or six chords I could play, until I heard a series which sounded particularly good to me. After this, I set the music to a suitable rhythm, (usually dependent on my mood at the time), and ran through the tune until I could play it fairly easily. Only after this section was complete did I go on to writing lyrics, which generally followed along the lines of the current popular songs on the radio.

At the time of the writing, I felt that my songs were, in themselves, an original creation of my own; that is, I, alone, made them. However, I now see that, in this sense of the word, I was not creative. The songs themselves seem to be an oversimplified form of the music I listened to at the time.

In a more fitting sense, however, I *was* being creative. Since I did not purposely copy my favorite songs, I was, effectively, originating my songs from my own "process of creativity." To achieve my goal, I needed what a composer would call "inspiration" for my piece. In this case the inspiration was the current hit on the radio. Perhaps with my present point of view, I feel that I used too much "inspiration" in my songs, but, at that time, I did not.

Creativity, therefore, is a process which, in my case, involved a certain series of "small creations" if you like. As well, it is something, the appreciation of which varies with one's point of view, that point of view being set by the person's experience, tastes, and his own personal view of creativity. The less experienced tend to allow for less originality, while the more experienced demand real originality to classify something a "creation." Either way, a term as abstract as this is perfectly correct, and open to interpretation.

This writer is consistently and dramatically conscious of herself forming something to say out of what has been said *and* out of what she has been saying in the act of writing this paper. "Creativity" begins, in this paper, as "original creation." What she thought was "creativity," however, she now calls "imitation" and, as she says, "in this sense of the word" she was not "creative." In another sense, however, she says that she *was* creative since she didn't purposefully copy the songs but used them as "inspiration."

The writing in this piece (that is, the work of the writer within the essay) goes on in spite of, or against, the language that keeps pressing to give another name to her experience as a song writer and to bring the discussion to closure. (Think of the quick closure of the football shoes paper in comparison.) Its style is difficult, highly qualified. It relies on quotation marks and parody to set off the language and attitudes that belong to the discourse (or the discourses) it would reject, that it would not take as its own proper location.[6]

In the papers I've examined in this essay, the writers have shown a varied awareness of the codes—or the competing codes—that operate within a discourse. To speak with authority student writers have not only to speak in another's voice but through another's "code"; and they not only have to do this, they have to speak in the voice and through the codes of those of us with power and wisdom; and they not only have to do this, they have to do it before they know what they are doing, before they have a project to participate in and before, at least in terms of our disciplines, they have anything to say. Our students may be able to enter into a conventional discourse and speak, not as themselves, but through the voice of the community. The university, however, is the place where "common" wisdom is only of negative value; it is something to work against. The movement toward a more specialized discourse begins (or perhaps, best begins) when a student can both define a position of privilege, a position that sets him against a "common" discourse, and when he can work self-consciously, critically, against not only the "common" code but his own.

The stages of development that I've suggested are not necessarily marked by corresponding levels in the type or frequency of error, at least not by the type or frequency of sentence level errors. I am arguing, then, that a basic writer is not necessarily a writer who makes a lot of mistakes. In fact, one of the problems with curricula designed to aid basic writers is that they too often begin with the assumption that the key distinguishing feature of a basic writer is the presence of sentence level error. Students are placed in courses because their placement essays show a high frequency of such errors and those courses are designed with the goal of making those errors go away. This approach to the problems of the basic writer ignores the degree to which error is not a constant feature but a marker in the development of a writer. Students who can write reasonably correct narratives may fall to pieces when faced with more unfamiliar assignments. More importantly, however, such courses fail to serve the rest of the curriculum. On every campus there is a significant number of college freshman who require a course to introduce them to the kinds of writing that are required for a university education. Some of these students can write correct sentences and some cannot, but as a group they lack the facility other freshmen possess when they are faced with an academic writing task.

The "White Shoes" essay, for example, shows fewer sentence level errors than the "Clay Model" paper. This may well be due to the fact, however, that the writer of that paper stayed well within the safety of familiar territory. He kept himself out of trouble by doing what he could easily do. The tortuous syntax of the more advanced papers on my list is a syntax that represents a writer's struggle with a difficult and unfamiliar language, and it is a syntax that can quickly lead an inexperienced writer into trouble. The syntax and punctuation of the "Composing Songs" essay, for example, shows the effort that is required when a writer works against the pressure of conventional discourse. If the prose is inelegant (although I'll confess I admire those dense sentences), it is still correct. This writer has a command of the linguistic and stylistic resources (the highly embedded sentences, the use of parentheses and quotation marks) required to complete the act of writing. It is easy to imagine the possible pitfalls for a writer working without this facility.

There was no camera trained on the "Clay Model" writer while he was writing, and I have no protocol of what was going through his mind, but it is possible to speculate that the syntactic difficulties of sentences like the following are the result of an attempt to use an unusual vocabulary and to extend his sentences beyond the boundaries that would be "normal" in his speech or writing:

> In past time I thought that an incident was creative was when I had to make a clay model of the earth, but not of the classical or your everyday model of the earth which consists of the two cores, the mantle and the crust. I thought of these things in a dimension of which it would be unique, but easy to comprehend.

There is reason to believe, that is, that the problem is with this kind of sentence, in this context. If the problem of the last sentence is a problem of holding together these units—"I thought," "dimension," "unique," and "easy to comprehend"—then the linguistic problem is not a simple matter of sentence construction.

I am arguing, then, that such sentences fall apart not because the writer lacks the necessary syntax to glue the pieces together but because he lacks the full statement within which these key words are already operating. While writing, and in the thrust of his need to complete the sentence, he has the key words but not the utterance. (And to recover the utterance, I suspect, he will need to do more than revise the sentence.) The invisible conventions, the prepared phrases remain too distant for the statement to be completed. The writer must get inside of a discourse he can only partially imagine. The act of constructing a sentence, then, becomes something like an act of transcription, where the voice on the tape unexpectedly fades away and becomes inaudible.

Mina Shaughnessy speaks of the advanced writer as a writer with a more facile but still incomplete possession of this prior discourse. In the case of the advanced writer, the evidence of a problem is the presence of dissonant, redundant, or imprecise language, as in a sentence such as this: "No education can be total, it must be continuous." Such a student Shaughnessy says, could be said to hear the "melody of formal English" while still unable to make precise or exact distinctions. And, she says, the pre-packaging feature of language, the possibility of taking over phrases and whole

sentences without much thought about them, threatens the writer now as
before. The writer, as we have said, inherits the language out of which he
must fabricate his own messages. He is therefore in a constant tangle with
the language, obliged to recognize its public, communal nature and yet
driven to invent out of this language his own statements (19).

For the unskilled writer, the problem is different in degree and not
in kind. The inexperienced writer is left with a more fragmentary record
of the comings and goings of academic discourse. Or, as I said above, he
often has the key words without the complete statements within which
they are already operating.

It may very well be that some students will need to learn to crudely
mimic the "distinctive register" of academic discourse before they are
prepared to actually and legitimately do the work of the discourse, and
before they are sophisticated enough with the refinements of tone and
gesture to do it with grace or elegance. To say this, however, is to say that
our students must be our students. Their initial progress will be marked by
their abilities to take on the role of privilege, by their abilities to establish
authority. From this point of view, the student who wrote about constructing the clay model of the earth is better prepared for his education than
the student who wrote about playing football in white shoes, even though
the "White Shoes" paper was relatively error-free and the "Clay Model"
paper was not. It will be hard to pry the writer of the "White Shoes" paper
loose from the tidy, pat discourse that allows him to dispose of the question of creativity in such a quick and efficient manner. He will have to be
convinced that it is better to write sentences he might not so easily control,
and he will have to be convinced that it is better to write muddier and
more confusing prose (in order that it may sound like ours), and this will
be harder than convincing the "Clay Model" writer to continue what he
has begun.[7]

NOTES

1. This article represents an abridged version of a chapter in *When A
   Writer Can't Write: Studies in Writer's Block and Other Composing
   Problems*. Ed. Mike Rose. New York: The Guilford Press, 1985.

2. David Olson has made a similar observation about school-related
   problems of language learning in younger children. Here is his conclusion: "Hence, depending upon whether children assumed lan-

guage was primarily suitable for making assertions and conjectures or primarily for making direct or indirect commands, they will either find school texts easy or difficult" (107).

3. For Aristotle there were both general and specific commonplaces. A speaker, says Aristotle, has a "stock of arguments to which he may turn for a particular need."

> If he knows the *topic* (regions, places, lines of argument)—and a skilled speaker will know them—he will know where to find what he wants for a special case. The general topics, or *common*places, are regions containing arguments that are common to all branches of knowledge. ... But there are also special topics (regions, places, *loci*) in which one looks for arguments appertaining to particular branches of knowledge, special sciences, such as ethics or politics. (154–155)

And, he says, "The topics or places, then, may be indifferently thought of as in the science that is concerned, or in the mind of the speaker." But the question of location is "indifferent" *only* if the mind of the speaker is in line with set opinion, general assumption. For the speaker (or writer) who is not situated so comfortably in the privileged public realm, this is indeed not an indifferent matter at all. If he does not have the commonplace at hand, he will not, in Aristotle's terms, know where to go at all.

4. See especially Bartholomae and Rose for articles on curricula designed to move students into university discourse. The movement to extend writing "across the cirriculum" is evidence of a general concern for locating students within the work of the university: see especially Bizzell and Maimon et al. For longer works directed specifically at basic writing, see Ponsot and Dean, and Shaughnessy. For a book describing a course for more advanced students, see Coles.

5. See especially Bizzell, and Bizzell and Herzberg. My debt to Bizzell's work should be evident everywhere in this essay.

6. In support of my argument that this is the kind of writing that does the work of the academy, let me offer the following excerpt from a recent essay by Wayne Booth ("The Company We Keep: Self-Making in Imaginative Art, Old and New"):

> I can remember making up songs of my own, no doubt borrowed from favorites like "Hello, Central, Give Me Heaven," "You Can't Holler Down My Rain Barrel," and one about the ancient story of a sweet little "babe in the woods" who lay down and died, with her brother.
>
> I asked my mother, in a burst of creative egotism, why nobody ever learned to sing my songs, since after all I was more than willing to learn theirs. I can't remember her answer, and I can barely remember snatches of two of "my" songs. But I can remember dozens of theirs, and when I sing them, even now, I sometimes feel again the emotions, and see the images, that they aroused then. Thus who I am now—the very shape of my soul—was to a surprising degree molded by the works of "art" that came my way.
>
> I set "art" in quotation marks, because much that I experienced in those early books and songs would not be classed as art according to most definitions. But for the purposes of appraising the effects of "art" on " life" or "culture," and especially for the purposes of thinking about the effects of the "media," we surely must include every kind of artificial experience that we provide for one another
>
> In this sense of the word, all of us are from the earliest years fed a steady diet of art ... (58–59).

While there are similarities in the paraphrasable content of Booth's arguments and my student's, what I am interested

in is each writer's method. Both appropriate terms from
a common discourse about (*art* and *inspiration*) in order to
push against an established way of talking (about tradition
and the individual). This effort of opposition clears a space
for each writer's argument and enables the writers to establish their own "sense" of the key words in the discourse.

7. Preparation of this manuscript was supported by the Learning
    Research and Development Center of the University of Pittsburgh,
    which is supported in part by the National Institute of Education.
    I am grateful also to Mike Rose, who pushed and pulled at this
    paper at a time when it needed it.

WORKS CITED

Aristotle. *The Rhetoric of Aristotle.* Trans. L. Cooper. Englewood Cliffs, NJ:
Prentice, 1932.

Bartholomae, David. "Teaching Basic Writing: An Alternative to Basic
Skills." *Journal of Basic Writing* 2(1979): 85-109.

———. "Writing Assignments: Where Writing Begins." *Forum.* Ed. P. Stock.
Montclair, NJ: Boynton/ Cook, 1983. 300-312.

Bartholomae, David and Anthony Petrosky. *Facts, Artifacts and Counter-
facts: A Basic Reading and Writing Course for the College Curriculum.* Montclair, NJ: Boynton/ Cook, forthcoming.

Bizzell, Patricia. "The Ethos of Academic Discourse." *College Composition
and Communication* 29(1978): 351-55.

———. "Cognition, Convention and Certainty: What We Need to Know
About." *Pre/Text* 3(1982): 213-244.

———. "College Composition: Initiation Into the Academic Discourse
Communities." *Curriculum Inquiry* 12(1982): 191-207.

Bizzell, Patricia and Bruce Herzberg. " 'Inherent' Ideology, 'Universal' History, 'Empirical' Evidence, and 'Context-Free' Writing: Some Problems
with E.D. Hirsch 's *The Philosophy of Composition.*" *Modern Language
Notes* 95(1980): 1181-1202.

Booth, Wayne. "The Company We Keep: Self-Making in Imaginative Art,
Old and New." *The Pushcart Prize, VIII: Best of the Small Presses.* Ed. Bill
Henderson. Wainscott, NY: Pushcart, 1983. 57-95.

Coles, William E., Jr. *The Plural I*. New York: Holt, 1978.

Flower, Linda S. "Revising Writer-Based Prose." *Journal of Basic Writing* 3(1981): 62-74.

Foucault, Michel. *The Archaeology of Knowledge*. Trans. A.M. Sheridan Smith. New York: Harper, 1972.

Maimon, Elaine P., G.L. Belcher, G.W. Hearn, B.F. Nodine, and F.X. O'Connor. *Writing in the Arts and Sciences*. Cambridge, MA: Winthrop, 1981.

Olson, David R. "Writing: The Divorce of the Author From the Text." *Exploring Speaking-Writing Relationships: Connections and Contrasts*. Eds. B. Kroll and R. Vann. Urbana, IL: NCTE, 1981.

Ponsot, Marie and Rosemary Deen. *Beat Not the Poor Desk*. Montclair, NJ: Boynton/ Cook, 1982.

Rose, Mike. "Remedial Writing Courses: A Critique and a Proposal." *College English* 45(1983): 109-128.

———. *When A Writer Can't Write: Studies in Writer's Block and Other Composing Problems*. New York: Guilford, 1985.

Shaughnessy, Mina. *Errors and Expectations*. New York: Oxford UP, 1977.

Identity and Interaction:
A Sociocultural Linguistic Approach

Mary Bucholtz and Kira Hall

ABSTRACT

The article proposes a framework for the analysis of identity as produced
in linguistic interaction, based on the following principles: (1) identity is
the product rather than the source of linguistic and other semiotic practices and therefore is a social and cultural rather than primarily internal
psychological phenomenon; (2) identities encompass macro-level demographic categories, temporary and interactionally specific stances and
participant roles, and local, ethnographically emergent cultural positions;
(3) identities may be linguistically indexed through labels, implicatures,
stances, styles, or linguistic structures and systems; (4) identities are
relationally constructed through several, often overlapping, aspects of
the relationship between self and other, including similarity/difference,
genuineness/artifice and authority/delegitimacy; and (5) identity may be in
part intentional, in part habitual and less than fully conscious, in part an
outcome of interactional negotiation, in part a construct of others' perceptions and representations, and in part an outcome of larger ideological
processes and structures. The principles are illustrated through examination of a variety of linguistic interactions.

KEYWORDS

agency, emergence, identity, ideology, indexicality, interaction, intersubjectivity, positioning, sociocultural linguistics, stance, style

INTRODUCTION

In this article, we propose a framework for the analysis of identity as constituted in linguistic interaction. The need for such a framework has become apparent in recent years, as linguistic research on identity has become increasingly central within sociolinguistics, linguistic anthropology, discourse analysis, and social psychology. But the concomitant development of theoretical approaches to identity remains at best a secondary concern, not a focused goal of the field. We argue for the analytic value of approaching identity as a relational and sociocultural phenomenon that emerges and circulates in local discourse contexts of interaction rather than as a stable structure located primarily in the individual psyche or in fixed social categories. We believe that the approach we propose here, which draws together insights from a variety of fields and theorists, allows for a discussion of identity that permits researchers to articulate theoretical assumptions about identity often left implicit in scholarship, while avoiding the critiques of this concept that have arisen in the social sciences and humanities in the past two decades. Given the scope of such scholarly research, our definition of identity is deliberately broad and open-ended: *Identity is the social positioning of self and other.*

Before describing our approach, we must first acknowledge our debt to a wide variety of research in several fields that has informed our own view of identity. Such work includes speech accommodation theory (Giles et al., 1991) and social identity theory (Meyerhoff, 1996; Meyerhoff and Niedzielski, 1994; Tajfel and Turner, 1979) in social psychology, theories of language ideology (Irvine and Gal, 2000; Silverstein, 1979) and indexicality (Ochs, 1992; Silverstein, 1976, 1985) in linguistic anthropology, and theories of style (Eckert and Rickford, 2001; Mendoza-Denton, 2002) and models of identity (Le Page and Tabouret-Keller, 1985) in sociolinguistics, among others. In addition, we have drawn on a number of different social theories that are especially relevant to an understanding of the intersubjective construction of identity within local interactional contexts.

The framework we outline here synthesizes key work on identity from all these traditions to offer a general sociocultural linguistic perspective on identity—that is, one that focuses on both the details of language and the workings of culture and society. By *sociocultural linguistics*, we mean the broad interdisciplinary field concerned with the intersection of language, culture, and society. This term encompasses the disciplinary subfields of sociolinguistics, linguistic anthropology, socially oriented forms of discourse analysis (such as conversation analysis and critical discourse analysis), and linguistically oriented social psychology, among others.[1] In incorporating these diverse approaches under a single label, our purpose is neither to deny the differences among them nor to impose new disciplinary boundaries; rather, it is to acknowledge the full range of work that falls under the rubric of language and identity and to offer a shorthand device for referring to these approaches collectively. The interdisciplinary perspective taken here is intended to help scholars recognize the comprehensive toolkit already available to them for analyzing identity as a centrally linguistic phenomenon. As our examples below illustrate, identity does not emerge at a single analytic level—whether vowel quality, turn shape, code choice, or ideological structure—but operates at multiple levels simultaneously. Our own approach privileges the interactional level, because it is in interaction that all these resources gain social meaning. Our goal is to assemble elements of sociocultural linguistic work on identity into a coherent model that both describes the current state of research and offers new directions for future scholarship.

We propose five principles that we see as fundamental to the study of identity, drawing examples from our own research, as well as studies by others. The first and second principles challenge narrowly psychological and static views of identity that have circulated widely in the social sciences. We argue instead, in line with abundant sociocultural linguistic research, that identity is a discursive construct that emerges in interaction. Further, we expand traditional macrosociological views of identity to include both local ethnographic categories and transitory interactional positions. The third principle inventories the types of linguistic resources whereby interactants indexically position self and other in discourse. The heart of the model is described in the fourth principle, which highlights the relational foundation of identity. To illustrate this principle, we briefly outline our own recently developed framework for analyzing identity as an intersubjective accomplishment. Finally, the fifth principle considers the limits and constraints on individual intentionality in the process of identity construction, while acknowledging the important role that deliberate social action may play in producing identity. Throughout the article, we argue for a view of identity that is intersubjectively rather than individually produced and interactionally emergent rather than assigned in an a priori fashion.

THE EMERGENCE PRINCIPLE

The first principle that informs our perspective addresses a traditional scholarly view of identity as housed primarily within an individual mind, so that the only possible relationship between identity and language use is for language to reflect an individual's internal mental state. While individuals' sense of self is certainly an important element of identity, researchers of individuals' language use (e.g. Johnstone, 1996) have shown that the only way that such self-conceptions enter the social world is via some form of discourse. Hence, accounts that locate identity inside the mind may discount the social ground on which identity is built, maintained, and altered.

Our own view draws from the sustained engagement with the concept of emergence in linguistic anthropology and interactional linguistics. The idea of emergence was promoted early on in linguistic anthropology by Dell Hymes, whose view of artful linguistic performance as dialogic rather than monologic led him to call for an understanding of 'structure as sometimes emergent in action' (Hymes, 1975: 71). Subsequent anthropologists, notably Richard Bauman and Charles Briggs, moved the field further away from the analysis of performance as mere reiteration of an underlying textual structure that was traditionally taken to be primary. In both their individual and collaborative work (Bauman, 1977; Bauman and Briggs, 1990; Briggs, 1988), these scholars demonstrated that performance is instead emergent in the course of its unfolding in specific encounters. These ideas also inform Bruce Mannheim and Dennis Tedlock's (1995) view of culture as emergent through dialogical processes; that is, culture is produced as speakers draw on multiple voices and texts in every utterance (Bakhtin, 1981). Moreover, in functional and interactional linguistics, scholars have argued against static structuralist and generativist formulations of grammar, proposing instead that linguistic structure emerges in the course of interaction (e.g. Bybee and Hopper, 2001; Ford et al., 2002; Hopper, 1987).

We extend the insights of this previous linguistic work on emergence to the analysis of identity. As with performance, culture, and grammar itself, we maintain that identity emerges from the specific conditions of linguistic interaction:

1. Identity is best viewed as the emergent product rather than the pre-existing source of linguistic and other semiotic practices and therefore as fundamentally a social and cultural phenomenon.

This is a familiar idea within several very different branches of socio-cultural linguistics: the ethnomethodological concept of 'doing' various kinds of identity (e.g. Fenstermaker and West, 2002; Garfinkel, 1967; West and Zimmerman, 1987) and the related conversation-analytic notion of identity as an interactionally relevant accomplishment (e.g. Antaki and Widdicombe, 1998; Aronsson, 1998; Auer, 1998; Kitzinger, n.d.; Moerman, 1993; Sidnell, 2003); the poststructuralist theory of performativity (Butler, 1990), developed from the work of J.L. Austin (1962), as taken up by researchers of language, gender, and sexuality (e.g. Barrett, 1999; Cameron, 1997; Livia and Hall, 1997); and more generally the semiotic concepts of creative indexicality (Silverstein, 1979) and referee design (Bell, 1984). Despite fundamental differences among these approaches, all of them enable us to view identity not simply as a psychological mechanism of self-classification that is reflected in people's social behavior but rather as something that is constituted through social action, and especially through language. Of course, the property of emergence does not exclude the possibility that resources for identity work in any given interaction may derive from resources developed in earlier interactions (that is, they may draw on 'structure'—such as ideology, the linguistic system, or the relation between the two).

Although nearly all contemporary linguistic research on identity takes this general perspective at its starting point, it is perhaps easiest to recognize identity as emergent in cases where speakers' language use does not conform with the social category to which they are normatively assigned. Cases of transgender identity and cross-gender performance (Barrett, 1999; Besnier, 2003; Gaudio, 1997; Hall and O'Donovan, 1996; Kulick, 1997; Manalansan, 2003) and ethnic, racial, and national boundary crossing (Bucholtz, 1995, 1999a; Chun, 2001; Cutler, 1999; Hewitt, 1986; Lo, 1999; Piller, 2002; Rampton, 1995; Sweetland, 2002) illustrate in diverse ways that identities as social processes do not precede the semiotic practices that call them into being in specific interactions. Such cases are striking only because they sever the ideologically expected mapping between language and biology or culture; that is, they subvert essentialist preconceptions of linguistic ownership. While the emergent nature of identity is especially stark in cases where a biologically male speaker uses feminine gendered pronouns or a speaker phenotypically classified as nonblack uses African American English, identity is discursively produced even in the most mundane and unremarkable situations.

To illustrate the emergent quality of identity, we offer two examples involving very different groups of speakers. The first focuses on the discourse practices of hijras, a transgender category in India whose members, though predominantly born male, identify as neither men nor women. Hijras typically dress and speak like women, but violate gender norms of appropriate Indian femininity in other ways, such as through the use of obscenity (Hall, 1997). One of the resources available to hijras to distance themselves from masculinity is the linguistic gender system of Hindi, where verbal gender marking is often obligatory. In Example (1), taken from an ethnographic interview with Hall, a hijra we call Sulekha discusses her relationship with her family, who forced her out of the house in her early teens because of her effeminate behavior. Here, she reports the speech of her family members as referring to her in the masculine gender (marked with a superscripted *m* in the transcript), yet when speaking in her own voice, she uses the feminine form to refer to herself (marked with a superscripted *f* in the transcript):

(1)

K: *āpkā parivār kyā soctā hai?*

S: jab ghare nahĩ jātī[f] hũ- jātī[f] hũ to sab samajhte haĩ ki "mar gayā[m], (1.0) khatam ho gayā[m], (1.5) nātā riśtā khatam ho gayā."

K: *acchā. jab āp choṭī thī to āp ke bare me kyā socte the?*

S: kyā soctā log? kuch nahĩ soctā thā log. (0.5) kahtā hai log ki ((lowering voice)) "are, i kyā ho gayā[m]. hijṛā ho gayā[m]. (0.2) mar bhī nahĩ jātā[m] hai, (0.2) are nikal bhī nahĩ jātā[m] hai, are bāp mahtārī kā nām khatam ho gayā."

K: *hameśā bolte the?*

S: hã. (4.0) beizzatī kā ghar ho gayā. "kaise zindagī calegā iskā. mar jātā to acchā rahtā." (2.0) maĩ sab suntī[f] thī[f] apnā nikal gayī[f]. (5.0) jhūṭh kah rahī[f] hũ? (6.0) maĩ jhūṭh nahĩ boltī[f]. (5.0) jahã par bāt gayā to jhūṭh bolkar kyā karũgī[f]? (1.0) hã? (1.0) hamẽ to koī lauṭ āyegā nahĩ. maĩ kaise kah dũ ki nahĩ.

K: *What does your family think?*

S: *When I don't go home–when I don't go[f] everybody thinks, "He died[m]! He's[m] finished! All of our ties [with him] are finished!"*

K: *Oh. But what were they thinking about you when you were small?*

S: *What could people think? People didn't think anything. Or people said ((lowering voice)), "Oh, what has he become[m]? He became[m] a hijra. Why doesn't he just die[m]! Oh, why doesn't he just go away[m]! Oh, the name of his father and mother is finished!"*

K: *They always said that?*

S: *Yes. It became a house of dishonor. [They said,] "How can his life go on? It would have been better if he had just died[m]!" I used[f] to listen[f] to all of that, and then I just ran[f] away. Am I lying[f]? I don't lie[f]. When no one cares what I say anyway, what would I gain[f] by lying? Right? Nobody will take me back anyway, so why should I tell you otherwise?*

For Sulekha, feminine gender marking does not reflect a straightfor-
wardly assigned feminine identity; indeed, as the reported speech of her
relatives makes clear, her gender identity is contested by her family. Under
these circumstances, gender marking becomes a powerful tool used by
Sulekha to constitute herself as feminine in opposition to her family's
perception of her gender. Such identity positioning is therefore occasioned
by the interactional demands of her narrative. It is important to note that
hijras do not use feminine self-reference in an automatic or predetermined
way; in other contexts, hijras alternate between feminine and masculine
forms in referring to themselves and other hijras in order to construct a
variety of rhetorical effects (Hall and O'Donovan, 1996). Though not as
dramatic or as recognizable as this example, a similar process of identity
construction takes place every time a speaker assigns social gender to
another human being. It is the constant iteration of such practices that
cumulatively produce not only each individual's gender identity, but gender itself as a socially meaningful system (Butler, 1990; West and
Zimmerman, 1987).

The second example is taken from the work of Elaine Chun (2001) on
Korean American men's identities. Chun points out that unlike African
Americans, most Asian Americans do not have access to a variety of
English invested with ethnically specific meaning. She argues that for this
reason some of the Asian American men in her study draw on elements of
African American Vernacular English (AAVE) in order to locate them-
selves against racial ideologies that privilege whiteness. This phenomenon
is illustrated in Example (2):

(2) (Chun, 2001: 60)

2368	Jin:	i think white people just don't keep it real and that's why
2369	Dave:	that is = that's true man?
2370	Jin:	cause that's why they always back stabbin like
		my roommate who wasn't gonna pay the last
		month's // rent
2371	JH:	white.
2372	Jin:	he kicks us out [of
2373	Eric:	[the prototypical *whitey*.
2374	Jin:	ye:::ah ma::n?
2375	JH:	no social skills.
2376	Jin:	but that's not true for everyone i don't think.

2377   EC: uh huh
2378   Jin: cause all those <u>ghetto whiteys</u> in my neighborhood
               i think they're cool

The speakers use various elements associated with African American youth language, including idiomatic phrases like *keep it real* (line 2368) and lexical items like *whitey* (lines 2373, 2378), as well as a few emblematic grammatical structures such as the zero copula (*they always back stabbin*, line 2370). None of the participants in this interaction is a fluent speaker of AAVE, and indeed not all participants use AAVE features. But in the context of this discussion—a critique of whiteness—AAVE becomes an effective instrument for rejecting dominant racial ideologies. At the same time, an antiracist Asian American identity emerges in the discourse in alliance with other people of color.

Despite the vast difference in cultural contexts, this example bears a strong resemblance to the hijra example above in that the speakers in both cases appropriate linguistic forms generally understood not to 'belong' to them. Both the use of feminine grammatical gender forms by hijras, who are usually assigned to the male sex at birth, and the use of African American youth style by Korean Americans actively produce new forms of identity through language by disrupting naturalized associations between specific linguistic forms and specific social categories. Yet even these innovative identities should not be understood as ontologically prior to the discourse that calls them forth. While the macro categories of hijra and Korean American have a certain ideological coherence, their actual manifestation in practice is dependent on the interactional demands of the immediate social context. Such interactions therefore highlight what is equally true of even the most predictable and non-innovative identities: that they are only constituted as socially real through discourse, and especially interaction.

THE POSITIONALITY PRINCIPLE

The second principle challenges another widely circulating view of identity, that it is simply a collection of broad social categories. This perspective is found most often in the quantitative social sciences, which correlate social behavior with macro identity categories such as age, gender, and social class. Within sociocultural linguistics, the concern with identities as broader social structures is particularly characteristic of early variationist sociolinguistics (e.g. Labov, 1966) and the sociology of language (see Fishman, 1971, among others). The traditional forms of these approaches have been valuable for documenting large-scale sociolinguistic trends; they are often less effective in capturing the more nuanced and flexible kinds of identity relations that arise in local contexts (but see, e.g. Labov, 1963). This analytic gap points to the importance of ethnography. Linguistic ethnographers have repeatedly demonstrated that language users often orient to local identity categories rather than to the analyst's sociological categories and that the former frequently provide a better empirical account of linguistic practice.

In addition, more recent sociocultural linguistic work has begun to investigate the micro details of identity as it is shaped from moment to moment in interaction. At the most basic level, identity emerges in discourse through the temporary roles and orientations assumed by participants, such as evaluator, joke teller, or engaged listener. Such interactional positions may seem quite different from identity as conventionally understood; however, these temporary roles, no less than larger sociological and ethnographic identity categories, contribute to the formation of subjectivity and intersubjectivity in discourse. On the one hand, the interactional positions that social actors briefly occupy and then abandon as they respond to the contingencies of unfolding discourse may accumulate ideological associations with both large-scale and local categories of identity. On the other, these ideological associations, once forged, may shape who does what and how in interaction, though never in a deterministic fashion.

Our own perspective therefore broadens the traditional referential range of identity to encompass not only more widely recognized constructs of social subjectivity but also local identity categories and transitory interactional positions:

> 2. Identities encompass (a) macro-level demographic categories; (b) local, ethnographically specific cultural positions; and (c) temporary and interactionally specific stances and participant roles.

Examples (3) and (4) illustrate how these different levels of identity emerge in discourse. Both are taken from ethnographic interviews Bucholtz conducted with middle-class European American 17-year-old girls who grew up in the same city and were attending the same California high school. The girls therefore had access to very similar kinds of linguistic resources. Yet they habitually positioned themselves as different kinds of teenagers through their differential use of language. This point could be illustrated through a wide variety of linguistic markers; the one we consider here is the use of innovative quotative forms. Quotative markers introduce represented discourse; some forms may mark nonlinguistic affective expressions as well. The prototypical quotative form is *say*, but *go* has also entered widespread use to perform quotative functions. In more recent years, the form *be like* has been widely adopted by young people in the United States (Blyth et al., 1990; Dailey-O'Cain, 2000). Two of these quotatives are found in Example (3):

(3)

1	Claire:	Then you say the magic word,
2		"I have a tutor." h
3	Mary:	Mm.
4	Christine:	Everyone goes,
5		"O::::h,"
6		and they're all jealous and they're like,
7		"Oh wow,
8		I wish I had a tutor." hh

In addition to these quotative markers, another form has emerged, especially on the West Coast: *be all* (Waksler, 2001). Because of its more recent appearance in youth discourse, it is more semiotically marked than *be like* or the older quotative forms. Whereas in Example (3), Christine uses the well-established quotative markers *go* and *be like*, in Example (4), Josie uses only one quotative form, the innovative *be all*:

(4)

1	Josie:	They would <u>not</u> let me join their club by the way.
2	Mary:	You tried and they woul[dn't let you]?
3	Josie:	[Oh I was all,]
4		"Can I join your club?"
5		<lower volume> {Of course I'd been sitting in the corner laughing at them for the last twenty minutes.}
6		And they're all,
7		"<u>No</u>:,"
8		And I was all,
9		"I don't like you either."

Christine and Josie both index their youth through their use of these innovative quotative markers, but their choice of different markers indexes more local dimensions of their identity. Christine is a self-described nerd, who values intelligence and nonconformity and, unlike cool students, is not interested in pursuing the latest trends, whether in fashion or language; Josie, by contrast, is one of the most popular girls in the school, and her exclusive use of the innovative quotative marker signals her consummate trendiness.[2] These local identities are also relevant to the content of the discourse: Claire and Christine are complaining that they have to pretend to have a tutor in order to avoid explaining their high grades to their less intelligent peers, and Josie is describing her joking attempt to join the high school's Macintosh Computer Club, which is widely recognized as a bastion of nerdiness.

In the analysis of these girls' speech, classification along demographic lines of gender, age, race, and class provides part of the picture, but more can be learned by considering other ways in which these girls position themselves and others subjectively and intersubjectively. First, by viewing the girls as members of a single age cohort, we can recognize the importance of age—specifically youthfulness—as a shared social identity that is expressed through the use of innovative quotative markers. Second, through ethnographically obtained information about these girls' affiliation with contrasting, locally developed social styles at the high school, we can make sense of their divergent quotative choices. Third, scrutiny of the interactional work the speakers are accomplishing reveals how through represented discourse they make negative evaluations of other types of people (and, implicitly, positively evaluate themselves). For example, in lines 4 and 5, Christine's utterance *Everyone goes O::::h* both prosodically and lexically marks the quoted speakers' collective stance of awe and jealousy. But because this utterance is represented discourse, it also signals Christine's orientation of disdain toward her classmates' desire for a tutor and their obliviousness to her deception.

Such examples demonstrate that different kinds of positions typically occur simultaneously in a single interaction. From the perspective of the analyst, it is not a matter of choosing one dimension of identity over others, but of considering multiple facets in order to achieve a more complete understanding of how identity works.

THE INDEXICALITY PRINCIPLE

While the first two principles we have discussed characterize the ontological status of identity, the third principle is concerned with the mechanism whereby identity is constituted. This mechanism, known as indexicality, is fundamental to the way in which linguistic forms are used to construct identity positions. In its most basic sense, an index is a linguistic form that depends on the interactional context for its meaning, such as the first-person pronoun *I* (Silverstein, 1976). More generally, however, the concept of indexicality involves the creation of semiotic links between linguistic forms and social meanings (Ochs, 1992; Silverstein, 1985). In identity formation, indexicality relies heavily on ideological structures, for associations between language and identity are rooted in cultural beliefs and values—that is, ideologies—about the sorts of speakers who (can or should) produce particular sorts of language.

Indexical processes occur at all levels of linguistic structure and use. The third principle outlines some of these different linguistic means whereby identity is discursively produced:

> 3. Identity relations emerge in interaction through several related indexical processes, including: (a) overt mention of identity categories and labels; (b) implicatures and presuppositions regarding one's own or others' identity position; (c) displayed evaluative and epistemic orientations to ongoing talk, as well as interactional footings and participant roles; and (d) the use of linguistic structures and systems that are ideologically associated with specific personas and groups.

The most obvious and direct way that identities can be constituted through talk is the overt introduction of referential identity categories into discourse. Indeed, a focus on social category labels has been a primary method that nonlinguistic researchers have used to approach the question of identity. Researchers in sociocultural linguistics contribute to this line of work a more precise and systematic methodology for understanding labeling and categorization as social action (e.g. McConnell-Ginet, 1989, 2002; Murphy, 1997; Sacks, 1995). The circulation of such categories within ongoing discourse, their explicit or implicit juxtaposition with other categories, and the linguistic elaborations and qualifications they attract (predicates, modifiers, and so on) all provide important information about identity construction. For example, in (1) above, Sulekha quotes her family as condemning her in childhood as a 'hijra', a term that carries an extreme derogatory force in non-hijra Indian society: 'Oh, what has he become? He became a hijra. Why doesn't he just die! . . . Oh, the name of his father and mother is finished!' The term acquires this force through its ideological association with impotence (in fact, *hijra* is often used to mean 'impotent' in everyday discourse). This stands as the ultimate insult within normative Indian family structures, for the widespread belief that hijras are impotent positions them outside of reproductive kinship. In short, it is precisely the invocation of the identity label *hijra* that motivates the quoted speakers' lamentations. A somewhat different labeling process is seen in Example (2), where the racial label *whitey*, also generally understood to be derogatory, takes on different valences within the interaction through the use of contrastive modifiers. While Eric negatively characterizes Jin's roommate as a 'prototypical whitey', Jin describes the 'ghetto whiteys' in his working-class neighborhood as 'cool'. In this interaction, adjectives and predication reorient the social meaning of *whitey* from a fixed racial refer-ence term to an intersubjectively negotiated identity category.

Less direct means of instantiating identities include such pragmatic pro-cesses as implicature and presupposition, both of which require additional inferential work for interpretation. For example, as Anita Liang (1999) has argued, lesbians and gay men who fear reprisal for openly displaying their sexual identity may use implicatures (such as gender-neutral references to lovers) to convey this information to savvy listeners while excluding possibly hostile outgroup members. Indeed, the ability to interpret such implicatures is recognized in gay and lesbian communities with a special term: *gaydar*. A similarly indirect strategy for positioning self or other in discourse is presupposition. In the college rape tribunal hearings analyzed by Susan Ehrlich (2001), for example, the defense exploits presupposi-tion to situate the alleged rape victims as powerful and in sexual control. Repeated references to the attacked women's purported options and choices presuppose that they could have prevented their rapes, thus fram-ing them as agents in contrast to the prosecution's representations of them as passive victims. Here identity is located in the situated social positions of rape survivor versus willing participant.

Recent work on stance—that is, the display of evaluative, affective, and epistemic orientations in discourse—has made explicit the ways in which other dimensions of interaction can be resources for the construction of identity. In his framework for the analysis of stance as both a subjective and an intersubjective phenomenon, John Du Bois (2002) characterizes stance as social action in the following terms: 'I evaluate something, and thereby position myself, and align [or disalign] with you.' Similar concepts have emerged in related fields, including assessment (Goodwin and Goodwin, 1992; Pomerantz, 1984) and epistemic authority (Heritage and Raymond, 2005) in conversation analysis, positioning in both discursive social psychology (Davies and Harré, 1990) and language and gender research (Eckert and McConnell-Ginet, 2003), and evaluation in discourse analysis (Hunston and Thompson, 2000). All these share an analytic focus on the linguistic marking of a speaker's orientation to ongoing talk. A related but somewhat different approach considers the interactional roles speakers and listeners inhabit in conversation, as laid out in Erving Goffman's (1974, 1981) groundbreaking work on footing, participant roles, and participation frameworks.

All of these scholars' insights—and work that builds on them— are productive for the study of identity because they show how even in the most fleeting of interactional moves, speakers position themselves and others as particular kinds of people. Moreover, stances can build up into larger identity categories. In an influential paper, Elinor Ochs (1992) extends the concept of indexicality by arguing that the indexical connection between a given linguistic form and a particular social identity is not direct (see also Ochs, 1993). Rather, linguistic forms that index identity are more basically associated with interactional stances such as forcefulness, uncertainty, and so on, which in turn may come to be associated with particular social categories, such as gender. Within interactional linguistics, Mirka Rauniomaa (2003) has developed Du Bois's (2002) concept of *stance accretion* to capture the way in which stances accumulate into more durable structures of identity. It is important to emphasize that the process of creating indexical ties of this kind is inherently ideological, creating in bottom-up fashion a set of interactional norms for particular social groups. Conversely, in the process of *indexical inversion* described by Miyako Inoue (2004), indexical associations can also be imposed from the top down by cultural authorities such as intellectuals or the media. Such an imposed indexical tie may create ideological expectations among speakers and hence affect linguistic practice.

Example (5), taken from a study of family dinnertime narratives by Elinor Ochs and Carolyn Taylor (1995), illustrates how interactional identities emerge in discourse. The following excerpt is from an interaction between a middle-class European American heterosexual couple. The wife ('Mom') has been telling her husband ('Dad') about her new assistant at work:

(5) (Ochs and Taylor, 1995: 108)

Dad: ((*eating dessert*)) Well – I certainly think that – you're a-
        you know you're a fair bo?ss – You've been working there
        how long?

Mom: fifteen years in June ((*as she scrapes dishes at kitchen sink*))

Dad: fifteen <u>years</u> – and you got a guy ((*turns to look directly at Mom
        as he continues*)) that's been workin there a few <u>weeks</u>? And you
        do (it what) the way <u>he</u> wants.

Mom: hh ((*laughs*))
        (0.6) ((*Dad smiles slightly?, then turns back to eating his dessert*))

Mom: It's not a matter of my doin it the way <u>he: wa:nt</u> – It <u>does</u>
        help in that I'm getting more <u>work</u>? done
        It's just that I'm workin too <u>hard</u>? I don't wanta <u>work</u> so hard

Dad: ((*rolls chair around to face Mom halfway*)) Well – You're the <u>bo:ss</u>
        It's up to you to set the standards . . .

Ochs and Taylor identify a number of interactional roles in such narratives, including protagonist, primary teller, and primary recipient. They also found that the narratives in their sample tended to involve negative evaluation of the protagonist by the primary recipient, a role pair they term *problematizee/ problematizer*. In Example (5), Dad assumes the role of problematizer and assigns Mom the role of problematizee at several points. Moreover, the authors discovered that the gendered distribution of interactional roles in this example was a general feature of other interactions they recorded between demographically similar married couples. In this way, gendered identities are built not only locally within couples, but more broadly across (some kinds of) couples. Through the repetition of such processes, the interactional identities produced via stance taking accrue into more enduring identities like gender, as well as forming ideologies of gender-appropriate interactional practice.[3]

A somewhat related set of insights comes from the concept of style in variationist sociolinguistics. This term traditionally refers to intra-speaker variation in language use (Labov, 1972), but more contemporary approaches (Bucholtz, 1999a, 1999b; California Style Collective, 1993; Eckert, 2000; Eckert and Rickford, 2001; Mendoza-Denton, forthcoming; Schilling-Estes, 2004), along with earlier work by Bell (1984) and Coupland (1980), understand style as a repertoire of linguistic forms associated with personas or identities. Whereas scholars concerned with stance concentrate on conversational acts such as evaluative expressions, sociolinguists of style typically look instead to linguistic structures below the discursive level, such as grammar, phonology, and lexis.[4] In an indexical process similar to what both Ochs and Rauniomaa describe for stance, these features become tied to styles and hence to identity through habitual practice (Bourdieu, 1977, [1972] 1978). Thus through their repeated choice of one quotative form over another in interactions such as Examples (3) and (4) earlier, teenagers in California display their identity as nerdy or popular. As these examples show, one of the important insights of the style literature is that the social meanings of style often require ethnographic investigation to uncover groups that may seem homogeneous through a wider analytic lens, but become sharply differentiated when ethnographic details are brought into close focus.

In addition to micro-level linguistic structures like stance markers and style features, entire linguistic systems such as languages and dialects may also be indexically tied to identity categories. This phenomenon—long the mainstay of a wide range of sociocultural linguistic scholarship—has been especially well theorized in the literature on language, nationalism, and ideology (e.g. Gal and Irvine, 1995; see also contributions to Kroskrity, 2000; Schieffelin et al., 1998). In addition, work on language choice has also begun to appear in the emerging field of language and globalization. Given the vast scale of such phenomena as nationalism and globalization, much of the research on these issues is not interactional in its approach. However, some current studies, especially on the latter topic (e.g. Besnier, 2004; Hall, 2003; Park, 2004), consider how largescale social processes such as globalization shape identity in interaction. Example (6) is taken from one such study, carried out by Niko Besnier (2004) in Tonga. The interaction takes place between a Tongan seller and customer at a second-hand market, or *fea*:

(6) (Besnier, 2004: 29–30)
Seller: *Sai ia kia koe, Sōnia.*
                       "Looks good on you, Sōnia."

Customer:	Yeah- if it fits =
Seller:	((ignoring customer's contingency)) =
	Ni::ce. (10.0)
	What size is it? (2.0)
Customer:	Eight. (3.0)
Seller:	Ohh. (4.0) Too small. (2.0)
	'E hao 'ia Mālia. (2.0) 'Ia me'a. (2.0)
	"It'll fit Mālia. I mean, what's-her-name."
	It's might fit you, cuz it looks big!
Customer:	'Io?
	"Yes?"
Seller:	Yeah! (2.0) The waist, look!
Customer:	I know-
Seller:	I think it's one of those one that it has to show
	the bellybutton.
Customer:	No way!
Seller:	Aaaha-ha-haa!
Customer:	.Haa-ha-hah!
Seller:	That's the in-thing in New Zealand now. Even my
	kids say,
	"Mummy, see, it has to show the b-!" Huh! I say,
	"No::::,no::!" Ahahahuh-hh! Cuz that's the look now!

What is most striking about this exchange is the use of English rather than Tongan for much of the interaction. Besnier demonstrates that this language choice constructs the speakers as modern and cosmopolitan. He notes that the seller also uses a markedly New Zealand pronunciation of certain words by centralizing the vowel [i] as [ə], a highly local New Zealand speech style that further displays her cosmopolitan identity. (The knowledgeable epistemic stance the seller takes toward current fashion similarly undergirds this identity project.) In such situations, we vividly see how the vast workings of global processes, and the languages carried with them, settle into the everyday lives of ordinary people around the world.

The range of phenomena discussed in this section attests to the wealth of linguistic resources that contribute to the production of identity positions. Disparate indexical processes of labeling, implicature, stance taking, style marking, and code choice work to construct identities, both micro and macro, as well as those somewhere in between. By considering identity formation at multiple indexical levels rather than focusing on only one, we can assemble a much richer portrait of subjectivity and intersubjectivity as they are constituted in interaction.

THE RELATIONALITY PRINCIPLE

The first three principles we have discussed focus on the emergent, positional, and indexical aspects of identity and its production. Building on these points, the fourth principle emphasizes identity as a relational phenomenon. In calling attention to relationality, we have two aims: first, to underscore the point that identities are never autonomous or independent but always acquire social meaning in relation to other available identity positions and other social actors; and second, to call into question the widespread but oversimplified view of identity relations as revolving around a single axis: sameness and difference. The principle we propose here suggests a much broader range of relations that are forged through identity processes:

> 4. Identities are intersubjectively constructed through several, often overlapping, complementary relations, including similarity/difference, genuineness/artifice, and authority/delegitimacy.

We have described these relations at length elsewhere as what we have termed *tactics of intersubjectivity* (Bucholtz and Hall, 2004a, 2004b); we briefly summarize those discussions here. The list of identity relations we outline in this and our earlier work is not intended to be exhaustive but rather suggestive of the different dimensions of relationality created through identity construction. In addition, it is important to note that although we separate the concepts for purposes of exposition we do not view them as mutually exclusive; indeed, since these are relational processes two or more typically work in conjunction with one another.[5]

Adequation and distinction

The first two complementary identity relations we describe, similarity and difference, are also the most widely discussed in social-scientific research on identity. To highlight the ways we depart from traditional views of these relations, we use the terms *adequation* and *distinction*.

The term *adequation* emphasizes the fact that in order for groups or individuals to be positioned as alike, they need not—and in any case cannot—be identical, but must merely be understood as sufficiently similar for current interactional purposes. Thus, differences irrelevant or damaging to ongoing efforts to adequate two people or groups will be downplayed, and similarities viewed as salient to and supportive of the immediate project of identity work will be foregrounded. The relation of adequation can be seen earlier in Examples (1) and (2). In Example (1), Sulekha's use of feminine gender marking reflects neither her view of herself as a woman nor her attempt to be so viewed. Instead, it allows her to claim just enough of the semiotic trappings of femininity to produce herself as a hijra in an interaction in which—by her own report—the gendered nature of such an identity is explicitly contested. Likewise, in Example (2), when Jin uses the grammatical and lexical resources of African American youth language, he positions himself not as black but as both nonwhite and as antagonistic to white racism, and hence as sufficiently similar to African Americans to make common cause with them.

A rather different example of adequation comes from unpublished work by Adam Hodges (n.d.), who investigates the Bush administration's rhetorical strategies to gain the American public's support for the war the United States eventually waged against Iraq in 2003. In his critical discourse analysis of a speech given by President George W. Bush in Cincinnati in October 2002, Hodges finds that Bush used the relation of adequation to effectively create an association in listeners' minds between President Saddam Hussein of Iraq and the terrorist network Al Qaeda, which claimed responsibility for the attack on the World Trade Center and the Pentagon on September 11, 2001. Example (7) is taken from Bush's speech:

(7) (Hodges ms.)
1   the attacks of September the 11th
2   showed our country that vast oceans
3   no longer protect us from danger
4   before that tragic date
5   we had only hints of al Qaeda's plans
6   and designs
7   today in Iraq
8   we see a threat whose outlines
9   are far more clearly defined
10   and whose consequences

11   could be far more deadly
12   Saddam Hussein's actions have put us on notice
13   and there is no refuge
14   from our responsibilities

Hodges notes that the repeated juxtaposition of the names *Al Qaeda* and *Saddam Hussein* in this and other speeches itself establishes a discursive ground for the production of adequation between the two entities. Moreover, the framing of both of them as morally and politically equivalent—for instance, as variously a 'danger' (line 3) or a 'threat' (line 8)—further adequates Al Qaeda with the Iraqi government as represented in the person of Saddam Hussein; indeed, Bush suggests that the primary difference between these two menacing entities is one of degree, not kind. The crudeness of such rhetorical strategies offers an especially extreme example of adequation by demonstrating how speakers—and here, by extension, entire governments—position not themselves but others as sufficiently similar for a given purpose, such as identifying a target for military attack.

The counterpart of adequation, distinction, focuses on the identity relation of differentiation.[6] The overwhelming majority of sociocultural linguistic research on identity has emphasized this relation, both because social differentiation is a highly visible process and because language is an especially potent resource for producing it in a variety of ways. Just as adequation relies on the suppression of social differences that might disrupt a seamless representation of similarity, distinction depends on the suppression of similarities that might undermine the construction of difference.

Because distinction is such a familiar identity relation, we provide only a brief illustration of how it operates. While processes of social differentiation may be found at some level in all of the examples given earlier, we return here to Example (6), the exchange in the Tongan marketplace. This interaction offers a clear instance of adequation with modern English-speaking cosmopolitanism. Moreover, by means of some of the same resources, it produces distinction as well. Besnier points out that the seller's use of centralized New Zealand-like vowels creates a relation of distinction with certain other Tongans: 'She also distances herself from Tongan-accented English (with some difficulty at the level of syntax) and all that it represents in the New Zealand context, including the stigma of being an underclass "Islander," whose vowels are never centralized' (2004: 32). In this example, even a linguistically slight similarity to the transna-

tional prestige variety of English is sufficient to align this Tongan seller
of second-hand western clothes with modernity and simultaneously to
separate her from a local lower-class identity.

Authentication and denaturalization

The second pair of relations, *authentication* and *denaturalization*, are the
processes by which speakers make claims to realness and artifice, respec-
tively. While both relations have to do with authenticity, the first focuses
on the ways in which identities are discursively verified and the second on
how assumptions regarding the seamlessness of identity can be disrupted.
Like the focus on distinction, a concern with authenticity—that is, what
sorts of language and language users count as 'genuine' for a given purpose—has pervaded the sociocultural linguistic literature, although ana-
lysts have not always separated their own assumptions about authenticity
from those of the speakers they study (Bucholtz, 2003). We call attention
not to authenticity as an inherent essence, but to authentication as a social
process played out in discourse. The interaction we have selected to illustrate this phenomenon is taken from Bauman's (1992) analysis of Icelandic
legends about the *kraftaskáld*, a poet thought to have magical powers. In
his analysis of this narrative genre as polyvocalic and dynamic, Bauman
points to the opening and closing of the narrative as sites where the narrator authenticates not only his story, but also himself as the teller of it:

(8) (Bauman, 1992: 130–31)

HÖE	1	*Voru nokkrir fleiri. . . voru fleiri kraftaskáld talin* *þarna í Skagafirði?* Were any others. . . were others reputed to be kraftaskálds in Skagafjord?
JN	2	*Ég man að nú ekki núna í augnabliki,* I don't remember that now, just now at the moment,
	3	*en eitt ég nú sagt þér ef. . . ef þú koerir þig um.* but I can tell you now if. . . if you care (to hear it).
	4	*það er nú ekki beint úr Skagafirði,* It is, now, not exactly from Skagafjord,
	5	*og þó, það er í sambandi við Gudrúnu,* although it is connected with Gudrún,
	6	*dóttur séra Páls skálda í Vestmannaeyjum.* daughter of Reverend Páll the Poet in the Westman Islands.

7 *Páll skáldi þótti nú kraftaskáld,*
 Páll the Poet was thought, now, to be a kraftaskáld
[. . .]
25 *Nú Gudrún dottir hans sagði föður minum þessa sögu.*
 Now Gudrún, his daughter, told my father this story.

Bauman notes that the detailing of the chain of narration whereby the teller heard the tale also provides evidence for his right to tell it, thus authenticating both the narrative and his interactional identity as its narrator. Bauman describes this process, which he terms *traditionalization*, as an 'act of authentication akin to the art or antique dealer's authentication of an object by tracing its provenience' (1992: 137). This useful metaphor highlights the temporal dimension of authentication, which often relies on a claimed historical tie to a venerated past.

In denaturalization, by contrast, such claims to the inevitability or inherent rightness of identities is subverted. What is called attention to instead is the ways in which identity is crafted, fragmented, problematic, or false. Such aspects often emerge most clearly in parodic performance and in some displays of hybrid identity (e.g. Bucholtz, 1995; Jaffe, 2000; Woolard, 1998), but they may also appear whenever an identity violates ideological expectations (e.g. Barrett, 1999; Rampton, 1995).

As an example of denaturalization, we turn to work by Benjamin Bailey (2000) on just such an identity: that of Dominican Americans. Bailey points out that in the US racial context, Dominican Americans' own language-based identities as Hispanic (or 'Spanish') are displaced by ideologically motivated perceptions of their identity as African American or black based on their phenotype. In Example (9), two Dominican American teenage boys in a Rhode Island high school, Wilson and JB, jokingly conspire against a Southeast Asian American classmate, Pam, to convince her that Wilson is black, not Spanish:

(9) (Bailey, 2000: 571)
(Wilson has just finished explaining to JB, in Spanish, the function of the wireless microphone he is wearing.)

Wilson: ((singing)) Angie Pelham is a weird person (2.5)
Wilson: *Me estoy miando yo,'mano.* ['I have to piss, man.'] (2.0)
JB: (   ) (2.0)

Pam:	Yo, the first time I saw you, I never thought you were Spanish. (.5)
Wilson:	[Who?]
JB:	[(He's)] Black.
Pam:	I never-
Wilson:	Cause I'm Black.
JB:	( )
Wilson:	Cause I'm Black.
Pam:	No
JB:	His father [is Black], her mother is-, his mother is uh-
Wilson:	[I'm Black]
Pam:	(Can he) speak Spanish?
JB:	No
Wilson:	Cause I was- [I was]
Pam:	[Yeah!]
JB:	So why (d- ?)
Wilson:	No, no seriously, I'm Black and I was raised in the Dominican Republic. (.5)
Wilson:	For real.
Pam:	Your mother's Black?
Wilson:	My mom? No, my father.
Pam:	Your father's Black, your [mother's Spanish?]
Wilson:	[My mom's Spanish]
JB:	His mom is Black- and she's Spanish.
Wilson:	Is mix(ed)
JB:	His mom was born over here.
	(2.0) ((Wilson smiles at Pam and throws a piece of paper at her))
JB:	Wilson, don't t(h)row anything to her.
Wilson:	*Excúsame, se me olvidó, que es la heva tuya* ['Sorry, I forgot that she is your girlfriend.']
JB:	*Cállate, todavía no.* ['Be quiet, not yet!']
Pam:	English!
JB:	English, yeah!
Wilson:	I said I'm sorry.
JB:	He can't speak Spanish.
Pam:	I saw you were talking to him ( )

Wilson: I understand, but I don't speak everything.
                (2.2) ((Wilson smiles broadly at Pam))
JB: I'm teaching him. (5.5)
Wilson: *¿Qué tú vas (a) hacer en tu casa hoy, loco?* ((slaps JB
                on the back))
                ['What are you going to do at your house today, man?']

Bailey's analysis shows that in this interaction Wilson and JB collab-
oratively construct an absurd and implausible (to them) representation of
Wilson's ethnic identity as black and non-Spanish-speaking. By the end
of the excerpt, Wilson blatantly violates his own immediately previous
identity claims by speaking in fluent Spanish, thereby unmasking himself as not 'really' black according to the Dominican cultural framework.
This jointly produced prank undermines essentialized assumptions that
black skin necessarily entails a black identity and thus denaturalizes the
dominant racial paradigm in the United States. In both Examples (7) and
(8), then, what is at stake, in very different ways, is what counts as a 'real'
identity. But where the Icelandic narrator puts forth his identity bona fides
in order to produce himself as an authentic and legitimate teller of the
kraftaskáld tale, Wilson knowingly offers false credentials only to withdraw
them later, and thus unsettles the naturalized links between phenotype
and ethnic identity.

Authorization and illegitimation

The final pair of intersubjective relations that we describe considers the
structural and institutional aspects of identity formation. The first of
these, authorization, involves the affirmation or imposition of an identity through structures of institutionalized power and ideology, whether
local or translocal. The counterpart of authorization, illegitimation,
addresses the ways in which identities are dismissed, censored, or simply
ignored by these same structures. To illustrate authorization, we return
to Bush's speech leading up to the Iraq war (Example 7). Throughout his
speech, Bush uses the first-person plural pronoun to conflate the Bush
Administration with the United States as a whole. Drawing on the shared
national identity that emerged in the wake of the September 11 attacks,
Bush invokes 'our country' at the beginning of the passage, but then uses
the same pronoun to refer to the specialized knowledge available only to

members of his Administration (and later revealed to be false). By the end
of this excerpt, 'our responsibilities' are imposed not only on Bush and
his advisors but on the American people as well. This sort of conflation is
reinforced by Bush's ability as President to metonymically position himself
as speaking on behalf of the nation. Just as he authoritatively adequates
Saddam Hussein to Al Qaeda, he likewise uses his presidential authority
to create an identification of a shared moral stance between himself and
the American public. (The effectiveness of such strategies, Hodges notes,
can be seen in the strong expressions of public support for Bush's position
after this speech.)

Structures of authority need not be as all-encompassing as in this
situation. In our final example, we demonstrate how interactional dynamics may shore up ideological structures even in the absence of a locatable
powerful authority. This is the process that Antonio Gramsci (1971)
calls *hegemony*. Example (10) comes from Joseph Park's (2004) multisited
investigation of ideologies of English in Korea. Park shows that these
ideologies permeate ordinary interactions in a variety of contexts. Example
(10) illustrates one of these ideologies: that it is, in some sense, culturally
inappropriate or unKorean to speak English fluently. The example takes
place among Korean nationals attending graduate school in the United
States. The speakers jointly mock a nonpresent Korean friend, who has
left a message on one participant's answering machine in which he uses an
Americanized pronunciation of the word *Denver*:

(10) (from Park, 2004; slightly simplified transcript)

24	Hyeju:	<@[/tɛnvʌ=r/]-ga eodi-ya?@>
		Denver-SUB where-IE
		"Where is Denver ([tɛnvʌ=r])?"
25	Junho:	/tɛnvʊ=r/-e iss-[<@eo@>]@
		Denver-LOC exist-IE
		"I'm in Denver ([tɛnvʌ=r])."
26	Hyeju:	/tɛn]bʌ/ ani-gu /tɛnvʌ=r/-ga eodi-ya
		<@ileohge@>
		Denver NEG-CONN Denver-SUB
		where-IE like:this
		"Where is Denver ([tɛnvʌ=r]), not
		Denver ([tɛnbʌ])?" Something like that.
27	All:	@@@@

28	Junho:	/tɛnvʊ=r/-eseo mweo hae-ss-eulkka @@@
		Denver-LOC what do-PST-IR
		What did he do in Denver ([tɛnvʊ=r])?
29	All:	@@@@@@

Here the repeated iterations of the forms [tɛnvʌr] and [tɛnvʊr] with exaggerated lengthening of the second syllable, coupled with frequent laughter (marked by @), signal the speakers' sense that such a pronunciation is inappropriate for a Korean speaker. In line 26, Hyeju contrasts this unacceptably American pronunciation with the usual Korean realization of the word, [tɛnbʌ]. These speakers draw on a shared national language ideology of Koreanness to illegitimate the inappropriately Americanized identity that, in their view, their friend's pronunciation projects.

The tactics of intersubjectivity outlined here not only call attention to the intersubjective basis of identity, but also provide a sense of the diverse ways that relationality works through discourse. Relationality operates at many levels. As many sociocultural linguists have argued, including several whose work is cited earlier, even genres traditionally thought of as monologic are fundamentally interactional. Whether one's interlocutor is a lower-class Tongan woman or the entire world, the earlier examples show that identities emerge only in relation to other identities within the contingent framework of interaction.

THE PARTIALNESS PRINCIPLE

The final principle draws from voluminous literature in cultural anthropology and feminist theory over the past two decades that has challenged the analytic drive to represent forms of social life as internally coherent. This challenge, inspired by the postmodern critique of the totalizing master narratives characteristic of previous generations, surfaces in ethnography in the realization that all representations of culture are necessarily 'partial accounts' (Clifford and Marcus, 1986). This idea has long been central to feminist analysis—as well as to the early work of female ethnographers who predated the emergence of second-wave feminism in the 1970s—in which there is an ethical commitment to recognizing the situatedness and partialness of any claim to knowledge (see Behar and Gordon, 1995; Visweswaran, 1994). The feminist commitment to explicitly positioning oneself as a researcher rather than effacing one's presence in the research process, a practice which echoes the politics of location in reflexive ethnography, has exposed the fact that reality itself is intersubjec-tive in nature, constructed through the particulars of self and other in any localized encounter. This idea fits well with postmodern theorizings of identity as fractured and discontinuous, for as anthropologist Kamala Visweswaran has noted, 'Identities are constituted by context and are themselves asserted as partial accounts' (1994: 41).

Whereas the critique of ethnography has been most interested in the partialness construed by one kind of identity relation – that of researcher and subject – our fifth principle attempts to capture not only this dynamic, but the entire multitude of ways in which identity exceeds the individual self. Because identity is inherently relational, it will always be partial, produced through contextually situated and ideologically informed configurations of self and other. Even seemingly coherent displays of iden-tity, such as those that pose as deliberate and intentional, are reliant on both interactional and ideological constraints for their articulation:

5. Any given construction of identity may be in part deliberate and intentional, in part habitual and hence often less than fully conscious, in part an outcome of interactional negotiation and contestation, in part an outcome of others' perceptions and repre-sentations, and in part an effect of larger ideological processes and material structures that may become relevant to interaction. It is therefore constantly shifting both as interaction unfolds and across discourse contexts.

Particular kinds of analysis will often bring to the forefront one of these aspects over others. However, the rich possibilities of the broad interdisciplinary research we include under the rubric of sociocultural linguistics are most fully realized when multiple dimensions of identity are considered in a single analysis or when complementary analyses are brought together.

The principle stated above helps to resolve a central and longstanding issue regarding research on identity: the extent to which it is understood as relying on agency. From the perspective of an interactional approach to identity, the role of agency becomes problematic only when it is concep-tualized as located within an individual rational subject who consciously authors his identity without structural constraints. (Our gendered pro-noun choice here is quite deliberate and corresponds to the fact that male

subjectivity was taken as unmarked by many scholars in earlier generations.) Numerous strands of social theory from Marxism to poststructural-
ism have rightly critiqued this notion of agency, but the litany of dubious
qualities associated with the autonomous subject now functions more as
caricature than critique of how agency is currently understood. Indeed,
current researchers, particularly within sociocultural linguistics, have
found ways of theorizing agency that circumvent the dangers identified by
critics while exploiting its utility for work on identity. Sociocultural linguists are generally not concerned with calibrating the degree of autonomy
or intentionality in any given act; rather, agency is more productively
viewed as the accomplishment of social action (cf. Ahearn, 2001). This way
of thinking about agency is vital to any discipline that wants to consider
the full complexity of social subjects alongside the larger power structures
that constrain them. But it is especially important to sociocultural linguistics, for the very use of language is itself an act of agency (Duranti, 2004).
Under this definition, identity is one kind of social action that agency
can accomplish.

Such a definition of agency does not require that social action be
intentional, but it allows for that possibility; habitual actions accom-
plished below the level of conscious awareness act upon the world no less
than those carried out deliberately. Likewise, agency may be the result
of individual action, but it may also be distributed among several social
actors and hence intersubjective. The phenomenon of what could be called
distributed agency, though not as well documented as that of distributed
cognition (Hutchins, 1995), has begun to receive attention in some areas
of sociocultural linguistics, often under the label of *joint activity* or *co-con-
struction* (e.g. Eckert and McConnell-Ginet, 1992; C. Goodwin, 1995; M.
Goodwin, 1990; Ochs and Capps, 2001). Finally, agency may be ascribed
through the perceptions and representations of others or assigned through
ideologies and social structures. As we have emphasized throughout this
article, it is not a matter of choosing one of these aspects of identity over
others, but of considering how some or all of them may potentially work
with and against one another in discourse.

The interactional view that we take here has the added benefit of
undoing the false dichotomy between structure and agency that has long
plagued social theory (see discussion in Ahearn, 2001). On the one hand,
it is only through discursive interaction that large-scale social structures
come into being; on the other hand, even the most mundane of everyday

conversations are impinged upon by ideological and material constructs that produce relations of power. Thus both structure and agency are intertwined as components of micro as well as macro articulations of identity.

CONCLUSION

Different research traditions within sociocultural linguistics have particular strengths in analyzing the varied dimensions of identity outlined in this article. The method of analysis selected by the researcher makes salient which aspect of identity comes into view, and such 'partial accounts' contribute to the broader understanding of identity that we advocate here. Although these lines of research have often remained separate from one another, the combination of their diverse theoretical and methodological strengths—including the microanalysis of conversation, the macroanalysis of ideological processes, the quantitative and qualitative analysis of linguistic structures, and the ethnographic focus on local cultural practices and social groupings—calls attention to the fact that identity in all its complexity can never be contained within a single analysis. For this reason, it is necessary to conceive of sociocultural linguistics broadly and inclusively.

The five principles proposed here—Emergence, Positionality, Indexicality, Relationality, and Partialness—represent the varied ways in which different kinds of scholars currently approach the question of identity. Even researchers whose primary goals lie elsewhere can contribute to this project by providing sophisticated conceptualizations of how human dynamics unfold in discourse, along with rigorous analytic tools for discovering how such processes work. While identity has been a widely circulating notion in sociocultural linguistic research for some time, few scholars have explicitly theorized the concept. The present article offers one way of understanding this body of work by anchoring identity in interaction. By positing, in keeping with recent scholarship, that identity is emergent in discourse and does not precede it, we are able to locate identity as an intersubjectively achieved social and cultural phenomenon. This discursive approach further allows us to incorporate within identity not only the broad sociological categories most commonly associated with the concept, but also more local positionings, both ethnographic and interactional. The linguistic resources that indexically produce identity at all these levels are therefore necessarily broad and flexible, including labels, implicatures, stances, styles, and entire languages and varieties. Because these tools are put to use in interaction, the process of identity construction does not reside within the individual but in intersubjective relations of sameness and difference, realness and fakeness, power and disempowerment. Finally, by theorizing agency as a broader phenomenon than simply individualistic and deliberate action, we are able to call attention to the myriad ways that identity comes into being, from habitual practice to interactional negotiation to representations and ideologies.

It is no overstatement to assert that the age of identity is upon us, not only in sociocultural linguistics but also in the human and social sciences more generally. Scholars of language use are particularly well equipped to provide an empirically viable account of the complexities of identity as a social, cultural, and—most fundamentally—interactional phenomenon. The recognition of the loose coalition of approaches that we call sociocultural linguistics is a necessary step in advancing this goal, for it is only by understanding our diverse theories and methods as complementary, not competing, that we can meaningfully interpret this crucial dimension of contemporary social life.

ACKNOWLEDGEMENTS

We are grateful to the many audiences and readers who have provided feedback at various stages in the development of this project, and particularly to Dick Bauman, Niko Besnier, Elaine Chun, Barbara Fox, Barbara Johnstone, and Sally McConnell-Ginet for suggestions and encouragement. Special thanks are also due to Sandro Duranti for incisive comments as well as for his original invitation to us to present our joint work at the UCLA symposium Theories and Models of Language, Interaction, and Culture, which spurred us to think more deeply about the interactional grounding of identity. Naturally, we alone are responsible for any remaining weaknesses.

NOTES

1. The term *sociolinguistics* sometimes carries this referential range, but for many scholars it has a narrower reference. *Sociocultural linguistics* has the virtue of being less encumbered with a particular history of use.

2. In other parts of the country, these markers may have very different—indeed, reversed—semiotic valences. Thus, Maryam Bakht-Rofheart (2004) has shown that at one Long Island high school a group that self-identifies as the 'Intellectual Elite' and that is identified by others as nerds rejected the use of *be like* as undesirably trendy and embraced *be all* as a form that lacked such associations.

3. It is important to note that interactional roles such as problematizer/problematizee (or primary storyteller or recipient) are not merely the building blocks of more persistent forms of identity such as gender; rather, they are situational identities in their own right—that is, they serve to socially position speakers and hearers.

4. Penelope Eckert (2000, 2004), for instance, links the realization of vowel quality to discourse topics and interactional goals (e.g. 'doing drama').

5. Indeed, in some situations the same person can enact both dimensions of a contrastive identity pairing, especially in performance contexts (e.g. Pagliai and Farr, 2000).

6. We take the term *distinction* from Pierre Bourdieu (1984), whose own conceptualization of it is concerned with the production of social-class difference by members of the bourgeoisie. We broaden its reference to include any process of social differentiation.

REFERENCES

Ahearn, L. (2001) 'Language and Agency', *Annual Review of Anthropology* 30: 109-37.

Antaki, C. and Widdicombe, S. (eds) (1998) *Identities in Talk*. London: Sage.

Aronsson, K. (1998) 'Identity-in-Interaction and Social Choreography', *Research on Language and Social Interaction* 31(1): 75-89.

Auer, P. (ed.) (1998) *Code-Switching in Conversation: Language, Interaction, and Identity*. London: Routledge.

Austin, J.L. (1962) *How to Do Things with Words*. Cambridge, MA: Harvard University Press.

Bailey, B. (2000) 'Language and Negotiation of Ethnic/Racial Identity among Dominican Americans', *Language in Society* 29(4): 555-82.

Bakht-Rofheart, M. (2004) 'Not So Elite Anymore: Shifting Ideologies and Language Choice in a Long Island Friendship Cohort', paper presented at the third International Gender and Language Association Conference, Cornell University, New York.

Bakhtin, M.M. (1981) *The Dialogic Imagination*. Austin: University of Texas Press.

Barrett, R. (1999) 'Indexing Polyphonous Identity in the Speech of African American Drag Queens', in M. Bucholtz, A.C. Liang and L.A. Sutton (eds) *Reinventing Identities: The Gendered Self in Discourse*, pp. 313–31. New York: Oxford University Press.

Bauman, R. (1977) 'Verbal Art as Performance', in *Verbal Art as Performance*, pp. 3–58. Prospect Heights, IL: Waveland Press.

Bauman, R. (1992) 'Contextualization, Tradition, and the Dialogue of Genres: Icelandic Legends of the *Kraftaskáld*', in A. Duranti and C. Goodwin (eds) *Rethinking Context: Language as an Interactive Phenomenon*, pp. 125–45. Cambridge: Cambridge University Press.

Bauman, R. and Briggs, C.L. (1990) 'Poetics and Performance as Critical Perspectives on Language and Social Life', *Annual Review of Anthropology* 19: 59–88.

Behar, R. and Gordon, D.A. (eds) (1995) *Women Writing Culture*. Berkeley: University of California Press.

Bell, A. (1984) 'Language Style as Audience Design', *Language in Society* 13: 145–204.

Besnier, N. (2003) 'Crossing Gender, Mixing Languages: The Linguistic Construction of Transgenderism in Tonga,' in J. Holmes and M. Meyerhoff (eds) *The Handbook of Language and Gender*, pp. 279–301. Oxford: Blackwell.

Besnier, N. (2004) 'Consumption and Cosmopolitanism: Practicing Modernity at the Secondhand Marketplace in Nuku'alofa, Tonga', *Anthropological Quarterly* 77(1): 7–45.

Blyth, C., Recktenwald, S. and Wang, J. (1990) 'I'm Like, "Say What?!": A New Quotative in American Oral Narrative', *American Speech* 65(3): 215–27.

Bourdieu, P. (1977) 'The Economics of Linguistic Exchanges', *Social Science Information* 16(6): 645–68.

Bourdieu, P. ([1972] 1978) *Outline of a Theory of Practice*. Trans. R. Nice. Cambridge: Cambridge University Press.

Bourdieu, P. (1984) *Distinction: A Social Critique of the Judgment of Taste*. Cambridge, MA: Harvard University Press.

Briggs, C.L. (1988) *Competence in Performance: The Creativity of Tradition in Mexicano Verbal Art*. Philadelphia: University of Pennsylvania Press.

Bucholtz, M. (1995) 'From Mulatta to Mestiza: Passing and the Linguistic Reshaping of Ethnic Identity', in K. Hall and M. Bucholtz (eds) *Gender Articulated: Language and the Socially Constructed Self*, pp. 351–73. New York: Routledge.

Bucholtz, M. (1999a) 'You da Man: Narrating the Racial Other in the Linguistic Production of White Masculinity', *Journal of Sociolinguistics* 3(4): 443–60.

Bucholtz, M. (1999b) '"Why Be Normal?": Language and Identity Practices in a Community of Nerd Girls', *Language in Society* 28(2): 203–23.

Bucholtz, M. (2003) 'Sociolinguistic Nostalgia and the Authentication of Identity', *Journal of Sociolinguistics* 7(3): 398–416.

Bucholtz, M. and Hall, K. (2004a) 'Language and Identity', in A. Duranti (ed.) *A Companion to Linguistic Anthropology*, pp. 369–94. Malden, MA: Blackwell.

Bucholtz, M. and Hall, K. (2004b) 'Theorizing Identity in Language and Sexuality Research', *Language in Society* 33(4): 501–47.

Butler, J. (1990) *Gender Trouble: Feminism and the Subversion of Identity*. New York: Routledge.

Bybee, J. and Hopper, P. (eds) (2001) *Frequency and the Emergence of Linguistic Structure*. Amsterdam: John Benjamins.

California Style Collective (1993) 'Personal and Group Style', paper presented at the annual meeting of the Conference on New Ways of Analyzing Variation, Ottawa.

Cameron, D. (1997) 'Performing Gender Identity: Young Men's Talk and the Construction of Heterosexual Masculinity', in S. Johnson and U.H. Meinhof (eds) *Language and Masculinity*, pp. 47–64. Oxford: Basil Blackwell.

Chun, E.W. (2001) 'The Construction of White, Black, and Korean American Identities through African American Vernacular English', *Journal of Linguistic Anthropology* 11(1): 52–64.

Clifford, J. and Marcus, G.E. (eds) (1986) *Writing Culture: The Poetics and Politics of Ethnography*. Berkeley: University of California Press.

Coupland, N. (1980) 'Style-Shifting in a Cardiff Work-Setting', *Language in Society* 9(1): 1–12.

Cutler, C.A. (1999) 'Yorkville Crossing: White Teens, Hip Hop, and African American English', *Journal of Sociolinguistics* 3(4): 428–42.

Dailey-O'Cain, J. (2000) 'The Sociolinguistic Distribution of and Attitudes toward Focuser *Like* and Quotative *Like*', *Journal of Sociolinguistics* 4(1): 60–80.

Davies, B. and Harré, R. (1990) 'Positioning: The Discursive Production of Selves', *Journal for the Theory of Social Behaviour* 20(1): 43–63.

Du Bois, J.W. (2002) 'Stance and Consequence', paper presented at the annual meeting of the American Anthropological Association, New Orleans.

Duranti, A. (2004) 'Agency in Language', in A. Duranti (ed.) *A Companion to Linguistic Anthropology*. Malden, MA: Blackwell.

Eckert, P. (2000) *Language Variation as Social Practice*. Oxford: Basil Blackwell.

Eckert, P. (2004) 'Sound Change and Gendered Personae on the Preadolescent Social Market', paper presented at the third International Gender and Language Association Conference, Cornell University, New York.

Eckert, P. and McConnell-Ginet, S. (1992) 'Think Practically and Look Locally: Language and Gender as Community-Based Practice', *Annual Review of Anthropology* 21: 461–90.

Eckert, P. and McConnell-Ginet, S. (2003) *Language and Gender*. Cambridge: Cambridge University Press.

Eckert, P. and Rickford, J.R. (eds) (2001) *Style and Sociolinguistic Variation*. Cambridge: Cambridge University Press.

Ehrlich, S. (2001) *Representing Rape: Language and Sexual Consent*. New York: Routledge.

Fenstermaker, S. and West, C. (eds) (2002) *Doing Gender, Doing Difference: Social Inequality, Power, and Resistance*. New York: Routledge.

Fishman, J.A. (ed.) (1971) *Advances in the Sociology of Language*. 2 vols. The Hague: Mouton.

Ford, C.E., Fox, B.A. and Thompson, S.A. (eds) (2002) *The Language of Turn and Sequence*. Oxford: Oxford University Press.

Gal, S. and Irvine, J.T. (1995) 'The Boundaries of Languages and Disciplines: How Ideologies Construct Difference', *Social Research* 62: 967–1001.

Garfinkel, H. (1967) *Studies in Ethnomethodology*. Cambridge: Polity.

Gaudio, R.P. (1997) 'Not Talking Straight in Hausa', in A. Livia and K. Hall (eds) *Queerly Phrased: Language, Gender, and Sexuality*, pp. 416–29. New York: Oxford University Press.

Giles, H., Coupland, J. and Coupland, N. (eds) (1991) *Contexts of Accommodation: Developments in Applied Sociolinguistics*. Cambridge: Cambridge University Press.

Goffman, E. (1974) *Frame Analysis*. Boston: Northeastern University Press.

Goffman, E. (1981) *Forms of Talk*. Philadelphia: University of Pennsylvania Press.

Goodwin, C. (1995) 'Co-Constructing Meaning in Conversations with an Aphasic Man', *Research on Language and Social Interaction* 28(3): 233–60.

Goodwin, M.H. (1990) *He-Said-She-Said: Talk as Social Organization among Black Children*. Bloomington: Indiana University Press.

Goodwin, C. and Goodwin, M.H. (1992) 'Assessments and the Construction of Context', in A. Duranti and C. Goodwin (eds) *Rethinking Context: Language as an Interactive Phenomenon*, pp. 147–89. Cambridge: Cambridge University Press.

Gramsci, A. (1971) *Selections from the Prison Notebooks*. Trans. and ed. by Q. Hoare and G. Nowell Smith. New York: International Publishers.

Hall, K. (1997) '"Go Suck Your Husband's Sugarcane!": Hijras and the Use of Sexual Insult', in A. Livia and K. Hall (eds) *Queerly Phrased: Language, Gender, and Sexuality*, pp. 430–60. New York: Oxford University Press.

Hall, K. (2003) 'English, Sexuality, and Modernity in Hindi-Speaking India', paper presented at the Workshop on Language, Gender, and Political Economy, University of Toronto, October.

Hall, K. and O'Donovan, V. (1996) 'Shifting Gender Positions among Hindi-Speaking Hijras', in V.L. Bergvall, J.M. Bing and A.F. Freed (eds) *Rethinking Language and Gender Research: Theory and Practice*, pp. 228–66. London: Longman.

Heritage, J. and Raymond, G. (2005) 'The Terms of Agreement: Indexing Epistemic Authority and Subordination in Talk-in-Interaction', *Social Psychology Quarterly* 68(1): 15–38.

Hewitt, R. (1986) *White Talk Black Talk: Inter-Racial Friendship and Communication amongst Adolescents*. Cambridge: Cambridge University Press.

Hodges, A. (n.d.) '"The Battle of Iraq": The Adequation of Saddam Hussein and Osama Bin Laden in the Bush War on Terror Narrative', unpublished manuscript.

Hopper, P. (1987) 'Emergent Grammar', *Proceedings of the Berkeley Linguistics Society* 13: 139–57.

Hunston, S. and Thompson, G. (eds) (2000) *Evaluation in Text: Authorial Stance and the Construction of Discourse*. Oxford: Oxford University Press.

Hutchins, E. (1995) *Cognition in the Wild*. Cambridge, MA: MIT Press.

Hymes, D. (1975) 'Breakthrough into Performance', in D. Ben-Amos and K.S. Goldstein (eds) *Folklore: Performance and Communication*, pp. 11–74. The Hague: Mouton.

Inoue, M. (2004) 'What Does Language Remember?: Indexical Inversion and the Naturalized History of Japanese Women', *Journal of Linguistic Anthropology* 14(1): 39–56.

Irvine, J.T. and Gal, S. (2000) 'Language Ideology and Linguistic Differentiation', in P.V. Kroskrity (ed.) *Regimes of Language: Ideologies, Polities, and Identities*, pp. 35–84. Santa Fe, NM: School of American Research Press.

Jaffe, A. (2000) 'Comic Performance and the Articulation of Hybrid Identity', *Pragmatics* 10(1): 39–59.

Johnstone, B. (1996) *The Linguistic Individual: Self-Expression in Language and Linguistics*. New York: Oxford University Press.

Kitzinger, C. (n.d.) 'Speaking as a Heterosexual: (How) Does Sexuality Matter for Talk-in-Interaction?' unpublished manuscript.

Kroskrity, P.V. (ed.) (2000) *Regimes of Language: Ideologies, Polities, and Identities*. Santa Fe, NM: School of American Research Press.

Kulick, D. (1997) 'The Gender of Brazilian Transgendered Prostitutes', *American Anthropologist* 99(3): 574–85.

Labov, W. (1963) 'The Social Motivation of a Sound Change', *Word* 19: 273–309.

Labov, W. (1966) *The Social Stratification of English in New York City*. Washington, DC: Center for Applied Linguistics.

Labov, W. (1972) 'The Isolation of Contextual Styles', in *Sociolinguistic Patterns*, pp. 70–109. Philadelphia: University of Pennsylvania Press.

Le Page, R.B. and Tabouret-Keller, A. (1985) *Acts of Identity: Creole-Based Approaches to Language and Ethnicity*. Cambridge: Cambridge University Press.

Liang, A.C. (1999) 'Conversationally Implicating Lesbian and Gay Identity', in M. Bucholtz, A.C. Liang and L.A. Sutton (eds), *Reinventing Identities*, pp. 293–310. New York: Oxford University Press.

Livia, A. and Hall, K. (1997) '"It's a Girl!": Bringing Performativity Back to Linguistics', in A. Livia and K. Hall (eds), *Queerly Phrased: Language, Gender, and Sexuality*, pp. 3–18. New York: Oxford University Press.

Lo, Adrienne (1999) 'Codeswitching, Speech Community Membership, and the Construction of Ethnic Identity', *Journal of Sociolinguistics* 3(4): 461– 79.

Manalansan, M.F. (2003) *Global Divas: Filipino Gay Men in the Diaspora*. Durham, NC: Duke University Press.

Mannheim, B. and Tedlock, D. (1995) 'Introduction', in D. Tedlock and B. Mannheim (eds) *The Dialogic Emergence of Culture*, pp. 1–32. Urbana: University of Illinois Press.

McConnell-Ginet, S. (1989) 'The Sexual (Re)Production of Meaning: A Discourse-Based Theory', in F. Wattman Frank and P.A. Treichler (eds) *Language, Gender, and Professional Writing: Theoretical Approaches and Guidelines for Nonsexist Usage*, pp. 35–50. New York: Modern Language Association.

McConnell-Ginet, S. (2002) 'Queering Semantics: Definitional Struggles', in K. Campbell-Kibler, R.J. Podesva, S.J. Roberts and A. Wong (eds) *Language and Sexuality: Contesting Meaning in Theory and Practice*, pp. 137–60. Stanford, CA: CSLI Publications.

Mendoza-Denton, N. (2002) 'Language and Identity', in J.K. Chambers, P. Trudgill and N. Schilling-Estes (eds) *The Handbook of Language Variation and Change*, pp. 475–99. Oxford: Blackwell.

Mendoza-Denton, N. (forthcoming) *Homegirls: Symbolic Practices in the Making of Latina Youth Styles*. Malden, MA: Blackwell.

Meyerhoff, M. (1996) 'Dealing with Gender Identity as a Sociolinguistic Variable', in V.L. Bergvall, J.M. Bing and A.F. Freed (eds) *Rethinking Language and Gender Research: Theory and Practice*, pp. 202–27. London: Longman.

Meyerhoff, M. and Niedzielski, N. (1994) 'Resistance to Creolization: An Interpersonal and Intergroup Account', *Language and Communication* 14(4): 313–30.

Moerman, M. (1993) 'Ariadne's Thread and Indra's Net: Reflections on Ethnography, Ethnicity, Identity, Culture, and Interaction', *Research on Language and Social Interaction* 26(1): 85–98.

Murphy, M.L. (1997) 'The Elusive Bisexual: Social Categorization and Lexico-Semantic Change', in A. Livia and K. Hall (eds) *Queerly Phrased: Language, Gender, and Sexuality*, pp. 35–57. New York: Oxford University Press.

Ochs, E. (1992) 'Indexing Gender', in A. Duranti and C. Goodwin (eds) *Rethinking Context: Language as an Interactive Phenomenon*, pp. 335–58. Cambridge: Cambridge University Press.

Ochs, E. (1993) 'Constructing Social Identity: A Language Socialization Perspective', *Research on Language and Social Interaction* 26(3): 287–306.

Ochs, E. and Capps, L. (2001) *Living Narrative: Creating Lives in Everyday Storytelling*. Cambridge, MA: Harvard University Press.

Ochs, E. and Taylor, C. (1995) 'The "Father Knows Best" Dynamic in Dinnertime Narratives', in K. Hall and M. Bucholtz (eds) *Gender Articulated: Language and the Socially Constructed Self*, pp. 97–120. New York: Routledge.

Pagliai, V. and Farr, M. (eds) (2000) *Pragmatics* 10(1). *Special issue: Art and the Expression of Complex Identities: Imagining and Contesting Ethnicity in Performance.*

Park, J.S.-Y. (2004) 'Globalization, Language, and Social Order: Ideologies of English in South Korea', unpublished dissertation, University of California, Santa Barbara.

Piller, I. (2002) 'Passing for a Native Speaker: Identity and Success in Second Language Learning', *Journal of Sociolinguistics* 6(2): 179–206.

Pomerantz, A. (1984) 'Agreeing and Disagreeing with Assessments: Some Features of Preferred/Dispreferred Turn Shapes', in J. Maxwell Atkinson and J. Heritage (eds) *Structures of Social Action: Studies in Conversation Analysis*, pp. 57–101. Cambridge: Cambridge University Press.

Rampton, B. (1995) *Crossing: Language and Ethnicity among Adolescents*. London: Longman.

Rauniomaa, M. (2003) 'Stance Accretion', paper presented at the Language, Interaction, and Social Organization Research Focus Group, University of California, Santa Barbara, February.

Sacks, H. (1995) *Lectures on Conversation*. 2 vols. Oxford: Basil Blackwell.

Schieffelin, B.B., Woolard, K.A. and Kroskrity, P.V. (eds) (1998) *Language Ideologies: Practice and Theory*. New York: Oxford University Press.

Schilling-Estes, N. (2004) 'Constructing Ethnicity in Interaction', *Journal of Sociolinguistics* 8(2): 163–95.

Sidnell, J. (2003) 'Constructing and Managing Male Exclusivity in Talk-in-Interaction', in J. Holmes and M. Meyerhoff (eds) *The Handbook of Language and Gender*, pp. 327–52. Oxford: Blackwell.

Silverstein, M. (1976) 'Shifters, Linguistic Categories, and Cultural Description', in K.H. Basso and H.A. Selby (eds) *Meaning in Anthropology*, pp. 11–55. Albuquerque: University of New Mexico Press.

Silverstein, M. (1979) 'Language Structure and Linguistic Ideology', in P.R. Clyne, W.F. Hanks and C.L. Hofbauer (eds) *The Elements: A Parasession on Linguistic Units and Levels*, pp. 193–247. Chicago: Chicago Linguistic Society.

Silverstein, M. (1985) 'Language and the Culture of Gender: At the Intersection of Structure, Usage, and Ideology', in E. Mertz and R.J. Parmentier (eds) *Semiotic Mediation: Sociocultural and Psychological Perspectives*, pp. 219–59. Orlando, FL: Academic Press.

Sweetland, J. (2002) 'Unexpected but Authentic Use of an Ethnically-Marked Dialect', *Journal of Sociolinguistics* 6(4): 514–36.

Tajfel, H. and Turner, J.C. (1979) 'An Integrative Theory of Intergroup Conflict', in W.G. Austin and S. Worchel (eds) *The Social Psychology of Intergroup Relations*, pp. 33–47. Monterey, CA: Brooks/Cole.

Visweswaran, K. (1994) *Fictions of Feminist Ethnography*. Minneapolis: University of Minnesota Press.

Waksler, R. (2001) 'A New All in Conversation', *American Speech* 76(2): 128–38.

West, C. and Zimmerman, D.H. (1987) 'Doing Gender', *Gender and Society* 1(2): 125–51.

Woolard, K.A. (1998) 'Simultaneity and Bivalency as Strategies in Bilingualism', *Journal of Linguistic Anthropology* 8(1): 3–29.

117
+ 141
‾‾‾‾‾
258

How Dual Identity Processes
Foster Creativity

Małgorzata A. Gocłowska and Richard J. Crisp

ABSTRACT

We propose a theoretical model explaining when and why possessing two inconsistent social identities can foster superior creativity. The framework describes how during cultural adaptation individuals (1) *alternate* their identities across contexts, (2) *integrate* elements of their distinct (i.e., remote and uncorrelated) identities, and, having formed cognitive and emotional links with the new group (3) *broaden* their self-definition. We explain how these processes of cultural adaptation map onto three fundamental creative processes: (1) an ability to quickly and effortlessly switch between cognitive strategies and semantic categories, (2) an apparent ease in integrating distant and conflicting ideas, and finally, (3) the widening of ones' creative idea base. Our model explains how the challenges involved in managing complex self-definitions enhance creativity, and increase potential for novel problem solutions. Understanding this dynamic brings a new perspective to debates on the value of diversity.

KEYWORDS

Acculturation, Diversity, Tolerance, Flexibility, Creativity, Cognition

In the era of global economy, where financial markets force individuals and companies to constantly re-structure and implement new strategies, thinking flexibly and creatively is essential to personal and professional success. Creativity allows people to develop new, innovative products

(IBM, 2010; Lombardo & Roddy, 2010), negotiate business solutions (Maddux & Galinsky, 2009) manage complex power relations (Sligte, De Dreu, & Nijstad, 2011), and avoid painful losses (Baas, De Dreu, & Nijstad, 2011; Roskes, De Dreu, & Nijstad, 2012). Creativity is thus essential to tackling problems, fostering change, and innovation. Moreover, recent findings suggest that rather than being a stable trait, this unique human ability can be developed and fostered in response to the *experience of social diversity* (Crisp & Turner, 2011; Maddux, Adam, & Galinsky, 2010; Plaut, 2010; Ritter et al., 2012; Simonton, 1997). This is a tantalizing thought: As our societies become increasingly diverse - changing from the provincial, homogenized worlds that have characterized much of human history - could such a shift have profound benefits for the way individuals think and behave? This article is about the link between diversity and creativity, and how considering the dynamics of cultural adaptation provides some important new insights in to cultural evolution and social change.

DIVERSITY AND DUAL IDENTITIES

In homogenous societies, peoples' identities are highly overlapping (Crisp & Hewstone, 2007; Homan, van Knippenberg, Van Kleef, & De Dreu, 2007): individuals are members of highly correlated groups, for instance the manager in a company will be White, middle-class, male and highly educated, while his cleaner may be a Latino, working-class, uneducated and female. But with increased social mobility in multicultural societies, diversity fault-lines break down, and many individuals gain the opportunity of entering new groups that they have traditionally been barred from[1]. As a result, they develop dual identities such as Chinese- American, business-woman, secular-Buddhist. Our review focuses on the intra-individual consequences of adopting such identities. We argue that the cultural adaptation to living in new groups - groups that have traditionally been unrelated to ones' initial identity - provides a challenge to people's self-definition, and the manner in which individuals process information. Throughout the paper, when we talk of dual identifiers, we consider individuals who belong to two (or more) different groups, regardless of those groups category domain. We do so because different types of cultures can characterize all sorts of social categories - such as gender, profession, social status, or personal interest (Cohen, 2009) - and not just national or ethnic cultural groups.

Being a member of two traditionally unrelated groups is not an easy task. Dual identifiers, such as female-engineers, or Chinese-Americans, are forced to adopt and negotiate between various, often opposing sets of cultural proscriptions. A Chinese-American will adopt different identities and sets of behaviors depending on whether they find themselves in a Chinese or American cultural context (Benet-Martínez, Leu, Lee, & Morris, 2002; Hong, Morris, Chiu, & Benet-Martínez, 2000; Morris, Menon, & Ames, 2001; Morris & Mok, 2011). This will be similar to the experience of a working class background academic assuming a middle-class set of behaviors when attending an academic conference, but changing their language and behavior while back in the family home. Both have, in the course of their lives, become simultaneous members of culturally distinct groups, and this experience necessitated the development of new skills and abilities (Benet-Martínez, 2012; Cohen, 2009).

Compared to their more "homogenous" peers, dual identity individuals, throughout their cultural adaptation experience, learn to alternate between their two identities, reconcile inconsistent values or cognitions, and broaden their self-definition. When individuals are highly attached to one salient identity only, this imposes limitations on how they generate (Adarves-Yorno, Postmes, & Haslam, 2007), and assess (Adarves-Yorno, Postmes, & Haslam, 2006) creative ideas. But changes from managing narrow, correlated identities, to creating a more complex identity structure, pose a challenge for everyday functioning, and self-definition, and can, if successfully addressed, lead to the development of more creativity. As a result, we argue that individuals who enter new groups, and develop deep relationships with those groups, become better at cognitive switching (for review see Bialystok & Craik, 2010), integrating apparently inconsistent ideas (Benet-Martínez, Lee, & Leu, 2006; Tadmor & Tetlock, 2009), and recruiting from a wider base of cognitions in idea generation (Leung & Chiu, 2010). When generating creative ideas, these individuals show an enhanced tendency to use multiple semantic categories (Maddux & Galinsky, 2009), their ideas are rated as more novel and original (Fee & Gray, 2012; Kharkhurin, 2011; Tadmor, Galinsky, & Maddux, 2012), their

---

[1]   That people can be affiliated to multiple social groups is not a new or exclusively social psychological idea. For instance Georg Simmel (Simmel, 1950) observed that in the Australian Aborigine culture the whole population is divided into five 'gentes' with members of the various gentes found across many different tribes.

negotiation solutions are more creative (Maddux & Galinsky, 2009), they display higher levels of innovation, and even a higher rate of promotion at work (Tadmor et al., 2012).

These findings suggest that something about the experience of simultaneously belonging to two (or more) distinct groups has beneficial impact on creativity. But what aspects of possessing a dual identity are necessary for such benefits to be realized? To address this question, we first define dual identity experiences by calling upon their three characteristics: depth, dual engagement, and the combination of identities that are culturally distinct. Then, we define creativity, and consider *how* the dynamic of dual identity adaptation leads to the development of creative cognition.

Developmental models of multiple identity adaptation (Amiot, de la Sablonnière, Terry, & Smith, 2007) describe how acquiring new social identities prompts an intra-individual development processes, allowing individuals to manage and integrate their old and new identities. Building on this perspective, we argue that as individuals progress through their cultural adaptation experience, they develop different strategies for managing and integrating their new and old identities, and progressively train cognitive faculties that are conducive to creativity. Each stage of dual identity development involves the use of specific cognitive skills that, if practiced extensively, could generalize to increased flexible and creative thinking in other domains, unrelated to the dual identity. Illuminating when and how this happens sheds a new light on the value of diversity and multiculturalism in the workplace, and for the society at large (Mendoza-Denton & España, 2010; Plaut, Thomas, & Goren, 2009; Verkuyten, Thijs, & Bekhuis, 2010; Verkuyten, 2007).

Characteristic Conditions

Before we go on to describe how developing a dual identity affects creative thinking, it is necessary to define *what kind* of experiences are at the center of our focus. Membership in two groups will most likely lead to enhanced flexible and creative thought when characterized by the following three components: depth, dual engagement, and cultural distance.

Depth

First of all, benefits to creativity, including benefits from dual identity experiences, are most likely when individuals develop a deeper relationship with the two (or multiple) groups that they belong to. Depth entails the length and/or degree of engagement with one's two identities, and is a prerequisite for individuals to thoroughly process the information related to their new role. Consistent with this idea, uplifts to creativity due to dual identity experiences are mostly found in individuals who had the opportunity to immerse themselves in the culture of the new group (e.g., host nation), and develop a strong identification with both their old group (e.g., home culture), as well as their new group. For instance, in the studies of Tadmor and colleagues (2009, 2012), membership in two cultural groups lead to increased creative thought only in individuals who developed a deep engagement with both (instead of only one, or none) of their identities. Across five studies, in those who were exposed to two cultures, but only identified with one of them, creativity remained at a level comparable to that of the assimilated or separated one-group identifiers (Tadmor et al., 2012; Tadmor & Tetlock, 2009). In a similar vein, in the studies of Maddux and Galinsky (2009) individuals who underwent a deep acculturation experience, such as when living abroad, performed better on a range of creativity tasks, but this uplift was *only* observed in those who lived abroad, rather than simply stayed abroad for a short visit or vacation (Maddux et al., 2010; Maddux & Galinsky, 2009). "Depth" effects have also been observed in individuals exposed to many cultural groups, where the level of engagement with a multicultural environment positively predicted creative flexibility, innovation, and performance at work (Godart, Maddux, Shiplov, & Galinsky, 2014; Maddux, Bivolaru, Hafenbrack, Tadmor, & Galinsky, 2013).

So something about the depth of one's diversity experience, such as living in and adopting to a host culture, or developing a strong identification with the new group (Morris, Mok, & Mor, 2011), and the social, psychological, and behavioral adjustments that such adaptations require, leads to the kinds of fundamental changes seen in the literature on cultural diversity and creativity (Benet-Martínez et al., 2006; Leung & Chiu, 2010; Maddux & Galinsky, 2009; Tadmor et al., 2012; Tadmor & Tetlock, 2009). Structural features of the situation, and the newcomers' skills can give us an idea about potential for depth. For instance, while living in an asylum seekers' detention centre, or a ghettoised part of the city, isolated migrants often have insufficient opportunity to learn about the new culture and will not undergo full cultural adaptation. On the other end of the spectrum, highly mobile and educated "citizens of the world", with superior communication skills and cultural intelligence (Imai & Gelfand,

2010; Mor, Morris, & Joh, 2013), or high levels of openness to experience (Leung & Chiu, 2008), are more likely to quickly and efficiently engage with their new group, and, as long as they maintain the original link with their home culture, they are likely to benefit from their experience. La Fromboise, Coleman & Gerton (1993) summarize this well by listing several skills necessary for developing a deep relationship with ones' new and old reference group: knowledge of beliefs and values of the new group, positive attitude to both groups, bicultural efficacy, communication ability, knowledge of culture-appropriate behaviours, and social groundedness (La Fromboise, Coleman, & Gerton, 1993). One can imagine that without those competencies, no newcomer will fully and successfully be able to engage with a group.

Dual Engagement

A second characteristic condition is dual engagement. Benefits to flexible and creative thought have been found in individuals who belong to at least two different cultural or social groups, for instance bilingual or bicultural adults. To put it differently, to experience benefits to creativity, people need to have the opportunity to see the world through the eyes of different social identities. For instance, a Chinese person living in China will not be dually engaged, unless, in addition to being identified with their original culture, they develop interpersonal links with individuals from a second culture, and see the world through a new set of cultural lenses. In other words, a dually engaged person is someone who has undergone the process of adaptation to living and functioning in a new group, but at the same time has remained identified with their original culture. In this sense, dual engagement entails identifying with, and interacting with, (at least) two cultures.

The most widely adopted framework for understanding psychological reactions to such diversity experiences is the *acculturation model*. Acculturation, in the more narrow sense, describes the process through which immigrants moving to a new country psychologically react to their new social reality, a reality in which they must resolve potential conflicts between their original cultural identity and their new identity (Berry & Annis, 1974; Sam & Berry, 2010). In a broader sense, acculturation can also refer to psychological changes and adaptations that result from the influence and contact with another cultural group. Although acculturation literature has typically been applied to understand the experience of immigrants, the basic principles underling the model - how people deal with adapting to a new group membership - can help define how dual identity experiences, more generally, stimulate creativity.

Central to the model are acculturation strategies. These strategies, proposed by Berry (1974), reflect differences in the extent to which the acculturating individual is motivated to engage with the host culture, and/or motivated to maintain a link with their original culture. The strategies range from assimilation (forgoing one's original culture in favor of the new) to separation (maintaining one's home culture with no engagement with the host culture). For instance a Muslim arriving in Canada, who is strongly motivated to fit in, may assume an *assimilation strategy*: decide to distance themselves from their home culture, and get as close as possible to becoming a Canadian person. On the other hand, a political refugee whose primary motivation for arriving in Canada is survival, may not be interested in the Canadian home culture, and follow a *separation strategy* – organize their life in a Muslim-only community that is separated from the mainstream culture of the home country. Acculturation research has argued for disadvantages of assimilation and separation to immigrants' well-being (La Fromboise et al., 1993), and that the strategy allowing for most beneficial outcomes is an *integration strategy* - where the individual engages with both category representations of the host and home cultures; this strategy is also most endorsed among minority members (Dovidio, Gaertner, & Saguy, 2009; Verkuyten, 2005), and leads to the development of the type of dual engagement that is at the heart of the current model.

This "dual engagement" of host and home culture is indeed important for peoples' well-being (La Fromboise, Coleman, & Gerton, 1993). Individuals who adopt this strategy, and engage with both host and home (or original) cultures are often described as *bicultural* (Hong et al., 2000; La Fromboise et al., 1993; Nguyen & Benet-Martínez, 2007; Phinney & Devich-Navarro, 1997; Phinney, Horenczyk, Liebkind, & Vedder, 2001). There are a range of benefits that accrue from developing this sort of dual identity (rather than choosing to either assimilate or separate oneself from one or other culture). Bicultural individuals report feeling more at ease interacting with individuals from outside their ethnic minority group (Buriel et al., 1998), and demonstrate heightened well-being, health, sociocultural prowess, low stress, and cultural skills (La Fromboise et al., 1993; Linville, 1987; Sam, Vedder, Liebkind, Neto, & Virta, 2008). Most importantly, there is evidence that this type of dual engagement can enhance flexibility and creativity.

Benet-Martínez and colleagues (2006) found that compared to a mono-cultural control group, Chinese-American bi-culturals were more likely to integrate multiple perspectives in which different ideas were compared and contrasted (rather than relying on the first, dominant, response that came to mind). Relatedly, Gutierrez and Sameroff (1990) presented Mexican-American mothers with vignettes which described a family in which a child had behavioral problems. They found that compared to mono-cultural mothers, bi-cultural mothers were more likely to sample a wider range of behaviors by identifying the interacting role of environmental, constitutional, and psychological influences, rather than identifying a singular cause (e.g., environmental factors). Also in the studies of Tadmor and colleagues (2009; 2012) cited above, dual identifiers, but not individuals identifying with one culture only, showed higher levels of *integrative complexity* - the capacity and willingness to acknowledge the legitimacy of competing perspectives on an issue, and to forge conceptual links among these perspectives (Suedfeld & Tetlock, 2001). In addition, these dual identifying individuals performed more creatively in laboratory settings, were more innovative in their workplace, and registered the highest promotion rate at work, compared to low identifiers, and their assimilated or separated peers (Tadmor et al., 2012). In studies tracing multicultural experiences (but not specifically dual identities) breadth of experiences – operationalized as the number of countries that one lived in – has also been positively (at the lower end of a curvilinear relationship) associated with creativity improvements (Godart et al., 2014).

Cultural Distance

Even when it comes to deep dual engagement with two different groups or cultures, not all diversity experiences are created equal. Most importantly, groups can differ in cultural distance. Cultural distance is the degree to which the values, customs, and characteristics predominant in two groups diverge (Benet-Martínez & Haritatos, 2005; Benet-Martínez et al., 2002). Imagine a Brit spending a year in the USA. She will probably not face as many conflicts in customs, values, and ideas as a Brit spending a year in China. Similarly, a bank employee will not find it too challenging if he or she is asked to relocate and work in a different branch of the same bank. If cultural distance is low, as in this case, it is easy to engage with both cultures; in fact, the similarities between the two cultures may be so unchallenging that *de facto* assimilation occurs. With low cultural distance dual engagement makes no functional difference because the values, customs and characteristics of both cultures converge to such an extent. It is only when individuals experience some *dissonance* between the host and home culture, will they be compelled to seek integratively complex solutions to problems (see Tadmor et al. 2012).

This issue is well illustrated in studies on Bicultural Identity Integration and cognitive complexity (Benet-Martínez, Lee, Leu, 2006). These researchers compared cognitive performance of individuals high and low in BII (note that here BII was used as a unitary construct). Chinese-American participants were asked to answer questions about the degree to which the two cultures in which they participate are conflicted with one another (Bicultural Identity Integration), and were subsequently asked to write 10 statements about the American culture, Chinese culture, or a neutral landscape. Bicultural participants who reported that their identities remained in conflict wrote more dense and complex descriptions of cultures, compared to those who did not think their identities were in conflict (Benet-Martínez, Lee, Leu, 2006, Study 2), suggesting that *perceived* cultural distance, or inconsistency between one's two identities, forces individuals to think hard about, and elaborate on cultural issues.

One reason for the importance of cultural distance is that as long as the norms of the two groups remain in conflict, this encourages individuals to elaborate on that conflict, and form integratively complex solutions. For instance a lawyer working at an environmental NGO may at first be quite startled to see that many of their work colleagues have a criminal record, and this is not condoned by the organization. However, if the newcomer remains deeply engaged and pursues this issue further, they may discover that criminal record is linked to their colleague's environmental activism, and, within the culture of the organization, is considered something to be proud of, rather than frowned upon. Having a legal background, and working in an NGO, the lawyer has now acquired two contradictory sets of beliefs about the meaning of having a criminal record. As we argue in further sections of our paper, this can prompt a process of resolving inconsistent norms and values, which can benefit individuals' creativity during identity integration – the second stage outlined in our model (see Figure 1).

To summarize, next to *depth* and *dual engagement, cultural distance* is a third important characteristic of the sort of diversity experiences that may enhance creativity. Without the involvement of tangible differences, uplifts to creativity would simply not exist. In short, in order for dual engagement to be functionally relevant for creative thought, the norms and values of the two groups must be different in ways that trigger (and require) a new way of thinking.

CREATIVITY

Before we explain how the adaptation to dual identity experiences influences creativity, it is good to briefly define creativity, and explain what cognitive processes lead to creative ends. Creativity is the process of bringing into being something that is novel and useful (Amabile, 1996; Baas et al., 2011; De Dreu, Baas, & Nijstad, 2008; Roskes et al., 2012). Creative insights and products result from ordinary cognitive processes (Ward, Smith, & Finke, 2008), that include the ability to flexibly and effortlessly switch between various sets and approaches to a problem (Ashby, Isen, & Turken, 1999; Heilman, Nadeau, & Beversdorf, 2003; Nijstad, De Dreu, & Rietzschel, 2010; Schank & Abelson, 1977), to integrate inconsistent ideas (Kunda, Miller, & Claire, 1990, Leung & Chiu, 2010; Tadmor et al., 2012; Thagard, 1997; Wan & Chiu, 2002), and to recruit ideas from a broad knowledge base (Eysenck, 1993; R. S. Friedman, Fishbach, Förster, & Werth, 2003; Isen & Daubman, 1984). In the cognitive literature, these types of thought processes are often labelled as creative cognition (Ward et al., 2008; Ward, Smith, & Vaid, 1997), and in social-psychology, they are equivalent to creative flexibility (but not creative persistence, see Dual Pathway to Creativity Model; De Dreu et al., 2008; Nijstad et al., 2010). Importantly, these types of creative processes are limited by what people have learned – habits and knowledge acquired in the family or via the education system, as well as cultural proscriptions that people have been exposed to in their initial group (Adarves-Yorno et al., 2007; S. M. Smith, Ward, & Schumacher, 1993; Ward, Smith, & Finke, 2007). However, we argue, because the adaptation to ones' own diversity is associated with exposure to new norms, and the necessary change of old thinking habits, it can help individuals overcome barriers to flexible and creative performance. Thus, by learning to navigate a new reality, where old knowledge is no longer useful, and new cultural scripts need to be applied instead, dual identity individuals train cognitive skills that are conducive to "thinking out of the box".

CHANGES IN CATEGORIZATION

So far we have argued that experiences of adapting to new groups, that are
deep, involve dual engagement, and involve two groups that espouse significant cultural differences, can change the way people behave and think.
These conditions provide the basis for understanding not only when, but
also *how* such experiences can stimulate creative thought. This is because
these characteristic conditions require an individual to adopt a novel way
of thinking (for reviews see Crisp & Meleady, 2012; Crisp & Turner, 2011;
Leung, Maddux, Galinsky, & Chiu, 2008) in order to operate effectively
in their (somewhat unique) social environment. This is apparent in the
early stages of adapting to a second group membership, when *alternation*
allows perceivers to compartmentalize cultural knowledge, bringing with
it enhanced-sensitivity to environmental cues and rapid adaptation in
the form of categorical frame-switching. As individuals begin to feel the
need to reconcile the two identities' characteristics into their self-concept,
reconciling conflicting values, ideas, and customs, they practice *integration* - a process in which attributes of seemingly irrelevant cognitions are
reconciled to form a new entity (Hampton, 1997; Thagard, 1997; Wan &
Chiu, 2002; Ward, Patterson, Sifonis, Dodds, & Saunders, 2002). Finally,
as dual identity individuals begin to think of themselves as members of a
more *inclusive* social category, they gain simultaneous mental access to a
broader range of cognitions, which enables them to recruit ideas from a
wider range of semantic categories, increasing their chance for creativity
(Leung & Chiu, 2010; Ward, Patterson, & Sifonis, 2004).

Alternation

In homogenous environments, knowing what group one belongs to,
and what norms and values that group espouses, can guide individuals'
behavior in an effortless and rapid fashion. But long-term sojourners and
immigrants, or employees following mergers find themselves simultaneous
members of two (or more) groups with visible differences in code of conduct or norms espoused. If, as a result of their experience, they develop a
dual identity, in any given situation, they are facing *multiple* potential ways
to categorize themselves, as well as *multiple* potential ways to behave.

As suggested by the dual engagement prerequisite, to function well dual
identity individuals must abide by the rules of both groups that they are
members of. Because, due to *cultural distance*, these rules will be different,
dual identity individuals must also quickly recognize when the norms of

one group are more appropriate than those of another. Not recognizing this could have severe consequences to their well-being, and position in the society. For instance a British expat living in Thailand must realize that while making jokes about the Royal Family may be considered harmless in the UK, it may lead to imprisonment in Thailand. In order to function in Thailand, the expat will constantly have to be aware of which situation they are in, in order to ensure they exhibit the appropriate behavior. Depending on the context, they will then activate one of their identities and the repertoire of beliefs and behaviors that come with it.

Dual identity individuals deal with their own diversity by alternating between the two relevant frames or identities - a process that has typically been referred to in the cross-cultural literature as *frame-switching* (Hong et al., 2000; L E Bell, 1990; Ramirez-Esparza, Gosling, Benet-Martínez, Potter, & Pennebaker, 2006 for an overview of studies see Table 2). Those who have become adept at frame-switching are able to independently activate meaning systems relevant to which of the two contexts they find themselves in (see Figure 1). For instance, Hong et al. (2000) showed that Chinese-American bi-culturals exposed to American primes made more internal attributions (a Western attributional style), while those exposed to Chinese primes made more external attributions (an East Asian attributional style). Examining this example more closely, we can imagine how, depending on the context, Chinese-Americans will speak English or Cantonese, exhibit more independent (American) or interdependent (Chinese) cultural norms, or type using American or Chinese characters on their keyboard. By dynamically varying the frame of reference, these individuals learn to more flexibly activate various ideas and meanings that are adaptive in a given context (E. R. Smith & Semin, 2007; Turner, Hogg, Oakes, Reicher, & Wetherell, 1987)[2]. This frame-switching can help them navigate the world. However developing superior switching skills in domains unrelated to culture may also be of benefit when performing tasks requiring creative thought.

Set-switching and creativity. Mental set shifting, which frame-switching is a special case of, involves the disengagement of a relevant task set, the subsequent active engagement of a relevant task set, and an ability to perform a new operation despite the interference from the previous task set (N. P. Friedman et al., 2006; Miyake et al., 2000). This type of skill is central to creativity (De Dreu et al., 2008; Nijstad et al., 2010; Nijstad, 2002). To perform creatively people need to "break set" (Duncker, 1945;

S. M. Smith & Blankenship, 1991) and easily move between different categorical frames of meaning (Nijstad et al., 2010). Set switching helps on tasks where the obvious solution stored in memory may hamper generation of the right answer (e.g., the Duncker candle problems, such as in the studies of Maddux & Galinsky, 2009), or in any other type of creative activity where it is relatively difficult to overcome obvious responses (Gocłowska, Crisp, & Labuschagne, 2013; Landau & Leynes, 2004; Marsh, Ward, & Landau, 1999; Sassenberg & Moskowitz, 2005).

In a divergent thinking task, a classic in the measurement of creativity, people are typically asked to generate different uses for an object (Guilford, 1950). While doing this, the originality of their answers will benefit from drawing on different conceptual categories, and easily switching between these categories (Gocłowska, Baas, Crisp, & De Dreu, 2014). If, while generating uses for a plastic bottle, participants come up with answers such as "to drink from", "carry water", "store liquid", "keep drink in", their answers stay within one conceptual category, indicative of low creativity. However, being able to effortlessly move among different semantic categories would render more original ideas, such as "use as a piggy bank" (storage), "throw at someone" (weapons), or "use instead of a football" (games), at a lower cognitive cost (Roskes et al., 2012; Roskes, Elliot, Nijstad, & De Dreu, 2013).

Consistent with this idea, creativity has been linked to improved performance on cognitive measures that require the suppression of immediately accessible responses, such as the paper version of the color Stroop test (Golden, 1975). More recently, creativity was linked to a decreased Stroop effect following a rule switch, suggesting that creative individuals have higher sensitivity to contextual demands, and can more easily switch to rules that are appropriate in a given context (Zabelina & Robinson, 2010). Thus, if individuals, in the course of their diversity experience were to gain an apparent ease in context-dependent activation of the right task set, this should increase their creativity (Baas et al., 2011; De Dreu, Nijstad, Baas, Wolsink, & Roskes, 2012; Roskes et al., 2012).

---

[2]   Although the discussion of the direction in which switching occurs is beyond the scope of the current paper, it is worth mentioning that researchers also registered cases of switching in the direction opposite to the culture primed (Benet-Martínez et al., 2002; Mok & Morris, 2010). This probably occurs, because in some contexts, individuals may want to distance themselves from one of their identities. Essentially however, the creative set-switching process that we discuss in this section is trained as a result of the act of switching itself, and not of the direction of the switch.

Facilitation of frame-switching abilities. Evidence of superior general-ized frame-switching in dual identity individuals is most apparent from the bilingualism literature (Bialystok, Craik, Klein, & Viswanathan, 2004; Bialystok & Martin, 2004; Bialystok, 1999; Kharkhurin & Samadpour Motalleebi, 2008; Martin-Rhee & Bialystok, 2008; Prior & Macwhin-ney, 2009; For an overview of studies see Table 2). Culture is expressed in terms of language, and the majority of frame-switching individuals will experience their different cultural frames as embedded in the use of a dif-ferent language (La Fromboise et al., 1993; Ramirez-Esparza et al., 2006). In fact, since the majority of bi-culturals are bilingual[3], and vice-versa, superior creative performance has been uncovered in both biculturalism and bilingualism studies (Kharkhurin, 2008, 2011; Maddux & Galin-sky, 2009; Tadmor et al., 2012). Bicultural and bilingual individuals are constantly required to monitor their environment in order to enact the relevant cultural scripts. This leads to improved sensitivities to the imme-diate social or cultural context (Hong, Benet-Martínez, Chiu, & Morris, 2003; Hong, Chiu, & Kung, 1997; Hong et al., 2000), but also to an appar-ent ease in the use of multiple categorical frameworks.

Research showed that bilingual children perform better (to mono-linguals) on the dimensional change card sort task, a task in which they are required to shift the sorting rule (color or shape; Bialystok, Craik, Klein, & Viswanathan, 2004). Adult bilinguals showed a smaller Simon effect – the interference of one rule with the other– compared to monolin-gual participants. Similar results were achieved with the use of the Navon task (1977) and the Trail Making Task (Wodka et al., 2008). More directly, Prior & Macwhinney (2009) have shown that it is specifically the switch cost that differentiates performance of bilingual and monolingual indi-viduals: when asked to perform a task in which the rule changed in sub-sequent trials, bilinguals were significantly faster to correctly perform on switch trials (Prior & Macwhinney, 2009). In a recent paper Kharkhurin

---

[3]   The overlap between bilingualism and biculturalism is well illustrated in the stud-ies of Bialystok & Martin (2004). In two experiments, conducted in Canada, English speaking monolingual children were contrasted with English-Cantonese bilingual children. Specifically, the bilingual sample "used Chinese regularly with their fami-lies, but English outside the home". While living in Canada and exposed to English speaking majority culture at school, these children also participated in a Chinese community, where "it is possible to function entirely in Chinese." (Bialystok & Mar-tin, 2004, pp. 335).

(2011) suggested that these abilities can contribute to the creative capacity of bilingual individuals. Indeed, the increased ease in task-switching ability in bilinguals seems to be accompanied by superior *creative* performance (Kharkhurin, 2008, 2009, 2010a). Studies have found that bilinguals (compared to monolinguals) score higher on the established Abbreviated Torrance Test of creativity (Kharkhurin, 2008), and draw more atypical pictures of alien creatures (Kharkhurin, 2009, 2010a). Echoing the principles of depth and dual engagement, improvements in creativity, in those studies, were more likely to occur in those with longer second-culture exposure (Kharkhurin, 2008), and those who became highly proficient in either of the languages (Kharkhurin, 2010a). In addition, in a sample of American-Middle Eastern University students, bilinguals with high English proficiency (akin to high depth of bicultural engagement) exhibited superior originality and invariance violation (drawing atypical features of aliens), compared to those with low English proficiency (low depth). They also displayed lower Stroop interference, which was correlated with creative performance, suggesting mediating role of switching ability (Kharkhurin, 2011).

In sum, creativity benefits from the ability to easily move between different frameworks of meaning, an ability that is developed when diversity experiences involve the maintenance of two cultural systems. However, creativity is also increased when individuals learn to re-combine ideas in entirely new ways (Amabile, 1996; Groborz & Nęcka, 2003). Also these skills are trained via adaptation to dual identity experiences. Below we discuss these dynamics of dual identity integration.

Integration

Although dual identity individuals can successfully navigate their social world by frame-switching, over time they may experience the need to achieve a more coherent sense of self. Imagine Ishrat, a daughter of Pakistani parents who attends a British school. There is considerable cultural distance between the two groups that Ishrat belongs to. To conform to the values of her peer group, during the day Ishrat may adopt a more Western style of clothing or behavior. Being simultaneously accountable to her British peers and Pakistani parents Ishrat will switch back to traditional garment and behavior when coming back from school. But this strategy remains functional only as long as the two worlds can be kept separate. When they collide, for instance when Ishrat is confronted by her grandparents for not wearing a hijab while at school, she will notice the conflict, and to maintain her belongingness to both social groups, become motivated to find a more satisfying resolution (Phinney & Devich-Navarro, 1997). Indeed, research has shown that when individuals realize the existence of two opposing identities and the cultural demands that follow, they experience this as an intra-individual conflict that they wish to resolve (Amiot et al., 2007; Gil, Vega, & Dimas, 1994; Leong & Ward, 2000; Walsh, Shulman, Feldman, & Maurer, 2005). To reconcile these opposing views and cultural norms Ishrat may attempt to find the creative "middle way" between her two conflicting identities. For instance, she can resolve the conflict by coming up with a different way of wearing her headscarf, to give it a more modern and "westernized" look (Khali, 2010; Somerville, 2008). In this process of conflict resolution, *novel, creative* qualities emerge (i.e., a new way of wearing the headscarf), that help resolve the conflicting cultural proscriptions associated with being British, and being a Muslim.

Inconsistency integration and creativity. Integrating conflicting cogni-tions has long been associated with the emergence of new, creative quali-ties (Goclowska et al., 2013; Huang & Galinsky, 2010; Miron-Spektor, Gino, & Argote, 2011; Wan & Chiu, 2002). According to Piaget (1971, 1975), when interactions or experiences do not easily fit within a child's existing world-view, they must reconcile this novel information with their current beliefs or creatively change these beliefs to fit this new informa-tion. In social categorization research, when being encouraged to think about individuals who belong to two, stereotypically incongruous catego-ries (e.g., a *Black* CEO, a *Gay* Soldier, a *Female* Mechanic), research par-ticipants have been shown to come up with novel, revised impressions of that target (Crisp, Hewstone, & Rubin, 2001; Hall & Crisp, 2005; Hastie, Schroeder, & Weber, 1990; Hutter & Crisp, 2005; Kunda et al., 1990). For instance, when describing a female-mechanic, rather than describ-ing her as a warm and nurturing (traits stereotypic of female), or greasy and crude (traits stereotypic of a mechanic), participants would use *novel* characteristics, not derived from either of the constituent categories: they would describe her as rebellious, or progressive, as only the use of such characteristic can explain the inconsistent combination of the cognitions female *and* mechanic.

Although conducted to investigate ways of reducing prejudiced behav-ior (Crisp, Ensari, & Hewstone, 2003; Crisp & Hewstone, 2007; Mullen,

Migdal, & Hewstone, 2001; Urban & Miller, 1998), the findings of coun-
ter-stereotype research seem to reflect what in the creativity literature is
known as *concept modification* (Amabile, 1996; De Dreu et al., 2008). Concept modification is a creative operation in which two inconsistent cognitions, when combined, lead to the emergence of new, creative qualities. As
people combine old words in new groupings, new vocabulary emerges (e.g.,
a "boomerang flu" to indicate a recurring flu pandemic; a "bait car" referring to a car used to catch carjackers; Wisniewski, 2001). When patterns
from nature are applied to everyday problems, new inventions, such as
the Velcro, are made (in fact, the invention was originally inspired by burr
seeds sticking to the inventors' dogs' fur). Finally, when features of existing
animals are recombined in unusual configurations, creatures of legends,
such as hippogriffs, sphinxes and centaurs are born (Canciarry, Levorato,
& Cicogna, 2001). Echoing the principle of cultural distance, these sort
creative concept modifications are especially likely when the two colliding
concepts are opposing and unrelated (Estes & Ward, 2002; S. M. Smith
et al., 1993).

Not only has it been shown that merging two inconsistent cognitions
leads to the emergence of creative qualities, but also that doing so can
carry over to a more creative way of thinking on an unrelated task. For
instance, in one set of studies, Wan and Chiu (2002) asked participants
to solve a set of novel (e.g., What is a piece of furniture that is also a kind
of fruit?) or ordinary (e.g., What is a piece of coat that is also a piece of
animal skin?) conceptual problems. Those primed in this way with incongruent conceptual combinations performed better on the Figural tests
of the Torrance Tests of Creativity Thinking (Experiment 1), and built
more creative LEGO models (Experiment 2) – tasks that were unrelated
to the initial cognitive inconsistency. Similar findings were obtained when
priming stereotypic and schematic inconsistencies (Gocłowska et al., 2013;
Vasiljevic & Crisp, 2013). In one study, thinking of a stereotypically inconsistent female mechanic lead to more flexible and creative thinking, on a
subsequent task, compared to a condition in which individuals thought
of a consistent "male mechanic" combination (Experiment 1, Gocłowska
et al., 2013). These types of primes also lead to the generation of more
creative ideas and posters (Experiment 2, Gocłowska et al., 2013), and better solutions to insight problems (Vasiljevic & Crisp, 2013 Experiment 3)[4].
Uplifts to creative and flexible cognitions have, furthermore, been found
when exposing participants to conflicting mental frames (Miron-Spektor

et al., 2011), bodily postures inconsistent with ones' mental state (Huang & Galinsky, 2010), or experiences (in a virtual reality lab) that were inconsistent with expectancies about the laws of physics (Ritter et al., 2012). Thus, across a multitude of situations, an apparent conflict between different cognitive frames was found to breed superior flexible and creative thought, beyond the task where the inconsistency was observed.

Superior generalized integration in dual identity individuals. Dual identity entails constant training in the resolution of conflicting categories, and one could thus expect dual identity individuals to exhibit a superior generalized skill at integrating conflicting cognitions. Indeed, in line with this prediction, the views of dual identity individuals tend to be more complex and integrated than those of assimilated or separated individuals. Bicultural individuals' descriptions of culture, and of a neutral landscape alike, were more differentiated: they included multiple perspectives and tended to more often compare and contrast various ideas (Benet-Martínez et al., 2006). In other research (Tadmor and Tetlock, 2009), biculturals were more integratively complex across domains: when describing a problem related to culture or work they were more likely to look at the issue from many perspectives, and accept the idea that these different perspectives or dimensions of the problem are valid (e.g., that some people view abortion as a civil liberties issue, while others see it as murder of helpless infants).

This seems to suggest that beyond being able to recognize and switch between various perspectives, bicultural individuals can more easily, or more readily, think of the reasons for why the two inconsistent cognitions are valid, and integrate those two inconsistent cognitions in one system. This type of superior ability to accommodate inconsistencies, contingent upon the development of a dual identity, was replicated across six experiments (Tadmor et al., 2012; Tadmor & Tetlock, 2009). Furthermore, integrative complexity mediated effects to superior creativity, additionally strengthening evidence that these effects can generalize beyond identity issues (Tadmor et al., 2012). Other studies have supported this assertion. Recently, a study of biculturals with blended identities (who are the most

---

[4]   It's important to note that these effects are conditional upon Personal Need for Structure, in such a way that individuals who are comfortable with uncertainty and inconsistencies (low PNS) are most likely to benefit from exposure to inconsistencies (Gocłowska et al., 2014; Gocłowska & Crisp, 2013).

likely to have developed a broader identification) showed that in the presence of multicultural cues, these individuals become more creative because they recruit more ideas on how to solve a problem (Saad, Damian, Benet-Martinez, Moons, & Robins, 2012). Another line of research, studying Asian-Americans, and female-engineers showed that individuals' whose identities are more integrated (high BII) are better able to combine ideas from their two identities to come up with creative products. For instance Asian-Americans whose identities were more integrated came up with more creative pizza recipes, when they could use ingredients related to either of their identities. In Study 2, female-engineers high in identity integration came up with more creative mobile devices when they knew that these devices would be used by other females (Cheng, Sanchez-Burks, & Lee, 2008).

It seems thus, that in addition to frame-switching, *immersive* membership in two *unrelated* social groups may increase individuals' ability to integrate and recombine existing concepts, leading to the emergence of novel, unique qualities - an ability that is central to creative endeavors. However alteration and inconsistency resolution are not the only solutions to managing complex self-definitions. Individuals have also been shown to deal with their dual group membership by assuming a broader sense of identification. Identifying oneself in terms of higher-order identities, we argue, could make it easier for individuals to access, simultaneously, a wide base of cognitions, increasing the likelihood that individuals will come up with novel solutions to problems.

Inclusion

While inconsistency resolution helps dual identity individuals resolve day-to-day practical issues, such as how to settle two conflicting cultural rules, this cognitive strategy may not be sufficient to address more general questions of personal identity. To achieve a more coherent sense of self dual identity individuals may rather attempt to shift perceptions of their own cultural and national identity (Amiot et al., 2007), by recognizing the simultaneous value of their two identities, and merging them within a more inclusive category (Gaertner & Dovidio, 2000): pan-national identity (e.g., European), pan-ethnic identity (Portes, 1997), or thinking in terms of "humanity", or "citizens of the world" (Amiot et al., 2007; McFarland, Brown, & Webb, 2013; Sussman, 2000). The development of such a broader identity, we argue, would support creativity of dual identifi-ers by widening the base of ideas, norms, and behaviours accessible at any one time.

To illustrate, a woman who, in the past, described herself primarily as a "mother", but who, throughout her work experience developed profes-sional identity "engineer", could integrate those two identities under a broader self-definition, for instance a "professional woman". When asked to think of behaviours characteristic of her in-group, she could easily access characteristics and behaviours linked to this broadened sense of self, and the associated wide base of cognitions, without the necessity of switching between two different mental sets. In other words, by integrat-ing being a mother and being an engineer under a higher-order identity – that of a "professional woman" – she would broaden the scope of cogni-tions, norms and values that she has immediate access to at any one time.

At the end of 1980's in the USA, Bell interviewed career-oriented African-American women. These women were the first among their com-munity to embrace high-status "White" professions, while maintaining links with their original African-American community. One of them said: "In many ways, I think white people are deprived. There is a richness from our duality that they will never have. (...) My world has a set of values, a set of expectations, a set of behaviour patterns, a language and a set of rewards. And that whole system was drawn from a broad base. Now parts of that system may be more particularly black in certain characteristics, while other parts are particularly white. But I think it is in that which I grew up with, it's not one or the other." (Bell, 1990, pp. 473).

Knowledge activation and creativity. To better understand how this type of broad identity described above breeds creativity, it is good to dis-cuss the effect of knowledge activation on creative thought. When generat-ing ideas and problem solutions, individuals are typically restrained by the activation of exemplars and narrow categories (Marsh, Ward, & Landau, 1999; Ward, Smith, & Vaid, 1997; Ward, 2007). This is because follow-ing the *path of least resistance* (Ward, 1994), people are drawn to retrieve typical and specific exemplars of known concepts, and assign the proper-ties of those concepts to their novel idea. For instance, when asked to draw a novel exemplar belonging to a certain category (e.g., a new kind of animal), 60 to 65 % of participants base their creations on specific known instances from those categories: when trying to think up a new animal, they draw on features of cats, and when trying to think up a new ritual, they draw on typical features of weddings (Ward et al., 2002). In a similar vein, when generating traits that could describe an individual, people typically generate those traits that are most strongly associated with the schemata or salient exemplars from the group that that person belongs to (Hutter & Crisp, 2005; Kunda & Thagard, 1996).

Although this type of thinking provides efficiency in information processing (Macrae, Milne, & Bodenhausen, 1994), it can, at the same time, stifle the range of ideas that one has access to at any one time (Gocłowska et al., 2013; Sassenberg & Moskowitz, 2005; S. M. Smith et al., 1993). For instance, in one line of research individuals were primed (or not) with examples of invented sport disciplines, and subsequently asked to come up with ideas for a new kind of sport. New ideas tended to draw on the characteristics of the primes: for instance, individuals primed with a game that contained a ball and a bat, were more likely, subsequently, to generate another game that contained a ball and a bat, but not games that had to do with rowing, flying, or climbing (S. M. Smith et al., 1993). In other words, activating an exemplar acted as a cognitive anchor, and inhibited individuals' ability to invent sports that did not contain a ball and a bat. Thus, the more people thought of concrete exemplars and narrow categories linked to those exemplars (e.g., ball sports), the more likely were they to draw ideas from a narrow cognitive base.

Since exemplars restrict idea generation to their immediate associates (Mednick, 1962), interventions that compel individuals to abandon the use of exemplars or low level categories should increase creativity. For instance, when participants considered abstract demands of a situation, such as the environmental properties of a planet, this lead to the generation of more creative exemplars of alien creatures (compared to a neutral baseline, and an experimental condition in which participants were asked to think of animals that already exist; Ward et al., 2004). In a similar vein, participants with higher abstract reformulation skills came up with more creative solutions to the problem "presence of mice in ones' basement" (Reiter-Palmon, Mumford, O'Connor Boes, & Runco, 1997). Thus, overreliance on narrowly defined concepts or self-definitions limits the ideas and problem solutions that individuals can draw upon when creating new things. However, broadening the categorical boundaries, such as when abandoning thinking in terms of a national identity, in favor of a European or pan-national identity, opens up the possibility of recruiting a wide range of problem solutions, leading to increased chances for creativity and innovation.

Evidence of broader self-definition. That dual identity individuals integrate their categorical representations in a wider, more inclusive identity is well illustrated in the development of pan-national or ethnic identities in immigrants (Amiot et al., 2007). Mobility within the European Union – a political structure that attempts to integrate the multitude of nationalities, languages, cultures and religions prevalent in Europe – has been shown to contribute to the development of a higher-order identity. For instance, British undergraduates who studied in another European country for a year, subsequently rated themselves as higher on belonging to a "European Cultural space", exhibited a higher partly European identity, and showed more interest in European issues (King & Ruiz-Gelices, 2003). These results have been echoed in large-scale sociological research where mobility within European states predicted the development of a broader European identity (Spannring, Wallace, & Datler, 2008).

Similar processes have been observed when members of ethnic minority groups became involved with the majority culture. For instance members of the Armenian community in Turkey who attended a Turkish (majority culture) school, were more likely (compared to their separated peers) to identify with the higher-order Turkish identity, as well as a global, "human" identity (Der-Karabetian & Balian, 1991). So participating in a second culture helped these minority individuals to develop a more encompassing, higher order identity. Such findings echo the idea of the common in-group identity model (Gaertner & Dovidio, 2000), a theoretical framework which argues that cross-group contact leads to a shift from categorization in terms of 'us' versus 'them', to a more inclusive 'we'. In this line of research, cooperation between two groups, and positive contact experiences, have been associated with developing a more inclusive, common in-group identity: both in multi-ethnic groups (Gaertner, Mann, Dovidio, Murrell, & Pomare, 1990), as well as organizational mergers (Gaertner, Dovidio, & Bachman, 1996). Although originally tested in inter-group settings, we argue, this phenomenon is very similar to what happens when individuals develop a broader identity – they become more inclusive of the concepts, norms and behaviors characteristic of their new group. This widens the base of cognitions from which they recruit ideas and creative problem solutions at any one time.

Broadening the scope of idea sampling. Developing a higher-order identification (Cinnirella, 1997) is associated with the broadening of one's social circle, interests, and an increased likelihood of recruiting a wider range of ideas. For instance career-oriented African-American women interviewed by Bell at the end of 1980's, reported increased variety of environmental, social and cultural contexts that they took advantage of, relatively to their assimilated peers. Recruitment of foreign ideas is, in fact, a natural element of cultural adaptation. While exposing themselves to out-group members and their culture, individuals form interpersonal and affective links with those cultures, and gain knowledge of the language, customs and culture of their new group (Aron et al., 2004; Carlson & Widaman, 1988; Douglas & Jones- Rikkers, 2001; Hadis, 2005; Schmid, Hewstone, & Al Ramiah, 2012; Verkuyten et al., 2010; Wright, Aron, & Tropp, 2002; Zhai & Scheer, 2004; Zorn, 1996).

This type of openness to other people's perspectives is a pivotal aspect of multicultural success (Leung & Chiu, 2008), and successful inter-cultural collaborations. For instance a study of managers showed that in intercultural collaborations, individuals high in affect-based trust (and thus more open to the "others'" ideas), are more likely to collaborate effectively, share ideas with their cross-cultural work partners, and together with them, come up with more creative idea solutions (Chua, Morris, & Mor, 2012).

Indeed, broadening one's self-definition strengthens the emotional ties with the new in-group and their culture, and increases the salience of universal values and behaviours in common with other people. In the words of Sampson and Smith (1957), diversity experiences lead individuals to becoming a world-minded person – someone who "favors a world-view of the problems of humanity, whose primary reference group is mankind, rather than Americans, English, Chinese etc."

Consistent with this idea, American students who had spent a year in Europe demonstrated (in a post-test, as well as compared to a matched control group) a subsequent increased concern in global politics and cooperation (international political concern; for similar evidence see Hadis, 2005; Zorn, 1996), increased intent to engage in contact with other cultures (cross-cultural interest), and a stronger respect for the values and traditions of other countries (cosmopolitan attitudes; Carlson, Carlson, & Widaman, 1988). In another line of research contact with individuals from other countries increased students' global perspective and positive attitudes towards cultural diversity (Zhai & Scheer, 2004). The effects observed were in line with the depth and cultural distance principles outlined earlier in our model. The longer the engagement with a second culture, the stronger the effects to cultural sensitivity (Medina-López-Portillo, 2003), and global mindedness (Kehl & Morris, 2005). The more significant the cultural differences between the host and home culture, the greater the increase in world-mindedness (Douglas & Jones-Rikkers, 2001).

The breath of one's interests has long been associated with creativity: for instance participating in broad extracurricular activities has been associated with divergent (creative) thought (Wallach & Wing, 1969; Kogan & Pankove 1974; Milgram 1978; Runco 1986), and openness to experience, a trait that entails increased receptivity and interest in various ideas and activities, counts among one of the strongest predictors of creative performance (McCrae, 1987). Beyond the increased interest in other cultures, individuals who experience diversity also are more likely, in a laboratory setting, to draw on foreign ideas in order to solve a concrete creative problem. In one line of research, participants were asked to think of a creative research idea, inspired by sayings on happiness attributed to various thinkers – from ones' own culture, and from abroad. Across three experiments, the degree of multicultural experience of the research participants was associated with more breadth in idea sampling: participants with more multicultural experience, on a creativity task, were more likely to sample ideas from various cultures, rather than just their own cultural group. In addition, participants with more multicultural experience rated foreign sayings as more positive, relative to individuals with less multicultural experience (Leung & Chiu, 2010), attesting to the idea that these dual identifiers are more receptive to a wide base of idea building blocks.

In sum, individuals who become members of new groups are more likely to move away from narrowly defined self-categorization, towards a broader self- definition, and display a tendency to retrieve and sample a wider base of cognitions. This development of a broader idea base should allow them to free themselves from restraints associated with prototypical problem solutions available within their initial group, and enhance their chances of producing more creative and innovative ideas.

TIME-COURSE OF INDIVIDUAL DUAL IDENTITY ADAPTATION

We have discussed three characteristics of dual identity experiences that are prerequisite to observing benefits to creativity. The experiences are *deep*, require *dual engagement*, and involve membership in groups that are *culturally distinct*. To manage these sort of experiences, individuals can employ three distinct cognitive strategies, all of which can come to benefit creativity in different ways. Individuals may *alternate* between host and home cultural frames, they may *integrate* elements from those two cultural frames in order to resolve conflicting values, customs and attitudes, and finally, they may come to construe themselves in a more *inclusive* manner, leading to the recruitment of a wide idea base (see Figure 1). We do not believe that these three processes are mutually exclusive, rather, we propose a *continuum* of adjustment whereby, over time, characteristics of the dual identity experiences (e.g., acculturation and conformity pressures), and intra-individual phenomena (e.g., need to achieve a coherent sense of self), come to progressively trigger each identity process. This cumulative model is consistent with recent research on how the dual identity experiences come to be incorporated into one's *self-concept* (Amiot et al., 2007; Amiot & de la Sablonniere, 2010).

Dual identity individuals usually talk about their diversity experience as being self-defining – it has become a part of *who they are*, internalized. Research has shown that as people develop wider social networks, and in particular networks that involve diverse and differentiated bases for identity, they develop a more complex social identity - an integrated self-concept - that includes their disparate identities (Amiot et al., 2007; Amiot & de la Sablonniere, 2010; Roccas & Brewer, 2002). In the context of multicultural experience, this means conceptually integrating host and home cultures, as we have discussed. Indeed, Maddux et al. (2009) suggest that dual identity experiences enhance creativity "because they help individuals *integrate* multiple cultures into their own personal and social identities" (p. 739; italics added).

Importantly, the different cognitive strategies and consequences that we have discussed may be triggered at different points in the internalization process. At first, dual identity individuals are unlikely to attempt conceptual integration, and unlikely to feel included in the wider group. They will more likely be focused on correctly responding to the immediate acculturation pressures by learning the behaviors and values of their new group, and enacting them when the circumstances require. As such, alternation between two identities will characterize early stages of the dual identity experience (Hong et al., 2000). However, as time goes by, dual identity individuals will become increasingly aware of the value, custom and cultural conflicts that exist between the two groups of which they are members. When the need to resolve intrapersonal conflicts arises, they will use *inconsistency resolution* to work out these conflicts between their original and new identity, or cultural norms associated with those, so that each identity can be considered part of the self (Amiot & de la Sablonniere, 2010, p. 40). In so doing, dual identity individuals will become practiced at the integration of inconsistent ideas – a psychological process that has been associated with conceptual expansion.

Finally, over time, individuals will gain more knowledge of and form interpersonal links with the new group, leading to the broadening of their self-definition. Amiot and de la Salbonierre (2010) capture the essence of this relationship and what it means for identity incorporation: "a ... way for the immigrant to integrate her different social identities would involve identifying with a superordinate social identity · such as being human or being a "world citizen," which would be highly inclusive and would incorporate the multitude of more specific identities she possesses." (p. 41). This inclusive way of thinking, we argue, will allow dual identity individuals to more easily recruit ideas from a wide conceptual network, increasing their likelihood of finding creative problem solutions.

RECOMMENDATIONS FOR FUTURE RESEARCH

The model presented in this paper may help develop specific, targeted tests of the cognitive consequences of dual identity processes. It can give us an indication of when, in the time-course of the dual identity experience, and in what individuals, increased set-switching, inconsistency resolution, and broad recruitment of ideas can be observed. For instance, researchers could ask about the extent to which the individual has maintained a sense of their home culture while living in the host culture, and the extent to which the two cultures are similar versus different (overlapping versus distinct). These dual engagement and cultural distance criteria should positively predict creativity. Relatedly, measures of common in-group identity are readily available from the literature on identity integration and can be used to obtain convergent evidence for the use of a wider base of ideas at later points in the time-course of adaptation (e.g., Roccas & Brewer, 2002; Geartner & Dovidio, 2000; Benet-Martinez & Haritatos, 2005).

Knowing what changes occur during dual identity adaptation may not just explain why boosts to creativity occur, but can illuminate other consequences of multiple group membership, that go beyond creativity. For instance, researchers could investigate whether dual group membership that involves frame switching, leads to improved simultaneous language interpretation, switching between driving on the left vs. right side of the road, or any other types of tasks that entail rapid change between multiple mental operations.

Dual identity development

Even though the model clarifies many issues and integrates several research threads, many questions remain unanswered. We discuss these issues in the paragraphs below. We begin by asking about the nature of dual identities and their cognitive development.

Operationalizing dual identities. Dual identities are studied from many angles: the psychology of multiple-, multicultural- , and bicultural identities, but also research on bilingual or multicultural adaptation. Cumulatively these studies indicate that experiences that involve exposure to, and deep engagement with a new group can increase creativity. However, it should be noted that various types of multicultural experiences are correlated, and isolating these processes in cross-section studies is very difficult. The clearest example is bilingualism and biculturalism: Most bilingual (vs. monolingual) participants are also bicultural (vs. monocultural). In other research, dual identities are often correlated with multicultural experience. For instance the Multicultural Experience Survey (Leung and Chiu, 2010) inquires about aspects of bicultural identity development (parents' cultural background, time spent living abroad) alongside being exposed to multicultural experiences (exposure to foreign food or music, social bonds). These issues are inherent to cross-sectional research, however to gain a deeper understanding of the dual-identity–creativity link, it is important to develop methods and measures that can tease apart the psychological impact of different diversity experiences. Importantly, precise measurement would allow researchers to better understand the different samples that they are working with, and develop more detailed conceptual models. For instance, while studies have shown that merely living abroad can increase creativity (Fee & Gray, 2012; Maddux & Galinsky, 2009), this outcome may be enhanced with advanced language proficiency (Kharkhurin, 2008) and the engagement of social identification processes

(Cheng, Sanchez-Burks, & Lee, 2008; Tadmor, Galinsky, & Maddux, 2012). This suggest that researchers working with cross-sectional data should develop a better understanding of the various properties of their samples: for instance depth, dual engagement, and cultural distance.

Multiple group identifiers. Alongside more precise measures of dual identity, further investigation is needed in to the effects of belonging to more than two social groups. In this review we suggested that boosts to creativity are likely to be observed when individuals possess *at least* two identities that are inconsistent with one-another. What happens when people have more than two identities remains unknown. One possibility is that if one were to manage more than two inconsistent identities, this would strengthen the observed effects, but only up to a certain point. First of all, crossed categorization research suggested that people can typically hold only two identities in working memory at any one time (Crisp & Hewstone, 2007), and this would mean that once two identities are already conflicted, the addition of a third identity would have a minimal impact over and above the addition of the second identity. Secondly, one can imagine that having too many identities would undermine depth, because with a large number of identities, there is a limit to how deeply individuals can engage with those identities. Perhaps this is why in the studies by Godart et al (2014) breadth and creativity had a curvilinear association: individuals who had lived in more than one country showed enhanced creativity, but once they had lived in more than three countries, creativity began to drop again. Future research should test these predictions utilizing different research samples, and various measures of dual identification..

Many forms of culture. Throughout the paper we talked of individuals who belong to two social categories that are incongruent with one another. From a theoretical point of view, this made sense, as cultures are not limited to geographies and ethnicities, but extend to all groups and categories of people (Cohen, 2009): gender, profession, social status, or personal interest. However, the vast majority of studies reported in the present paper described the experiences of national or ethnic biculturals. One reason for this may be the prevalence of ethnic and national biculturalism in the world today. The number of international migrants has now moved beyond 190 million people (The United Nations, 2009), and many of these individuals have settled their families in the host country, raising a second generation bicultural children. However, given increased mobility across other social structures, understanding whether similar processes occur in gender counter-stereotypic individuals (e.g., female engineers), those who embrace new ethical systems (e.g., a Western Buddhist), or those who move up and down the social ladder (e.g., a working class academic), would greatly help us understand the nature of processes described in this literature.

One example, and perhaps one that we have not discussed throughout the paper, is of second language acquisition, in the absence of cultural exposure. Could this type of exposure also contributes to more creative thought? Some support to that idea can be found in the literature on bilingual education. For instance when Lambert, Tucker & d'Angeljan (1973) followed up Canadian elementary schoolchildren in a bilingual study program in Quebec, English-speaking pupils instructed in French (relative to their native English or French peers) demonstrated higher levels of creativity (Lambert et al., 1973). However, other studies suggest that when language is learned in isolation from the cultural environment, benefits to creativity are less profound (Kharkhurin, 2010b). Experimenters could attempt to establish to what extent, in the absence of a second cultural base, mere bilingualism could lead to superior set switching and creativity. A test like that could relatively easily be conducted in multilingual countries – Canada, Belgium – where bilingualism is imposed by the education system and political structures, but the two languages are (relatively) low in cultural distance.

Switching, integration, and inclusion. Our dual identity model outlines three stages of dual identity adaptation, and explains how these stages influence creativity. Future research should try to establish to what extent, and in what way particular processes outlined in the model compliment and build onto each other. For instance as individuals adapt to possessing a complex self-definition, one may expect them to be more likely to frame-switch, rather than integrate or form an inclusive identity. However, even at the inclusive stage, individuals are still bound to experience frame-switching in those domains where this strategy remains most adaptive. For instance, after 20 years spent in the U.S. a Chinese immigrant may have developed a broad identity, and may be displaying behaviors indicative of cultural blendedness via their lifestyle, beliefs or dress. However, they will still continue to switch languages or certain cultural norms when the context deems it appropriate, and since having developed extensive practice, they may be more proficient at it, than individuals who had not developed a blended identity. Consistent with this idea, individuals high in identity integration, tend to assimilatively switch more, compared to individuals low in identity integration (Mok & Morris, 2010). This means that the competencies or skills acquired at a previous stage do not necessarily dissipate with the next stage. They may rather build onto each other, leading to a broadening of the behavioral repertoire of the diversifying individual, and resulting in cumulative improvements in cognitive performance. Future studies may attempt to more carefully test these ideas.

Boundary Conditions

The idea that possessing two or more social identities can boost creativity is a relatively new thought, and studies begin to suggest that such effects are warranted by a number of prerequisites. Future research should help more precisely describe under what conditions possessing dual identities leads to increased flexible and creative thought.

Relations between depth, dual engagement, and cultural distance. First of all, we need to better understand how the three prerequisites of dual identity adaptation – depth, dual engagement, and cultural distance – interact with one another, and what constellations of these factors are needed to bring about creativity. In real life, dual engagement will often imply cultural distance, as two groups that one belongs to are bound to be different from one-another, even if just a little. This suggests that dual engagement and cultural distance should be positively correlated. However, their correlation with the third prerequisite - depth - may depend on particular operationalisations of depth. If depth is understood as deep engagement with a group or culture (for instance high identification with both the home and host culture), it will negatively correlate with dual engagement and cultural distance, because lots of different groups will make it too difficult to deeply engage with either of their cultures. Things do however look different when we operationalize depth as the time spent in a culture (as we suggested in the introduction, time is also a form of depth, because with time individuals are more likely to develop interpersonal links and absorb the norms of a group). For example, when Godart and colleagues (2014) ran archival analyses of the lives of great fashion designers, they found a positive correlation of depth – operationalized as time spent abroad – with breadth. In that study, designers who had lived in many countries had also spent a long time living abroad. In our review, we have discussed both length of stay abroad, and processing depth, under one label because we believe that both can lead to the same outcome – they allow individuals to get to know the new group/culture really well, and though that, can contribute to superior creativity. However, to really understand the dynamic of this relationship, and how that dynamic brings about superior creativity, researchers should attempt to more precisely measure various aspects of "depth", considering both the time of exposure to one group or culture, as well as ones' psychological engagement with that culture.

Drawbacks of dual identification. A separate question is one about the various consequences of dual identity dynamics that may offset the benefits discussed in our paper. Embracing dual identities brings not only benefits; it can also associate with tangible difficulties in various areas of life: cultural misunderstandings and differences of perspective (Morris & Leung, 2010), adverse linguistic effects (Zhang, Morris, Cheng, & Yap, 2013) acculturation stress, low power positions, or increased levels of experienced prejudice. These types of negative consequences may offset individual creativity gains acquired via dual identity adaptation. Future research should investigate to what extent the effects of dual identity adaptation are qualified by such factors (e.g., see Chua, 2012).

Painting the bigger picture

Two further inquiries can help us extent the current work beyond what is known and what is being researched. First of all, it's worth mentioning that because the current paper focuses on individual-level creativity, it does not consider an alternative route through which dual identity experiences can boost creativity. Even though this perspective may be played down in psychological research, creativity is often a social process: it occurs in groups of people, and involves exchanges of ideas and thoughts between and within social groups. Therefore, it is important that future studies investigate how dual identity individuals perform within and between teams, and whether their improved ability to switch, integrate and include can contribute to better creative outcomes on the group level (e.g., Cao, Galinski, & Maddux, 2014; Chua, Morris & Mor, 2012).

Related to that, it is worth asking whether the effects observed in the literature result from possessing two or more social identities, or from a decreased reliance on one social identity only. Tadmor and colleagues have shown that improvements to integrative flexibility and creativity are observed not only in highly identified biculturals, but also in marginal individuals – those who do not identify with either of the groups that they belong to. This could suggest that the dual identity-creativity links manifests a broader phenomenon, whereby creativity increases as a function of decreased reliance on one single identity. Consistent with this, social identities have been found to stifle creativity, when norms of those identities are associated with less creative outcomes, and when individuals' identification is high (Adarves-Yorno et al., 2006, 2007). Following from that finding, we can also imagine that when individuals rely on one identity only, this affects not only norms, but also information accessibility. Perhaps then, any identity structure that does not entail high identification with one culture only (e.g., developing personal, rather than social identities, possessing dual social identities), can make people more creative.

CONTRIBUTIONS TO THE MULTICULTURALISM DEBATE

Our model integrates notions of multicultural adaptation from cross-cultural and bilingualism literature, with cognitive models of category construal and intergroup relations. While the review focuses on cognitive outcomes, this integrated approach may also make an important contribution to the "multiculturalism debate" (Mendoza- Denton & España, 2010; Plaut et al., 2009; Verkuyten et al., 2010). Is dual identity a good thing? Should politicians, policy makers and the public, welcome our increasingly pluralistic society, or should they expect immigrants to assimilate, and become like everyone else? These questions have dominated scholarly, political and public discourse for the last 50 years (Lambert & Taylor, 1990; Rudmin, 2003; Schlesinger, 1992; Yinger, 1994). Our theoretical analysis contributes to this debate by explicitly linking models of bicultural identity adaptation development, with the creativity literature. The work we have reviewed shows that dual identity experiences *can* yield benefits for individuals and societies, and on a very real and important psychological, social and economic dimension – *creativity*, provided that individuals have the possibility to deeply identify, process, and interact with the cultures of both groups that they belong to.

Demonstration of the link between dual identity adaptation and creative thinking also feeds into specific debates on education policy. As Bowman (2010) notes, opponents of policies promoting multiculturalism argue that focusing on diversity in schools takes attention away from their true purpose - to foster academic excellence - because one comes at the expense of the latter (Rothman, Lipset, & Nevitte, 2003). The research described in our article stands in direct contravention of these views, and suggests that diversity is a critical component of academic attainment - and should be *fostered* in schools not only as personal and social education, but as an even more key part of the curriculum.

Finally, work that continues to elucidate the impact of dual identity development on creative thought, will not only provide scientific justification for multicultural policies, but provide new ways of looking at existing psychologically- informed interventions for promoting tolerance and positive intergroup attitudes. For instance, the theoretical analysis provided above suggests a new, beneficial outcome for interventions based on an implementation of the *common ingroup identity* model. Not only can a focus on shared identities reduce tendencies to favour in-groups over out-groups, it may also help to advance individuals' propensity for innovation and original thought through tendencies to adopt a wide idea base, conceptual integration and frame-switching strategies. Uncovering these new, unforeseen benefits of such interventions poses a range of new research questions, and some exciting new routes for future research and practical application.

CONCLUSIONS

In this article we have aimed to gain a better understanding of how individuals perceive, construe, and represent their various group memberships, and how this relates to the development of creativity. Our analysis provided a new theoretical lens through which to understand, interpret, and predict benefits resulting from dual identity experiences; experiences that, we argue, are encapsulated in extant categorical models of social relations. This theoretical analysis may help us understand the link between creativity and dual identities in several important ways. First, it enables a better understanding of how people mentally construe their identities, and how the nature of that construal has implications, not just for efforts to reduce prejudice, but for individuals' creativity, innovation and original thinking. Second, it highlights a conceptual link between two hitherto largely independent, but intensely researched areas in psychology: the psychology of creativity, and the models of multiple social categorization and prejudice reduction. Finally, it informs debate on the value in diversity characterized by dual identities, by illustrating the potential benefits, not only for tolerance and harmony between social groups, but for the personal, professional and social well-being of individuals, groups and organizations.

ACKNOWLEDGEMENTS

This research was supported by a Marie-Curie postdoctoral fellowship awarded to M. Gocłowska (FP7-PEOPLE-2011-IEF, 299852, CREA.DIV), and a British Academy Research Development Award (BARDA 47819) to R. J. Crisp. The authors would like to thank Matthijs Baas, Mariska Kret, and the three anonymous reviewers for their thoughtful comments on an earlier version of this manuscript.

Group Membership

Use of Conceptual Categories

Single: access to information from once conceptual framework only.

Alternation: there is only rapid access to information from identity A or B at any one time, but individuals become adept in *switching* between conceptual frameworks.

Integration: individuals need to resolve conceptual inconsistencies between identity A and B, and become, as a result, more adept at integrating inconsistent cognitions.

Inclusion: developing a broader self-definition (C) allows individuals to simultaneously draw from a broader range of ideas, decreasing reliance on more narrowly defined concepts constituent of identity framework A or B.

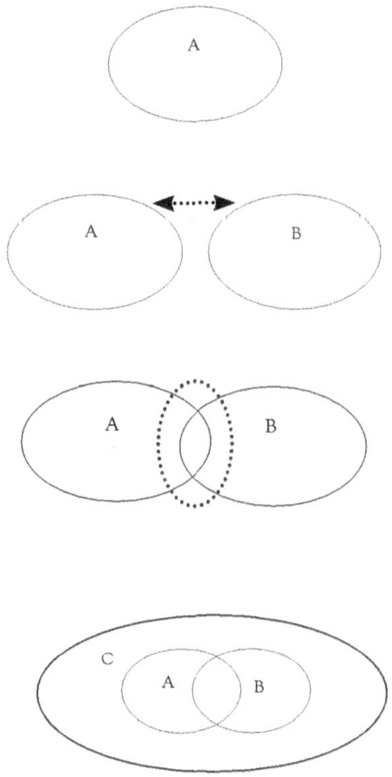

Figure 1 Dual identity affects concept use. People who belong to relatively uniform groups access knowledge structures associated with one group only. But managing two diverse identities allows individuals to practice novel cognitive skills involving (1) alternation of conceptual frameworks, (2) integration of inconsistent cognitions, and (3) increased inclusiveness.

Table 1 Changes in creative performance resulting from dual identity experiences.

Study	Sample	Measure of Dual Engagement	Outcome Variable
Fee & Gray, 2012	Australians and New Zealanders living in Asia, Africa or the Pacific.	Performance 12 months after departure > performance before departure.	Abbreviated Torrance Test (ATTA) overall creativity and flexibility.
Tadmor, Galinsky & Maddux, 2012	MBA students from a European (S1) or US (S2) university who have previously lived abroad.	Integrated > assimilated and separated international students.	Fluency, flexibility and novelty on the multiple uses task (S1) and rating of innovations at work (S2).
Kharkhurin, 2011	Arabic/Urdu/Farsi speakers living in the United Arab Emirates.	Bilinguals with high second language proficiency > moderate second language proficiency.	Originality and violation of invariants (typical features) in drawings of alien creatures.
Leung & Chiu, 2010	European American undergraduates.	High multicultural experience > low multicultural experience score.	Infrequent/original ideas for a gift (S2).
Kharkhurin, 2010a	Russian-English speakers and English speakers living in the US.	Ethnic bilinguals > monolinguals.	Nonverbal creativity on the ATTA.
Kharkhurin, 2010b	Russian-English speakers & English speakers living in the US; Farsi-English speakers living in the UAE and Farsi speakers living in Iran.	Ethnic bilinguals > monolinguals.	ATTA fluency, flexibility and originality.

Table 1 Changes in creative performance resulting from dual identity experiences.

Study	Sample	Measure of Dual Engagement	Outcome Variable
Maddux, Adam, & Galinsky, 2010	Students from a European (S1) or US (S2) university who have previously lived abroad. Home and internationalstudents from a US university (S3).	Multicultural learning > control primes.	Overcoming activated solutions (S1), Remote Associates Test (RAT) performance (S2), Duncker-candle problem (S3).
Kharkhurin, 2009	Farsi-English Bilinguals living in the United Arab Emirates > Farsi Monolinguals living in Iran.	Ethnic bilinguals > monolinguals.	ATTA originality, increased violation of invariants (typical features) in drawings of alien creatures.
Maddux &Galinsky, 2009	International and American MBA students from a US university (S1 & S2),	Long > short time living abroad (S1, S2, & S4); Living abroad prime > control (S3, S5).	Insight tasks (S1, S2 & S4), RAT (S3), drawing alien creatures (S5).
Leung & Chiu, 2008	European American undergraduates.	High multicultural experience > low multicultural experience.	Fluency and flexibility on the unusual uses test; retrieval of non-normative exemplars.
Kharkhurin, 2008	Russian-speaking and English-speaking students at a US college.	Ethnic bilinguals > monolinguals.	ATTA fluency and flexibility.

Table 2 Cultural and cognitive switching in dual identity individuals.

Study	Sample	Measure of Dual Engagement	Outcome Variable
		Cultural frame switching	
Ramirez-Esparza, Gosling, Benet-Martinez, Potter & Pennbaker, 2006	Spanish-English adult bilinguals living in the US.	Priming Hispanic/English culture via the use of language.	Responses on personality test in line with primed culture.
Hong, Morriss, Chiu & Benet-Martinez, 2000	Westernized Chinese students in Hong Kong.	Priming American/Chinese culture.	Attribution style in line with primed culture.
Hong, Chiu & Kung, 1997	Westernized Chinese students in Hong Kong.	Priming American/Chinese culture.	Attribution style in line with primed culture (S2 & S3).
Bell, 1990	African-American career-oriented women working in a White US-majority culture.		Self-reports of compartmentalization and switching between cultures.
		Cognitive switching	
Kharkhurin, 2011	Arabic/Urdu/Farsi speakers living in the UAE.	High > moderate second language proficiency.	Color-naming Stroop test.
Bialystok, 2010	In Canda, English speaking children and children who additionally speak a second language at home (e.g., Cantonese, Italian).	Ethnic bilinguals > monolinguals.	Global-local (S1, S2 & S3) and trail making task (S1, S2 & S3).

Study	Sample	Measure of Dual Engagement	Outcome Variable
Prior & Macwhinney, 2009	US college students speaking English only, or speaking two languages continuously from the age of six (or earlier).	Ethnic bilinguals > monolinguals.	Reduced switching cost in a task-switching paradigm.
Martin-Rhee & Bialystok, 2008	In Canada, English speaking children, and children additionally speaking French, Chinese, Spanish, Hebrew, or Russian in their home.	Ethnic bilinguals > monolinguals.	Simon task (S1 & S2) and day-night Stroop task (S3).
Bialystok & Martin, 2004	In Canada, English speaking children, and children additionally speaking Chinese or French in their home.	Ethnic bilinguals > monolinguals.	Dimensional change card sort task (S1, S2 & S3).
Bialystok, Craik, Klein & Viswanathan, 2004	English-speaking Canadian adults, Tamil-English bilinguals living in India, Cantonese-English bilinguals living in Hong-Kong, and French-English bilinguals living in Canada.	Ethnic bilinguals > monolinguals.	Simon task.
Bialystok 1999	In Canada, English speaking children and children speaking English at school and Chinese at home.	Ethnic bilinguals > monolinguals.	Dimensional change card sort task.

Table 2 Cultural and cognitive switching in dual identity individuals.

Table 3 Identity conflict and conceptual integration skills in dual identity individuals.

Study	Sample	Measure of Dual Engagement	Outcome Variable
		Identity Conflict	
Walsh, Shulman, Feldman & Maurer, 2005	Non immigrant Israeli adolescents, and Russian-Israeli immigrant adolescents.	Immigrants > non-immigrants.	Conflicted sense of self.
Leong & Ward, 2000	Chinese sojourners in Singapore.	Higher contact with host nationals > lower contact with host nationals.	Identity conflict.
Phinney & Devich-Navarro, 1997	African-Americans and Latino-Americans in the US.	Blended (integrated) identity > separated and alternating individuals.	Increased perceptions of acculturation pressures (e.g., to be "more ethnic" and "less white").
		Conceptual Integration	
Maddux, Bivolaru, Hafenbrack, Tadrmor & Galinsky, 2014	MBA students in an international environment	High multicultural engagement > low multicultural engagement	Increase (over time) in integrative complexity on the topic of multicultural cooperation
Saad, Damian, Benet-Martinez, Moons & Robins, 2012	Chinese-American students primed with a bicultural context	High > Low identity blendedness	Increase in fluency and originality of ideas on the brick task.

Table 3 Identity conflict and conceptual integration skills in dual identity individuals.

Study	Sample	Measure of Dual Engagement	Outcome Variable
Tadmor, Galinsky & Maddux, 2012	MBA students from a European or US university who have previously lived abroad (S1 & S2). Israeli professionals working in the US (S3).	Integrated > assimilated and separated individuals.	Integrative complexity (S1-S3).
Tadmor & Tetlock, 2009	Asian undergraduates studying in the US (S1). Israeli professionals working in the US (S2).	Integrated > assimilated and separated individuals.	Integrative complexity (S1 & S2).
Benet-Martinez, Lee, & Leu, 2006	Anglo-American Monoculturals and Chinese-American Biculturals living in the US.	Biculturals > monoculturals.	Culture/landscape descriptions comparing and contrasting multiple perspectives (S1).
Cheng, Sanchez-Burks & Lee, 2008	Asian-Americans (S1) and female-engineers (S2)	High BII > low BII	More fluency and more originality on creativity tasks that enabled people to draw ideas from both their identities.

Table 4 Breadth of identification and breadth of idea sampling in dual identity individuals.

Study	Sample	Measure of Dual Engagement	Outcome Variable
Breadth of Identification			
Spanring, Wallace & Datler, 2008	Europeans with high and low European mobility experiences.	High > low mobility experience.	Development of a European identity.
King & Ruiz-Gelices, 2003	British students who lived (or not) abroad for 1 year.	Living abroad experience > no living abroad experience.	Belonging to a "European cultural space" & possessing a "partly-European" identity.
Der Karabetian & Balian, 1991	Armenian ethnic minority members attending a Turkish (or Armenian) school in Turkey.	Engagement with majority > minority culture education.	Higher-order "Turkish" and global "human" identity.
Breadth of Idea Sampling			
Leung & Chiu, 2010	European American undergraduates.	High multicultural experience > low multicultural experience score.	Sampling sayings from foreign cultures (S3 - S5).
Hadis, 2005	US students who did (before and after) and did not spend a year studying in Europe.	Living abroad experience > no living abroad experience; Living abroad experience > before departure.	Interest in international news and politics; knowledge of the politics, geography and economics of the visited country; frequency of travel abroad; participation in foreign cultures.

Table 4 Breadth of identification and breadth of idea sampling in dual identity individuals.

Study	Sample	Measure of Dual Engagement	Outcome Variable
Kehl & Morris, 2005	Students participating in a semester-long or short-term study abroad program.	Longer stay abroad > shorter stay abroad.	World-mindedness scores (favoring global concerns over national interests).
Zhai & Scheer, 2004	Students with various degrees of contact with individuals from other countries.	More > less contact.	Global perspective & positive attitudes towards diversity.
Medina-Lopez-Portillo, 2004	Students who participated (or not) in a study abroad program.	Post > pre departure.	Intercultural sensitivity.
King & Ruiz-Gelices, 2003	British students who lived (or not) abroad for 1 year.	Living abroad experience > no living abroad experience.	Interest in European affairs.
Douglas & Jones-Rikkers, 2001	US students who participated (or not) in a study abroad program.	Living abroad experience > no living abroad experience.	World-mindedness scores (favoring global concerns over national interests).
Zorn, 1996	Students who participated in short or long study abroad program.	Long > short stay abroad.	International perspective.
Carlson & Widaman, 1988	US students who spent (or not) their junior year abroad.	Living abroad experience > no living abroad experience.	International political concern and increased crosscultural interest.

REFERENCES

Adarves-Yorno, I., Postmes, T., & Haslam, S. A. (2006). Social identity and the recognition of creativity in groups. *The British Journal of Social Psychology, 45*, 479-97. doi:10.1348/014466605X50184

Adarves-Yorno, I., Postmes, T., & Haslam, S. A. (2007). Creative innovation or crazy irrelevance? The contribution of group norms and social identity to creative behavior. *Journal of Experimental Social Psychology, 43*(3), 410-416. doi:10.1016/j.jesp.2006.02.013

Amabile, T. M. (1996). *Creativity in context. Update to the social psychology of creativity.* Oxford: Westview Press.

Amiot, C. E., & de la Sablonniere, R. (2010). Facilitating the development and integration of multiple social identities. The case of immigrants in Quebec. In R. Crisp (Ed.), *The Psychology of Cultural Diversity*. Wiley-Blackwell.

Amiot, C. E., de la Sablonnière, R., Terry, D. J., & Smith, J. R. (2007). Integration of social identities in the self: toward a cognitive-developmental model. *Personality and Social Psychology Review, 11*(4), 364-88. doi:10.1177/1088868307304091

Aron, A., Mclaughlin-Volpe, T., Lewandowski, G., Wright, S. C., Aron, E. N., & Mashek, D. (2004). Including others in the self. *European Review of Social Psychology, 15*(1), 101-132. doi:10.1080/10463280440000008

Ashby, F. G., Isen, A. M., & Turken, A. U. (1999). A neuropsychological theory of positive affect and its influence on cognition. *Psychological Review, 106*(3), 529-50. doi:10.1037/0033-295X.106.3.529

Baas, M., De Dreu, C. K. W., & Nijstad, B. A. (2011). When prevention promotes creativity: the role of mood, regulatory focus, and regulatory closure. *Journal of Personality and Social Psychology, 100*(5), 794-809. doi:10.1037/a0022981

Bell, L. E. (1990). The bicultural life experience of career- oriented black women. *Journal of Organizational Behavior, 11*(6), 459-477.

Benet-Martínez, V. (2012). Multiculturalism: Cultural, social, and personality processes. In K. Deaux & M. Snyder (Ed.), *Handbook of Personality and Social Psychology* (Oxford Univ., pp. 623-648).

Benet-Martínez, V., & Haritatos, J. (2005). Bicultural Identity Integration (BII): Components and psychosocial antecedents. *Journal of Personality, 73*(4), 1015- 1050. doi:10.1111/j.1467-6494.2005.00337

Benet-Martínez, V., Lee, F., & Leu, J. (2006). Biculturalism and cognitive complexity: Expertise in cultural representations. *Journal of Cross-Cultural Psychology, 37*(4), 386–407. doi:10.1177/0022022106288476

Benet-Martínez, V., Leu, J. X., Lee, F., & Morris, M. W. (2002). Negotiating biculturalism. Cultural frame switching in biculturals with oppositional versus compatible cultural identities. *Journal of Cross-Cultural Psychology, 33*(5), 492–516. doi:10.1177/0022022102033005005

Berry, J. W., & Annis, R. C. (1974). Acculturative stress. *Journal of Cross-Cultural Psychology, 5*(4), 382–406. doi:10.1177/002202217400500402

Bialystok, E. (1999). Cognitive Complexity and Attentional Control in the Bilingual Mind. *Child Development, 70*(3), 636–644. doi:10.1111/1467-8624.00046

Bialystok, E., & Craik, F. I. M. (2010). Cognitive and Linguistic Processing in the Bilingual Mind. *Current Directions in Psychological Science, 19*(1), 19–23. doi:10.1177/0963721409358571

Bialystok, E., Craik, F. I. M., Klein, R., & Viswanathan, M. (2004). Bilingualism, aging, and cognitive control: Evidence from the Simon task. *Psychology and Aging, 19*(2), 290–303. doi:10.1037/0882-7974.19.2.290

Bialystok, E., & Martin, M. M. (2004). Attention and inhibition in bilingual children: evidence from the dimensional change card sort task. *Developmental Science, 7*(3), 325–339. doi:10.1111/j.1467-7687.2004.00351.x

Buriel, R., Perez, W., Dement, T. L., Chavez, D. V, Virginia, R., De Ment, T. L., & Moran, V. R. (1998). The relationship of language brokering to academic performance, biculturalism, and self-efficacy among Latino adolescents. *Hispanic Journal Of Behavioral Sciences, 283*(3), 283–297. doi:10.1177/07399863980203001

Carlson, J. S., & Widaman, K. F. (1988). The effects of study abroad during college on attitudes toward other cultures. *International Journal of Intercultural Relations, 12*(1), 1–17. doi:10.1016/0147-1767(88)90003-X

Cheng, C.-Y., Sanchez-Burks, J., & Lee, F. (2008). Connecting the dots within: creative performance and identity integration. *Psychological Science, 19*(11), 1178–84. doi:10.1111/j.1467-9280.2008.02220.x

Chua, R. Y. J. (2012). The Costs of Ambient Cultural Disharmony: Indirect Intercultural Conflicts in Social Environment Undermine Creativity. *Academy of Management Journal, 56*(6), 1545–1577. doi:10.5465/amj.2011.0971

Chua, R. Y. J., Morris, M. W., & Mor, S. (2012). Collaborating across cultures: Cultural metacognition and affect-based trust in creative collaboration.*Organizational Behavior and Human Decision Processes, 118*(2), 116–131. doi:10.1016/j.obhdp.2012.03.009

Cinnirella, M. (1997). Towards a European identity? Interactions between the national and European social identities manifested by university students in Britain and Italy. *British Journal of Social Psychology, 36*(1), 19–31. doi:10.1111/j.2044- 8309.1997.tb01116.x

Cohen, A. B. (2009). Many forms of culture. *American Psychologist, 64*(3), 194–204. doi:10.1037/a0015308

Crisp, R. J., Ensari, N., & Hewstone, M. (2003). A dual-route model of crossed categorisation effects. *European Review of Social Psychology, 13*(1), 35–73.

Crisp, R. J., & Hewstone, M. (2007). Multiple social categorization. In M. P. Zanna (Ed.), *Advances in Experimental Social Psychology* (Vol. 39, pp. 163–254). Orlando: FL: Academic Press.

Crisp, R. J., Hewstone, M., & Rubin, M. (2001). Does multiple categorization reduce intergroup bias? *Personality and Social Psychology Bulletin, 27*(1), 76–89. doi:10.1177/0146167201271007

Crisp, R. J., & Meleady, R. (2012). Adapting to a multicultural future. *Science, 336*(6083), 853–855. doi:10.1126/science.1219009

Crisp, R. J., & Turner, R. N. (2011). Cognitive adaptation to the experience of social and cultural diversity. *Psychological Bulletin, 137*(2), 242–66. doi:10.1037/a0021840

De Dreu, C. K. W., Baas, M., & Nijstad, B. A. (2008). Hedonic tone and activation level in the mood-creativity link: toward a dual pathway to creativity model. *Journal of Personality and Social Psychology, 94*(5), 739–56. doi:10.1037/0022- 3514.94.5.739

De Dreu, C. K. W., Nijstad, B. A., Baas, M., Wolsink, I., & Roskes, M. (2012). Working memory benefits creative insight, musical improvisation, and original ideation through maintained task-focused attention. *Personality & Social Psychology Bulletin, 38*(5), 656–669. doi:10.1177/0146167211435795

Der-Karabetian, A., & Balian, N. (1991). Ingroup, outgroup, and global-human identities of Turkish-Armenians. *The Journal of Social Psychology, 132*(4), 498– 504.

Douglas, C., & Jones-Rikkers, C. G. (2001). Study abroad programs and American student worldmindedness. *Journal of Teaching in International Business, 13*(1), 37–41.

Dovidio, J. F., Gaertner, S. L., & Saguy, T. (2009). Commonality and the complexity of "we": Social attitudes and social change. *Personality and Social Psychology Review, 13*(1), 3–20. doi:10.1177/1088868308326751

Duncker, K. (1945). On problem solving. *Psychological Monographs, 58*(5, Serial No. 270).

Estes, Z., & Ward, T. B. (2002). The emergence of novel attributes in concept modification. *Creativity Research Journal, 14*(2), 149–156. doi:10.1207/S15326934CRJ1402_2

Eysenck, H. J. (1993). Creativity and personality: suggestions for a theory. *Psychological Inquiry, 4*(3), 147–178.

Fee, A., & Gray, S. J. (2012). The expatriate-creativity hypothesis: A longitudinal field test. *Human Relations, 65*(12), 1515–1538. doi:10.1177/0018726712454900

Friedman, N. P., Miyake, A., Corley, R. P., Young, S. E., Defries, J. C., & Hewitt, J. (2006). Not all executive functions are related to intelligence. *Psychological Science, 17*(2), 172–179.

Friedman, R. S., Fishbach, A., Förster, J., & Werth, L. (2003). Attentional priming effects on creativity. *Creativity Research Journal, 15*(2/3), 277.

Gaertner, S. L., & Dovidio, J. F. (2000). Reducing intergroup bias: The common ingroup identity model. Philadephia, PA: Psychology Press.

Gaertner, S. L., Dovidio, J. F., & Bachman, B. A. (1996). Revisiting the contact hypothesis: the induction of a common ingroup identity. *International Journal of Intercultural Relations, 20*(3), 271–290.

Gaertner, S. L., Mann, J. A., Dovidio, J. F., Murrell, A. J., & Pomare, M. (1990). How does cooperation reduce intergroup bias? *Journal of Personality and Social Psychology, 59*(4), 692–704.

Gil, A. G., Vega, W. A., & Dimas, J. M. (1994). Acculturative stress and personal adjustment among hispanic adolescent boys. *Journal of Community Psychology, 22*(1), 43–54.

Gocłowska, M. A., Baas, M., Crisp, R. J., & De Dreu, C. K. W. (2014). Whether Social Schema Violations Help or Hurt Creativity Depends on Need for Structure. *Personality & Social Psychology Bulletin*, 40(8), 959–971. doi:10.1177/0146167214533132

Gocłowska, M. A., & Crisp, R. J. (2013). On counter-stereotypes and creative cognition: When interventions for reducing prejudice can boost divergent thinking. *Thinking Skills and Creativity*, 8, 72–79. doi:10.1016/j. tsc.2012.07.001

Gocłowska, M. A., Crisp, R. J., & Labuschagne, K. (2013). Can counter-stereotypes boost flexible thinking? *Group Processes & Intergroup Relations*, 16(2), 217– 231. doi:10.1177/1368430212445076

Godart, F. C., Maddux, W. W., Shiplov, A. V, & Galinsky, A. D. (2014). Fashion with a foreign flair: professional experiences abroad facilitate the creative innovations of organizations. *Academy of Management Journal, in press.*

Golden, C. J. C. J. (1975). The measurement of creativity by the Stroop color word test. *Journal of Personality Assessment*, 39(5), 502. doi:10.1207/ s15327752jpa3905_9

Groborz, M., & Nęcka, E. (2003). Creativity and cognitive control: Explorations of generation and evaluation skills. *Creativity Research Journal*, 15(2-3), 183–197. doi:10.1207/S15326934CRJ152&3_09

Guilford, J. P. (1950). Creativity. *American Psychologist*, 5(9), 444–454

Gutierrez, J., & Sameroff, A. (1990). Determinants of complexity in Mexican-American and Anglo-American mothers' conceptions of child development. *Child Development*, 61(2), 384. doi:10.1111/1467-8624.ep5878987

Hadis, B. F. (2005). Gauging the impact of study abroad: how to overcome the limitations of a single cell design. *Assessment & Evaluation in Higher Education*, 30(1), 3–19. doi:10.1080/0260293042003243869

Hall, N. R., & Crisp, R. J. (2005). Considering multiple criteria for social categorization can reduce intergroup bias. *Personality and Social Psychology Bulletin*, 31(10), 1435–1444. doi:10.1177/0146167205276084

Hampton, J. A. (1997). Emergent attributes in combined concepts. In T. B. Ward, S.

M. Smith, & J. Vaid (Eds.), *Creative Thought: An Investigation of Conceptual Structures and Processes* (pp. 83–110). Washington, DC: APA.

Hastie, R., Schroeder, C., & Weber, R. (1990). Creating complex social conjunction categories from simple categories. *Bulletin of the Psychonomic Society, 28*(3), 242–247.

Heilman, K. M., Nadeau, S. E., & Beversdorf, D. O. (2003). Creative innovation: possible brain mechanisms. *Neurocase, 9*(5), 369–79. doi:10.1076/neur.9.5.369.16553

Homan, A. C., van Knippenberg, D., Van Kleef, G. A., & De Dreu, C. K. W. (2007). Bridging faultlines by valuing diversity: Diversity beliefs, information elaboration, and performance in diverse work groups. *Journal of Applied Psychology, 92*(5), 1189–1199. doi:10.1037/0021-9010.92.5.1189

Hong, Y.-Y., Benet-Martínez, V., Chiu, C.-Y., & Morris, M. W. (2003). Boundaries of cultural influence. *Journal of Cross-Cultural Psychology, 34*(4), 453–464. doi:10.1177/0022022103034004005

Hong, Y.-Y., Chiu, C. Y., & Kung, T. M. (1997). Bringing culture out in front: Effects of cultural meaning system activation on social cognition. In K. Leung, Y. Kashima, U. Kim, & S. Yamaguchi (Eds.), *Progress in Asian Social Psychology* (Vol. 1, pp. 135–146). Singapore: Wiley.

Hong, Y.-Y., Morris, M. W., Chiu, C.-Y., & Benet-Martínez, V. (2000). Multicultural minds: A dynamic constructivist approach to culture and cognition. *American Psychologist, 55*(7), 709–720. doi:10.1037//0003-066X.55.7.709

Huang, L., & Galinsky, A. D. (2010). Mind-body dissonance: Conflict between the senses expands the mind's horizons. *Social Psychological and Personality Science, 2*(4), 351–359. doi:10.1177/1948550610391677

Hutter, R. R. C., & Crisp, R. J. (2005). The composition of category conjunctions. *Personality and Social Psychology Bulletin, 31*(5), 647–657. doi:10.1177/0146167204271575

IBM. (2010). *Capitalizing on Complexity. Insights from the Global Chief Executive Officer Study.*

Imai, L., & Gelfand, M. J. (2010). The culturally intelligent negotiator: The impact of cultural intelligence (CQ) on negotiation sequences and outcomes. *Organizational Behavior and Human Decision Processes, 112*(2), 83–98. doi:10.1016/j.obhdp.2010.02.001

Isen, A. M., & Daubman, K. A. (1984). The influence of affect on categorization. *Journal of Personality and Social Psychology, 47*(6), 1206–1217.
doi:10.1037/0022-3514.47.6.1206

Kehl, K., & Morris, J. (2005). Differences in global-mindedness between
short-term and semester-long study abroad participants at selected private universities. *The Interdisciplinary Journal of Study Abroad,* 67–81.

Khali, S. (2010). Muslim designers mix the hijab with latest fashions. *BBC
World Service.* Retrieved from http://www.bbc.co.uk/news/10105062

Kharkhurin, A. V. (2008). The effect of linguistic proficiency, age of
second language acquisition, and length of exposure to a new cultural
environment on bilinguals' divergent thinking. *Bilingualism: Language
and Cognition, 11*(02), 225–243. doi:10.1017/S1366728908003398

Kharkhurin, A. V. (2009). The role of bilingualism in creative performance on divergent thinking and invented alien creatures tests. *Journal
of Creative Behavior, 43*(1), 59–71.

Kharkhurin, A. V. (2010a). Bilingual verbal and nonverbal creative
behavior. *International Journal of Bilingualism, 14*(2), 211–226.
doi:10.1177/1367006910363060

Kharkhurin, A. V. (2010b). Sociocultural differences in the relationship
between bilingualism and creative potential. *Journal of Cross-Cultural
Psychology, 41*(5- 6), 776–783. doi:10.1177/0022022110361777

Kharkhurin, A. V. (2011). The role of selective attention in bilingual creativity. *Creativity Research Journal, 23*(3), 239–254. doi:10.1080/1040041
9.2011.595979

Kharkhurin, A. V, & Samadpour Motalleebi, S. N. (2008). The impact
of culture on the creative potential of American, Russian, and Iranian college students. *Creativity Research Journal, 20*(4), 404–411.
doi:10.1080/10400410802391835

King, R., & Ruiz-Gelices, E. (2003). International student migration and
the European Year Abroad: effects on European identity and subsequent migration behaviour. *International Journal of Population Geography,
9*(3), 229–252. doi:10.1002/ijpg.280

Kunda, Z., Miller, D. T., & Claire, T. (1990). Combining social concepts:
The role of causal reasoning. *Cognitive Sciece, 14,* 551–577. doi:10.1207/
s15516709cog1404_3

Kunda, Z., & Thagard, P. (1996). Forming impressions from stereotypes, traits, and behaviors: A parallel-constraint-satisfaction theory. *Psychological Review, 103*(2), 284–308. doi:10.1037/0033-295X.103.2.284

La Fromboise, T., Coleman, H. L. K., & Gerton, J. (1993). Psychological impact of biculturalism: Evidence and theory. *Psychological Bulletin, 114*(3), 395–412.

Lambert, W. E., & Taylor, D. M. (1990). *Coping with Cultural and Racial Diversity in Urban America.* New York: Praeger.

Landau, J. D., & Leynes, P. A. (2004). Manipulations that disrupt generative processes decrease conformity to examples: Evidence from two paradigms. *Memory, 12*(1), 90–103. doi:10.1080/09658210244000388

Leong, C.-H., & Ward, C. (2000). Identity conflict in sojourners. *International Journal of Intercultural Relations, 24*(6), 763–776. doi:10.1016/S0147-1767(00)00030-4

Leung, A. K.-Y., & Chiu, C.-Y. (2008). Interactive effects of multicultural experiences and openness to experience on creative potential. *Creativity Research Journal, 20*(4), 376–382. doi:10.1080/10400410802391371

Leung, A. K.-Y., & Chiu, C.-Y.-Y. (2010). Multicultural experience, idea receptiveness, and creativity. *Journal of Cross-Cultural Psychology, 41*(5-6), 723–741. doi:10.1177/0022022110361707

Leung, A. K.-Y., Maddux, W. W., Galinsky, A. D., & Chiu, C.-Y. (2008). Multicultural experience enhances creativity: the when and how. *The American Psychologist, 63*(3), 169–81. doi:10.1037/0003-066X.63.3.169

Linville, P. W. (1987). Self-complexity as a cognitive buffer against stress-related illness and depression. *Journal of Personality and Social Psychology, 52*(4), 663–76.

Lombardo, B. J., & Roddy, D. J. (2010). *Cultivating organizational creativity in an age of complexity. A companion study to the IBM 2010 Global Chief Human Resource Officer Study.*

Macrae, C. N., Milne, A. B., & Bodenhausen, G. V. (1994). Stereotypes as energy- saving devices - a peek inside the cognitive toolbox. *Journal of Personality and Social Psychology, 66*(1), 37–47. doi:10.1037/0022-3514.66.1.37

Maddux, W. W., Adam, H., & Galinsky, A. D. (2010). When in Rome ... Learn why the Romans do what they do: how multicultural learning experiences facilitate creativity. *Personality & Social Psychology Bulletin*, *36*(6), 731–41. doi:10.1177/0146167210367786

Maddux, W. W., Bivolaru, E., Hafenbrack, A. C., Tadmor, C. T., & Galinsky, A. D. (2013). Expanding opportunities by opening your mind: Multicultural engagement predicts job market success through longitudinal increases in integrative complexity. *Social Psychological and Personality Science*, *5*(5), 608– 615. doi:10.1177/1948550613515005

Maddux, W. W., & Galinsky, A. D. (2009). Cultural borders and mental barriers: The relationship between living abroad and creativity. *Journal of Personality and Social Psychology*, *96*(5), 1047–1061. doi:10.1037/a0014861

Marsh, R. L., Ward, T. B., & Landau, J. D. (1999). The inadvertent use of prior knowledge in a generative cognitive task. *Memory & Cognition*, *27*(1), 94–105.

Martin-Rhee, M. M., & Bialystok, E. (2008). The development of two types of inhibitory control in monolingual and bilingual children. *Bilingualism: Language and Cognition*, *11*(01), 81–93. doi:10.1017/S1366728907003227

McCrae, R. R. (1987). Creativity, divergent thinking, and openness to experience. *Journal of Personality and Social Psychology*, *52*(6), 1258–1265. doi:10.1037/0022-3514.52.6.1258

McFarland, S., Brown, D., & Webb, M. (2013). Identification with all humanity as a moral concept and psychological construct. *Current Directions in Psychological Science*, *22*, 192–196.

Medina-López-Portillo, A. (2003). Intercultural learning assessment: The link between program duration and the development of intercultural sensitivity. *Frontiers: The Interdisciplinary Journal of Study Abroad*, *10*, 179–200.

Mednick, S. A. (1962). The associative basis of the creative process. *Psychological Review*, *69*(3), 220–232. doi:10.1037/h0048850

Mendoza-Denton, R., & España, C. (2010). Diversity science: What is it? *Psychological Inquiry*, *21*(2), 168–174. doi:10.1080/1047840X.2010.492753

Miron-Spektor, E., Gino, F., & Argote, L. (2011). Paradoxical frames and creative sparks: Enhancing individual creativity through conflict and integration. *Organizational Behavior and Human Decision Processes, 116*(2), 229-240. doi:10.1016/j.obhdp.2011.03.006

Miyake, A., Friedman, N. P., Emerson, M. J., Witzki, a H., Howerter, A., & Wager, T. D. (2000). The unity and diversity of executive functions and their contributions to complex "Frontal Lobe" tasks: a latent variable analysis. *Cognitive Psychology, 41*(1), 49-100. doi:10.1006/cogp.1999.0734

Mok, A., & Morris, M. W. (2010). Asian-Americans' Creative Styles in Asian and American Situations: Assimilative and Contrastive Responses as a Function of Bicultural Identity Integration. *Management and Organization Review, 6*(3), 371-390. doi:10.1111/j.1740-8784.2010.00190.x

Mor, S., Morris, M. W., & Joh, J. (2013). Identifying and Training Adaptive Cross- Cultural Management Skills : The Crucial Role of Cultural Metacognition. *Academy of Management Learning and Education, 12*(3), 153-475.

Morris, M. W., & Leung, K. (2010). Creativity East and West: Perspectives and Parallels. *Management and Organization Review, 6*(3), 313-327. doi:10.1111/j.1740-8784.2010.00193.x

Morris, M. W., Menon, T., & Ames, D. R. (2001). Culturally conferred conceptions of agency: A key to social perception of persons, groups, and other actors. *Personality and Social Psychology Review, 5*(2), 169-182. doi:10.1207/s15327957pspr0502_7

Morris, M. W., & Mok, A. (2011). Isolating effects of cultural schemas: Cultural priming shifts Asian-Americans' biases in social description and memory. *Journal of Experimental Social Psychology, 47*(1), 117-126. doi:10.1016/j.jesp.2010.08.019

Morris, M. W., Mok, A., & Mor, S. (2011). Cultural Identity Threat: The Role of Cultural Identifications in Moderating Closure Responses to Foreign Cultural Inflow. *Journal of Social Issues, 67*(4), 760-773. doi:10.1111/j.1540- 4560.2011.01726.x

Mullen, B., Migdal, M. J., & Hewstone, M. (2001). Crossed categorization versus simple categorization and intergroup evaluations: a meta-analysis. *European Journal of Social Psychology, 31*(6), 721-736. doi:10.1002/ejsp.60

Navon, D. (1977). Forest before trees: The precedence of global features in visual perception. *Cognitive Psychology, 9*(3), 353–383.

Nguyen, A.-M. D., & Benet-Martínez, V. (2007). Biculturalism unpacked: Components, measurement, individual differences, and outcomes. *Social and Personality Psychology Compass, 1*(1), 101–114. doi:10.1111/j.1751-9004.2007.00029.x

Nijstad, B. A. (2002). Cognitive stimulation and interference in groups: Exposure effects in an idea generation task. *Journal of Experimental Social Psychology, 38*(6), 535–544. doi:10.1016/S0022-1031(02)00500-0

Nijstad, B. A., De Dreu, C. K. W., & Rietzschel, E. F. (2010). The dual pathway to creativity model: Creative ideation as a function of flexibility and persistence. *European Review of Social Psychology, 21*(1), 37–41.

Phinney, J. S., & Devich-Navarro, M. (1997). Variations in bicultural identification among African American and Mexican American adolescents. *Journal of Research on Adolescence, 7*(1), 3–32.

Phinney, J. S., Horenczyk, G., Liebkind, K., & Vedder, P. (2001). Ethnic identity, immigration, and well-being: An interactional perspective. *Journal of Social Issues, 57*(3), 493–510. doi:10.1111/0022-4537.00225

Piaget, J. (1971). The theory of stages in cognitive development. In D. R. Green, M. P. Ford, & G. B. Flamer (Eds.), *Measurement and Piaget* (pp. 1–111). New York: McGraw-Hill.

Piaget, J. (1975). *The equilibration of cognitive structures: The central problem of intellectual development.* Chicago: University of Chicago Press.

Plaut, V. C. (2010). Diversity Science: Who Needs It? *Psychological Inquiry, 21*(2), 168–174. doi:10.1080/1047840X.2010.492753

Plaut, V. C., Thomas, K. M., & Goren, M. J. (2009). Is multiculturalism or color blindness better for minorities? *Psychological Science, 20*(4), 444–6.

Portes, A. (1997). Immigration theory for a new century: Some problems and opportunities. *International Migration Review, 31*(4), 799–825.

Prior, A., & Macwhinney, B. (2009). A bilingual advantage in task switching. *Bilingualism: Language and Cognition, 13*(02), 253. doi:10.1017/S1366728909990526

Ramirez-Esparza, N., Gosling, S. D., Benet-Martínez, V., Potter, J. P., & Pennebaker, J. W. (2006). Do bilinguals have two personalities? A special case of cultural frame switching. *Journal of Research in Personality, 40*(2), 99–120. doi:10.1016/j.jrp.2004.09.001

Reiter-Palmon, R., Mumford, M. D., O'Connor Boes, J., & Runco, M. A. (1997). Problem construction and creativity: The role of ability, cue consistency, and active processing. *Creativity Research Journal, 10*(1), 9–23.

Ritter, S. M., Damian, R. I., Simonton, D. K., Van Baaren, R. B., Strick, M., Derks, J., & Dijksterhuis, A. (2012). Diversifying experiences enhance cognitive flexibility. *Journal of Experimental Social Psychology, 48*(4), 961–964. doi:10.1016/j.jesp.2012.02.009

Roccas, S., & Brewer, M. B. (2002). Social identity complexity. *Personality and Social Psychology Review, 6*(2), 88–106. doi:10.1207/s15327957pspr0602_01

Roskes, M., De Dreu, C. K. W., & Nijstad, B. A. (2012). Necessity is the mother of invention: Avoidance motivation stimulates creativity through cognitive effort. *Journal of Personality and Social Psychology, 103,* 242–256. doi:10.1037/a0028442

Roskes, M., Elliot, A. J., Nijstad, B. A., & De Dreu, C. K. W. (2013). Avoidance motivation and conservation of energy. *Emotion Review, 5*(3), 264–268.

Rothman, S., Lipset, S. M., & Nevitte, N. (2003). Does enrollment diversity improve university education? *International Journal of Public Opinion Research, 15*(1).

Rudmin, F. W. (2003). Critical history of the acculturation psychology of assimilation, separation, integration, and marginalization. *Review of General Psychology, 7*(1), 3–37. doi:10.1037/1089-2680.7.3.250

Saad, C. S., Damian, R. I., Benet-Martinez, V., Moons, W. G., & Robins, R. W. (2012). Multiculturalism and Creativity: Effects of Cultural Context, Bicultural Identity, and Ideational Fluency. *Social Psychological and Personality Science, 4*(3), 369–375. doi:10.1177/1948550612456560

Sam, D. L., & Berry, J. W. (2010). Acculturation: When individuals and groups of different cultural backgrounds meet. *Perspectives on Psychological Science, 5*(4), 472–481. doi:10.1177/1745691610373075

Sam, D. L., Vedder, P., Liebkind, K., Neto, F., & Virta, E. (2008). Acculturation and the paradox of adaptation in Europe. *European Journal of Immigration, 5*(2), 138–158.

Sampson, D. L., & Smith, H. P. (1957). A scale to measure world-minded attitudes *Journal of Social Psychology, 45,* 99–106.

Sassenberg, K., & Moskowitz, G. B. (2005). Don't stereotype, think different! Overcoming automatic stereotype activation by mindset priming. *Journal of Experimental Social Psychology, 41*(5), 506-514. doi:10.1016/j.jesp.2004.10.002

Schank, R., & Abelson, R. (1977). *Scripts, plans, goals and understanding.* Hillsdale, N.J.: Erlbaum.

Schlesinger, A. (1992). *The Disuniting of America.* New York: W. W. Norton.

Schmid, K., Hewstone, M., & Al Ramiah, A. (2012). Neighborhood diversity and social identity complexity: Implications for intergroup relations. *Social Psychological and Personality Science.* doi:10.1177/1948550612446972

Simmel, G. (1950). *The sociology of Georg Simmel.* New York, NY: Free Press.

Simonton, D. K. (1997). Foreign influence and national achievement: The impact of open milieus on Japanese civilization. *Journal of Personality and Social Psychology, 72*(1), 86-94. doi:10.1037/h0082846

Sligte, D. J., De Dreu, C. K. W., & Nijstad, B. A. (2011). Power, stability of power, and creativity. *Journal of Experimental Social Psychology, 47*(5), 891-897. doi:10.1016/j.jesp.2011.03.009

Smith, E. R., & Semin, S. R. (2007). Situated social cognition. *Current Directions in Psychological Science, 16*(3), 132-135. doi:10.1111/j.1467-8721.2007.00490.x

Smith, S. M., & Blankenship, S. E. (1991). Incubation and the persistence of fixation in problem solving. *The American Journal of Psychology, 104*(1), 61-87.

Smith, S. M., Ward, T. B., & Schumacher, J. (1993). Constraining effects of examples. *Cognition, 21*(6), 837-845.

Somerville, K. (2008). Transnational belonging among second generation youth : Identity in a globalized world. *Journal of Social Sciences, 10*(23-33).

Spannring, R., Wallace, C., & Datler, G. (2008). What leads young people to identify with Europe? An exploration of the impact of exposure to Europe and political engagement on European identity among young Europeans. *Perspectives on European Politics and Society, 9*(4), 480-498.

Suedfeld, P., & Tetlock, P. (2001). Individual Differences in Information Processing. In A. Tesser & N. Schwarz (Eds.), (pp. 284–304).

Sussman, N. M. (2000). The dynamic nature of cultural identity throughout cultural transitions: Why home is not so sweet. *Personality and Social Psychology Review*, 4(4), 355–373. doi:10.1207/S15327957PSPR0404_5

Tadmor, C. T., Galinsky, A. D., & Maddux, W. W. (2012). Getting the most out of living abroad: Biculturalism and integrative complexity as key drivers of creative and professional success. *Journal of Personality and Social Psychology*. doi:10.1037/a0029360

Tadmor, C. T., & Tetlock, P. E. (2009). Acculturation strategies and integrative complexity: The cognitive implications of biculturalism. *Journal of Cross- Cultural Psychology*, 40(1), 105–139. doi:10.1177/0022022108326279

Thagard, P. (1997). Coherent and creative conceptual combinations. An investigation of conceptual structures and processes. In T. B. Ward, C. P. Smith, & J. Vaid (Eds.), (pp. 129–141). Washington DC: APA.

The United Nations. (2009). International Migration 2009. *International Migration*.

Turner, J. C., Hogg, M. A., Oakes, P. J., Reicher, S., & Wetherell, M. S. (1987). *Rediscovering the social group: A self-categorization theory*. Oxford: Basil Blackwell.

Urban, L. M., & Miller, N. (1998). A theoretical analysis of crossed categorization effects: A meta-analysis. *Journal of Personality and Social Psychology*, 74(4), 894–908.

Vasiljevic, M., & Crisp, R. J. (2013). Tolerance by surprise: Evidence for a generalized reduction in prejudice and increased egalitarianism through novel category combination. *PLOS One*, 8(3). doi:10.1371/journal.pone.0057106

Verkuyten, M. (2005). Ethnic Group Identification and Group Evaluation Among Minority and Majority Groups: Testing the Multiculturalism Hypothesis. *Journal of Personality and Social Psychology*, 88(1), 121–138. doi:10.1037/0022- 3514.88.1.121

Verkuyten, M. (2007). Social psychology and multiculturalism. *Social and Personality Psychology Compass*, 1(1), 280–297. doi:10.1111/j.1751-9004.2007.00011.x

Verkuyten, M., Thijs, J., & Bekhuis, H. (2010). Intergroup contact and ingroup reappraisal: examining the deprovincialization thesis. *Social Psychology Quarterly, 73*(4), 398–416. doi:10.1177/0190272510389015

Walsh, S., Shulman, S., Feldman, B., & Maurer, O. (2005). The impact of immigration on the internal processes and developmental tasks of emerging adulthood. *Journal of Youth and Adolescence, 34*(5), 413–426. doi:10.1007/s10964-005-7259-7

Wan, W. W. N., & Chiu, C.-Y. (2002). Effects of novel conceptual combination on creativity. *The Journal of Creative Behavior, 36*(4), 227–240. doi:10.1002/j.2162-6057.2002.tb01066.x

Ward, T. B., Patterson, M. J., & Sifonis, C. M. (2004). The Role of Specificity and Abstraction in Creative Idea Generation. *Creativity Research Journal, 16*(1), 1–9. doi:10.1207/s15326934crj1601_1

Ward, T. B., Patterson, M. J., Sifonis, C. M., Dodds, R. A., & Saunders, K. N. (2002). The role of graded category structure in imaginative thought. *Memory & Cognition, 30*, 199–216. doi:10.3758/BF03195281

Ward, T. B., Smith, S. M., & Finke, R. A. (2007). Creative Cognition. In *Creativity* (pp. 189–212).

Ward, T. B., Smith, S. M., & Finke, R. A. (2008). Creative Cognition. In R. J. Sternberg (Ed.), . New York: Cambridge University Press.

Ward, T. B., Smith, S. M., & Vaid, J. (1997). Conceptual structures and processes in creative thought. Washington DC: APA.

Wodka, E. L., Loftis, C., Mostofsky, S. H., Prahme, C., Larson, J. C. G., Denckla, M. B., & Mahone, E. M. (2008). Prediction of ADHD in boys and girls using the D-KEFS. *Archive of Clinical Neuropsychology, 23*(3), 283–293. doi:10.1016/j.acn.2007.12.004

Wright, S. C., Aron, A., & Tropp, L. R. (2002). Including others (and groups) in the self: self-expansion and intergroup relations. In K. D. W. J.P. Forgas (Ed.), (Vol. 350). New York: Psychology Press.

Yinger, J. M. (1994). *Ethnicity: Source of Strength? Source of Conflict?* New York: State University of New York Press.

Zabelina, D. L., & Robinson, M. D. (2010). Creativity as flexible cognitive control. *Psychology of Aesthetics, Creativity, and the Arts, 4*(3), 136–143. doi:10.1037/a0017379

Zhai, L., & Scheer, S. D. (2004). Global perspectives and attitudes toward cultural diversity among summer agriculture students at the Ohio State University. *Journal of Agricultural Education, 45*(2), 39–50.

Zhang, S., Morris, M. W., Cheng, C., & Yap, A. J. (2013). Heritage-culture images disrupt immigrants' second-language processing through triggering first- language interference. *Proceedings of the National Academy of Sciences, 110*(28), 1–6.

Zorn, C. R. (1996). The long-term impact on nursing students of participating in international education. *Journal of Professional Nursing, 12*(2), 106–10.

How Multiple Social Identities Are Related to Creativity

Niklas K. Steffens, Małgorzata A. Gocłowska, Tegan Cruwys, and Adam D. Galinsky

ABSTRACT

The present research examined whether possessing multiple social identities (i.e., groups relevant to one's sense of self) is associated with creativity. In Study 1, the more identities individuals reported having, the more names they generated for a new commercial product (i.e., greater idea fluency). In Study 2, multiple identities were associated with greater fluency and originality (mediated by cognitive flexibility, but not by persistence). Study 3 validated these findings using a highly powered sample. We again found that multiple identities increase fluency and originality, and that flexibility (but not persistence) mediated the effect on originality. Study 3 also ruled out several alternative explanations (self-affirmation, novelty seeking, and generalized persistence). Across all studies, the findings were robust to controlling for personality, and there was no evidence of a curvilinear relationship between multiple identities and creativity. These results suggest that possessing multiple social identities is associated with enhanced creativity via cognitive flexibility.

KEYWORDS

creativity, fluency, identity, social identity, self-categorization

Although he passed away nearly 200 years ago, Johann Wolfgang von Goethe continues to inspire people today through his novels and dramas such as *The Sorrows of Young Werther and Faust*. Goethe was by all standards an exceptionally creative novelist, playwright, and poet. What is sometimes forgotten is that being a writer constituted only one of many facets of his spirited way of life. He also was an active botanist, optometrist, anatomist, mineralogist, aesthetician, natural philosopher, impresario, painter, university custodian, politician—someone who would act as State Minister of Finance, write an essay on the *theory of colors*, and create more than 2,000 paintings. We suggest that Goethe's creativity was not unrelated to his multiple identities; instead, we posit that having multiple identities may in fact be positively associated with his and our levels of creativity.

The identities that people derive from being members of social groups have profound effects on their behavior. Indeed, the salient norms, values, and ideals of social groups shape and direct every aspect of thought and behavior (for a review, see Ellemers, 2012). The literature on social identity and selfcategorization argues that people are able to self-categorize not only in terms of a personal identity (as "I" and "me") but also in terms of a social identity that is shared with other people (as "we" and "us"; Turner, Hogg, Oakes, Reicher, & Wetherell, 1987). More specifically, this literature asserts that when people categorize themselves in terms of a shared social identity (e.g., "us psychological scientists"), then this structures creativity, both in terms of the way people *generate* and *evaluate* creative products (for a review, see S. A. Haslam, Adarves-Yorno, Postmes, & Jans, 2013). For instance, in terms of the generation of creative ideas, evidence indicates that individuals come up with new products that are consistent with the normative boundaries of a shared group membership (Adarves-Yorno, Postmes, & Haslam, 2007) and that people in the workplace are particularly creative to the extent that they identify with the social category of "creative employees" (Farmer, Tierney, & Kung-McIntyre, 2003). Moreover, in terms of the evaluation of creative products, there is evidence that people regard new proposals to be more creative if such proposals are aligned with the norms and values of an ingroup, and if they are created by ingroup rather than outgroup members (Adarves-Yorno, Haslam, & Postmes, 2008; Adarves-Yorno, Postmes, & Haslam, 2006), while disregarding those ideas that undermine such norms and values (Tetlock, Kristel, Elson, Green, & Lerner, 2000), or proposals by people who do not fit the prototype of "creative professionals" (as found in judgments of creativity of screenwriters during Hollywood pitches; Elsbach & Kramer, 2003). In sum, social identity research on creativity has demonstrated that identifying with a particular group motivates an individual to seek creative solutions to the group's problems.

From this past work, however, it is *not* clear what the creative consequences are for people with multiple social identities. If one social identity is a source of inspiration and motivation, perhaps multiple identities offer multiple sources of inspiration and motivation. Because creative thought benefits from a variety of ideas and perspectives on a problem (Damian & Simonton, 2014; Simonton, 1997b), we propose that drawing on multiple social identities might be particularly beneficial for an individual's capacity to embrace and generate a large number of novel and creative ideas.

MULTIPLE IDENTITIES AND CREATIVITY

Recent findings from cross-cultural psychology offer support to the idea that multiple *cultural* identities enhance creativity. For example, individuals who have lived abroad (vs. those who have not) have been found to show greater creativity (Godart, Maddux, Shipilov, & Galinsky, 2015; Maddux & Galinsky, 2009), to be more receptive to ideas from foreign cultures (Leung & Chiu, 2010), to score higher on measures of cognitive complexity (Benet-Martínez, Lee, & Leu, 2006; Tadmor & Tetlock, 2006), and to demonstrate greater innovation across a variety of life domains (Leung, Maddux, Galinsky, & Chiu, 2008; Maddux, Leung, Chiu, & Galinsky, 2009). Other work found that bicultural individuals were more generative and original compared with their single-identifying counterparts (Tadmor, Galinsky, & Maddux, 2012) and that experience with two different cultures fosters creativity to the extent that individuals are motivated to delve into, and learn about, the culture associated with a national identity (Maddux, Adam, & Galinsky, 2010; Maddux, Bivolaru, Hafenbrack, Tadmor, & Galinsky, 2014). Finally, recent research has shown that priming individuals with thoughts of their own multiracial identities induces creativity (Gaither, Remedios, Sanchez, & Sommers, 2015) and that living in multiple countries—that is, having broad multicultural experiences—can increase creativity (Godart et al., 2015). Overall, research to date has shown strong evidence for a link between dual identities and creativity (and to a lesser extent multiple identities), but so far, this evidence has been limited to cultural, ethnic, and national identities (for a detailed review, see Gocłowska & Crisp, 2014).

Yet social identities vary on many dimensions other than national or ethnic culture—including an individual's gender, profession, social status, or organizational membership. We propose that creativity may be attributable not only to national or ethnic diversity (Cohen, 2009; Gocłowska & Crisp, 2014) but rather to multiple identities more generally. This raises an important question: Does the link between bicultural experiences and creativity reflect a more general relationship between multiple social identities and creativity? In other words, is the number of social identities that one possesses (in any domain) linked with more creative performance? We suggest that the answer is yes.

Some indirect support for this idea can be garnered from social identity research that has looked at multiple identity processes in other domains. Specifically, this research has shown that possessing multiple identities (regardless of group type) promotes mental well-being (Cruwys et al., 2013) and adjustment after life transitions (Iyer, Jetten, Tsivrikos, Postmes, & Haslam, 2009; for reviews, see Jetten, Haslam, & Haslam, 2012; Jetten, Haslam, Haslam, Dingle, & Jones, 2014). Moreover, this research has also found evidence that multiple identities prevent decline in memory functioning in the elderly (C. Haslam, Jetten, Haslam, Pugliese, & Tonks, 2011) and in people who have suffered from a stroke (C. Haslam et al., 2008).

We propose that possessing multiple social identities extends to the domain of creative performance. Our hypothesis builds off self-categorization work that shows that a particular social identity is associated with a unique set of experiences and provides a unique lens through which to make sense of the world. By being a member of many social groups, people will be able to draw on ideas and input across a variety of domains (e.g., geographical regions, professions, religions, political groups, leisure groups), and this should boost their ability not only to produce *many* ideas but also to produce ideas that are more *original*. Thus, we argue that people's ability to draw on multiple social identities is associated with greater creativity.

One key element of creativity is the ability to generate many ideas and products over time (Simonton, 1997a). Creative productivity (i.e., fluency) can be considered as the most basic form of creative achievement. In addition to the number of ideas, creativity is also defined by what kind of ideas people produce. In this regard, creative products and ideas are typically defined as those that are novel or original (Amabile, 1983). We, therefore, predicted that multiple group membership would be associated with greater fluency and originality in idea generation—two key indicators of creative production.

CREATIVE PRODUCTS AND PROCESSES

If multiple social identities are linked to creativity, how would this link be produced? Cognitively oriented approaches consider the various thought *processes* that lead to the generation of novel, original ideas. According to the Dual Pathway to Creativity Model (DPCM; De Dreu, Baas, & Nijstad, 2008), creative products can be generated via the process of cognitive flexibility, and/or via the process of persistence in generating ideas (see also Nijstad, De Dreu, Rietzschel, & Baas, 2010). It is important to note, too, that these two different processes are not mutually exclusive, but they can operate in concert (Nijstad et al., 2010). The first process, flexibility, refers to the ease with which people are able to overcome functional fixedness (Smith & Blankenship, 1991), invoke ideas that are remote from one another (Mednick, 1962), and use a wide range of semantic categories when generating ideas and problem solutions (Maddux et al., 2010). Because being a member of many social groups allows individuals to draw from a broader idea base (see also Godowska & Crisp, 2014), multiple group membership should be associated with greater originality via more flexible idea generation.

However, flexibility is not the only way in which people reach creative ends. Creativity can also be achieved via persistence, defined as "the degree of sustained and focused task-directed cognitive effort" that individuals exert (Nijstad et al., 2010, p. 42). The persistence pathway to creativity has often been operationalized as the degree to which individuals explore ideas within a narrow set of semantic categories (Baas, De Dreu, & Nijstad, 2011; Rietzschel, De Dreu, & Nijstad, 2007; Roskes, De Dreu, & Nijstad, 2012). Experimental research shows that creative ends are achieved via the persistence pathway especially when individuals are highly motivated to avoid negative ends, and when increased effort is functional in the context of a specific task (Roskes et al., 2012; Sligte, Nijstad, & De Dreu, 2013). Because multiple identities are associated with greater persistence and endurance in the face of difficult physical tasks (Jones & Jetten, 2011), and because multiple identities constitute a psychological resource (see also Jetten et al., 2015) that increases general motivation and perseverance, it is also possible that multiple identities may be related to creativity due to greater persistence. Overall, then, our studies examined the role of flexibility and persistence as potential mediators that could explain why people with multiple group memberships are more creative.

OVERVIEW OF THE PRESENT RESEARCH

In three studies, we tested the hypotheses that multiple identities will be positively associated with (Hypothesis 1 [H1]) greater creative fluency and (Hypothesis 2 [H2]) greater originality in idea generation. In addition, we examined whether the relationship between multiple identities and originality was mediated by an effect on flexibility (Hypothesis 3a [H3a]; that is, increased number of semantic categories used) or persistence (Hypothesis 3b [H3b]; that is, greater number of ideas generated per semantic category; Nijstad et al., 2010).

To establish the robustness of the multiple identities–creativity relationship, we used different methodologies across the three studies. In Study 1, participants completed a Multiple Group Memberships scale (C. Haslam et al., 2008) and were asked to generate various names for a commercial product (De Dreu et al., 2014). In this study, we tested whether the extent to which people self-reported being members of many groups would be associated with a greater number of ideas generated (fluency), indicative of greater creative productivity (testing H1).

In Studies 2 and 3, we conceptually replicated and extended the first study in two important ways. First, we used a well-established variant of the Multiple Uses Task (Tadmor et al., 2012), allowing us to measure both creative fluency and originality (examining H1 and H2), as well as the two chief cognitive processes implied in the generation of original ideas: cognitive flexibility and persistence (testing H3). Second, we used different measures of multiple identities: In Study 2, an "identity mapping task" was used to obtain a concrete assessment of people's multiple identities (Best et al., 2014), and in Study 3, a group membership grid (Jetten et al., 2012) was used. Third, we reversed the order in which participants completed the creativity and multiple identity measures to rule out sequence effects. Finally, in Study 3, we used a highly powered sample, allowing us to run a series of additional robust sensitivity analyses. Specifically, we also examined whether the multiple identities–creativity relationship holds (a) when controlling for self-affirmation, novelty seeking, and an additional persistence measure (to establish whether the effect of multiple identities on creativity could be attributed to these third variables), and (b) when including only those (multiple) identities that participants feel are important to self.

Across all three studies, we ran sensitivity analyses to examine the extent to which multiple identities predict creativity above and beyond personality (the Big Five; Studies 1-3). This allowed us to rule out the possibility that our focal relationship could be explained by personality (Feist, 1998) and that the possession of multiple group memberships is confounded with personality. Furthermore, across all studies, we conducted additional analyses to test whether a curvilinear relationship existed, and whether multiple identities show diminishing marginal benefits.

Our studies offer potential integration of previous research on the relationships between identity, culture, and creativity by suggesting that multiple social identities enhance creative thinking, because this diversity of experience allows people to think flexibly. In short, we propose that creativity is pronounced among those who share an identity, have dual national identification, or, perhaps particularly parsimoniously, have multiple social identities.

STUDY 1

Method
Participants. A total of 208 students (75% female) from a large Australian university completed the study online for course credit (M_{age} = 19.53, SD = 4.21).

Procedure and measures. Participants completed a creativity task followed by a multiple group membership measure, a personality questionnaire, and demographic information (for verbatim responses and power analyses for all studies, see the online appendix).

Creativity measure. To assess creativity, we asked participants to generate within 3 min as many names as possible for a new kind of commercial product (a new kind of pasta; DeDreu et al., 2014; Dijksterhuis & Meurs, 2006; Gocłowska, Baas, Crisp, & De Dreu, 2014). Because the ability to produce many ideas (fluency) is an essential element of creativity, we used this task to assess the total number of ideas that participants generated as an indicator of *fluency*[1] (M = 12.04, SD = 5.93; 2,518 in total; Gilford, 1950; Saad, Damian, Benet-Martínez, Moons, & Robins, 2013).

Multiple identities measure. Participants next completed a measure of multiple identities. They responded to four items of a Multiple Group Memberships scale on 7-point Likert-type scales ranging from 1 (*strongly agree*) to 7 (*strongly disagree*; for example, "I belong to lots of different groups" and "I have strong ties with lots of different groups"; α = .85; C. Haslam et al., 2008; Jetten et al., 2012). Participants agreed moderately strongly with items of the Multiple Group Memberships scale (M = 4.17, SD = 1.31; comparable with previous studies using student populations; Cruwys, South, Greenaway, & Haslam, 2015).

Personality measure. For the purpose of conducting sensitivity analyses, participants completed a short measure assessing the Big Five traits: extraversion, agreeableness, conscientiousness, emotional stability, and openness to experience—10 items from the short version of the Big Five Inventory; scale ranging from 1 (*strongly disagree*) to 5 (*strongly agree*); Rammstedt and John (2007); rs ranged from .06 to .44.

Table 1 Study 1: Means, Standard Deviations, and Intercorrelations Between Measures.

Variable	M	SD	1	2	3	4	5	6	7	8a	8b
1. Multiple identities	4.17	1.31	—								
2. Extraversion	3.17	0.88	.31**	—							
3. Agreeableness	3.66	0.67	.03	.14*	—						
4. Conscientiousness	3.35	0.76	.11	.20**	.12	—					
5. Emotional stability	2.83	0.95	.13†	.22**	.11	.07	—				
6. Openness to experience	3.31	0.80	.06	.08	-.02	.20*	-.08	—			
7. Creativity: Fluency	12.04	5.93	.18**	.10	-.15*	.07	-.16*	-.03	—		
8a. Divergent ideas	4.40	4.56	-.03	.10	-.06	-.02	-.02	.02	.56**	—	
8b. Convergent ideas	7.64	5.09	.23**	.02	-.12†	.09	-.17*	-.06	.67**	-.24**	—

Note. n = 208; due to missing data, n = 203 for bivariate correlations involving control variables.
†p < .10. *p < .05. **p < .01.

Table 2 Study 1: Hierarchical Regression Analyses Assessing Effect of Multiple Identities on Fluency Including Sensitivity Analysis (With the Big Five as Control Variables).

Variable	Main analysis					Sensitivity analysis (adding control variables)				
	b	SE	95% CIs	β	t	b	SE	95% CIs	β	t
Multiple identities	0.81	.31	[0.19, 1.42]	.18	2.60*	0.78	.33	[0.13, 1.43]	.17	2.63*
Extraversion						0.66	.51	[-0.34, 1.66]	.10	1.31
Agreeableness						-1.40	.61	[-2.61, -0.19]	-.16	-2.29*
Conscientiousness						0.61	.56	[-0.49, 1.71]	.08	1.09
Emotional stability						-1.23	.44	[-2.10, -0.36]	-.20	-2.78**
Openness to experience						-0.62	.52	[-1.65, 0.41]	-.08	-1.18
R^2					.03*					.10**

Note. n = 208 for main analysis; due to missing data, n = 203 for analysis including control variables.

CI = confidence interval. †p < .10. *p < .05. **p < .01.

Results

Multiple identities and creativity. Descriptive statistics and bivariate correlations are shown in Table 1. To test H1, we conducted a series of linear regressions comprising (a) main analysis to estimate the direct relationship between multiple identities and fluency in idea generation and (b) additional sensitivity analysis by controlling for personality and by examining the extent to which the present relationship is curvilinear. Results are presented in Table 2. Linear regression results supported H1 by revealing a positive association between multiple identities and creative fluency, suggesting that the more identities individuals felt they belong to, the greater the number of names for a new commercial product they came up with.

Sensitivity analysis. As presented in Table 2, an additional sensitivity analysis that controlled for personality (the Big Five) yielded a virtually identical pattern of results—multiple identities were positively associated with fluency. In sum, the anticipated positive relationship between multiple identities and idea generation holds even when accounting for the impact of personality.

We examined whether there is evidence for a curvilinear relationship, that is, a diminishing marginal return of having multiple identities (see also Swaab, Schaerer, Anicich, Ronay, & Galinsky, 2014). To this end, we conducted an analysis in which we entered the quadratic term of multiple identities (to reduce collinearity between the linear and quadratic terms, multiple identities were Z-standardized before calculating the quadratic term) as a predictor in addition to the linear term. Analysis indicated that the quadratic term was not related to fluency, and did not account for significant variance beyond that accounted for by the linear term in predicting fluency, $b = -0.04$, 95% confidence intervals (95% CIs) = $[-.72, .63]$, $\beta = -.01$, $\Delta R^2 = .001$, $p = .899$. Together, results do not provide evidence for a curvilinear relationship between multiple identities and fluency.

In addition, we followed previous research that used the present task (De Dreu et al., 2014; Gocłowska et al., 2014) and coded participants' responses to assess divergent and convergent thinking. We divided the overall number of ideas into those that ended with the letter "i" (e.g., "paragoni"; in line with five provided examples and common pasta names; convergent items) and those that ended with a letter other than "i" (divergent items; De Dreu et al., 2014). Analyses indicated that multiple identities were unrelated to divergent items, $b = -0.10$, 95% CIs = $[-0.58, 0.38]$,

$\beta = -.03$, $p = .684$, while they were positively related to convergent items, b = 0.91, 95% CIs = [0.39, 1.42], $\beta = .23$, $p = .001$. In sum, there was evidence that multiple identities led to greater convergent thinking, while there was no evidence that they led to greater divergent thinking.

Discussion

Supporting H1, results from Study 1 indicated that multiple identities were positively related to greater creative fluency. To the extent that individuals felt connected to many social identities, they produced more ideas. Moreover, there was no evidence for a curvilinear relationship, ruling out diminishing marginal returns of having multiple identities and that multiple identities ever become negatively related to creativity. Finally, findings also demonstrated that multiple identities explained creative fluency over and above the contribution of personality. In sum, the results provided support for our core hypothesis.

Nevertheless, these findings also raised a few additional questions. First, while Study 1 suggested that multiple identities are related to greater creative productivity, the "pasta" task did not allow us to test whether the ideas generated by participants were also more *original*. Furthermore, this task does not allow for an assessment of creative persistence and/or flexibility. First, the instructions of the present task have been designed to anchor participants on an initial set of solutions (i.e., ideas ending with the letter "i"), and thus may have artificially restricted the range of participants' flexibility. Indeed, the present version of the task (following De Dreu et al., 2014; Gocłowska et al., 2014) differs from the original version of this task used by Marsh, Ward, and Landau (1999), where people were explicitly asked to avoid using features of the provided examples, and from common brainstorming tasks that are used to assess flexibility, such as versions of the Multiple Uses Task (Guilford, 1967), where no restraining instructions are provided.

Second, convergent and divergent thinking (as assessed in the present task) and persistence and flexibility (as defined earlier) differ conceptually. Convergent and divergent thinking, as assessed in the present task, focus on the extent to which people follow a superficial *lexical* rule, while the concepts of creative persistence and flexibility refer to the production of ideas across various *semantic* categories. Given these differences, on the basis of the present results, we can only draw limited implications for persistence and flexibility.

Thus, in Study 2, we used the established "brick" variant of the Multiple Uses Task (Tadmor et al., 2012) as a more suitable test of H2 concerning the link between multiple group membership and greater creative, original idea generation. Moreover, this variant of the Multiple Uses Task allows not only testing the effects to fluency and originality but also examining H3 concerning the processes (flexibility and/or persistence) by which the effect on originality occurs (De Dreu et al., 2008).

Moreover, to rule out the possibility that participants in the present study only *thought* they belonged to many groups (rather than actually belonged to many groups), we used a different multiple identity assessment, in which participants explicitly indicated each group that they regarded as important to self. To better control for random variance, we also reversed the order of the creativity and multiple identity tasks in Study 2, and conducted the study in a laboratory, rather than an online environment.

STUDY 2

Method

Participants. A total of 136 participants took part in exchange for AU$10. Four participants who did not complete the multiple identities task as instructed and one participant who did not complete the creativity task were excluded, resulting in a final sample of 131 participants (68% female; M_{age} = 22.49, SD = 5.06).

Procedure and measures. Participants completed a multiple identity measure followed by a creativity task, a personality measure, and demographic information.

Multiple identities measure. Participants completed an identity mapping task (Best et al., 2014) that involved participants indicating all social groups they belonged to, and saw as important to self. The instructions listed many different types of groups (e.g., work or recreational) as examples to facilitate a representative retrieval of all the groups that participants saw as central to self, and to rule out the possibility that indicating groups required creativity or cognitive effort. Participants identified the groups that they belonged to, and regarded as relevant to their self, by indicating the name of each group on a separate post-it note. Participants also provided a range of other details about their group memberships (e.g., length of association) that were not central to the present research project and are thus not reported in further detail here.

Creativity measure. Participants completed a variant of the Multiple Uses Task (the "brick task"). Specifically, participants had 2 min to come up with as many ideas as possible for the different ways in which one could use a brick. *Fluency* (M = 7.02, SD = 2.95; 941 ideas in total) was assessed by counting the number of ideas that each person generated (Saad et al., 2013). To obtain *flexibility* (M = 4.53, SD = 1.79), an independent coder, who was blind to the hypotheses, assigned each of the 941 ideas generated to one of 19 predefined semantic categories developed by Markman, Lindberg, Kray, and Galinsky (2007; using a brick as a measurement tool, a weapon, etc.) and computed the number of categories that a participant used. Next, the number of ideas that a participant generated was divided by the number of semantic categories used, to yield within-category fluency or *persistence* (M = 1.63, SD = 0.76; De Dreu et al., 2008).

Moreover, we used an established point-coding scheme to assess idea *originality* (Runco, Okuda, & Thurston, 1987). Specifically, an independent coder assigned weights to each idea as a function of originality or relative frequency by giving one point to the most common uses for a brick (mentioned by around 55% of participants; for example, paperweight, building block, build a house, weapon). The rater gave two points for uses that were slightly more unusual in their function but still common (mentioned by around 40%; for example, break a window, exercise weight, drum, pillow, toy). Three points were given to uses which take advantage of physical properties of a brick other than hardness, weight, and stackability, or use one of those in a very unorthodox way, or are very unusual (mentioned by around 5%; for example, sundial, grind to make powder, submerge to test density/volume, chia pet, metaphor, prop for movie). Finally, four points were given for uses which are extremely unusual, unique, and innovative (around one or two ideas). Points were summed to obtain an indicator of overall originality (M = 10.78, SD = 5.30). A second rater coded 10% of the material. This yielded a satisfactory, high degree of interreliability (coders agreed in 88% of assigned points), providing evidence of reliable data coding.

Personality measure. Finally, participants responded to the same 10 items as in Study 1 that assessed personality (Rammstedt & John, 2007; r s ranged from .08 to .51). Afterward, they provided demographic information.

Table 3 Study 2: Means, Standard Deviations, and Intercorrelations Between Measures.

Variable	M	SD	1	2	3	4	5	6	7	8	9	10
1. Multiple identities	7.50	4.02	—									
2. Extraversion	3.36	0.91	.08	—								
3. Agreeableness	3.57	0.72	-.02	.14	—							
4. Conscientiousness	3.22	0.79	-.01	.16	.10	—						
5. Emotional stability	3.13	0.98	.01	.29**	.06	.09	—					
6. Openness to experience	3.30	0.79	.13	-.01	-.11	.08	-.17*	—				
7. Creativity: Fluency	7.02	2.95	.24**	.01	-.01	.25**	.09	.18*	—			
8. Creativity: Flexibility	4.53	1.79	.28**	.03	.05	.03	.13	.18*	.70**	—		
9. Creativity: Persistence	1.63	0.76	-.06	-.03	-.07	.11	-.02	.03	.37**	-.29**	—	
10. Creativity: Originality	10.78	5.30	.24**	.05	-.01	.23*	.15†	.19*	.92**	.80**	.12	—

Note. n = 131; due to missing data, n = 129 for bivariate correlations involving control variables.
†p < .10. *p < .05. **p < .01.

Table 4 Study 2: Hierarchical Regression Analyses Assessing Effect of Multiple Identities on Fluency, Originality, Flexibility, and Persistence (Within-Category Fluency) Including Sensitivity Analysis (With the Big Five as Control Variables).

Variable	Main analysis					Sensitivity analysis (adding control variables)				
	b	SE	95% CIs	β	t	b	SE	95% CIs	β	t
Fluency										
Multiple identities	0.17	.06	[0.05, 0.30]	.24	2.74**	0.16	.06	[0.04, 0.28]	.22	2.56*
Extraversion						−0.30	.29	[−0.87, 0.27]	−.09	−1.04
Agreeableness						−0.07	.35	[−0.75, 0.62]	−.02	−.20
Conscientiousness						0.98	.32	[0.34, 1.61]	.26	3.04**
Emotional stability						0.37	.27	[−0.16, 0.91]	.12	1.40
Openness to experience						0.63	.32	[−0.01, 1.27]	.17	1.95†
R^2					.06**					.16**
Originality										
Multiple identities	0.32	.11	[0.10, 0.54]	.24	2.84**	0.19	.10	[0.07, 0.50]	.22	2.66**
Extraversion						−0.45	.51	[−1.46, 0.55]	−.08	−.89
Agreeableness						−0.13	.61	[−1.33, 1.08]	−.02	−.21
Conscientiousness						1.60	.57	[0.47, 2.72]	.24	2.82**
Emotional stability						1.00	.47	[0.07, 1.94]	.19	2.12*
Openness to experience						1.32	.57	[0.19, 2.45]	.20	2.95*
R^2					.06**					.18**

Table 4 Study 2: Hierarchical Regression Analyses Assessing Effect of Multiple Identities on Fluency, Originality, Flexibility, and Persistence (Within-Category Fluency) Including Sensitivity Analysis (With the Big Five as Control Variables).

	Main analysis					Sensitivity analysis (adding control variables)				
Flexibility										
Multiple identities	0.12	.04	[0.05, 0.20]	.28	3.27**	0.11	.04	[0.04, 0.19]	.26	3.01**
Extraversion						-0.15	.18	[-0.50, 0.19]	-.09	-.83
Agreeableness						0.14	.21	[-0.28, 0.56]	.06	.65
Conscientiousness						0.27	.20	[-0.12, 0.66]	.12	1.38
Emotional stability						0.31	.16	[-0.01, 0.63]	.17	1.89†
Openness to experience						0.43	.20	[0.04, 0.82]	.19	2.16*
R^2					.08**					.15**
Persistence										
Multiple identities	-0.01	.02	[-0.04, 0.02]	-.06	-.62	-0.01	.02	[-0.04, 0.02]	-.06	-.64
Extraversion						-0.02	.08	[-0.18, 0.14]	-.03	-.27
Agreeableness						-0.08	.01	[-0.27, 0.11]	-.08	-.84
Conscientiousness						0.12	.09	[-0.06, 0.30]	.12	1.35
Emotional stability						-0.02	.07	[-0.16, 0.13]	-.02	-.21
Openness to experience						0.02	.09	[-0.16, 0.20]	.02	.21
R^2					.01					.02

Note. n = 131 for main analysis; due to missing data, n = 129 for analysis including control variables. CI = confidence interval. †p < .10. *p < .05. **p < .01.

Results

Multiple identities and creativity. Means, standard deviations, and bivariate correlations are presented in Table 3. Linear regression results concerning fluency, originality, flexibility, and persistence (within-category fluency) are presented in Table 4. Supporting H1 and H2, multiple identities were positively associated with fluency as well as originality, suggesting that people who have many social identities generate more uses for a brick and that the uses that they generate are more original. Moreover, multiple identities were positively related to flexibility indicating that the greater number of identities that people had, the broader the semantic categories that their generated ideas fell into. However, multiple identities did not predict persistence (within-category fluency).

Sensitivity analysis. We also ran sensitivity analyses by controlling for personality. Results were largely identical. As presented in Table 4, multiple identities remained a significant predictor of fluency, originality, and flexibility, even after controlling for individual differences.

In addition to overall originality, we also examined average originality as a second indicator of originality or quality of an idea by dividing overall originality by fluency (the overall number of generated ideas; Diehl & Stroebe, 1987; Rietzschel, Nijstad, & Stroebe, 2007). Analysis revealed that multiple identities were a marginally significant predictor of average originality, $b = 0.012$, 95% CIs = [−0.001, 0.025], $\beta = .16$, $p = .074$.

We also examined evidence for a curvilinear relationship by computing the quadratic term of the number of group memberships (to reduce collinearity between predictors, the number of group memberships was standardized prior to calculating the quadratic term), and by adding it to the linear term number of group memberships as predictor of creativity. Analysis revealed that adding the quadratic term was unrelated to, and did not account for additional variance beyond that accounted for by the linear term predicting, fluency, $b = 0.24$, 95% CIs = [−0.08, 0.55], $\beta = .17$, $\Delta R^2 = .016$, $p = .139$; flexibility, $b = −0.07$, 95% CIs = [−0.26, 0.12], $\beta = −.08$, $\Delta R^2 = .01$, $p = .473$; and originality, $b = 0.21$, 95% CIs = [−0.36, 0.77], $\beta = .08$, $\Delta R^2 = .004$, $p = .469$. Therefore results did not provide evidence for a curvilinear relationship.

Mediation analysis. Finally, in line with our theorizing and building on the DPCM model by De Dreu and colleagues (2008; Nijstad et al., 2010), we examined flexibility (H3a) and persistence (H3b) as two competing mediators of the effect of multiple group memberships on originality. We conducted multiple mediation analysis using bias-corrected bootstrapping with 5,000 resamples (using PROCESS parallel mediation Model 4; Hayes, 2013). Mediation analysis indicated that, consistent with H3a, there was a significant indirect path from multiple identities to originality via flexibility, γ = .33, SE = .10, 95% CIs = [0.15, 0.54]. The indirect path from multiple identities via persistence (H3b) was not significant, γ = −.03, SE = .05, 95% CIs = [−0.13, 0.09]. The mediation is presented in Figure 1. Multiple mediation analysis of average originality yielded similar results with evidence that flexibility was a significant mediator, γ = .008, SE = 0.003, 95% CIs = [0.003, 0.016], but persistence was not, γ = .001, SE = .003, 95% CIs = [−0.004, 0.007].

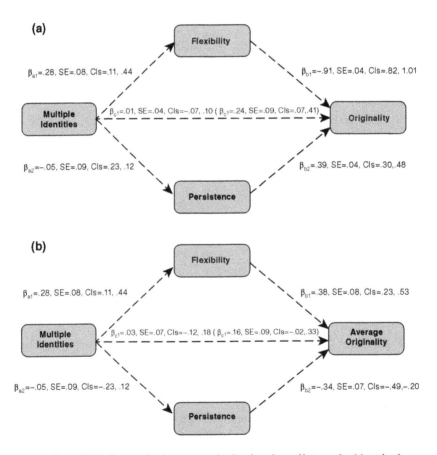

Figure 1 Study 2: Mediation displaying standardized path coefficients for (a) paths from multiple identities through the two mediating processes, flexibility (category diversity) and persistence (within-category fluency), to overall originality and (b) path from multiple identities through the two mediating processes, flexibility (category diversity) and persistence (within-category fluency), to average originality (originality per generated idea). Note. Numbers in parentheses are path coefficients after controlling for the mediator. CI = confidence interval.

Discussion

Study 2 replicated the findings of Study 1 by demonstrating that multiple identities are positively related to creative fluency (H1). Moreover, Study 2 extended previous findings by showing that multiple identities are also positively associated with creative originality (H2), and that this is mediated by more flexibility (but not more persistence) in creative thinking (H3a).

As in Study 1, the evidence supported a multiple identities–creativity link that goes beyond the impact of personality. Results also indicated that the relationship between multiple identities and creativity was linear, but not curvilinear. Furthermore, Study 2 demonstrated that the multiple identities–creativity link holds across variations in measurement of multiple identities (i.e., when using a more concrete index of group memberships).

Finally, Study 2 also provided insight into process by testing two different pathways to originality—that is, persistence (within-category fluency) on one hand and cognitive flexibility on the other (see also De Dreu et al., 2008; Nijstad et al., 2010). There was evidence that multiple identities enhanced originality of ideas via increased flexibility (H3a), while there was no evidence that this link was accounted for by greater persistence. This pattern was found for both overall and average originality. In sum, results suggest that the multiple identities–creativity link cannot be reduced to mere persistence, but instead is in part accounted for by a more diverse range of ideas generated by those with a greater number of social identities.

STUDY 3

Study 3 extended our investigation of the multiple identities–creativity link using a larger sample with an expanded design and sufficient statistical power to conduct additional sensitivity analyses. We validated previous findings using a concrete measure of multiple group memberships and the multiple uses paradigm. In addition, as in Studies 1 and 2, we assessed individual differences as alternative explanations. Study 3 also set out to demonstrate that the multiple identity–creativity link cannot be attributed to (a) self-affirmation (which could be related to possessing multiple identities and that sets free their capacity to think creatively) and (b) preference to seek novelty (i.e., a factor that could be argued would enhance both the ease with which people take up new group memberships and creativity). Moreover, building on the process data of Study 2, we also set out to assess more rigorously whether the effects are due to persistence by using an additional explicit measure of generalized persistence that is assessed independently from responses in the creativity task (assessed by time spent on unsolvable anagrams). Finally, to provide firmer evidence for our theorizing, we examined the nature of groups that matter for creativity by testing to what extent the present relationship is still supported when honing only on those identities that people feel are important to their sense of self (Tadmor et al., 2012).

Method

Participants. We recruited participants via Amazon's Mechanical Turk (Buhrmester, Kwang, & Gosling, 2011; Goodman, Cryder, & Cheema, 2013). We aimed for a total sample size of 400 to ensure that the design has enough statistical power (.80) to detect a reliable correlation as small as .15. To address any practice effects among MTurkers, we recruited only participants who had not completed the brick task previously (an additional 239 participants indicated that they had completed the brick task before and were ineligible). Participants were reimbursed US$1.50 upon study completion. Nine participants failed to accurately respond to two control questions as instructed ("This is a control question—please select '2'/'not at all' "), resulting in a final sample of 480 participants (47% female; M_{age} = 34.61, SD = 10.63).

Procedure and measures. Participants completed the following measures and provided their demographic data in an online procedure.

Creativity measure. Consistent with Study 2, we used the brick task in which participants generate ideas for uses of a brick in 2 min. In an identical fashion to Study 2, we recorded fluency (the number of generated ideas; M = 6.93, SD = 2.57, 3382 ideas in total) and originality (using the same point-coding scheme as in Study 2; M = 13.82, SD = 6.98) as measures of creative production. Coding of 10% of the data by a second coder yielded a satisfactory, high degree of agreement in assigned points (87%), providing evidence of reliable coding. As in Study 2, to capture the creative process, we also computed (a) flexibility in idea generation (i.e., the number of different semantic categories that participants generated using the same coding scheme as in Study 2; M = 4.25, SD = 1.57), and (b) persistence or within-category fluency (i.e., the number of ideas divided by the number of semantic categories; M = 1.72, SD = 0.69).

Multiple identities measure. Participants completed a group membership listing task (C. Haslam et al., 2008) in which they were asked to write down up to 10 groups that they belonged to (M = 5.49, SD = 2.44). To reduce the influence of creativity or persistence in this task, the instructions explicitly referred to the "groups that you belong to" and provided an extended list (even more comprehensive than in Study 2) of types and examples of groups to facilitate retrieval.[2] In addition, participants also indicated the importance of each group to their sense of self ("Indicate how important each group is to who you are") on a scale ranging from 1 (*not at all important*) to 7 (*very important*).

Personality measure. As in Studies 1 and 2, we assessed the Big Five traits—using the 10 items from the short version of the Big Five Inventory that participants responded to on a scale ranging from 1 (*strongly disagree*) to 5 (*strongly agree*); Rammstedt and John (2007); *r*s ranged from .30 to .60.

Self-affirmation. To rule out that effects can be attributed to self-affirmation (by being related to possessing many identities and by strengthening individuals' capacity to think freely), participants responded to five items on 7-point Likert-type scales ranging from 1 (*not at all*) to 7 (*completely*) assessing self-affirmation (e.g., "This survey made me think about positive aspects of myself" and "This survey made me focus my attention on who I am"; α = .95; from Napper, Harris, & Epton, 2009).

Novelty seeking. We assessed novelty seeking with a view of ruling out the possibility that a general preference to seek novelty might facilitate people's propensity to join new groups and their creative ability. Participants responded to five items on 7-point Likert-type scales ranging from 1 (*not at all*) to 7 (*completely*; that is, "I am always interested in finding new things to try" and "I usually seek out new opportunities"; α = .83; Gordon & Luo, 2011).

Generalized persistence. The second measure of persistency was calculated based on the amount of time people spent trying to solve unsolvable anagrams using the task developed by Ciarocco, Sommer, and Baumeister (2001). In this task, participants are provided with three anagrams that are solvable and three anagrams that are unsolvable. We recorded the overall amount of time (in seconds) that people spent on this task (M = 178.33, SD = 172.62).

Table 5 Study 3: Means, Standard Deviations, and Intercorrelations Between Measures.

Variable	M	SD	1	2	3	4	5	6	7	8	9	10	11	12	13
1. Multiple identities	5.49	2.44	—												
2. Extraversion	2.82	1.07	-.01	—											
3. Agreeableness	3.49	0.90	-.01	.16**	—										
4. Conscientiousness	3.80	0.83	-.02	.21**	.21**	—									
5. Emotional stability	3.39	1.01	-.01	.35**	.30**	.31**	—								
6. Openness to experience	3.70	0.85	.09	.13**	-.01	.14**	.04	—							
7. Self-affirmation	4.67	1.68	.08†	.10*	.11*	.18**	.15**	.10*	—						
8. Novelty seeking	4.60	1.06	.03	.32**	.13**	.19**	.29**	.25**	.19**	—					
9. Generalized persistence	178.33	172.62	.14**	.03	-.02	.02	.08	.09†	.10*	.05	—				
10. Creativity: Fluency	6.93	2.57	.15**	.08†	.03	-.04	.01	.16**	.01	.08†	-.12**	—			
11. Creativity: Flexibility	4.25	1.57	.10*	.04	.01	-.04	-.01*	.16**	-.03	.06	-.11*	.69**	—		
12. Creativity: Persistence	1.72	0.69	.06	.07	.01	.01	.01	-.01	.05	.01	.01	.31**	-.36**	—	
13. Creativity: Originality	13.82	6.98	.15**	.13**	.03	-.04	.01	.17**	.03	.09*	-.11*	.89**	.62**	.28**	—

Note. n = 480.

†p < .10. *p < .05. **p < .01.

Table 6 Study 3: Hierarchical Regression Analyses Assessing Effect of Multiple Identities on Fluency, Originality, Flexibility, and Persistence (Within-Category Fluency) Including Sensitivity Analysis (With the Big Five as Control Variables).

Variable	Main analysis					Sensitivity analysis (adding control variables)				
	b	SE	95% CIs	β	t	b	SE	95% CIs	β	t
Fluency										
Multiple identities	0.16	.05	[0.06, 0.25]	.15	3.28**	0.16	.05	[0.07, 0.26]	.16	3.46**
Extraversion						0.18	.12	[-0.05, 0.41]	.07	1.51
Agreeableness						0.08	.14	[-0.05, 0.41]	.03	0.58
Conscientiousness						-0.27	.15	[-0.56, 0.03]	-.09	-1.78†
Emotional stability						-0.01	.13	[-0.26, 0.25]	-.01	-0.07
Openness to experience						0.46	.14	[0.19, 0.74]	.15	3.29**
Self-affirmation						-0.01	.07	[-0.15, 0.13]	-.01	-0.10
Novelty seeking						0.08	.12	[-0.16, 0.32]	.03	0.65
Generalized persistence						-0.002	.001	[-0.004, -0.001]	-.15	-3.46**
R^2					.02**					0.08**

Table 6 Study 3: Hierarchical Regression Analyses Assessing Effect of Multiple Identities on Fluency, Originality, Flexibility, and Persistence (Within-Category Fluency) Including Sensitivity Analysis (With the Big Five as Control Variables).

Variable	Main analysis					Sensitivity analysis (adding control variables)				
	b	SE	95% CIs	β	t	b	SE	95% CIs	β	t
Originality										
Multiple identities	0.43	.13	[0.18, 0.69]	.15	3.34**	0.45	.13	[0.20, 0.70]	.16	3.49**
Extraversion						0.79	.32	[0.16, 1.41]	.12	2.45*
Agreeableness						0.21	.36	[-0.51, 0.92]	.03	0.73
Conscientiousness						-0.77	.40	[-1.56, 0.02]	-.09	-1.86†
Emotional stability						-0.10	.35	[-0.79, 0.60]	-.03	-0.52
Openness to experience						1.32	.38	[0.57, 2.06]	.15	3.22**
Self-affirmation						0.04	.19	[-0.34, 0.41]	.03	0.67
Novelty seeking						0.22	.33	[-0.42, 0.86]	-.01	-0.07
Generalized persistence						-0.006	.002	[-0.010, -0.002]	-.15	-3.34**
R^2					.02**					0.09**
Flexibility										
Multiple identities	0.06	.03	[0.01, 0.12]	.10	2.08*	0.06	.03	[0.01, 0.12]	.10	2.20*
Extraversion						0.05	.07	[-0.01, 0.19]	.03	0.62
Agreeableness						0.04	.08	[-0.13, 0.20]	.02	0.42
Conscientiousness						-0.13	-.09	[-0.31, 0.05]	-.07	-1.45
Emotional stability						-0.01	.08	[-0.17, 0.15]	-.01	-0.14
Openness to experience						0.30	.09	[0.13, 0.47]	.16	3.46**
Self-affirmation						-0.04	.04	[-0.12, 0.05]	-.04	-0.88

Table 6 Study 3: Hierarchical Regression Analyses Assessing Effect of Multiple Identities on Fluency, Originality, Flexibility, and Persistence (Within-Category Fluency) Including Sensitivity Analysis (With the Big Five as Control Variables).

Variable	Main analysis					Sensitivity analysis (adding control variables)				
	b	SE	95% CIs	β	t	b	SE	95% CIs	β	t
Novelty seeking						0.05	.07	[-0.09, 0.20]	.04	0.72
Generalized persistence						-0.001	.01	[-0.002, -0.001]	-.13	-2.87**
R^2					.01**					.06**
Persistence										
Multiple identities	0.02	.01	[-0.01, 0.04]	.06	1.24	0.02	.01	[-0.01, 0.04]	.06	1.25
Extraversion						0.06	.03	[-0.01, 0.12]	.09	1.69
Agreeableness						0.01	.04	[-0.07, 0.08]	.01	0.03
Conscientiousness						-0.01	.04	[-0.09, 0.07]	-.01	-0.27
Emotional stability						-0.01	.04	[-0.08, 0.06]	-.01	-0.24
Openness to experience						-0.02	.04	[-0.10, 0.06]	-.03	-0.55
Self-affirmation						0.02	.02	[-0.02, 0.06]	.05	1.03
Novelty seeking						-0.01	.03	[-0.08, 0.05]	-.02	-0.40
Generalized persistence						0.00	.00	[0.00, 0.00]	-.01	-0.21
R^2					.00					.01

Note. n = 480. CI = confidence interval.
$^{†}p < .10$. $^{*}p < .05$. $^{**}p < .01$.

Results

Multiple identities and creativity. Descriptive statistics and bivariate correlations between variables are presented in Table 5. Linear regression results concerning the creativity indices are shown in Table 6. Consistent with Studies 1 and 2, multiple identities were positively associated with fluency (H1), suggesting that people who felt they belong to many groups came up with a greater number of ideas than their counterparts who had few groups. Furthermore, as in Study 2, multiple identities were also positively associated with originality (H2), indicating that to the extent that people felt they belonged to many groups, the more original the ideas they generated. Finally, consistent with Study 2, results showed a positive association between multiple identities and flexibility, such that participants who felt they belong to many groups generated ideas from more diverse categories than their counterparts with few groups. However, there was a nonsignificant relationship between multiple identities and persistence.

Sensitivity analysis. As presented in Table 6, sensitivity analyses controlling for personality (the Big Five), self-affirmation, novelty seeking, and generalized persistence (time spent on unsolvable anagrams) yielded largely identical results.

In further sensitivity analyses, and as in Study 2, we examined the relationship between multiple identities and average originality (Diehl & Stroebe, 1987). Analysis indicated that multiple identities were also associated with average originality, b = 0.021, 95% CIs = [0.004, 0.038], β = .11, p = .015.

Furthermore, to rule out the alternative explanation that creative people are good at coming up with lots of groups that they belong to, we conducted sensitivity analyses examining only those social identities people rated as highly important to self (i.e., groups that were rated above the midpoint of the scale). Analysis yielded largely identical results. Multiple important identities were positively associated with fluency, b = 0.18, 95% CIs = [0.07, 0.29], β = .15, p = .001; flexibility, b = 0.08, 95% CIs = [0.01, 0.14], β = .10, p = .030; overall originality, b = 0.52, 95% CIs = [0.22, 0.82], β = .15, p = .001; and average originality, b = 0.025, 95% CIs = [0.005, 0.045], β = .11, p = .013. When controlling for personality, self-affirmation, novelty seeking, and generalized persistence, multiple important identities remained a predictor of fluency, b = 0.19, 95% CIs = [0.08, 0.31], β = .15, p = .001; flexibility, b = 0.84, 95% CIs = [0.01, 0.15], β = .11, p = .019; overall originality, b = 0.52, 95% CIs = [0.21, 0.83], β = .15, p = .001; and average originality, b = 0.022, 95% CIs = [0.002, 0.043], β = .10, p = .034.

As in Studies 1 and 2, analysis indicated that the quadratic term was unrelated to fluency, b = −0.03, 95% CIs = [−0.24, 0.18], β = −.01, ΔR^2 = .000, p = .793; flexibility, b = 0.02, 95% CIs = [−0.11, 0.15], β = .01, ΔR^2 = .000, p = .788; and originality, b = 0.13, 95% CIs = [−0.45, 0.71], β = .02, ΔR^2 = .000, p = .658, providing no evidence for a curvilinear relationship between multiple identities and creativity.

Mediation analysis. As in Study 2, we examined issues of process by analyzing to what extent the multiple identities–creativity link is accounted for by flexibility and/or persistence. Using bias-corrected bootstrapping with 5,000 resamples (using PROCESS Model 4; Hayes, 2013), multiple mediation analysis revealed that the path from multiple identities to originality via flexibility (H3a) was statistically significant, γ = .22, SE = .10, 95% CIs = [0.02, 0.42], while the path via persistence (H3b) was not statistically significant, γ = .09, SE = .07, 95% CIs = [−0.06, 0.24]. The mediation is shown in Figure 2. Moreover, mediation analysis of average originality yielded similar results and a significant indirect path from multiple identities through flexibility to average originality, γ = .005, SE = .003, 95% CIs = [0.001, 0.013], and a nonsignificant path through persistence, γ = .003, SE = .002, 95% CIs = [−0.001, 0.008].

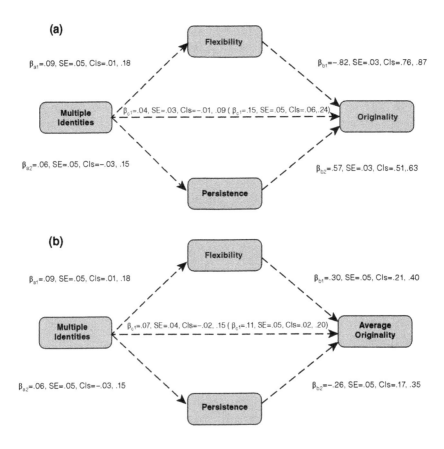

Figure 2. Study 3: Mediation displaying standardized path coefficients for (a) paths from multiple identities through the two mediating processes, flexibility (category diversity) and persistence (within-category fluency), to overall originality and (b) path from multiple identities through the two mediating processes, flexibility (category diversity) and persistence (within-category fluency), to average originality (originality per generated idea). Note. Numbers in parentheses are path coefficients after controlling for the mediator. CI = confidence interval.

Discussion

Study 3 replicated the previous findings in a large sample with high statistical power. In addition, it extended previous findings by demonstrating that the proposed relationship also holds (a) when focusing on only those identities that people feel are important to who they are, and (b) when controlling for plausible confounding variables: the strength of the relationship between multiple identities and enhanced creativity remained after accounting for participants' sense of self-affirmation, their tendency to seek novelty, and their generalized persistence.

GENERAL DISCUSSION

Results from three studies demonstrate that people with multiple social identities show greater creative productivity (Studies 1-3) and generate more original ideas (Studies 2-3). Speaking to the robustness of this relationship, the findings were consistent and of a similar effect size across variations in the assessment of both multiple identities and creativity. Addressing the issue of the process, flexibility, but not persistence, mediated the relationship between multiple group memberships and creativity (Studies 2-3). Across all three studies, multiple identities predicted creativity *above and beyond* personality variables (i.e., Big Five). Furthermore, there was no evidence that the multiple identities–creativity link could be attributed to the third variables of self-affirmation, novelty seeking, or generalized persistence (Study 3). At the same time, providing evidence for an identity-based explanation of the findings, creativity was also associated with those multiple groups that people felt are highly important to their sense of self (Study 3). Finally, across all studies, there was consistent evidence for a linear relationship, but no evidence for a curvilinear relationship, between multiple identities and creativity. This indicates that there were no diminishing marginal benefits associated with having multiple identities and that the relationship never turned negative.

The present findings make at least three significant contributions to the literatures on creativity and identity. First, our results demonstrate that while people's creative performance is related to enduring personality variables (Feist, 1998; Simonton, 2000), it is also related to social factors, as indicated by their connection to, and internalization of, social groups. Across the studies, we found that people who regard multiple (rather than few) groups as an integral part of who they are show greater creativity in coming up with new ideas. Our findings corroborate previous analyses that demonstrate that creative performance can be enhanced by reflecting on social experiences prior to engaging in creative tasks (Ybarra et al., 2008) and that innovation is fostered by people's social relationships and their networking skills (Baer, 2012). At the same time, these results extend previous analyses by revealing that creative idea generation is also positively associated with people's psychological sense of connectedness to social groups. In sum, while creativity is a skill that is expressed by individuals, it is nourished by the groups they belong to (see also Adarves-Yorno et al., 2007). Given the potential gains to organizations and wider society of enhancing creativity, these *modifiable* predictors have clear utility in the applied domain.

Second, the present findings expand upon the literature on multiple identities. In the last few years, a growing body of evidence indicates that multiple identities are a resource for people's health, well-being, and adjustment to challenges in life (Cruwys et al., 2013; Jetten et al., 2012; Jetten et al., 2014; Jones & Jetten, 2011). Our results demonstrate that in addition to feeding into psychological health and preventing cognitive decline (C. Haslam et al., 2008; C. Haslam et al., 2011), multiple identities can also be seen as a resource that allows for creative thought. Moreover, it is noteworthy that there was evidence that enhanced idea generation was accounted for by flexibility and not by persistence or effort, suggesting that benefits derive not only from people's motivation (e.g., trying harder) but also from their knowledge and experience associated with feeling connected to multiple identities (e.g., seeing the world differently; Gocłowska & Crisp, 2014). In this way, the findings reveal that the implications of multiple identities extend to the domain of creativity and thus open up an entirely new area for future investigations that examine the implications of multiple identities in a range of other (professional, artistic, and organizational) contexts.

At the same time, the present findings also align with previous assertions that issues of identity are key to the creativity process. Specifically, the findings substantiate previous research that has shown that creativity is fostered to the extent that (a) people share membership in a particular *single* social identity (Adarves-Yorno et al., 2006, 2007; S. A. Haslam et al., 2013) and (b) people have engaged with *two different cultural* identities (Maddux & Galinsky, 2009; Maddux et al., 2009; Saad et al., 2013; Tadmor et al., 2012) by demonstrating that creativity is also fostered to the extent that people have *multiple social* identities. Indeed, our findings not only are consistent with these previous literatures but also allow us to integrate important and distinctive findings that each of these literatures had revealed. In short, creativity is prevalent among people who share an identity, have dual national or cultural identification, or, perhaps particularly parsimoniously, have multiple social identities.

Third, the present findings have important implications for organizational behavior. Indeed, the present research aligns with recent suggestions that organizational behavior is influenced not only by a person's relevant work or organizational identity but also by his or her various other non-work identities that he or she holds dear (Godart et al., 2015; Ramarajan & Reid, 2013). Our findings dovetail with other research suggesting that efforts to enhance creativity may be limited if organizations undermine the co-expression of members' multiple identities by focusing exclusively on strengthening a single identity associated with a work group or an organization (at the expense of others; see also Fiol, Pratt, & O'Connor, 2009). Instead, it appears that organizations that aim to promote creative thinking are more likely to be successful to the extent that they encourage practices and structures that allow for the development and enactment of members' multiple identities that they feel are important to self.

Limitations and future research

It is important to mention some limitations of the present set of studies. First, our article did not make claims concerning directionality of the present relationship but instead focused on a general association between multiple identities and enhanced creativity. More generally, we believe that both pathways from multiple identities to creativity, and from creativity to multiple identities are likely to operate across different settings. Indeed, this perspective is consistent with research that suggests that while the influence of social factors on creativity may explain the larger part of the shared variance of this relationship, a part of the variance may also be due to the possibility that creative people are more likely to be invited to participate in social activities (Perry-Smith, 2006; Perry-Smith & Shalley, 2003). In the future, researchers could design longitudinal studies to provide insight into the ways in which the relationship between many social identities and creativity unfolds. Social group memberships are not fixed, and to provide evidence of directionality, it would be fruitful for future research to develop interventions that focus on facilitating people's efforts to take up memberships in new groups and quantify their long-term impact on creativity and innovation.

Second, results from the pasta task in Study 1 indicated a relationship with measures of convergent, and not with divergent, thinking. As discussed earlier, there are differences between convergent thinking (as assessed in Study 1) and persistence. Nevertheless, it is also important to note that various cognitive processes can account for creative performance, and that these different processes are not mutually exclusive (e.g., for some tasks and measures, people who have multiple identities may also show greater persistence in addition to enhanced flexibility; Nijstad et al., 2010).

Finally, it is noteworthy that we ruled out a number of alternative explanations that one might believe have a role to play in accounting for the variance of the multiple identities–creativity relationship—notably personality, self-affirmation, and novelty seeking—which could be argued to enhance creativity as well as people's propensity to join new groups. In addition, we can rule out that a significant proportion of the variance can be explained by people's ability to generate names of multiple groups—for at least three important reasons. Indeed, this possibility cannot explain why creativity is related to a scale measure of multiple identities (Study 1), to only those multiple identities that people feel are important to who they are (Study 3), and why multiple identities are associated with greater (overall and average) originality (Studies 2-3). Nevertheless, future work should examine additional boundary conditions of the relationship. For instance, there would be value in shedding light on whether the relationship becomes amplified to the extent that the social identities in question are diverse and unrelated (Goclowska & Crisp, 2014), the degree of complexity associated with different social identities increases (Roccas & Brewer, 2002; Swann, Jetten, Gómez, Whitehouse, & Bastian, 2012), and the relevance of identities to a particular task or aspect of creativity becomes more pronounced (in terms of both mini c and Big C creativity; Beghetto & Kaufman, 2007).

CONCLUSION

The present research covers new conceptual and empirical ground by revealing an association between people's multiple identities and greater creativity. The more identities a person feels he or she belongs to, the more ideas he or she was able to generate (fluency), and the more creative those ideas were (originality). Indeed, our findings expand upon, and allow for potential integration of, previous research on the relationships between identity, culture, and creativity by suggesting that people who feel they belong to multiple social identities show enhanced creative thinking because this diversity of experience allows them to think flexibly. In sum, it appears that—like Goethe with whom we began—those who embrace multiple social connections are more creative in their thinking about the world.

NOTES

1. Preliminary results indicated that the creativity data in all studies were slightly positively skewed. Because linear regression is largely robust against violations of normality and because results were identical when the raw data were log-transformed; for ease of interpretation, we report and discuss results based on original untransformed data.

2. We also manipulated whether participants wrote down and explained why their groups are important to them by focusing on one group, three groups, or on a group-unrelated meal they have had. This manipulation did not influence creativity, $Fs(2,477) <$ 1.09. Controlling for this reflection exercise did not alter he significance of any of the key results.

SUPPLEMENTAL MATERIAL

The online supplemental material is available at http://pspb.sagepub.com/supplemental.

REFERENCES

Adarves-Yorno, I., Haslam, S. A., & Postmes, T. (2008). And now for something completely different? The impact of group membership on perceptions of creativity. *Social Influence, 3,* 248-266.

Adarves-Yorno, I., Postmes, T., & Haslam, S. A. (2006). Social identity and the recognition of creativity in groups. *British Journal of Social Psychology, 45,* 479-497.

Adarves-Yorno, I., Postmes, T., & Haslam, S. A. (2007). Creative innovation or crazy irrelevance? The contribution of group norms and social identity to creative behavior. *Journal of Experimental Social Psychology, 43,* 410-416.

Amabile, T. M. (1983). The social psychology of creativity: A componential conceptualization. *Journal of Personality and Social Psychology, 45,* 357-376.

Baas, M., De Dreu, C. K. W., & Nijstad, B. A. (2011). When prevention promotes creativity: The role of mood, regulatory focus, and regulatory closure. *Journal of Personality and Social Psychology, 100,* 794-809.

Baer, M. (2012). Putting creativity to work: The implementation of creative ideas in organizations. *Academy of Management Journal, 55,* 1102-1119.

Beghetto, R. A., & Kaufman, J. C. (2007). Toward a broader conception of creativity: A case for "mini-c" creativity. *Psychology of Aesthetics, Creativity, and the Arts, 1,* 73-79.

Benet-Martinez, V., Lee, F., & Leu, J. (2006). Biculturalism and cognitive complexity expertise in cultural representations. *Journal of Cross-Cultural Psychology, 37,* 386-407.

Best, D., Lubman, D., Savic, M., Wilson, A., Dingle, G., Haslam, S. A., & Jetten, J. (2014). Social and transitional identity: Exploring social networks and their significance in a therapeutic community setting. *Therapeutic Communities: The International Journal of Therapeutic Communities, 35,* 10-20.

Buhrmester, M., Kwang, T., & Gosling, S. D. (2011). Amazon's Mechanical Turk: A new source of inexpensive, yet high-quality, data? *Perspectives on Psychological Science, 6,* 3-5.

Ciarocco, N. J., Sommer, K. L., & Baumeister, R. F. (2001). Ostracism and ego depletion: The strains of silence. *Personality and Social Psychology Bulletin, 27,* 1156-1163.

Cohen, A. B. (2009). Many forms of culture. *American Psychologist, 64,* 194-204.

Cruwys, T., Dingle, G. A., Haslam, C., Haslam, S. A., Jetten, J., & Morton, T. A. (2013). Social group memberships protect against future depression, alleviate depression symptoms and prevent depression relapse. *Social Science & Medicine, 98,* 179-186.

Cruwys, T., South, E. I., Greenaway, K. H., & Haslam, S. A. (2015). Social identity reduces depression by fostering positive attributions. *Social Psychological & Personality Science, 6,* 65-74.

Damian, R. I., & Simonton, D. K. (2014). Diversifying experiences in the development of genius and their impact on creative cognition. In D. K. Simonton (Ed.), *The Wiley handbook of genius* (pp. 375-394). Oxford, UK: Wiley-Blackwell.

De Dreu, C. K., Baas, M., & Nijstad, B. A. (2008). Hedonic tone and activation level in the mood-creativity link: Toward a dual pathway to creativity model. *Journal of Personality and Social Psychology, 94,* 739-756.

De Dreu, C. K., Baas, M., Roskes, M., Sligte, D. J., Ebstein, R. P., Chew, S. H., . . . Shamay-Tsoory, S. G. (2014). Oxytonergic circuitry sustains and enables creative cognition in humans. *Social Cognitive and Affective Neuroscience, 9,* 1159-1165.

Diehl, M., & Stroebe, W. (1987). Productivity loss in brainstorming groups: Toward the solution of a riddle. *Journal of Personality and Social Psychology, 53,* 497-509.

Dijksterhuis, A., & Meurs, T. (2006). Where creativity resides: The generative power of unconscious thought. *Consciousness and Cognition, 15,* 135-146.

Ellemers, N. (2012). The group self. *Science, 336,* 848-852.

Elsbach, K. D., & Kramer, R. M. (2003). Assessing creativity in Hollywood pitch meetings: Evidence for a dual-process model of creativity judgments. *Academy of Management Journal, 46,* 283-301.

Farmer, S. M., Tierney, P., & Kung-McIntyre, K. (2003). Employee creativity in Taiwan: An application of role identity theory. *Academy of Management Journal, 46,* 618-630.

Feist, G. J. (1998). A meta-analysis of personality in scientific and artistic creativity. *Personality and Social Psychology Review, 2,* 290-309.

Fiol, C. M., Pratt, M. G., & O'Connor, E. J. (2009). Managing intractable identity conflicts. *Academy of Management Review, 34,* 32-55.

Gaither, S. E., Remedios, J. D., Sanchez, D. T., & Sommers, S. R. (2015). Thinking outside the box: Multiple identity mindsets affect creative problem solving. *Social Psychological & Personality Science, 6,* 596-603.

Gocłowska, M. A., Baas, M., Crisp, R. J., & De Dreu, C. K. (2014). Whether social schema violations help or hurt creativity depends on need for structure. *Personality and Social Psychology Bulletin, 40,* 959-971.

Gocłowska, M. A., & Crisp, R. J. (2014). How dual identity processes foster creativity. *Review of General Psychology, 18,* 216-236.

Godart, F. C., Maddux, W. W., Shipilov, A. V., & Galinsky, A. D. (2015). Fashion with a foreign flair: Professional experiences abroad facilitate the creative innovations of organizations. *Academy of Management Journal, 58,* 195-220.

Goodman, J. K., Cryder, C. E., & Cheema, A. (2013). Data collection in a flat world: The strengths and weaknesses of Mechanical Turk samples. *Journal of Behavioral Decision Making, 26,* 213-224.

Gordon, C. L., & Luo, S. (2011). The Personal Expansion Questionnaire: Measuring one's tendency to expand through novelty and augmentation. *Personality and Individual Differences, 51,* 89-94.

Guilford, J. P. (1950). Creativity. *American Psychologist, 5,* 444-454.

Guilford, J. P. (1967). *The nature of human intelligence.* New York, NY: McGraw-Hill.

Haslam, C., Holme, A., Haslam, S. A., Iyer, A., Jetten, J., & Williams, W. H. (2008). Maintaining group memberships: Social identity continuity predicts well-being after stroke. *Neuropsychological Rehabilitation*, *18*, 671-691.

Haslam, C., Jetten, J., Haslam, S. A., Pugliese, C., & Tonks, J. (2011). "I remember therefore I am, and I am therefore I remember": Exploring the contributions of episodic and semantic self-knowledge to strength of identity. *British Journal of Psychology*, *102*, 184-203.

Haslam, S. A., Adarves-Yorno, I., Postmes, T., & Jans, L. (2013). The collective origins of valued originality: A social identity approach to creativity. *Personality and Social Psychology Review*, *17*, 384-401.

Hayes, A. F. (2013). *Introduction to mediation, moderation, and conditional process analysis: A regression-based approach*. New York, NY: Guilford Press.

Iyer, A., Jetten, J., Tsivrikos, D., Postmes, T., & Haslam, S. A. (2009). The more (and the more compatible) the merrier: Multiple group memberships and identity compatibility as predictors of adjustment after life transitions. *British Journal of Social Psychology*, *48*, 707-733.

Jetten, J., Branscombe, N. R., Haslam, S. A., Haslam, C., Cruwys, T., Jones, J. M., . . . Zhang, A. (2015). Having a lot of a good thing: Multiple important group memberships as a source of self-esteem. *PLoS ONE*, *10*, e0124609.

Jetten, J., Haslam, C., & Haslam, S. A. (Eds.). (2012). *The social cure: Identity, health and well-being*. New York, NY: Psychology Press.

Jetten, J., Haslam, C., Haslam, S. A., Dingle, G., & Jones, J. M. (2014). How groups affect our health and well-being: The path from theory to policy. *Social Issues and Policy Review*, *8*, 103-130.

Jones, J. M., & Jetten, J. (2011). Recovering from strain and enduring pain multiple group memberships promote resilience in the face of physical challenges. *Social Psychological & Personality Science*, *2*, 239-244.

Leung, A. K. Y., & Chiu, C. Y. (2010). Multicultural experience, idea receptiveness, and creativity. *Journal of Cross-Cultural Psychology*, *41*, 723-741.

Leung, A. K. Y., Maddux, W. W., Galinsky, A. D., & Chiu, C. Y. (2008). Multicultural experience enhances creativity: The when and how. *American Psychologist*, *63*, 169-181.

Maddux, W. W., Adam, H., & Galinsky, A. D. (2010). When in Rome . . . Learn why the Romans do what they do: How multicultural learning experiences facilitate creativity. *Personality and Social Psychology Bulletin, 36,* 731-741.

Maddux, W. W., Bivolaru, E., Hafenbrack, A. C., Tadmor, C. T., & Galinsky, A. D. (2014). Expanding opportunities by opening your mind: Multicultural engagement predicts job market success through longitudinal increases in integrative complexity. *Social Psychological & Personality Science, 5,* 608-615.

Maddux, W. W., & Galinsky, A. D. (2009). Cultural borders and mental barriers: The relationship between living abroad and creativity. *Journal of Personality and Social Psychology, 96,* 1047-1061.

Maddux, W. W., Leung, A. K.-Y., Chiu, C.-Y., & Galinsky, A.D. (2009). Toward a more complete understanding of the link between multicultural experience and creativity. *The American Psychologist, 64,* 156-158.

Markman, K. D., Lindberg, M. J., Kray, L. J., & Galinsky, A. D. (2007). Implications of counterfactual structure for creative generation and analytical problem solving. *Personality and Social Psychology Bulletin, 33,* 312-324.

Marsh, R. L., Ward, T. B., & Landau, J. D. (1999). The inadvertent use of prior knowledge in a generative cognitive task. *Memory & Cognition, 27,* 94-105.

Mednick, S. (1962). The associative basis of the creative process. *Psychological Review, 69,* 220-232.

Napper, L., Harris, P. R., & Epton, T. (2009). Developing and testing a self-affirmation manipulation. *Self and Identity, 8,* 45-62.

Nijstad, B. A., De Dreu, C. K., Rietzschel, E. F., & Baas, M. (2010). The dual pathway to creativity model: Creative ideation as a function of flexibility and persistence. *European Review of Social Psychology, 21,* 34-77.

Perry-Smith, J. E. (2006). Social yet creative: The role of social relationships in facilitating individual creativity. *Academy of Management Journal, 49,* 85-101.

Perry-Smith, J. E., & Shalley, C. E. (2003). The social side of creativity: A static and dynamic social network perspective. *Academy of Management Review, 28,* 89-106.

Ramarajan, L., & Reid, E. (2013). Shattering the myth of separate worlds: Negotiating nonwork identities at work. *Academy of Management Review, 38*, 621-644.

Rammstedt, B., & John, O. P. (2007). Measuring personality in one minute or less: A 10-item short version of the Big Five Inventory in English and German. *Journal of Research in Personality, 41*, 203-212.

Rietzschel, E. F., De Dreu, C. K. W., & Nijstad, B. A. (2007). Personal need for structure and creative performance: The moderating influence of fear of invalidity. *Personality and Social Psychology Bulletin, 33*, 855-866.

Rietzschel, E. F., Nijstad, B. A., & Stroebe, W. (2007). Relative accessibility of domain knowledge and creativity: The effects of knowledge activation on the quantity and originality of generated ideas. *Journal of Experimental Social Psychology, 43*, 933-946.

Roccas, S., & Brewer, M. B. (2002). Social identity complexity. *Personality and Social Psychology Review, 6*, 88-106.

Roskes, M., De Dreu, C. K. W., & Nijstad, B. A. (2012). Necessity is the mother of invention: Avoidance motivation stimulates creativity through cognitive effort. *Journal of Personality and Social Psychology, 103*, 242-256.

Runco, M. A., Okuda, S. M., & Thurston, B. J. (1987). The psychometric properties of four systems for scoring divergent thinking tests. *Journal of Psychoeducational Assessment, 5*, 149-156.

Saad, C. S., Damian, R. I., Benet-Martinez, V., Moons, W. G., & Robins, R. W. (2013). Multiculturalism and creativity: Effects of cultural context, bicultural identity, and ideational fluency. *Social Psychological & Personality Science, 4*, 369-375.

Simonton, D. K. (1997a). Creative productivity: A predictive and explanatory model of career trajectories and landmarks. *Psychological Review, 104*, 66-89.

Simonton, D. K. (1997b). Foreign influence and national achievement: The impact of open milieus on Japanese civilization. *Journal of Personality and Social Psychology, 72*, 86-94.

Simonton, D. K. (2000). Creativity: Cognitive, personal, developmental, and social aspects. *American Psychologist, 55*, 151-158.

Sligte, D. J., Nijstad, B. A., & De Dreu, C. K. W. (2013). Leaving a legacy neutralizes negative effects of death anxiety on creativity. *Personality and Social Psychology Bulletin, 39,* 1152-1163.

Smith, S. M., & Blankenship, S. E. (1991). Incubation and the persistence of fixation in problem solving. *The American Journal of Psychology, 104,* 61-87.

Swaab, R. I., Schaerer, M., Anicich, E. M., Ronay, R., & Galinsky, A. D. (2014). The too-much-talent effect: Team interdependence determines when more talent is too much or not enough. *Psychological Science, 25,* 1581-1591.

Swann, W. B., Jr., Jetten, J., G.mez, A., Whitehouse, H., & Bastian, B. (2012). When group membership gets personal: A theory of identity fusion. *Psychological Review, 119,* 441-456.

Tadmor, C. T., Galinsky, A. D., & Maddux, W. W. (2012). Getting the most out of living abroad: Biculturalism and integrative complexity as key drivers of creative and professional success. *Journal of Personality and Social Psychology, 103,* 520-542.

Tadmor, C. T., & Tetlock, P. E. (2006). Biculturalism: A model of the effects of second-culture exposure on acculturation and integrative complexity. *Journal of Cross-Cultural Psychology, 37,* 173-190.

Tetlock, P. E., Kristel, O. V., Elson, S. B., Green, M. C., & Lerner, J. S. (2000). The psychology of the unthinkable: Taboo tradeoffs, forbidden base rates, and heretical counterfactuals. *Journal of Personality and Social Psychology, 78,* 853-870.

Turner, J. C., Hogg, M. A., Oakes, P. J., Reicher, S. D., & Wetherell, M. S. (1987). *Rediscovering the social group: A self-categorization theory.* Cambridge, MA: Basil Blackwell.

Ybarra, O., Burnstein, E., Winkielman, P., Keller, M. C., Manis, M., Chan, E., & Rodriguez, J. (2008). Mental exercising through simple socializing: Social interaction promotes general cognitive functioning. *Personality and Social Psychology Bulletin, 34,* 248-259.

ACKNOWLEDGMENTS

Bartholomae, David. "Inventing the University" from *Journal of Basic Writing*, 5.1 (1986). Reprinted with permission. All rights reserved.

Bucholtz, Mary, and Kira Hall. "Identity and Interaction: A Sociocultural Linguistic Approach" from *Discourse Studies*, 7.4-5 (2005). Reprinted with permission of Sage Publishing. All rights reserved.

Edwards, Dustin W. "Framing Remix Rhetorically: Toward a Typology of Transformative Work" from *Computers and Composition*, 39 (2016). Reprinted with permission of Elsevier B.V. All rights reserved.

Gocłowska, Małgorzata A., and Richard J. Crisp. "How Dual-Identity Processes Foster Creativity" from *Review of General Psychology*, 18.3 (2014). Reprinted with permission of the American Psychological Association. All rights reserved.

Joy, Janet E., Stanley J. Watson, Jr., and John A. Benson, Jr., Editors. "Executive Summary" from *Marijuana and Medicine: Assessing the Science Base*. Institute of Medicine, 1999. Reprinted with permission of The National Academies Press. All rights reserved.

Larsson, Anna, Andrew D. Oxman, Cheryl Carling, and Jeph Herrin. "Medical Messages in the Media–Barriers and Solutions to Improving Medical Journalism" from *Health Expectations*, 6.4 (2003). Reprinted with permission of John Wiley and Sons. All rights reserved.

Lethem, Jonathan. Excerpt(s) from *The Ecstasy of Influence: Nonfictions, Etc.* Copyright © 2011 by Jonathan Lethem. Used by permission of Doubleday, an imprint of the Knopf Doubleday Publishing Group, a division of Penguin Random House LLC. All rights reserved.

Matsuda, Paul Kei, and Christine M. Tardy. "Voice in Academic Writing: The Rhetorical Construction of Author Identity in Blind Manuscript Review" from *English for Specific Purposes*, 26.2 (2007). Reprinted with permission of Elsevier B.V. All rights reserved.

Matsuda, Paul Kei, and Christine M. Tardy. "Continuing the Conversation on Voice in Academic Writing" from *English for Specific Purposes*, 27.1 (2008). Reprinted with permission of Elsevier B.V. All rights reserved.

Randall, Marilyn. "Introduction: What is Plagiarism?" from *Pragmatic Plagiarism: Authorship, Profit, and Power*, edited by Marilyn Randall. Copyright © 2001 by University of Toronto Press. All rights reserved.

Stapleton, Paul, and Rena Helms-Park. "A Response to Matsuda and Tardy's 'Voice in Academic Writing: The Rhetorical Construction of Author Identity in Blind Manuscript Review'" from *English for Specific Purposes*, 27.1 (2008). Reprinted with permission of Elsevier B.V. All rights reserved.

Steffens, Niklas, Małgorzata A. Goclowska, Tegan Cruwys, and Adam D. Galinksky. "How Multiple Social Identities are Related to Creativity" from *Personality and Social Psychology Bulletin*, 42.2 (2015). Copyright © 2017 by Society for Personality and Social Psychology, Inc. All rights reserved.

Stolberg, Sheryl Gay. "Government Study of Marijuana Sees Medical Benefits" from *The New York Times*. Reprinted with permission. All rights reserved.

COVER ARTIST BIOGRAPHY

The cover art for *Re:Mix* was designed by Misty Fuller.

Misty Fuller obtained her Associate in Arts from FSCJ when it was still FCCJ. She earned her Bachelor's and Master's degrees in English from the University of North Florida. As a former couch surfer and lover of small, furry animals she's made a lucrative career out of dog sitting and aimlessly creates with no desire for production. Misty resides in Jacksonville, FL as a collection of stardust.